A Worldwide Heart

A WORLDWIDE HEART

THE LIFE OF MARYKNOLL
FATHER JOHN J. CONSIDINE

Robert Hurteau

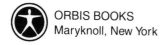

ORBIS BOOKS
Maryknoll, New York

ORBIS BOOKS
Maryknoll, New York 10545

Fathers and Brothers
MARYKNOLL™

Founded in 1970, Orbis Books endeavors to publish works that enlighten the mind, nourish the spirit, and challenge the conscience. The publishing arm of the Maryknoll Fathers and Brothers, Orbis seeks to explore the global dimensions of the Christian faith and mission, to invite dialogue with diverse cultures and religious traditions, and to serve the cause of reconciliation and peace. The books published reflect the views of their authors and do not represent the official position of the Maryknoll Society. To learn more about Maryknoll and Orbis Books, please visit our website at www.maryknollsociety.org.

Library of Congress Cataloging-in-Publication Data

Hurteau, Robert.
    A worldwide heart : the life of Maryknoll Father John J. Considine / by Robert Hurteau.
        pages cm
    Includes bibliographical references (pages   ) and index.
    ISBN 978-1-62698-021-1 (pbk.)
    1. Considine, John Joseph, 1897-1982. 2. Missiologists—United States—Biography. 3. Catholic Foreign Mission Society of America—Biography. I. Title.
BV2072.2.C66H87   2013
271'.79—dc23
[B]
                                                                2012049629

*For Riji—always my friend,
always my love and delight*

Contents

Abbreviations

For ease of reference, the list below offers an abbreviated key for certain archival materials presented throughout the following text. For full citations and allusions to further reading, please refer to the footnotes as well as the bibliography following the main text.

CD   Considine Diary entry. These entries are included in the Maryknoll Mission Archives in "Considine Papers," Boxes 4-7.

Archives

ACUA   Archives of the Catholic University of America

ASPF   Archivio Storico "de Propaganda Fide" (English: Historical Archives "de Propaganda Fide")

ASV   Archivio Segreto Vaticano (English: Vatican Secret Archives)

MMA   Maryknoll Mission Archives

UNDA   Archives of the University of Notre Dame

RPA   Redemptorist Provincial Archives

Acknowledgments

THE WRITING OF any book is always a collaborative venture that involves many people, many conversations. The significance of the subject matter is shaped in those conversations, leading to the discovery of materials that tell the story. Only thus did the biography of Maryknoll Fr. John J. Considine that you have in your hands come into existence. It goes without saying that due to Fr. Considine's extraordinary creativity at networking and research, keeping up with the ground he covered in his long and productive career has similarly involved extensive conversations with many individuals across a range of institutions and geographies. Along the way, the invitation has always been there for me to do what Fr. Considine did—go deeper and deeper into the story of twentieth-century Christian expansion, an expansion that drew in the stories of the Christian peoples of Asia, Africa, Latin America, and Oceania in an ever more comprehensive way.

There are therefore many people to thank, people who helped guide the project in big ways, and people who helped provide resources throughout the three and a half years I dedicated to the project.

In the first place, I offer a word of thanks to my wife, Riji, with whom I shared many conversations about the cross-cultural and ecclesial implications of the research on Fr. Considine. Whether it was over pasta at a café near the Vatican or coffee in our home, Riji in a sense welcomed Fr. Considine into our lives, and being able to talk over with her points in his life story was extremely helpful—especially when my own research and writing seemed unproductive. In a practical sense, the welcome she offered to this work meant adjustments in our routine over a long period of time, a sacrifice she took on with characteristic helpfulness; she always has been able to keep me going on the right track in regard to the project.

In the Maryknoll Society and at Orbis Books there were several people who championed the value of a biography of Fr. Considine. A small editorial committee composed of Bill Burrows, former managing editor at Orbis, and Maryknoll Frs. Gerard McCrane and Stephen Judd guided the early research; these colleagues were always available for consultation on the tone, scope, and trajectory of the book. As the project came to a close, Orbis publisher Robert Ellsberg has offered helpful suggestions for the improvement of the work. Four Maryknollers reviewed the first draft of the book and offered invaluable suggestions and corrections: Frs. Edward Hayes, Joseph Healy, Stephen Judd, and Laurence Murphy. I am also grateful to the two Maryknoll Superior Generals who shepherded the work on the project: Fr. John Sivalon, M.M. (2002–2008) and Fr. Edward Dougherty, M.M. (2008–present)

The key person who offered unqualified support and expertise to the editorial committee was the late Fr. William D. McCarthy, M.M. Working in the Maryknoll Society History Project until his untimely death in 2009, Fr. Bill was convinced of the treasure that Maryknoll had in Fr. Considine, and he offered abundant suggestions and bibliographic resources during our consultations. In addition to his cheerful and welcoming disposition, Fr. Bill was an example of a historian with a strong grasp of missions.

A word of thanks to Loyola Marymount University (LMU) in Los Angeles, my academic home, is also in order. My boss, Provost Joseph Hellige, encouraged me to consider the project and facilitated my one-year leave from the university for research and writing. I am also grateful to my colleagues Ben Hayes, Michael McNaught, and Elsy Arévalo and my former colleague Dr. Cherie Schenck for their hard work of keeping the Center for Religion and Spirituality in LMU Extension running smoothly during the year I was away.

LMU also provided me with the help of a Graduate Assistant, Ms. Lovely Hammett, whose formidable abilities as a researcher and proofreader I came to appreciate. Lovely was also keenly interested in the topic, and she became a collaborator on whom I could rely for understanding the nature and significance of many details in the Considine story.

At the Maryknoll Mission Archives, I would especially like to thank Ms. Ellen Pierce, archivist, and Fr. Michael Walsh, M.M., assistant archivist. They and their capable staff did abundant digging out of resources and kept me busy during my research trips to the Maryknoll headquarters. The Society library staff—Frs. Charles Cappel and Ernie Brunelle and Bro. Kevin Dargan—provided generous assistance. I am also grateful to Fr. John Casey for opening many doors to his own research on the Maryknoll Society's educational institutions. Fr. Frank McGourn also read a chapter and provided important feedback.

Maryknoll Sisters Ellen McDonald, Claudette Laverdiere, and Camilla Kennedy made themselves available for consultations on relations between the Maryknoll Society and the Maryknoll Sisters during the 1930s and 1940s. Sisters Joan Peltier and Camille Marie Black reviewed drafts of chapters and provided invaluable suggestions.

Numerous other Maryknoll priests and brothers made themselves available for interviews and consultations and also made me feel welcome during my research trips to the Maryknoll Society Center. A word of thanks to Patricia Healy and Holly Brown in the Council Secretariat and Maureen Toohey in the Maryknoll Society History Project for their help in facilitating access to historical materials.

Everywhere I conducted archival research I was greeted with helpfulness and expert advice. At Fordham University Archives, Vivian Shen, Fr. Henry Bertels, S.J., and Patrice Kane were most helpful. At the Archives of the Catholic University of America, John Shepherd, Jane Stoeffler, and Maria Mazzenga were both efficient and knowledgeable about the university's immense collection, as well as many questions of twentieth-century U.S. Catholic history.

Fr. Barry Wall, archivist of the Fall River Diocese, offered invaluable insight into the church context of southeastern Massachusetts in the early twentieth century and generously supplied me with photocopied materials. Suzanne Sullivan, Debbie Pelletier, and Fr. Mark Chmurski at St. Lawrence Martyr Church in New Bedford, Massachusetts, did a bit of digging to provide me with a copy of John Considine's 1915 high school transcript. Similarly, Fr. Carl Hoegerl of the Redemptorist Archives in Brooklyn, New York, supplied me with materials on *Pilate's Daughter,* the passion play run at the Mission Church in Roxbury, Massachusetts.

I was especially fortunate to have access to Considine family histories and good chunks of the family archive. Mary Lou Considine, Fr. Considine's niece, is largely responsible for the composition of the well-documented family histories and the amassing of the archival materials. Some years ago, she turned the archive over to her nephew, Matthew Considine, who generously supplied me with high-quality copies of more than ten years of correspondence between John Considine and his mother, Alice Murphy Considine. Later, Matthew and his brother Frank supplied high-quality reproductions of photos found in the family archive. They and other members of the family have been most gracious to me and helped me to shape an idea of what family life may have been like for Fr. Considine.

At the University of Notre Dame Archives, Kevin Cawley and Sharon Sumpter took my many requests with cheerfulness and at every turn offered expert advice on making good use of their ample collection. On a hot July afternoon when the air conditioning failed, Sharon and the rest of the staff kept lining up electric fans so that the group of us conducting research that day would not lose valuable time. Travel funds to and from Notre Dame in order to conduct research in the university archives were generously provided by the Cushwa Center for the Study of American Catholicism.

Frs. Robert Pelton and Paul Kollman at Notre Dame made themselves available for consultations. I am grateful to Fr. Bob for his personal knowledge of Fr. Considine and of many leaders in Latin America in the latter half of the twentieth century, and Fr. Paul gave me an orientation to bibliographic resources on Africa. Fr. Pelton also reviewed several chapters of the book and provided insightful suggestions on the long-term impact of Considine's work at the Latin America Bureau in the 1960s. Timothy Matovina also made himself available for a consultation on Hispanic ministry in the United States in relation to Latin America during the mid-twentieth century.

There are numerous other colleagues to thank—first among them is Wilbert Shenk, senior professor of Mission History and Contemporary Culture at Fuller Theological Seminary. Wilbert took an immense interest in this project, encouraged me to take it up, and over the years always made time to consult with me and read parts of the manuscript. More than anything, Wilbert offered invaluable assistance for understanding the place of Considine in the history of Christian mission during the twentieth century.

Similarly, historian of U.S. Catholic missions Sister Angelyn Dries, OSF, has been a fellow traveler on the journey of interpreting the history of Maryknoll. She generously made herself available to read parts of the manuscript and offered helpful insight into the question of Considine's career ambitions. I was especially grateful to Angie for her earlier research on Considine.

Thomas Quigley, formerly of the USCCB, served on the staff of the Latin America Bureau under Fr. Considine. He reviewed drafts of chapters, and I was fortunate to be able to consult with him on many occasions. Tom is an authority on Latin America and the U.S. Catholic bishops during the second half of the twentieth century, and I have been grateful for his deep interest in this project.

Mary Elizabeth Brown of the Center for Migration Studies, New York, assisted with bibliography on nineteenth-century Irish migration to the United States. Similarly, Fr. Thomas Ahearn, M.M., offered a world of sociological insight on Irish-American communities in Massachusetts.

Fr. David Endres of Mt. St. Mary's Seminary, Cincinnati, offered perspectives on the Catholic Student Mission Crusade, and Fr. Tom Stransky, C.S.P., helped me to contact Fr. Leo Declerck for consultations on Ivan Illich at Vatican II. Similarly, Todd Hartch of Eastern Kentucky University was very generous with his time and his thinking on the Illich–Considine relationship.

Fr. James Kroeger, M.M., gave me access to his considerable research on the Considine–Latourette relationship. We also happened to find ourselves in Rome at the same time during the spring of 2011, and so he was helpful in getting me oriented to conducting research in various Roman archives.

The research in Rome was a new venture for me, and so I am grateful to many people who opened doors—or gave me advice on getting doors opened—and helped me locate the needed archival and bibliographic resources. Before I departed for Rome, Carlos Parra Pirela at the University of Toronto gave me a crash course in what I needed to bring and what to expect; Carlos previously had researched late-nineteenth-century inter-religious perspectives of the Holy See. Archbishop José H. Gomez of Los Angeles and LMU's Fr. Thomas Rausch, S.J., graciously provided me with letters of introduction for the various archives in Rome; once in Rome, Archbishop Joseph A. DiNoia, O.P., also assisted me with a recommendation.

Fr. Clyde Philips, M.M., was a gracious host to me at Collegio Mary-knoll in Rome, and Fr. Joseph McCabe, M.M., was a font of ideas on how the Vatican works. At the Pontifical Urbanian University, Fr. Francis Ane-kwe Oborji gave me a warm welcome and a practical orientation on how to navigate the bureaucratic aspects of gaining access to Roman archives. At the university's library, Dr. Antonio Alesiani, assistant librarian, offered consistent help with locating obscure items or alerted me to where else I could find them.

At the Missionary Ethnological Museum of the Vatican, Fr. Nicola Mapelli, P.I.M.E., curator of Ethnological Collections, and Dr. Nadia Fius-sello provided generous help with the museum's archives.

My thanks also go to the helpful staff at the Archivio Storico di Pro-paganda Fide: Msgr. Luis Manuel Cuña Ramos, archivist; Dr. Giovanni Fosci, assistant archivist, and Dr. Roberta Ciocci, conservator. At the Vatican Secret Archives, I am grateful to the secretary general, Dr. Luca Carboni, for his assistance with a petition for access to records of the 1929 Pontifical Mission to the Court of the emperor of Ethiopia. Also at the Vatican Secret Archives, Mr. Edoardo Amtinucci, assistente di sala, always offered kind and intelligent help.

There are several colleagues whom I have met only in cyber space but who have read drafts of my work and endeavored to help me understand the historical context of Pius XI: Lucia Ceci, Università degli Studi di Roma "Tor Vergata"; Alberto Melloni and Mara Dissegna of the working group on Pius XI, Fondazione per le sciencie religiose Giovanni XXIII; and Alessandro Bausi, co-editor of the *Encyclopaedia Aethiopica*. Fr. Daniel Assefa, OFM Cap., Rector of St. Francis Major Seminary, Addis Ababa, also read a draft of the section on Ethiopia.

On a personal note, my parents, Art and Ann, and my mother-in-law Yeon Wha Kim, along with numerous family members and friends offered patient support as I proceeded with the project and missed various family celebrations along the way. Special thanks go to my niece, Jihye Kim, whose visit was a great support to Riji while I was away from home on one of the longer research trips undertaken during the project. Thanks also go out to Matt Williamson for all the computer troubleshooting he did for me and for being there and keeping me sane, as only an old and trusted friend can.

While I have all of these and more to thank for their assistance and helpful perspectives, the work that follows is solely my responsibility. The persons named here have graciously assisted me with insights and even direction, but any and all errors in the text are mine.

Introduction

"CONSIDINE WAS BIG," said historian Christopher Kauffman at the other end of the phone line in December of 2010.[1] Indeed, Maryknoll Father John J. Considine (1897–1982) was as large as the worldwide perspective found in the questions he asked, always with a view to strengthening the church's ability to engage human cultures everywhere. He understood that the missioner's task was of a scale both small and large, simultaneously concerned with how the efforts of catechists in a Chinese village would be organized and with the advent of the space age.[2]

As a Vatican insider, Maryknoll Father John J. Considine was a large enough figure to be pursued for high office in the Vatican diplomatic corps on several occasions. However, as a missionary, he demurred from such possibilities in order to remain focused on enterprises where he could be most effective for the mission cause.

In the mid-twentieth century, Considine's writings, conferences, and organizing style reflected the sensibilities of someone who understood both the concerns of the Vatican and the context of mission around the world. He was thus able to assist the church in the United States to understand and stay in tune with the mission concerns of the universal church. The inverse was also true—his colleagues in Rome understood him to be a reliable source of information on the growing U.S. Catholic mission enterprises. Who was John Considine?

Born in New Bedford, Massachusetts, John Joseph Considine joined the new Catholic Foreign Mission Society of America (Maryknoll) in 1915 and was ordained in 1923. From 1924 to 1934 he worked in Rome under the Sacred Congregation of Propaganda Fide (SCPF), the Vatican office that since 1622 has supervised Catholic missionary work worldwide (in 1969 it was renamed "Congregation for the Evangelization of Peoples"). He served in the leadership of the Maryknoll Society from 1934 to 1946 and was an editor of *Maryknoll: The Field Afar* from 1936 to 1960. Between 1960 and 1968, Considine served as the director of the U.S. Bishops' Latin

---

1. December 16, 2010.
2. Eugene C. Kennedy, "Didn't You See It? It Happened," *Interchange* 31, no. 2 (2011): 4.

America Bureau, and in his retirement at Maryknoll, New York, he continued to research and write on mission.

In world affairs, the growing ascendancy of the United States parallels Fr. Considine's career. The same period in the church was a time of great growth—a time of expansion of the U.S. Catholic mission effort, and a time when the church was increasing in numbers in non-Western areas. Over his long career, Considine was a strong voice for the cause of Catholic missions; he was the author of more than a dozen books and hundreds of articles on the subject.

Because Considine's life parallels significant moments of twentieth-century mission history, the narrative of his life offered here shifts at times from a sustained focus on what Considine did and said to an examination of the contexts in which he worked. Both foci are meant to elaborate details about Considine, either in regard to his own accomplishments and struggles or in regard to the world he inhabited.

At the end of this introduction I will offer a summary of the book's chapters. What follows immediately is a further introduction to significant aspects of Considine's thought and contributions: his sense of World Christianity; his work as a journalist and as an organizer of mission initiatives; nascent postcolonialism in missions; and a brief appreciation of how his characteristic optimism can be understood in the context of U.S. Catholicism in the twentieth century.

Fr. Considine was a researcher, a writer, and a teacher on mission topics; he was a tireless organizer of Catholic missions and their support institutions. But more than anything, he could explain why mission was important.

An Educator to World Christianity[3]

An example of how concrete and detailed Considine's efforts in educating Catholics to the new world Christian reality occurred on a cold February day in 1944, when John Considine was fired up over the sad state of geography textbooks in Catholic schools. The Teacher's Institute of the Archdiocese of New York asked him to review their textbooks, and he gave them an earful in his address about what was at stake in this matter.

He focused on Africa, and after reviewing both what he learned about Africa from the textbooks—the physical characteristics of the land, the

---

3. In a 1953 essay, Considine noted that the term "Education to World Christianity" was first used in 1944 as the title of a statement issued by the Mission Education Committee of the National Catholic Education Association. This terminology, which would become the title of one of Considine's most important books (*World Christianity*, 1945), is attributed in the 1953 article to Msgr. George Johnson, chair of Mission Education Committee during 1944 ("Education to World Christianity," 1953).

political divisions, a vague sense of the livelihood of Africans, a good deal about what Africa exports to the rest of the world—and what he did *not* learn (there was almost nothing about African culture, education, economics, and religions in the texts), he launched into what was for him the heart of the matter in regard to the study of geography:

> The greatest fact in Africa today is the existence of 120 million immortal souls on that continent. It is good to know where the rivers and mountains and deserts are, what products we get from the Congo, from East Africa, West Africa, South Africa. But is it proper to end a course with the impression left in the minds of our children (so far as the text book is concerned) that religion is to be ignored in the study of the peoples of the earth? Would it be improper in a Catholic classroom to have a text which notes that 10,000,000 Africans are Catholic? Is it not a sufficiently outstanding fact to explain that 20,000 Catholic priests, Brothers, and Sisters dedicate themselves to the spiritual and likewise to the temporal welfare of the African people? [4]

From there he went on to urge that Catholic schools should provide "an education to World Christianity," simultaneously cultivating knowledge of and regard for all peoples, as well as a devotion to the church's mission to bring "to all non-Catholics and non-Christians Christ's teaching and life of charity." For Considine, the key to all of this was a sense of brotherhood and sisterhood of the world's peoples:

> It is not enough for the Church to send out missioners. By the Christian theory of the universe, it is not enough to pay the way of men who will baptize our neighbor, the non-Christian; it is not enough to send our neighbor bread when he is starving, a cover when he is cold. The teachings of Christianity applied to the world require still more than *service* to all men; they require *brotherhood* with all men. "Thou shalt love thy neighbor as thyself." This love is not to apply in some vague, eschatological way; it is to apply in the daily life of each of us as individuals and in the daily life of the nation and the portion of human society to which we belong in its relations with all other nations and portions of human society. [5]

---

4. John J. Considine, "World Christianity in the Teaching of Geography and History." Conference at Teacher's Institute, Archdiocese of New York, February 21, 1944. MMA, Considine Papers, 8:7. Emphasis in original.

5. Ibid.

In 1944, in a world very much at war, Considine developed his ideas on World Christianity as a way to engage people in a vision of human life that would tie them more closely to each other and to all peoples everywhere. He spent his life promoting this simple point: if you are a believer in Christ, it is an inescapable conclusion that you are, because of Christ, in a relationship with the peoples of the world. In this view, it is only a matter of each believer fully taking responsibility for these relationships. These ideas impassioned Considine and motivated him throughout his career.

A Definite Goal in the Mission Line

Early in his career, Considine came to understand his service to mission as taking the path of a practical intellectual. In a 1926 letter to his friend, Maryknoll Father Francis X. Ford, who was serving in South China, Considine described how he was organizing his reading:

> I began last year, after getting hints from various missionaries here in Rome, to set for myself a definite goal in the mission line. The field is altogether too large for me to attempt to tackle it all—and altogether too vague to trust myself picking up what is of momentary interest. . . . I have picked up the period of the French Revolution to the present day for historical browsings, and hope to read the history of at least the important missionary societies during this approximate century and a quarter. Then I have set for myself as a goal a knowledge of the present day mission world in general and of the fields of the Maryknoll workers in particular, but I desire to move from the general to the less general, therefore during the past few months, I have been looking for synthetic treatments of the universe and its continents.[6]

In addition to mission history, Considine also read works of political history, such as Dennett's *Americans in Eastern Asia* (1922). However, to further the cause of mission, a wider range of knowledge was needed, and it would be important for Considine to not stick to the bibliographic limits established by the church at the time.

> You may be interested to know that I began by trying to get for myself a more grown-up concept of the God of the Universe: I read Aveling,[7] the god of philosophy, and at present am completing him by

---

6. John J. Considine, Rome, to Francis Ford, Kaying, China, October 14, 1926. MMA, Considine Papers, 2:9.

7. Aveling, 1920.

Sheen's "God and intelligence."[8] Then I made a move—slightly illicit, but one which I do not regret, though I shall be careful to whom I tell it: I read H.G. Wells's "Short History of the World,"[9] being led to it by having first read the criticisms of Hilaire Belloc published by the N.C.W.C.[10] As you already know, Wells has thoughts and ideas on many gravely important subjects, but so far as giving a synthetical view of all things material from the first moment of Creation down to 1920, his attempt is masterly.[11]

He also read Protestant missiologists such as Kenneth MacLennan, and J. H. Oldham's *Christianity and the Race Problem* (1924). And, of course, there was the poetry of Keats and Shelley. He read Joseph Conrad's works "quite thoroughly," savoring the atmosphere of his stories with a view to creating a Conradian sense in his own writing on missions. Considine admired Conrad's ability "to whip across two or three continents in the stroke of a pen."[12]

But the goal of the intellectual life for Considine was the building up of the ability of the church to be in mission to the world's peoples. He was particularly concerned to develop mission literature—for missioners, for mission supporters, and for the general public—that would present the church's mission efforts in all their depth.

In some future letter we will talk of the possibility of our combining with perhaps a few others in the Society or outside the Society, in the preparation of some worth while missionary productions. My stay in Rome has impressed me with the necessity of studying out carefully exactly what will be of most prominent value in printed matter. There is a glut of inconsequential material and there are many well prepared monographs; there are certain fields however, which should be entered in a more wide-visioned manner. I am wondering if in the course of the next twenty years we may not be able to do something in this line.[13]

---

8. Sheen, 1925.

9. Wells, 1922.

10. National Catholic Welfare Council, the forerunner of the U.S. Conference of Catholic Bishops.

11. Considine to Ford, October 14, 1926.

12. Ibid. Considine worked also in various yearbooks: the *China Year Book,* the *Negro Year Book,* the *Statesman Year Book,* the *World Almanac,* the *South American Handbook,* the *Japan Year Book,* the *Indian Year Book, Stuart's Year Book.*

13. Considine to Ford, October 14, 1926.

The Journalist

Considine was a journalist, and he used his journalistic talents to educate English-speaking audiences on the peoples of the world. Considine could digest quickly what was in front of him and turn it into a text that was simultaneously sympathetic to those it described and comprehensible to audiences that had no familiarity with the situation. His texts were therefore examples of high-quality interpretive journalism, but, more than that, they were effective means of educating Catholics and others about mission.

When it came to researching and writing about Catholic missions, he was a quick study. While serving in Rome near the beginning of his career, Considine conceived the idea of taking a fourteen-month mission study tour to Asia and Africa. He planned to tour missions on the two continents and write stories for Fides Service and *L'Osservatore Romano* based on his observations. When he approached Cardinal Van Rossum, the prefect of Propaganda, to seek approval of his journey, the cardinal had one word of advice: take your time. Van Rossum advised against a strict itinerary, adding that Considine should advance only when he had gained a sufficient glimpse of the missions on which he was standing.[14]

Considine either took his advice to heart or had already thought of it, because during that first study tour (November 1931–January 1933), the flow of articles for his series, "Other Men's Lands,"[15] poured forth in constant succession. In fact, Considine's traveling program included more than two months in India and three months in China, more than a month in Indochina and three and a half months in East, Central, and West Africa. Both within and in between those countries, Considine traveled extensively, speaking to as many missioners, church officials, and laity as he could in each place.

His particular talents—a curiosity about the world's peoples and the church around the world, an ability to write clearly and sympathetically, the ability to comprehend a situation quickly and to focus on a newsworthy topic, the gift of gab with the people he interviewed, and an ability to write while in transit—helped him time and again to produce his many articles, stories, and books.

Considine operated out of the regnant missiology of the time, that of the planting of the church in new contexts—*plantatio ecclesiae*. However, in his writing and teaching he was ever pushing the envelope on what that meant. For example, whether he was evaluating the church's approach to the Indonesian aesthetic or offering an appreciation of the ability of

---

14. CD, September 9, 1931.

15. Most of the articles were later compiled in a book: John J. Considine and Thomas Dickenson Kernan, *Across a World* (New York: Longmans, Green & Co., 1942).

mission work to keep up with population growth in China, Considine would expand the basic missiology of establishing the church among all the world's peoples into important practical questions about what the church needed to do to further the sharing of the gospel.

In keeping with his vocational call to connect the peoples of the world through education on mission, Considine catered to a general Catholic audience. He wrote mostly in English and sometimes in French; Fides Service, an international Catholic press service on missions, which he founded in 1927, distributed its publications in several languages.

One might ask, what was the purpose of producing these sympathetic texts on mission situations? Why educate Catholics about mission? Considine's writing fit squarely within an organized plan or idea of how the mission of Christ should be carried out. Accordingly, he would judge each account he wrote as helping or hindering the concrete cause of the church's mission. He strove to strike the right tone and reach the right audience in such a way as to enlist their energies in the mission enterprise.

Considine the Mission Organizer

Considine had great gifts as an organizer and networker for missions. Through the 1950s, he founded or helped organize four different missionary or academic enterprises,[16] and he was a collaborator or leader in the early development of four others.[17] (For a complete timeline on these and other activities, see p. xxiv.)

At the end of his career, at age sixty-two, in 1960 he accepted the position of director of the U.S. Bishops' Latin America Bureau (LAB), where he served until his retirement in 1968. The mission of the LAB was to invigorate and increase the U.S. Catholic mission effort in Latin America. In this "second career" he had to start from zero—the LAB was being revived after almost thirty years of inactivity. Nevertheless, in a short period of time Considine assembled a competent staff and worked to establish several more enterprises: a new lay missionary organization, the Papal Volunteers for Latin America, PAVLA (1960); the Center of Intercultural Formation, CIF, in Cuernavaca, Mexico (1961); and the Catholic Inter-American Cooperation Program, CICOP, a series of ten annual conferences in which thousands of North American Church people would gather each year to learn about the church in Latin America (1964). He also published the pro-

---

16. Fides International Service (1927); the U.S. Catholic Mission Secretariat (1949); the Fordham Mission Institute and the Fordham Conference of Mission Specialists (1953); the African Studies Association (1957).

17. The Catholic Student Mission Crusade, CSMC (1920–1923); the Catholic Medical Mission Board (1923); the Vatican Missionary Exposition (1925); and the Missionary Ethnological Museum at the Lateran (1927).

Considine at a Glance, 1897-1982

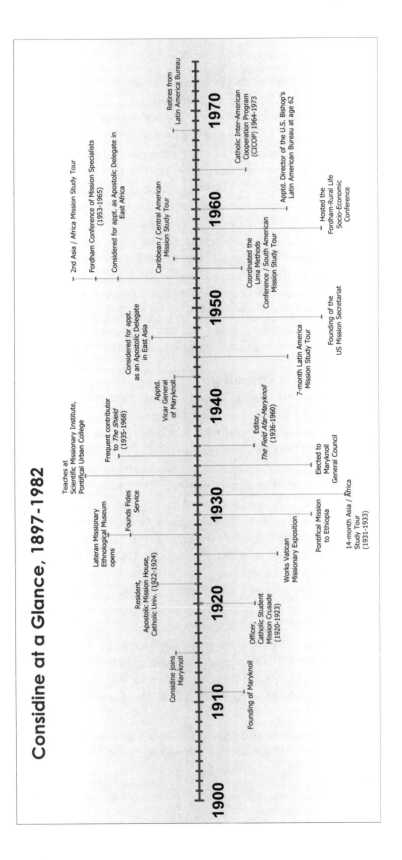

ceedings of each of those conferences in book form, in addition to initiating four smaller serials.

To accomplish all this, Considine and his staff networked with church leaders in many settings: bishops, religious superiors, and lay organizations in the United States; the Pontifical Commission for Latin America (CAL) in Rome; and the Latin American Bishops Conference (CELAM).

Such networking came naturally to Fr. Considine, whose study tours of Africa, Asia, and Latin America had brought him into direct contact with up-and-coming church leaders from many parts of the world. The long list of people he interviewed on his study tours includes three men who later became the first cardinals from their countries: Archbishop Caro of Santiago, Chile, whom Considine met in 1945; Bishop Laurean Rugambwa of Rutabo, Tanganyika, in 1953; and, also in 1953, Fr. Stephen Kim in Korea. In Rome, too, in 1925 he attended meetings of the Vatican Missionary Exposition with a young Msgr. Angelo Roncalli, the future Pope John XXIII.

Although he was never assigned to any particular mission station, John J. Considine was fundamentally a missionary. Following Ivan Illich's compact definition, a missionary is marked by the capacity to leave home and talk with strangers.[18] Fr. Considine spent his long career traveling the world and engaging people in conversation, studying their life situations and their relationships to Christ and the church. As he did so, he remained ever convinced that most of what he learned in those conversations carried significance for any member of the church—or even for any human being.

A Matter of Perspective

In the pages of his first book, *The Vatican Mission Exposition: A Window on the World* (1925), Fr. Considine led North American readers through the twenty-six halls of mission exhibits set up on the Vatican grounds. He was no stranger to the event; from not long after his arrival in Rome in November 1924, Fr. Considine walked visitors through the Exposition's displays as an English-speaking guide almost every day for his first eight months in Rome. By early summer 1925, Considine composed *The Vatican Mission Exposition*. He continued to walk the halls of the Exposition through its closing in January of 1926.

The Hall of History was one of the first pavilions described by Considine. The hall's designers had profiled four stages of mission history: (1) from the time of the apostles to that of St. Benedict (d. ca. 547); (2) from St. Benedict's time to the founding of the mendicant orders in the thirteenth

18. Ivan Illich, *The Church, Change, and Development* (Chicago: Urban Training Center Press, 1970), 113.

century; (3) from the thirteenth century to the discovery of the Americas; and (4) from the discovery of the Americas to the present.

"By far the greater part of the material found in the hall relates to the last period of missions," and Considine devoted the most space in his chapter to that period.[19] He comments on the depictions of the voyages of discovery and adds details about the first missionaries sent out with the explorers and navigators. St. Francis Xavier's legacy is described in detail, and a photo of a statue of him is included in the pages of this chapter.[20]

After Xavier are found descriptions of Matteo Ricci and his companions, and of Fr. Constantino, a Capuchin Franciscan among the first missionaries in Tibet. From India, de Nobili is recalled; the founders of the Paris Foreign Mission Society (de La Motte and Pallu) are also remembered. And from North America, Franciscan Fr. Hennepin and Jesuit Fr. Marquette are also described.

In Considine's telling, the exhibits of the Hall of History concerned with the modern period of mission provide exactly that, the history of missionaries going out. What he did not describe from that hall is also quite significant.

In no part of this chapter is found any version of the word "colonial." But for European observers at the time, the larger-than-life presence of colonialism in the Hall of History was the main event. The magazine of the Italian Society for the Propagation of the Faith reported that the

> description of the room devoted to missionary history shows us, for example, the four stages of this history, "brought to life by large wall maps." The fourth of these, dedicated to contemporary times, openly extols "the foundation of the vast colonial empires" that with the geographical discoveries "opened the way to Christianity even in the most distant regions of the earth."[21]

As will become clear in the pages ahead, the omission of a discussion on colonialism and mission in Considine's text was no accident. Certainly he had good reason to believe that his North American audience would have had limited interest in the topic of European colonialism. But beyond such considerations was a much deeper concern for Considine. Pope Benedict

---

19. John J. Considine, *The Vatican Mission Exposition: A Window on the World* (New York: Macmillan, 1925), 52–59.

20. St. Francis Xavier's statue stood in one of the India Halls of the Exposition.

21. G. de Rossi, "Una finestra aperta sul mondo," *La Propagazione della Fede nel Mondo* III-1 (1925): 21–42. Cited in Stefano Trinchese, *Roncalli e le missioni: l'opera della propagazione della fede tra Francia e Vaticano negli anni '20* (Brescia: Morcelliana, 1989), 180–81 (my translation).

XV and then Pius XI had been working on a nascent postcolonial mission agenda. It was 1925, and key leaders in the Catholic Church understood—correctly, as it turned out—that Christianity in the twentieth century had tremendous opportunities for growth in Asia, Africa, Latin America, and Oceania. But in the vision of Benedict XV and Pius XI, the church would have to free itself from colonialism, racism, and ethnocentrism if it hoped to share the gospel of Christ effectively with the peoples of the non-Western world.

As is evident from the contemporary account of the Exposition's Hall of History, not everybody understood this early postcolonialism or saw it as advantageous for mission. At its heart, the policy of the popes was calling for a brand-new set of relationships among the peoples of the world, in which peoples of all nations would be free to be themselves as they expressed faith in Christ, and the leaders among them would be recognized by the universal church. Many missionaries throughout the centuries had practiced such a vision, but it was clearly not the norm in the 1920s.

The effort to move the actual mission policy lived by Catholic missionaries in a postcolonial direction was a task to which Considine dedicated his life. Over the major periods of his life—from initial formation beginning in 1915 until his retirement from the U.S. Bishops' Latin America Bureau in 1968—Considine both advocated for a postcolonial mission policy and devised ways concretely to counter prejudice.

Considine's approach to countering prejudice was subtle rather than confrontational, but it was something he consciously thought of as part of his work throughout his career. His efforts usually took the form of disseminating correct information about a group of people either unknown to an audience or for which the audience may have held only stereotypes. Similarly, this approach always involved an appeal for basic human respect. For example, after giving a talk on Latin America to the Diocesan Council of Catholic Women in Bridgeport, Connecticut, in 1963, Considine's diary records the reactions of Carmen and Mercedes de Arango, two Cuban-Americans who "lost everything to Castro. It was my appeal for respect for the Latin American that counted most." Considine's strategies for countering prejudice will be explored further in chapter 5 and in the essay on missiography that follows chapter 6.

Considine the Optimist

William Halsey has advanced the notion of an American Catholic innocence, a noticeable optimism that emerged after World War I.[22] Americans

---

22. William M. Halsey, *The Survival of American Innocence: Catholicism in an Era of Disillusionment, 1920–1940* (Notre Dame, IN: University of Notre Dame Press, 1980).

in general were much more optimistic at this time than Europeans, but Halsey notes the specific contours of this sensibility among U.S. Catholics: the belief in a rational and ordered universe, a morality that is inherent in human life, and the triumph of progress.[23] These three characteristics permeated Fr. Considine's writing; they certainly undergird his argument in *World Christianity* (1945) that Christianity is the unique world institution capable of propagating in goodwill the ideas of the unity of the human race, the equality of all people, an equality of fellowship for all, and the universality of the fall.[24] Considine will ever display a sunny optimism about what the missionary church can do.

Considine's optimism was grounded in a reality with which he became well acquainted. It was perhaps in Rome during the 1925 Vatican Mission Exposition that he first had an experience of the church's ability to function among the world's cultures and peoples:

> I stood this afternoon in the Exposition and talked with a Negro priest of Ethiopia; and in the course of the last twenty-four hours have talked with, sat with, or passed by on the street, Catholics of India, China, Indo-China, and Japan. Read Christianity's story in each of these countries, meet their Christian children today, then go aside and dream awhile, and build a kingdom in your mind, a kingdom with a Savior leading all and a world-united people following— a people one, without rank, caste, class, or color-line. This is the true vision of the Kingdom of God.[25]

Because of the church's worldwide mission and because people on all the continents had embraced Christ and his church, Considine could confidently envision further expansions of the ministries and institutions of the church, bringing a sense of oneness in Christ to peoples of all races, classes, and cultures.[26]

A note of evaluation is in order in regard to U.S. Catholic innocence and Considine. Even though the choice for optimism is not unproblematic—Halsey notes that in a general sense it could not be sustained by U.S. Catholics into the 1960s—it does not follow that "a confident approach

---

23. Ibid., 2.

24. Considine, *World Christianity*, 24–32.

25. Considine, *Vatican Mission Exposition*, 172.

26. This optimistic sense does not, of course, solve all the problems of a world church, and Considine was a keen observer of the many difficulties experienced by the churches of Africa, Asia, Latin America, and Oceania during the twentieth century. For example, in an extensive report on East Asia in 1932, Considine discussed the problem of missioners with poor ability in Asian languages (John J. Considine, "Foreign Mission Sisters." MMA, Considine Papers, 12:2).

to reality" or the "close association between religion and American ideals" is a form of pathology.[27] Halsey's analysis of American Catholic innocence is helpful because it is descriptive, not because it offers a solution to any post–Vatican II dismay.

Indeed, a more recent focus on communities of narrative and theology would bid us to understand well how people like Considine and other leaders of the U.S. church 1920–1960 nourished faith communities within a shared narrative framework. It is not possible to relive a pre-1960 framework in today's context, but it is always interesting to ask if the sorts of qualities displayed and practices shared in other times can contribute to the church's life and mission today.

Essential Considine

Apart from his normal duties, from 1931 to 1955 Considine made five lengthy study tours, and from these travels he produced four major books on mission.[28] Since he was never assigned to a mission, the study tours allowed him to spend months at a time visiting Catholic missions in Asia, Africa, and Latin America. Each trip would be a combination of long conversations with bishops, missioners, students, lay leaders, and many others, sprinkled with hefty doses of life on the road—life aboard ship (and later on, in flight), and side trips on trains, buses, jeeps, river boats, and canoes. He read volumes of anthropology and history on these journeys and took copious notes in his diaries for future articles and books. Considine was especially vibrant when he was on the road, as he found that travel did not take any "pep" out of him; he often reported, as he did in a February 1932 letter to his mother from Tindivanam, India, that he felt "better than when I left."[29]

Over his long career, those conversations with strangers shaped his contributions to mission and to the church. But they also formed him as an individual believer and made his life a window on the growth of Christianity in non-Western contexts during the twentieth century. While Fr. Considine did not predict the twentieth-century growth of Christianity in Africa, Asia, Latin America, and Oceania, like many of his contemporaries in Rome in the 1920s and 1930s, he understood that in those areas of the world the twentieth century afforded the church abundant opportunities for expansion.

---

27. Halsey, *Survival of American Innocence,* 7.

28. *Across a World* (with Thomas Kernan, 1942); *Call for Forty Thousand* (1946); *Africa: World of New Men* (1954); and *New Horizons in Latin America* (1958).

29. John J. Considine, Tindivanum [Tindivanam], India, to Alice Considine, New Bedford, MA, February 7, 1932. Considine Family Archive.

Chapter Summary

As the story of Fr. Considine's life, this book explores both his contributions as such and also the way the trajectory of his career opens up important vistas for an understanding of the mission of the church in the twentieth century. The book is principally a narrative of his life, interspersed with essays that provide either context or a more detailed analysis of some part of his work.

Chapter 1 introduces the reader to the Considine family of New Bedford, Massachusetts, and tells the story of how his immigrant mother overcame the hardship of early widowhood and sent all six of her sons to college. Chapter 2 explores what is known of young John Considine's high school years, 1911–1915; as with many Catholics of the time, the church was important to John and his family, though there are clear indications that he was not overly deferential to religious authority. The chapter ends with a narrative of his vocational discernment and subsequent decision to become a missionary priest and join the new Catholic Foreign Mission Society of America at age seventeen in 1915.

Chapter 3 uses Considine's 1916–1917 diaries to describe the family environment of Maryknoll seminary life during his second year in Maryknoll, a time when the very youthful group was growing in number and in mission spirit, even though the first Maryknoll missioners had not yet been sent out. This was also a time when Considine's talents and leadership abilities came to the attention of his superiors.

Chapter 4, covering the years 1917–1924, narrates the end of his studies for the priesthood and his two years of graduate study in missiology at the Catholic University of America (1922–1924). It was also a time when the events of Considine's life brought him into significant contact with two important currents in U.S. Catholicism: the emergence of national Catholic organizations (Considine served on the board of the Catholic Student Mission Crusade 1920–1923) and a strain of Catholic Americanism that had survived the 1899 Vatican condemnation and was alive at Catholic University in the thinking of Msgr. John A. Ryan and others. The chapter closes with the telling of how Considine arranged for Maryknoll to send two exhibits to the 1925 Vatican Mission Exposition, setting the stage for the next significant phase of his work in Rome.

Chapter 5 describes roughly the first half (1924–1930) of Considine's ten-year sojourn in Rome, focusing on his accomplishments during these years but also on the formative impact the period had on him as he quickly learned the ropes of working in the church's central bureaucracy. During these years he was given the opportunity to embark on a career path aimed at an eventual appointment to high ecclesiastical office. It was an option he ultimately put aside, although he certainly learned how to thrive as a Vatican insider. In regard to his work, Fr. Considine was the founding director of Fides Service, a multilingual Catholic missions press agency. Fides had a large impact—what other Vatican press agency utilized a comparative religions perspective in 1927? Publishing weekly dispatches from around the world, the service became an immediate happening in the world of the Catholic press of the time.

Chapter 6 covers the period from 1930 until Considine's decision to return to Maryknoll to serve in the leadership of the Maryknoll Society at the end of 1934. By 1930, Considine had established Fides Service and was about to see it expanded to include an international Catholic missions think-tank. Over his more than seven years at Fides, Considine certainly did establish and improve the service, but he was ultimately unsuccessful in expanding its operations.

During his final years in Rome, he would try out his journalistic talents in a new way by taking a fourteen-month mission study tour of Asia and Africa. The trip allowed Considine firsthand knowledge of Catholic missions and began to further shape his vision of his own practical service to missions as an intellectual and as a journalist. Considine's decision to return to the United States was related to changes in leadership at Propaganda Fide, but was perhaps most greatly influenced by the needs of a growing Maryknoll in the United States.

A brief excursus follows chapter 6 on the topic of "missiography," which Considine defined as the study of the world's peoples and the study of the church's mission. Considine described himself as a missiographer, and a key document from the founding of Fides Service opens up the texture of what was for him a lifelong passion.

Appointed to serve on the leadership Council of the Maryknoll Society in 1934, Considine returned from Rome to Maryknoll's headquarters near Ossining, New York. Chapter 7 covers Considine's work as a mission executive (1934–1946). Since Maryknoll Co-Founder Bishop James Anthony Walsh died in 1936, these were years in which the first generation of Maryknollers led the still-young mission society for the first time. These were also years of crisis—World War II had severely limited Maryknoll's mission work in East Asia, and new missions were begun in Latin America. Considine and his fellow Council members played a crucial role in defining the importance of mission in mostly Catholic Latin America; up until this time Maryknollers had conceived of mission only in terms of outreach to those outside the church. Additionally, as the only Maryknoller at the time to have ever visited sub-Saharan Africa, Considine also played a large role in a seven-year process that led to the first Maryknollers being sent to Musoma, Tanganyika, in 1946. And because what happens in one's own house also marks a person, the chapter concludes with an exploration

of the sometimes-troubled relationship between the leadership of the two
U.S. missionary groups that share the name of Maryknoll. Fr. Considine's
successful and unsuccessful efforts to keep the leadership of the Maryknoll
Society and the Maryknoll Sisters Congregation in fruitful relationship
with each other and his work with a professional staff of Maryknoll Sister
writers, educators, and illustrators in the promotion department at Maryknoll headquarters are discussed.

Chapter 8, "Teaching and Organizing for Mission," backtracks a little
by covering the years 1942–1962, a time when Considine, still working on
the editorial staff of *The Field Afar*, continued to develop mission education
initiatives for U.S. Catholics and also took part in several key U.S.-based
mission initiatives outside of Maryknoll: the founding of a national Mission
Secretariat and its publication *Worldmission*; the Fordham Mission Institute
and the Fordham Conference of Mission Specialists; the Fordham Rural
Life Conference of 1958. In 1957 he became a founding member of the
African Studies Association. These were also years when the Vatican Diplomatic Corps tried unsuccessfully on four occasions to recruit Considine
for high ecclesiastical office. During these years, Considine also made four
more mission study tours—three to Latin America (1945, 1954, 1955), and
an extensive trip to Asia and Africa in 1953. The chapter also includes an
analysis of the work of the 1954 Lima Methods Conference, a gathering
of twenty Maryknoll priests working in South America to assess their first
twelve years of mission work on the continent and to plan future initiatives. Considine was the main organizer of the conference.

During this period, some of Considine's strongest statements on mission
were published in which he articulated a vision of world unity and the universality of Christian mission.[30] His writings during this period gave great
attention to the need to counter prejudice firmly, betraying his dependence
on such seminal thinkers as J. H. Oldham, Pius XI, and Jacques Maritain.
Considine also returned to the classroom during the late 1940s and the
1950s to teach a course on missiology at Maryknoll Seminary. There was
a persistent focus in the writings of this period: Christian mission would
benefit from greater and greater forms of cooperation in a world that was
becoming globalized.

Between chapters 8 and 9 an essay on Considine, ecumenism, and interreligious dialogue is inserted. Considine had a decades-long friendship with
Yale historian of missions Kenneth Scott Latourette, and key early Considine writings calling for greater ecumenical cooperation in foreign mis-

---

30. Considine, "Introduction," in *Across a World* (1942); *Outline of Missiography* and
World Christianity (1944); *Call for Forty Thousand* (1946); *Fundamental Catholic Teaching on the
Human Race* (1961); "The Church's Global Mission and the Future" (1962).

sions are also reviewed. Additionally, a parallel will be highlighted between Considine's stances toward ecumenism and toward interreligious matters. In both areas he pushed the envelope, describing or proposing activities that stop just short of attracting condemnation from those zealous of official Catholic teaching on Protestantism or other religions.

Chapters 9 and 10 review Considine's service as director of the U.S. Bishops' Latin America Bureau (LAB) and offer an assessment of the U.S. Catholic mission effort in Latin America in the 1960s.

The years 1960–1965, roughly corresponding to the administration of President John F. Kennedy, are profiled in chapter 9. During these years, Considine was surely considered one of the U.S. church's best and brightest. He was a recognized writer on foreign missions and was well versed in foreign affairs.[31] As has already been noted, this was a time in which Considine coordinated carefully with the U.S. bishops, the Latin American bishops (CELAM), and the Pontifical Commission for Latin America to build the LAB and its many initiatives from scratch. It was also a time of great ferment in Washington, and Considine interacted with Kennedy administration figures such as Sargent Shriver on the development of the Peace Corps and Teodoro Moscoso in regard to the Alliance for Progress, seeking cooperation between government and church efforts. Ever the networker, Considine started the "Latin America Supper Club," a monthly Dutch-treat think tank for academics, church people, and government officials concerned about Latin America.

Considine's final years at the LAB, 1965–1968, are considered in chapter 10. While many have suggested that Ivan Illich's 1967 essay "The Seamy Side of Charity" sparked a decline in the U.S. Catholic mission to Latin America, I offer three alternative views: I suggest a number of other factors that help to explain the decline in the number of U.S. missioners to Latin America after 1967; I examine the long-running conflict between Considine and Illich and suggest that Illich unfairly targeted Considine for criticism; and I suggest that Illich overreached in "Seamy" by claiming to speak for the Latin American church in his criticisms of Considine and the LAB. The chapter concludes with an appreciation of Considine's decision to retire and an assessment of what the LAB was able to accomplish in the way of hemispheric cooperation among Catholics during the period and beyond.

Chapter 11 offers perspectives on a couple of post-retirement projects, the Maryknoll Institute of Peoples and Cultures—which was never inaugurated—and his work as the founding editor of the Maryknoll Society's

---

31. Throughout the 1950s and 1960s, Considine was a member of the Council on Foreign Relations, and in 1957 was a founding member of the African Studies Association.

in-house publication, *Mission Bulletin.* The chapter also describes Considine's attitude toward developments such as the theology of liberation in post-conciliar Catholicism, in addition to his struggles with illness that took him into a more definitive retirement in 1976.

★ ★ ★

Shortly after New Year's day 1925, Considine was summoned to his first papal audience. Pope Pius XI was receiving the missioners who were responsible for exhibits at the Vatican Mission Exposition. The pope's remarks were dutifully recorded by Considine and transmitted to Maryknoll co-founder Fr. James Anthony Walsh, most likely with the intention that his account could be published in *The Field Afar.* The pope commented that he was convinced that people who had thought of missioners only as good priests or devoted and pious souls will be surprised to discover in the Exposition "the proportions not only of the religious activity but of the civilizing activity of the church in all parts of the world."[32]

As he imparted the apostolic blessing, the pope made brief mention of a characteristic of the missionary vocation: "You stand here as representatives of men who are not only lovers of the truth but who are willing to suffer and to die for the truth."

In those few words, Pius XI captured a sentiment that animated Considine throughout his career—that the special purpose of mission was the willingness to venture beyond borders and to risk all so that all peoples might be invited to the life of faith given by Christ and entrusted to the care of the church. Over his lifetime, Considine came to understand the missionary enterprise of the church as adaptable to changing times and a wide diversity of cultural milieu throughout the world. Nonetheless, he never wavered from the conviction that, whatever the places, times, or tasks at hand, and regardless of the results, the church's mission will always depend on the disposition of missioners willing to go forth and to risk everything. He counted himself fortunate to be a representative of those who not only are lovers of the truth but who are willing to suffer and die for the truth.

32. John Considine, Rome, to James A. Walsh, Ossining, NY, January 11, 1925. MMA, Rome House Correspondence, 2:2.

CHAPTER I

_____

The Considines of New Bedford

JOHN JOSEPH CONSIDINE was born in New Bedford, Massachusetts, on October 9, 1897, and the following day a five-day celebration began. New Bedford was celebrating the fiftieth anniversary of its city charter with fireworks, music, and other amusements. John was the first of seven children for John W. Considine (1869–1910) and Alice Murphy Considine (1869–1941), who had married the year before. John W. Considine was a successful businessman, whose key to success was a penchant both for hard work and for sniffing out advantageous opportunities. A favorite family story illustrates how these qualities were remembered by his children:

> The Star Store put a pony in their store window on Union Street. The pony was to be given away to the person who guessed its correct weight. One could enter the contest by buying a pair of sox and with each pair of sox could guess a number. Sox were selling at two pairs for twenty five cents.
>
> John W. Considine, whose drug store was located across the street from the Star Store no doubt had ample opportunity to observe the pony. . . . He thought that this pony was about the same size as his own pony named Annie. So he weighed Annie and then went to the Star Store and purchased ten dollars worth of sox for his children. The 80 pairs of sox gave them eighty chances to guess the correct weight.[1]

He won the pony—one can imagine him realizing that he could turn the contest to his advantage once he had calculated how relatively little it would cost him. And the story became treasured in the family, as both a fond memory of the father who died too young and as a marker of the way the Considine family valued cleverness and enterprise.

_____

1. Frank Considine, as quoted in Mary Lou Considine, "The Considines of New Bedford" (unpublished manuscript, Considine Family Archives), chapter 5, p. 93.

Perhaps because John W. Considine died at such a young age, the figure of Alice Murphy Considine loomed large in the upbringing of the couple's six sons (their one daughter had died as an infant). Alice is remembered as "very proper, very strict, very generous, and kind."[2] She was not above taking her boys to task. Frank Considine (1898–1995), the second son of the family, years later recalled this story about his mother attempting to reprimand his older brother John:

> Father John hated corned beef when he was a young boy.
> We always had corned beef on Saturday noon.
> One Saturday my mother said to John, "You are eating that corned beef before you leave the table." "No" he said, and started to leave. My mother chased him around and around the table but she could not catch him. No more corned beef for Father John.[3]

Alice was an educated woman, and her surviving eldest granddaughter, Mary Lou Considine, recalls her as a sophisticated woman who dressed fashionably. She was born in Kilcumney, County Carlow, in 1869, where her father, Arthur Murphy, was the holder of the lease to Kilcumney House and 133 acres of farmland, a property that had been in the family since 1788. Alice's father lost Kilcumney House in 1883 due to financial difficulties, the nature of which is currently unknown. In 1884, he immigrated to the United States. However, the report among the family has been that the rest of the Murphys who remained in Ireland continued to prosper, even into the twenty-first century. Although past generations of Considines in Ireland were not desperately poor, the Murphys in Ireland were understood to have been at a higher socioeconomic level than the Considines.[4]

Prior to emigrating, Alice completed her education at a convent school in Somain, France, and then came to the United States in 1887 to join her family in Philadelphia. After her father's death in November 1887, the family relocated to New Bedford; an old family friend had preceded them there.[5]

Alice ran a dress-making business out of the family home in New Bedford to make ends meet. After her marriage to John W., she would no longer need such employment. In their married life, he was in charge of the family businesses, and she of the home. Alice would also have the help of a live-in housekeeper for many years.

When John J. Considine was born in 1897, he was born into a family

2. Mary Lou Considine, interview with author, September 10, 2011.
3. Quoted in Mary Lou Considine, "The Considines of New Bedford," chapter 5, p. 96.
4. Mary Lou Considine, interview with author, September 10, 2011.
5. Ibid.

that had recently joined the entrepreneurial class in a bustling and still-growing New England city. The whaling industry was no longer as prominent as it had been prior to the 1870s, but the textile industry was thriving. With thousands of immigrants coming to New Bedford to work in the textile mills, the Catholic faith of his family in 1897 was becoming the religion of the majority of the population of New Bedford, a city that had been founded by Quakers.

The six brothers grew up in a city that peoples of many cultures called home. Even before all the immigration that came with the growth of the mills, the city had been a cosmopolitan whaling city, famously described by Herman Melville in *Moby Dick*. In the antebellum period, the town was also home to Frederick Douglass and many other fugitive slaves. The New Bedford public schools were integrated in the 1830s; all six Considine brothers attended those schools through grade eight.

The family started out in New Bedford's North End, where their neighbors were immigrants from French Canada and from Ireland. Other Considine and Murphy relatives lived nearby. The parish church, St. Kilian's, was on the same block as their home, and going to church was referred to as "going to Fr. Brady's."[6] The Considine children attended public grammar schools and would take the streetcar downtown to their father's drug stores, passing first at least ten different textile mills and then the whaling ships in New Bedford's harbor as they made the trip.

Their mother plied them with stories of Ireland, perhaps of the Battle of Kilcumney—the ballad of which mentions her great-grandfather's property. Their practice of weekly Mass and confession was surely augmented by stories of "the Murphy family Cardinals," Paul Cullen and Patrick Moran—Cardinal Cullen was a distant step-cousin to Alice, and Cardinal Moran was a second cousin of her father.[7]

The family's local geography changed significantly when they moved to

---

6. Frank Considine, quoted in Mary Lou Considine, "The Considines of New Bedford," chapter 5, p. 97.

7. In 1866, Cullen became the first Irishman elevated to the College of Cardinals; his nephew, Patrick Moran, later became archbishop of Sydney, Australia, and was elevated to the cardinalate in 1885. Two other Murphy relatives had notable ecclesiastical careers: Alice's great-grandfather's brother, Fr. Arthur Murphy, was acting bishop of Kildare and Leighlin in 1814; he was appointed bishop but did not accept the appointment. A fourth Murphy relative was a priest and seminary professor at Maynooth. Alice's uncle was Fr. James O'Donnell (1828–1861), who taught English and French at the seminary beginning in 1858 (Mary Lou Considine, interview with author; "The Record, Nui Maynooth Calendar 2009–2010," http://www.nuim.ie/calendar/almanac/documents/professors.pdf [accessed February 12, 2012]; Mary Lou Considine, "The Murphys of Kilcumney County Carlow" [unpublished manuscript, Considine Family Archives], chapter 2, pp. 2, 7).

Pearl Street in 1906.[8] The stately three-story house with seven bedrooms faced the Common, a parklike open space from which the views of the upper reaches of the New Bedford harbor are quite handsome. At the harbor end of Pearl Street was the train station. It was not the most exclusive neighborhood in New Bedford—that was a block west and further south along County Street—but it was a real step up from living in a two-family residence in the working-class North End.

Young John J. Considine, his younger brothers Frank and Walter (1900–1990), and perhaps also Raymond (1902–1996), could recall both residences. Arthur (1906–1991) was born just prior to the move, and the house on Pearl Street was the only family home that the youngest Considine brother, George (1909–1986), ever knew. John Considine lived with the family on Pearl Street from about his ninth birthday until he left to join Maryknoll in 1915, when he was seventeen.

When they lived on Pearl Street, their father's downtown drug stores were much closer, and they had a new parish (St. Lawrence Martyr) and a new public school. They now lived within blocks of a small African American neighborhood located to the east and south of their new home, but there was a color line that whites normally did not cross. Similarly, they probably would not have had occasion to visit the Azorean and Cape Verdean neighborhoods of New Bedford's South End.

In November 1910, John W. Considine passed away unexpectedly from tuberculosis. His son John J. Considine would later write:

> While I was in the eighth grade my father died (November 27, 1910).
> This did not immediately affect any home affairs but I went to the
> drug store more regularly.[9]

Were all the Considine brothers so reserved in describing their reactions to their father's death? Did they ever have occasion to talk about themselves? "I don't think they ever [did]; they didn't express their personal feelings," answers Mary Lou Considine. "They were very respectful of each other."

Even if they were reticent in their expressions about their feelings, it seems clear from family stories, diaries, and correspondence that there was a strong sense of unity and happiness in each other's company that characterized the family. As a Maryknoll priest, John Considine would spend many years away from his family; but throughout his life he was a frequent correspondent, and receiving news of the family was important to him.

---

8. Mary Lou Considine, "The Considines of New Bedford," chapter 4, p. 68.
9. John J. Considine autobiography, n.d. (but seemingly written between September 1917 and August 1922). MMA, Considine Papers, Box 1, Folder 1.

Returning to family gatherings in or near New Bedford was something he often did, and he usually regretted it when he could not.

For ninety-six years the family owned the large home on Pearl Street in New Bedford. As the site of so many Considine gatherings, the home was described by one family member as "embodying" the family.[10] Indeed, since it was sold in 2002, a similar center of Considine family life has yet to be identified.

Like many Irish immigrants in the United States of that period, both sides of the family sought and found better economic conditions in their new country. Charles R. Morris has noted that Irish-American prosperity was greater in Philadelphia than in Boston in the nineteenth and twentieth centuries. In Boston, the situation of the local elites locking out the Irish economically was more devastating than in other places.[11] In this regard, New Bedford's situation was more like Philadelphia than Boston, and when the Considines and Murphys found opportunities to advance, they took them readily.

How did the Considines prosper so quickly in New Bedford, even through tough economic times? A combination of practices and good timing seems to have favored the family's economy. In terms of their practices or decision making, three points come to mind: the families settled in a smaller thriving industrialized city where they had some contacts; there was a willingness to part with one type of livelihood and take up another in an entrepreneurial fashion; and the families had a devotion to thrift and valued the acquisition of property. In terms of timing, the histories of the Considine and Murphy families in New Bedford coincided with two economic booms in which the family secured more property or businesses.

The first economic boom from which the Considines benefited was the 1850s whaling boom. Indeed, New Bedford was the world's leading whaling port in the decades leading up to the Civil War. Before the widespread use of petroleum, whale oil was the product that furnished two vital needs: lubrication and oil for the making of candles. Michael Considine (father of John W. and grandfather of John J. Considine) was originally from County Carlow, Ireland. The first public record of Michael Considine in New Bedford dates from 1855, during the height of this boom. He purchased a farm in 1859 and found work in the New Bedford Copper Works.

The next generation lived through a second, lengthy economic boom. Michael Considine's three sons—Michael F., Daniel, and John W.—came of age in the 1870s and 1880s, a time when the population of New Bedford

---

10. Matthew Considine, interview with author, 21 August 2009.

11. Charles R. Morris, *American Catholic: The Saints and Sinners Who Built America's Most Powerful Church* (New York: Times Books, 1997), 168.

was growing rapidly as immigrants streamed into the city to find work in the textile mills. The population grew from 21,000 in 1870, to more than 40,000 in 1890, to its all-time peak of 120,000 in 1920.[12]

The most productive years of the lives of these three brothers would match the boom years of the mills, which ended in 1920. Known as "the Considine brothers," the three became entrepreneurs in this bustling atmosphere, operating a sporting goods store, drug stores, and a hotel. They also invested in real estate and race horses.[13] Not all of their enterprises prospered, however. In 1894, they built the Park Hotel on Weld Square in New Bedford's North End,[14] anticipating the construction of a railroad station that was never built. They sold the hotel in 1902, and it was razed in 1936 to make room for a gas station.[15]

By that time, however, their other enterprises were going well. In 1896, John W. Considine became a partner in C. H. and H. A. Lawton & Co., which operated two "apothecaries" (drug stores) in downtown New Bedford;[16] John had been working for that firm since 1885.[17] In just one generation, "the Considine brothers" had been able to move up from a working-class Irish background to a status of "well-known businessmen"[18] of New Bedford.

After John W. Considine's death, the family enterprises continued with even greater intensity. John W. had arranged for a $20,000 insurance policy, and the payout on the policy provided a nest egg for his widow. Alice took out a loan for another $30,000 and bought more property in the North End. When she had finished her building projects, she had twenty-two rental units—seven commercial units and fifteen apartment residences.[19] Income from the rental units would be key to the family's fortunes, and in fact Alice Murphy Considine was able to put all six of her sons through

---

12. Kingston Wm. Heath, *The Patina of Place: The Cultural Weathering of a New England Industrial Landscape* (Knoxville: University of Tennessee Press, 2001), 38–39.

13. Mary Lou Considine, "The Considines of New Bedford," chapter 4, p. 3.

14. "Weld Square Hotel Slated To Go To Building Wreckers," *Morning Mercury*, July 9, 1936, p. 14.

15. "Old Hotel Recalled," *New Bedford Standard Times*, January 13, 1952; "Old Hostelry Will Be Razed," *New Bedford Standard Times*, July 9, 1936.

16. "Weddings," *New Bedford Evening Standard*, November 17, 1896.

17. Mary Lou Considine, "The Considines of New Bedford," chapter 4, p. 65.

18. "Funeral," *New Bedford Evening Standard*, April 6, 1900 (the article describes the funeral of Michael Considine, grandfather of John J. Considine).

19. Mary Lou Considine records that Alice Considine even moved one of the houses she bought off of busy Acushnet Avenue to a spot around the corner, in order to make room for a new commercial and residential development on the parts of her property along Acushnet Avenue ("The Considines of New Bedford," chapter 4, p. 94). Because Acushnet Avenue had street car service, rental properties located on it were more desirable.

college. That education, in turn, provided economic security for the next generation.

The 1910s were the last good period of growth in New Bedford during the years in which the textile mills dominated the economic life of the city. Beginning in 1920, the mills would start a decline from which they never recover, as the enterprises were unable to compete with textile mills in the southern United States. Alice Considine was thus able to invest heavily during a period of economic growth in New Bedford, and the investments of those years continued to provide for her family's needs even in the hard times to come.

In the next generation, the enterprises of the family included the Catholic Church; from this family of six boys came three priests. In addition to John J. Considine becoming a Maryknoll priest, his brothers Raymond and Arthur were ordained priests of the Fall River Diocese. Frank became an accountant; Walter became a judge; and George became a successful antique dealer.

During his seminary years, young John J. Considine would comment that when they were small, the brothers did not mingle much with other children, "being satisfied to play with each other."[20] As will be portrayed in the next chapter, that would certainly change for John in high school, when he became much more gregarious with his classmates. But growing up together, the six boys shared ponies, played sports, and helped out in their father's drug stores. They were a tight-knit band of brothers.

The Considine brothers held their mother Alice in great esteem. Interestingly, as the Considines have told it, the history of the Considine side of the family is limited almost exclusively to the generation that emigrated from Ireland to New Bedford and their descendants, while the Murphy family history is much more extensive, going back many generations in Ireland. That history also includes Alice's visit to her native land in 1926 with sons Fr. John J. Considine, Ray, and young George, surely a triumphal return for an emigrant Irish woman who had done well in her new country. As Considine relatives today tell it, the connections to the Murphys of County Clare are still important to the family, all of which is a testament to the deep influence Alice Murphy Considine had on her six sons and their descendants.

---

20. John J. Considine autobiography, n.d.

CHAPTER 2

A Calling as an Opportunity for Enterprise 1911–1915

This awful world-war, which has already decimated the ranks of Catholic missioners and checked the supply of resources from Europe, will yet force us American Catholics to provide missioners and alms for the heathen lands. We believe that God will make our people realize the need and rouse us all effectively to a sense of duty.

The Field Afar, November 1914

THE DECISION TO become a priest and a foreign missioner, almost regardless of the age when the decision is made, is always a momentous decision. What were the circumstances that led young John Considine to choose that vocation and join the new Catholic Foreign Mission Society of America (Maryknoll) in 1915?

A personal diary kept during the months of his vocational discernment would be the preferred primary source for this moment in his life, but in Considine's case, no such diary describing a vocational decision has been found.[1] The sources for this period of his life are limited to a diary he

---

1. There is some evidence that Considine did not keep a diary during the time of his vocational decision making and his first year in Maryknoll (between July 1913—immediately following the end of his sophomore year in high school—and August 1916, the summer between his first and second year at preparatory seminary). In a letter to his mother in 1930, Considine requests that she send him another Ward's Line-A-Day diary and comments: "I have been keeping a Ward's 14 years now" (John J. Considine, Rome, to Alice Considine, New Bedford, MA, September 21, 1930, Considine Family Archives). Considine's diaries covering the aforementioned dates (prior to July 1913 and after August 1916) are located in the Maryknoll Mission Archives, Considine Papers, Box 4, Folder 1.

kept for a few months at the end of his sophomore year of high school (1913), an autobiographical essay written sometime after the fall of 1917,[2] and a 1983 essay by his younger colleague in Maryknoll, Bishop Edward McGurkin.[3] The 1913 diary is helpful for understanding Considine as an adolescent, and when the three sources are viewed together, a certain narrative emerges.

Considine had attended public schools through the end of the eighth grade, but for the fall of 1911 he planned to go to a Catholic high school. He particularly had his hopes set on Fairhaven College, a high school run by the Picpus Fathers (the Congregation of the Sacred Hearts of Jesus and Mary), located just across the Acushnet River from New Bedford. However, the high school closed, and so he entered Holy Family High School around the corner from St. Lawrence Catholic Church, his home parish.

The Picpus Fathers were and are a missionary order, and St. Damian of Molokai (Damien de Veuster [1840–1889]), though not yet recognized as Venerable in 1911, had given his life in the line of his missionary service to lepers. Nonetheless, it would appear that in 1911 the missionary background of the priests that ran Fairhaven College was not particularly on Considine's mind, for he makes no mention of it in his autobiographical essay. It was probably the case that his mind and heart had not yet been awakened to the world of Catholic missions.

Considine's 1913 diary does not portray him as inclined toward a priestly vocation, a fact that is consistent with his autobiography. The picture from this diary is that of a rambunctious teenager, a young man who is very much enjoying the social activities that come with youth. He smoked, and the diary records many outings with his friends. He seems quite fascinated with girls—in fact, in a May 27 entry he wrote about dating two girls at the same time. The autobiography glosses these social activities as the "other interests" of a high school student who particularly liked English class and had a love of reading—mainly popular novels but also the *Literary Digest* and the *Catholic World*. Although he was not the top student in

---

2. The autobiography was undated, but in its final paragraph, Considine notes, "I arrived at Maryknoll about the 6th of September, 1915. I spent two years at the Venard and entered the seminary in September, 1917." This seven-page hand-written autobiography provides a chronology of his path to making the decision to enter Maryknoll. The fact that it was found in his personnel file in the Maryknoll Mission Archives suggests that it was requested of him by his superiors (MMA, Considine Papers, 1:1).

3. This essay was composed by McGurkin and published by Maryknoll in a booklet in June 1983. However, with the exception of a few details, it seems apparent that McGurkin relied heavily on the autobiographical essay for his recollections of Considine's pre-Maryknoll vocation story (Edward A. McGurkin, "Father John J. Considine," in *Profiles of 12 Maryknollers*. MMA Research Room).

his class,[4] in his autobiography he said that he often spent afternoons in the library during high school. At the same time, the 1913 diaries do not portray a bookworm—the diaries record him on the go, involved in many activities.

While the Catholic parish and the practices of a regular Catholic life such as Mass and confession are found on the pages of the diary, Considine was also publishing what might be understood as a parish newspaper, called *The Gleaner*.[5] Additionally, he sent various correspondent articles to the Boston Catholic newspaper, *The Pilot*, for publication. He bubbled with ideas for new religious enterprises, such as a Catholic YMCA.[6] He is also somewhat profuse about a social club known as Entre Nous, which he and his circle of friends had started.

John was strikingly mobile; in 1913, private automobiles were still not very common, and in any case the Considine family did not own one at this time. Yet many of the pages of this diary record comings and goings with his friends in New Bedford, across the Acushnet River to Fairhaven and then down to the beaches on Sconticut Neck, up to Taunton (twenty-three miles north), and down to Onset Beach (twenty-one miles to the east). To get about town, Considine would walk or take a streetcar, and there was regular train service to Taunton. His friend Ed Galligan had use of his family's car, making possible their venture over to Onset Beach.

The diary depicts a carefree time in his young life, making evident that the premature death of his father did not impoverish Alice Considine and her six boys. Strikingly absent from these pages is any sense of urgency to think about an occupation that would enable him to help his mother economically. The autobiography, on the other hand, records that the following year he turned his thoughts more seriously to a career:

> The financial condition of the drug firm was becoming unsound and hence was an unpromising outlook for me for the future. By my third year of high school I commenced to consider other fields for a life work. I had always in mind the owning of some business which did not depend for operation solely on personal effort. I saw the advantages of this in my father's case, who on his death had things so established that those depending on him were not seriously affected. Journalism had the greatest appeal but it lacked this feature.[7]

---

4. Considine ranked fifth out of seventeen.

5. McGurkin, "Father John J. Considine," 13.

6. CD, June 8, 1913.

7. John Considine autobiography. MMA, Considine Papers, 1:1.

Even though the 1913 diary does not mention a vocation to the priest-hood, Considine's aspirations at this time revolve around Catholic life. He mentions his family in these pages, but the diary is mainly about a fifteen-year-old hanging out with his friends, playing pool, holding parties, going on dates, going to movies, and otherwise exploring his social world—and Considine's social world at this time was made up of Catholic friends from Holy Family High School. Nor would it have been common during this period in New Bedford for a boy in the second year of high school to be preparing for the priesthood in any formal sense. The Fall River Diocese neither operated nor made use of high school–level seminaries; the normal point at which a young man would begin preparation for the priesthood in the diocese was after graduation from high school. However, there is one episode recorded in the 1913 diary that gives a sense of how Considine understood Catholicism as a very human venture. In the middle of May, Considine organized a "Dutch supper"—presumably a Dutch-treat picnic supper—for the Entre Nous club at Pope's Beach, over on Sconticut Neck. Into the evening, after the supper, some of the young people paired off in spots on the beach, and other couples leisurely walked each other home. It took a couple of weeks, but Considine's diary entry of May 28 records a bitter response to this sort of event from Sister Cletus, one of the nuns who taught at Holy Family High School. She "gave the school a three-quarters of an hour sermon . . . on the vulgarities carried on at the Dutch supper." Considine added that Sister "gave the girls an awful going over," and in his writing, he first showed some ambivalence—Sister may have gone too far, but the girls might have deserved it.

But the next day Considine had a different attitude:

> Excitement was intent around the school and the topic of the hour was the call down of Sr. Cletus. In thinking it over and hearing it spo-ken of more she certainly did lay it on too strong when she called the girls rags and said they'd end up in the Good Shepherd Home.

Considine was a faithful Catholic, but that did not produce in him a blind deference to the religious authority of a Catholic nun who was also one of his teachers. Rather, she could be challenged when she was wrong, and Considine was eager to defend his friends. Though he did not mention it specifically, as the organizer of the Dutch supper, he could not but have felt implicated in Sister Cletus's recriminations. The attitude portrayed in this diary entry is one of little patience for her exaggerated accusations.

Vocational Discernment

Perhaps owing to the fact that his autobiography records the story of his early vocational development at least a few years after his decision to enter

Maryknoll, Considine's prose carries a matter-of-factness in his telling of how he decided to be a priest, how he learned about missions and Maryknoll, and about his decision to apply to Maryknoll for admission. The basic story line is that he found what he wanted to give his life to, and then he was spending his life in pursuit of that ideal.[8]

A significant turning point came during Considine's junior year in high school when he traveled, most likely with a group from his parish or high school, to Roxbury, Massachusetts, to see the annual Lenten passion play *Pilate's Daughter*.[9] The Redemptorists at the "Mission church" in Roxbury had first staged this play in 1902, and over its run of sixty-three Lents it was performed as many as thirty times during a single season.[10]

The five-act play was always a community production, and it told the fanciful story of Pontius Pilate's young daughter Claudia, who, from her palace balcony, threw a red rose to Christ. The rose touches Jesus' robe, falls to the ground, and is trampled by the crowd. When Claudia goes to retrieve it, it is in perfect condition. Years later in Rome, the play finds Claudia, now a Christian believer, still in possession of the rose, which she now discovers has miraculous powers to raise the dead, to heal the sick, and to inflict harm on the enemies of Christians. The play was always destined for a young audience and follows the fortunes of Claudia and three other main characters, all young women, as they make decisions in the face of adversity about what is true in their faiths and how they will live their lives. By 1914 when Considine saw it, *Pilate's Daughter* had already become an annual tradition. Considine's autobiography records that, after the play had concluded, Fr. Turner, one of the Redemptorists, told him, "I'll make a priest out of you." The idea stuck with him in a most persistent way.

McGurkin notes that the crucifixion scene in the play made a "lasting impression" on the young Considine. It would seem to have been a moment of sincere conversion. What type of conversion, however? Did the active and expansive mind of the young John Considine sense in Christ's crucifixion something of great significance, something without which human enterprises would lack meaning? *Pilate's Daughter* is certainly a pivotal moment in the autobiography. Could this moment be understood in

---

8. To inquire about any family stories of John Considine's decision to become a priest and missioner, the author interviewed surviving nieces and nephews of John Considine. However, each family member referred to the same "matter-of-factness" as characteristic of Considine's generation: "It was a different generation, and people did not talk that much about themselves" (David Considine interview, March 5, 2011).

9. Redemptorist Provincial Archives (Brooklyn, NY).

10. Chris Harding, "A legendary Lenten passion play may be revived in Roxbury 'Pilate's Daughter'," *Redemptorist Chronicle* (June 1984). Redemptorist Provincial Archives (Brooklyn, NY).

terms of a serious reorientation, as an experience that sparked in Considine the inspiration to live his life for God's purposes in the world? Considine's autobiography records no experience of, for example, emotional relief. What moved his heart and will in the direction of priesthood does not appear to have been a sense of being "saved" by Christ from some form of distress. What then? As we shall see presently, the text of Considine's autobiography moves quickly from the experience of the play to a sense of what he desired to do in the priesthood, in keeping with the matter-of-fact manner aforementioned.

Whatever the personal motivation may have been, Considine came away from that experience with a desire to become a priest. But what sort of life would he seek in the priesthood? In his autobiography he wrote:

> I felt sure I did not want diocesan work, but sought something where I could be active along some line where my work would mean gaining some particular end. One thought was that perhaps I could be a priest writer and as it seemed to me that the Jesuits did a large amount of writing, that order suggested itself.

About six weeks later he read a Society for the Propagation of the Faith column in *The Pilot* that particularly made him think. The article mentioned pleas for American priests to go to China. "The two thoughts that attracted me were, that what I did as a missioner would humanly speaking be otherwise left undone and, that there was opportunity for enterprise in such work," commented Considine. He immediately decided to become a missioner.

In November 1914, he saw *The Field Afar* for the first time. The first line of text in that edition read: "This paper is designed to make known the new American Seminary for Foreign Missions and the cause for which it stands—the conversion of heathen peoples to Christ." The magazine displayed large photos and featured letters from missioners; it was peppered with fund-raising pleas and contained cheerful stories of conversions in China. One article described Chinese customs, not without a sweeping generalization or two. But in several pieces the message was clearly relayed that the church in the United States is now being asked to take up an important new work, the work of foreign missions. In this particular issue that message was amplified by the concern that the war in Europe made foreign mission work by Catholics from the United States all the more urgent.

At that time a friend of Considine's, John Toomey, was a seminarian for the Fall River Diocese who was in the process of joining Maryknoll. Toomey got Considine a subscription to *The Field Afar*. Since Considine had his heart set on becoming a missionary priest, he went to see his pastor about his interest and also spoke with his mother. Based on Considine's autobiography, it would appear that his mother was not enthusiastic about her son becoming a missionary. However, Considine was able to reassure her that his decision was not based on any disregard for her. That seemed to keep their relationship on a good footing but did not convince her of the idea of her son working in a foreign country. It was an issue between them for many years.[11]

There was only one important decision left—which missionary group should he join?

> I still had made no choice between Maryknoll and the Jesuits as I felt becoming a Jesuit was a means of reaching the field. Maryknoll's shorter term of preparation decided me as my desire then was to get into active work.[12]

And so he made the decision to join Maryknoll. His contact with Maryknoll prior to entering was limited to what he learned about the group from his friend John Toomey and from his subscription to *The Field Afar*. Though he had corresponded with Maryknoll co-founder Fr. James A. Walsh, he had never met a Maryknoll priest, for, at that time, there were only three: Walsh, co-founder Fr. Thomas Frederick Price, and newly ordained Fr. Daniel McShane.

A more subtle point is present in the two sentences that describe John's choice of Maryknoll over the Jesuits—he displays a curiosity about the relative opportunities for work offered by different religious orders. While such curiosity is certainly expected among people who must choose one order or the other, in Considine's case it is a curiosity that he would carry with him throughout his lifetime. For example, while visiting Tanganyika in 1932, Considine acquainted himself with the missionary life and work of the White Fathers in that country. This led him to lament in his diary entry of October 28, 1932, that Maryknoll co-founder James A. Walsh had followed the individualistic missionary ethos of the Paris Foreign Mission Society and of the Mill Hill Fathers, seemingly without considering the

---

11. In 1921, Considine wrote to his mother regarding an upcoming trip to Cincinnati for meetings of the Catholic Student Mission Crusade. The scheduling of the meeting apparently forced Considine to cancel a visit in New York with his family. "Of course you must never place any hopes in this coming true but any aptitude which I may have in this work may lead to my being kept for some years on this side of the Pacific for propaganda activities. My one desire is to serve the missions in the way my superiors decide best so I never permit myself to give thought to such a thing as being placed in any particular line but nevertheless this is always a possibility" (John J. Considine, Ossining, NY, to Alice Considine, New Bedford, MA, March 20, 1921. Considine Family Archives).

12. John Considine autobiography.

more communitarian model of his present hosts, the White Fathers. Considine extolled aspects of their operation, such as the benefit of having a support community for the missioner in the field and a unified approach to mission.

It was a curiosity that would feed his ideas on missions, ideas that would always take into account the human situation of both the missioner and the people whom he or she is trying to call to faith in Christ. Considine would ever believe that Christ and the Holy Spirit will use human instruments to spread the gospel, and he would live his life studying and teaching the methods of mission that make what he considered to be the best use of those human instruments.

But to do all of that, he had to begin, and so the young John Considine himself began a journey of becoming an instrument of God's plans for humanity by joining the new Catholic Foreign Mission Society of America—Maryknoll—in the fall of 1915, when that group was just four years old.

CHAPTER 3

The Family Environment of Maryknoll Seminary 1916–1917

IN 1968, WHEN Fr. John J. Considine, M.M., retired from the Latin America Bureau of the USCC in Washington, the Maryknoll Society had 1,022 priests, 156 brothers, and 129 seminarians and brothers in formation. For those preparing for the priesthood, seminary life at that time was a large operation.

The Catholic Foreign Mission Society of America that young John J. Considine joined at age seventeen in 1915 was a much smaller operation, though sustained growth from those early years until the 1960s was the rule. "Maryknoll" at that time was a place near Ossining, New York, not yet the name of the mission society itself.

Considine's diary from 1915 is apparently lost, but his 1916 diary depicts the Vénard Apostolic School near Clark's Summit, Pennsylvania, and affords a "day-in-the-life" view of a small and youthful Maryknoll that, even though it was yet to send out any missioners, was full of missionary spirit and an atmosphere of family. The line between the ordained and those aspiring to orders, as in any seminary, was certainly present, but in such a youthful group with few priests of its own, the line was not very sharp or rigid. This was especially the case regarding matters of how this early and small formation community organized itself. There were twenty-nine students that year in a two-year course of study. To teach them, there was a regular faculty of just three priests and one layman: Fr. Fred Dietz, Fr. Brown, Fr. James E. Walsh (the rector), and Mr. Duffy. "Fr. Superior" (Maryknoll co-founder Fr. James A. Walsh) was a monthly visitor to "the Vénard," and took it upon himself to get to know the young seminarians as well as to supervise their program of studies and formation. Similarly, the young seminarians seemed confident enough to speak out about their concerns to the faculty and the superior.

Along the way they confronted physical hardship, a flu epidemic ("the grip"), and the death of the first Maryknoller—in addition to a full-time course of studies, a full schedule of manual labor to maintain and improve their new home, spiritual exercises, and sporting activities. This was the first year that Vénard students were studying on the property that would serve as a minor seminary for Maryknoll until 1967.[1] The building they occupied in 1916 was a large farmhouse. By 1916, Considine was a "senior"—in the second year of the two-year program of studies.

During this period, Considine kept two diaries—he was most faithful to "A Line-A-Day" five-year diary, in addition to jotting down an occasional longer entry in another diary. Let us allow John Considine's diary entries to take us back to the 1916–1917 school year, to a time when the trip from home to seminary was made by taking an overnight steamship from New Bedford to New York, then the ferry across the Hudson River to the Lackawanna Station in Hoboken, and finally the 10:20 train to Scranton.

Considine arrived at the Vénard on the morning of Wednesday, September 6; many in this group of mostly late-teen students had already arrived, and others would trickle in. There was much physical work to be done before classes began. Evidently, the seminary "rule" that governed student conduct was not immediately put into effect upon the arrival of the students.

Thursday, September 7, 1916: Slept in front room. [New wing] not finished. Manual labor morning & afternoon. Rest of fellows arrived. Eight new fellows & three of last year's did not arrive. . . . . The gang is even a better one than last year.

Friday, September 8, 1916: Slept in unfinished dorm. Six of the old gang together. No rule yet so there was a big racket. Manual labor morning & afternoon. I am assistant manual labor prefect, infirmarian, ground keeper, fire chief.

Saturday, September 9, 1916: Helped clean grounds in morning. The Vénard shower took place in the afternoon. About 300 people from Scranton visited & brought mite boxes. About $400 collected. Washed dishes all afternoon. The gang here is great. Slept in attic to-night.

---

1. John J. Casey, "The History of Maryknoll Formation/Education, 1911–2011: An Internal History of the Seminaries Built and Run by Maryknoll" (photocopy). MMA Research Room, Ossining, NY.

Tuesday, September 12, 1916: Manual labor morning & afternoon. Plenty of fun all day long.

Saturday, September 23, 1916: The seniors are to have the attic for their permanent dormitory. It looks like some breezy nights this winter.

Classes began on Tuesday, September 19. Just prior to that date, Maryknoll co-founder Fr. James A. Walsh came for the first of his monthly visits. Since the group had been in residence on the Maryknoll property near Ossining during the previous academic year,[2] this group of second-year students was already acquainted with him. However, it was probably the case that the many pressing responsibilities that Walsh experienced at the Maryknoll headquarters precluded him from spending much time with the students. Now that the Vénard had returned to the Scranton area, Considine was able to have "the first good talk I ever enjoyed with Father Superior."[3] The two had corresponded by letter over the summer, as Father Superior had urged Considine to skip the second year of preparatory studies at the Vénard and be advanced to the first year of studies in philosophy at Maryknoll Seminary in New York. Considine resisted this move—he told the Maryknoll co-founder that he did not feel sufficiently prepared academically, noting particularly his lack of ability with Latin. They talked for over an hour. Fr. Superior asked about his mother's disposition toward young Considine's vocation—and also about her livelihood.

> He indirectly brought up her affairs and I thought the opportunity ripe to ask him where he invested the society's money. He said his business went through the hands of a friend of his in the employ of Lee, Higginson & Co. and that bonds were all he dealt in,—five per cent. and sometimes six. He said he could arrange with this man— Mr. Curry I think his name is—to invest my mother's surplus if she cared. She is far from having a surplus at present as it took a loan of seventeen thousand to build her block but it may make her feel good if I tell her this. Father Superior is shrewd and watches his investments, I have no doubt. I find great interest in business affairs and it was just this afternoon that I was considering whether it might not be the Lord's will that I should become involved in business matters to some great extent when I reach the priesthood.

2. During the 1915–1916 school year—the year Considine entered Maryknoll—the Vénard Apostolic School had been temporarily relocated from Scranton to the Maryknoll property in Ossining, NY; the student dormitory was the hayloft of a barn.
3. CD, September 17, 1916.

They also discussed vocations, along with the concern that priests, bishops, and Catholic families be open to letting young vocations to the missions develop.

From that day until the day James A. Walsh died in 1936, the two carried on a lively correspondence. For many years, Considine would write more than the Maryknoll co-founder, but, particularly after Considine went to Rome in 1924, that was not always the case. Their correspondence carries the flavor of a father and son who are deeply involved in a family enterprise. For young Considine, who had lost his own father at such a young age, the relationship with James A. Walsh was probably a great consolation.

During January 1917, a flu epidemic hit the Vénard particularly hard, with nine members of the community, Considine among them, getting sick. There were no fatalities, but the flu epidemic was followed by two students being operated on for appendicitis, while a third was hospitalized for unspecified reasons. Additionally, Fr. Brown, one of the four faculty, was hospitalized for a week. Then, in February, news arrived of the first death of a Maryknoller. Miss Wholean was one of the original group of secretaries who, together with the Maryknoll Sisters' foundress, Mary Josephine Rogers, arrived at the new Maryknoll headquarters in 1912 to assist cofounders Frs. Price and Walsh with getting the new mission society off the ground. Though there was as yet no official founding of a women's foreign mission religious community, Miss Wholean and all the other young women had that foundation as their long-term goal. Her death at a young age came as a shock to the new mission enterprise—though some seminarians had stayed for a while and then left, almost everyone was young and very much alive, and there was a sense that solid growth was happening. At the same time, the missionary ethos was one in which giving your all, making sacrifices, and accepting the risk of even violent death were part of what had to be learned and inculcated. When Miss Wholean died, perhaps it became a real-life existential lesson for the community. In Considine's case, it is hard to tell, as his diary entries betray mainly a general concern to learn the details of her passing and of her funeral.

Considine also records significant tension with a faculty member during the year. Writing in June 1917 from Maryknoll headquarters in Ossining, New York, he recalled Fr. Brown as

a friend of Father Superior years ago, whose home is Newfoundland [and who] must be handled carefully. . . . Personally I admired his intentions and am sure he is a spiritual man. He was *not*, however, the man for the Vénard. He had none of the principles Maryknoll stands for and was too old to countenance them. To all appearances at least, his was the gospel of fear. I have it that he will never be a member of our society. I will watch his career and be sorry if things break badly for him but I can say truly that he is a type of man who is termed as born wrong.[4]

This passage reveals a couple of fascinating things. First, there is the way Considine sizes up people independently of their religious status. As was the case with Sister Cletus when Considine was in high school, the fact that Fr. Brown was a priest in no way stopped the young seminarian from laying things out plainly about the priest's character and behavior. And, once again, it is the issue of a perceived lack of fairness—Fr. Brown's use of fear as a power mechanism—to which Considine takes exception. Yet also noteworthy is a sense of calm and acceptance—justice will be done; Fr. Brown will not be with the group in the end; Maryknoll and John Considine will be all right. Although Considine's assessment of Fr. Brown is mostly negative, there is a reasonableness to Considine's entire portrayal of him—human compassion for him, but also a strength of conviction about the wisdom of not allowing Fr. Brown to have power over students.

Second, at age nineteen and still six years away from being a priest, how did Considine "have it"—and have it correctly—that Fr. Brown would not become a member of Maryknoll in the end? Is this an indication that the regimented lines between the ordained and the nonordained were porous in a Maryknoll nary six years established? Similarly, in such a community, where the emphasis was on raising up a new generation of missioners, did the traditional educational power arrangement—that is, faculty sitting in judgment of students' performance—get reversed? Who was more important to the future of that society, a priest professor willing to give a year or two to teach in the society's seminary, or a student who would spend his entire career in the group? And would there have been a sense of the students' being able to communicate to the superior about who they think is or is not apt for a position on the seminary faculty? In any case, the matter was crystal clear to Considine—Fr. Brown would not be part of Maryknoll's future.

While the Seminary Rule used at the Vénard regimented each day and every day of the week with hours for study, prayer, reflection, work, and recreation,[5] apparently certain aspects of formation for missionary priesthood were flexible. For example, the seminary faculty dispensed with reading during meals and gave a day off in honor of the visit of the Apostolic Delegate to Maryknoll headquarters in Ossining, New York.[6] The esprit de corps of a youthful group hoping to have an impact on the church's

---

4. CD, June 11, 1917 [emphasis as in original].
5. James E. Walsh, *Maryknoll Spiritual Directory* (New York: Field Afar Press, 1947), 3–30.
6. CD, October 17, 1916.

worldwide mission at times trumped many formalities, as on the occasion of Considine's nineteenth birthday:

> The most interesting event of this period was an escapade in the senior dormitory on the night of my birthday—October ninth. At the time only the nine seniors were up there; Ma sent me a cake. Tom O'Melia and I went down to get some milk to drink with it and Brother Greene . . . suggested, though he should not have, doing it I suppose out of the kindness of his heart, that we have a couple of cans of fruit. We had a can of peaches and one of pears, 2 boxes of Dromedary dates, 2 jars of jelly (these from Mrs. Mayrand) and a couple of pounds of cookies. Maybe that stuff didn't go down well. Father Brown, by accident, happened on the rubbish the next morning and smashed all our well planned secrecy. We had a table set between my and Murrett's beds and having undressed we prepared to the feast in our bath robes. Everything was spread out with candles to furnish the light. We never set a sound out of us, strange to say, though we laughed our heads off the whole time over every foolish joke that came up. It was a night to be remembered. Father Walsh was concerned, to say the least, as Father Brown told the faculty, treating it as a joke. I apologized to Father James E. and our pull, sad to say, as seniors blew the event over. I must admit none of us had any doubts but that we could get away with the thing.[7]

As the numbers of Maryknoll Society recruits are smaller at present, it is a particular challenge for those trained in the more institutionalized and regimented years when the group was larger to adapt to the conditions of a smaller community. In 2011, the Maryknoll Society had 357 priests, 49 brothers, and 10 seminarians and brothers in formation. Considine's Vénard diary seems to suggest that conditions can certainly be favorable for training new missioners in a smaller community when a family spirit prevails.

---

7. CD, November 6, 1916.

CHAPTER 4

An Americanism that Persisted 1917–1924

Between 1917 and 1924, Considine continued his formal studies at Maryknoll Seminary and Catholic University, and he was ordained a priest in May 1923. These were years in which he developed his ideas about mission methods, methods that were based on a sympathetic understanding of the culture of those with whom the missioner shares the gospel. These years gave Considine significant opportunities—to work on the leadership of the Catholic Student Mission Crusade, to earn a licentiate in sacred theology from Catholic University, and to organize Maryknoll's participation in the Vatican Mission Exposition. They were also years for deepening friendships and exercising leadership among his peers.

It is often thought that the seminary program of studies—two years of philosophical study followed by four years of theological studies, a program that young John Considine was allowed to complete in only five years—is rather unremarkable. Post–Vatican II lore among Roman Catholic priests describes seminary life in pre–Vatican II times as tightly regimented and indicates that the program of study—even the times when meals were scheduled—was uniform throughout the world. However, there were two factors that made Considine's years in major seminary a departure from such a rigid norm. One factor had its basis in the sort of "family" organization that Maryknoll was at the time, and the other factor had to do with the church in the United States adopting a national focus.

The Maryknoll Family in Ossining

A "family style" of organization pervaded the Maryknoll operation in those years. In the previous chapter I alluded to how this spirit was found in the relatively small community of young men in their first years of preparation for the missionary priesthood at the Vénard Apostolic School. That spirit carried over to life in the major seminary at the Maryknoll headquarters in Ossining.

It is important to understand, however, that the term "major seminary," in the case of Maryknoll prior to 1922, referred not to a grand building but to a large farmhouse that had been expanded several times. During these years, the seminarians, auxiliary brothers, faculty, and the several other priests in residence at Maryknoll lived in the farmhouse—dubbed "Rosary House"—and in a collection of other small buildings on the property. The "secretaries" or Teresians—women who had also joined the Maryknoll community but until 1920 would not be constituted as an official women's missionary congregation of the church—occupied several buildings on the north end of the property, one of which was called St. Teresa's.

Like the Vénard, the Maryknoll complex was a busy and almost self-contained operation; almost everyone was expected to do manual labor to keep this growing group of missioners-in-training fed and clothed, and to maintain and keep clean their places of residence, study, and work. Of course, there were also classes and homework, in addition to the tasks of producing and mailing out *The Field Afar*, Maryknoll's monthly mission publication. Maryknoll co-founder and father superior James A. Walsh oversaw the editorial content and did a chunk of the writing as well, but the young Maryknoll men and women would also have been involved in some of the creative tasks of writing, typesetting, and photography. Moreover, many more hands were needed to keep the subscription lists up to date and to do the labeling and mailing of the magazines eleven times a year.

The family spirit extended not only to the idea of everybody pitching in but also to morale. In January 1921, Considine felt enough confidence to send what he probably considered to be a necessary memo to Father Superior entitled simply "Suggestion." The memo was basically about improving morale in the community and began with the words "For the spirit." It offered two practical suggestions—that some extra privileges be granted during recreation and that places at table be changed every four weeks according to a system that would exclude the possibility of favoritism—but also contained a plea that Maryknoll Superior Fr. Walsh address issues of morale and community life in order to dispel erroneous ideas about the way missioners ought to relate to their peers. [1]

---

1. The privilege requested was permission "for smoking in St. Joseph's auditorium only, for every Wednesday evening." The second part, on the effect that erroneous ideas can have on community, is here quoted in its entirety:

That in an indirect way you make known to the community your ideas of what should be the spirit in general and what should be the individual's part in its develop-

It was another demonstration that Considine did not feel inhibited by the hierarchical situation that distinguished his status as a seminarian from that of the ordained priest who was the superior of the Maryknoll Society, and that he was capable of thinking expansively about what practical steps can be taken to improve a situation. Tellingly, although the heading of the memo states that it was from "J. J. Considine et al.," no other student's name is on it, reflecting again the self-confidence with which Considine approached such matters. If the "et al." part is true, it also suggests a leadership role for Considine among his peers.

Seminarians in Public Service to Mission:
The Catholic Student Mission Crusade

The second factor that distinguished Considine's experience in major seminary from those of major seminarians of just a few decades prior were the opportunities to be involved in extracurricular organizations and activities. For Considine and for many of his contemporaries at the Catholic Foreign Mission Seminary, this meant involvement in the Catholic Student Mission Crusade (CSMC), then a new national Catholic organization.[2]

David Endres has referred to the first decades of the twentieth century as American Catholicism's Organizational Revolution,[3] because of the many national Catholic organizations that were founded or were flourishing during this time. Extending the period back into the latter decades of the nineteenth century, the list of national Catholic organizations founded during this period is long: the Knights of Columbus (1882); the National Black Catholic Congress (1889); the American Federation of

---

ment. Failure to contribute to the spirit, it seems to us, can be attributed to numerous causes, most of them the outgrowth of a sincere following of wrong ideas.

V.g. –

A missioner should learn to find contentment in his own company.

A man should bind to him true friends who will have a close regard for him and remember him through his life.

Some are behind in their class work and feel they should give all possible time to it. Some are engaged in extra work and feel that there is no unselfishness in consecrating every moment to the success of undertakings that redound to the cause.

Some naturally are sensitive and feel they cannot approach but should wait until approached. Some have strong likes.

Some have the qualities for contributing to the spirit but lack the vision to see the need of it.

The memo ends with these words: "The majority are ready but need a reminder and increased opportunities" (J. J. Considine et al., Ossining, NY, to James A. Walsh, Ossining, NY, January 1, 1921. MMA, Considine Papers, Box 2, Folder 1).

2. David Jeffrey Endres, *American Crusade: Catholic Youth in the World Mission Movement from World War I through Vatican II* (Eugene, OR: Pickwick, 2010).

3. Ibid., 34.

Catholic Societies (1900); the Catholic Education Association (1904); the Catholic Hospital Association (1915); the National Conference of Catholic Charities (1910); and the National Catholic Rural Life Conference (1923). Additionally, a national Catholic Congress was held in Baltimore in 1889, followed by the Columbian Catholic Congress in Chicago in 1893.[4]

In terms of broader U.S. history, the 1910s and early 1920s were a time of increased nationalism, when allegiance to the nation state became a value that was much talked about. At the same time, it was a moment of greater international awareness in the United States—the nation state to which Americans gave their allegiance was taking a more active role in international affairs. The Spanish-American war had successfully launched the United States onto the world stage as a military and expansionist power. Within a generation the United States would join the Allies and be victorious in World War I.

For Catholics, there were two facets to their growing participation in this combined nationalistic patriotism and internationalist perspective—the persistent desire to communicate to their non-Catholic compatriots in the United States (who at times displayed nativist anti-Catholic tendencies) that Catholics were American and not a foreign element in U.S. society and the simultaneous desire to show to Catholics in the rest of the world that their American "style" of living their faith was a very useful pathway toward a truly modern and therefore internationalist catholicity.

Endres argues that the CSMC fostered a sense of the ability of the Catholic Church in the United States to effectively use scholasticism and the medieval ideal of a union between church and culture to attack secularism and materialism, the "ideologies at the root of unbelief." Scholasticism was understood as an "antidote to the errors of modernity." The CMSC was thus able simultaneously to understand American Catholic students as able to make use of modern industrial progress and material prosperity while rejecting a modern intellectual framework viewed as "unbelieving."

> The merging of the missionary ethos with dominant religious and nationalist rhetoric produced a synthesis that appealed to the idealistic and youthful Catholics of the interwar years, while articulating a vision consonant with more 'mature' scholastic thought and American political ideology.[5]

---

4. Alfred J. Ede, *The Lay Crusade for a Christian America: A Study of the American Federation of Catholic Societies, 1900–1919* (New York: Garland, 1988), 47–54.

5. Endres, *American Crusade,* 60–61.

Though it is unclear when John Considine began participating in CSMC, in 1920 he was elected to its executive board.[6] Although getting permission from his superiors at Maryknoll Seminary to travel to CSMC meetings was not always a simple matter, serving in the leadership of a national Catholic organization while still a seminarian in the United States would have been something unheard of before the turn of the twentieth century. In addition to the prospect of helping at the national level to mold the work of a growing Catholic organization, it afforded opportunities for travel when attending crusade activities.[7]

Endres characterizes the 1920s as the time when the leadership of the CSMC consolidated the crusader and "holy war" metaphors for foreign mission; Fr. Daniel A. Lord, S.J., is credited with connecting the CSMC to these powerful analogies.[8] The appeal of these medieval analogies fit early-twentieth-century Catholicism in the United States in a unique way—reference to medieval crusaders and crusades intentionally evoked a time of great harmony between church and culture. The symbolism of knights, shields, and swords also served to continue to capture the attention of youthful Catholics eager for adventure and heroism while at the same time reframing the horrors of modern warfare so recently experienced in World War I. It was a conscious effort to bring young people together for the adventure of peacefully conquering souls to create Christ's kingdom in a way that included all the world's peoples and cultures.[9]

The main CSMC activities were meetings and conventions at which rituals and drama were employed to communicate and solidify religious, missionary, and patriotic ideals.[10] Following the 1923 convention, the systematic study of mission countries or areas, as well as missionary opportunities, problems, and methods, was undertaken by the CSMC, a move Considine surely welcomed.[11]

A Close Friend

While still at the Vénard in the fall of 1916, Considine mentioned in his diary that he had received an eleven-page letter from Francis Ford.[12] The

---

6. Ibid., 120.

7. In the spring of 1921 alone, Considine traveled once to Cincinnati for a CSMC board meeting and then again to Dayton, Ohio, for the national convention that same year (John J. Considine, Ossining, NY, to Alice Considine, New Bedford, MA, March 20, 1921. Considine Family Archives).

8. Endres, *American Crusade,* 61.

9. Ibid., 59.

10. Endres credits Fr. Lord with developing several plays and rituals for the CSMC that were used consistently over the life of the organization (ibid., 63).

11. Ibid., 72.

12. CD, October 23, 1916. The letter from Ford could not be found.

two had met at Maryknoll's headquarters in Ossining, New York, during the previous fall, when Considine had recently joined Maryknoll. The letter was just the first of many lengthy dispatches between these two over the course of a long friendship.

Francis Xavier Ford was the first student to join Maryknoll in 1912; he was ordained in 1917, and in 1918 became one of four members of the first Maryknoll departure group for missions in China. After several years of parochial mission work in South China, in 1929 he was appointed prefect of the Kaying Prefecture, and then vicar apostolic of the same see when it became a vicariate in 1935. For this latter appointment, he was consecrated bishop. Bishop Ford died in 1952 during imprisonment after the Chinese communist revolution; he has long been considered by Maryknollers a martyr to the cause of the church in China.

In 1922, Ford was in the Yeungkong mission in South China, and he received a letter from Considine that spoke of Considine's desire not to be assigned to an overseas mission. The reasons Considine mentioned such a desire to Ford are unclear, although the year before he had written to his mother that any aptitude that Considine had for the work of promoting support for missions in the United States could lead to his being "kept for some years on this side of the Pacific. . . ."[13] Considine's letter to his mother had detailed his activities with the CSMC.

Ford answered Considine sympathetically—as a student, he too had dreaded the thought of being a missioner in a foreign land, but Ford added that ordination awakens in one the desire to work for souls. Then he added this wish:

> I hope for your own good that you will get at least five years on the missions, if only to shake your soul to its very roots. Without this mission training I might have been a better man in some ways but I don't think I would have seen as clearly as I do God's nearness and love.[14]

Graduate Studies at Catholic University

Ford may not have known at the time he wrote that letter that Considine was about to embark on a new stage in his preparation for mission. Seminarian John Considine was allowed to finish his studies at Maryknoll Seminary a year early, in 1922. He was ordained to the subdiaconate on June 10, 1922, and in July was assigned to further studies at Catholic University in Washington, DC, becoming part of the first group of six students

---

13. John Considine, Ossining, NY, to Alice Considine, New Bedford, MA, March 20, 1921. Considine Family Archives.

14. Francis Ford, Yeung Kong, China, to John Considine, Ossining, NY, August 22, 1922. MMA, Considine Papers, 2:9.

to be sponsored by the Maryknoll Society to undertake graduate studies.[15] Fr. Leopold Tibesar was assigned to accompany the group, which took up residence at the Apostolic Mission House on the grounds of Catholic University.

The Apostolic Mission House had been founded in 1902 by two Paulist priests, Walter Elliott and Alexander Doyle; it was designed to be a training center for missionary priests who would evangelize the United States, although at the founding there was also "some mention of those who would go to other countries."[16] According to Angelyn Dries, the founding of the Apostolic Mission House was one of the first concrete initiatives taken by the church in the United States toward foreign mission work, and it should be understood as part of the ecclesial and social environment from which soon emerged the founding of Maryknoll (1911) and the concurrent decision of the American Province of the Society of the Divine Word, which had been established in 1895 to work with African Americans, to prepare U.S. missioners for overseas service.[17]

Considine's purpose at Catholic University was to study missiology, though no such course of study existed at the university at the time. However, what Considine did was arrange a program of study leading to the licentiate degree in theology which covered a range of church history and the writing of a thesis on a mission history topic. As part of his program of study, he also earned a bachelor's degree in canon law.

A large part of the continued correspondence with Francis Ford during Considine's years at Catholic University centered on an evaluation of Protestant missions; the correspondence suggests that Considine was exposed to a tolerant attitude toward Protestants while at Catholic University in the early 1920s. Ford had written an article on the failure of Protestant missions in China; the piece was published as an unsigned article in *The Catholic World,* probably in late 1922.[18] Ford explained that the article represented a shift in his thinking; he reminded Considine how much he had previously admired Protestant missions. Living in China had changed Ford's view of the matter—what appealed to him about Protestant missions prior to com-

15. The other five were Patrick Cleary, Joseph Connors, Joseph McGinn, Tom O'Melia, and Francis Winslow.

16. Angelyn Dries, *The Missionary Movement in American Catholic History* (Maryknoll, NY: Orbis Books, 1998), 67.

17. Ibid., 74; see also eadem, "The Context for the Maryknoll Foundations: The Church and the United States in the Post-Civil War South, Urban North, and the Competition for a Foreign Missions Seminary, 1866–1911" (talk given at Maryknoll centennial celebration, Ossining, NY, January 26, 2011).

18. Francis Ford, Yeung Kong, China, to John Considine, Washington, January 13, 1923. MMA, Considine Papers, 2:9.

ing to China was their efficient use of mission resources to spread the gospel, but after a few years in China, doubts emerged about that effectiveness.

The correspondence continued through 1923, and at one point that year Considine sent Ford an eight-point letter, asking for Ford's opinion. The points were a mixture of responses to Ford and further questions:

1. Is it a Catholic practice to criticize Protestant methods?
2. Criticizing Protestant methods does little to rouse Catholics to take action.
3. Criticizing Protestant methods lessens the regard of Protestants for Catholics.
4. Criticizing Protestant methods is a drawback for those Protestants who might otherwise be interested in converting to Catholicism.
5. Are Protestant educational and medical work in China aimed at reaching the upper classes?
6. Are Protestants a factor in modern education in China?
7. Do Protestants have control of modern medicine in China?
8. Are the YMCA and YWCA influential in the political-business-social set of China?[19]

Ford answered Considine point by point, arguing mainly that the context of China is hard to understand from the outside. The two continued to discuss these matters for many years. A few years later, Considine wrote an article that offered a certain synthesis of the discussion with Ford on Protestant mission.[20] In the article, Considine laid out the differences between Catholic and Protestant ecclesiology and missiology that were coming to the fore as the trend toward an indigenization of the churches progressed in China. Because Catholics have in Rome a "supranational center," Catholicism has a workable way of indigenizing while maintaining a universal perspective. Protestants, however, have an ecclesiology that has always been local. Their missions have been an "astoundingly generous . . . and . . . colossal experiment at expansion," but it was unclear how they would retain Christian universality in China, where Chinese nationalism was growing.

In regard to the context of Catholic University in the 1920s, the eight points suggest that Considine at this time had an openness to Protestantism based on an overall idea of the actions of the church in mission. That is, he crafted his view of Protestantism less from a concern with Protestant departures from Catholic teaching—confessional questions—than from a

---

19. Considine's 1923 letter to Ford could not be located; however, Ford reproduced Considine's eight points in his reply. Francis Ford, Yeung Kong, China, to John Considine, Washington, February 14, 1924. MMA, Considine Papers, 2:9.

20. John J. Considine, "Protestantism and Self-Government in China," *Ecclesiastical Review* 79 (Summer 1928): 301–4.

concern about how best to keep the Catholic Church focused on its own identity as Catholic and missionary to all people, including Protestants.

That Considine possessed a broad-minded stance toward Protestantism would not have been unusual considering the professors in whose courses Considine enrolled for the fall of 1922. One of these, Fr. Edward A. Pace, taught "Methods of Teaching Religion" that semester.[21] Pace held a doctorate in psychology from the University of Leipzig, had previously served as the chair of the department of philosophy, and was both director of studies and general secretary of the university during Considine's years at Catholic University. He was convinced that the university should have academically credible specialists in many scientific disciplines, and he was elected president of the American Council of Education in 1925.[22] Msgr. John A. Ryan was also on the faculty, and more will be said about him presently.

Considine's two thesis advisors were Fr. Franz Cöln and Fr. James Hugh Ryan, both of whom went on to have considerable influence at Catholic University. A priest of the German diocese of Trier, Cöln was professor of Old Testament and was dean of the theological faculty from 1925 to 1931.[23] James H. Ryan had been secretary of the Department of Education at the NCWC before joining the Catholic University philosophy department in 1922. With Pace he co-founded the American Catholic Philosophical Association in 1926, and in its official publication, *The New Scholasticism*, gained notoriety in the concurrent Catholic revival of Thomism. James H. Ryan was the fifth rector of Catholic University (1928–1935). From 1935 until his death in 1947, he was bishop and then archbishop of Omaha, Nebraska.[24]

In April 1924, Franz Cöln and James Hugh Ryan reviewed Considine's licentiate thesis on the missionary methods of Blessed (now Saint) Ramon Lull. The thesis used sources from ecclesiastical history to tell not the entire story of Lull's life but rather how Lull argued for and acted upon the urgency for the church to make mission to Muslims a priority in the thirteenth century. Lull's proposal cut against the grain of the times; missions were carried out in Islamic lands throughout the thirteenth and the fourteenth centuries, but the numbers of missioners were in the hundreds. For many Christians, the journey to Muslim lands was too dangerous to contemplate. Lull advocated for a detailed mission program that included a sympathetic attitude toward Muslims and a thorough knowledge of their

21. John Considine, Washington, to Alice Considine, New Bedford, MA, October 4, 1922. Considine Family Archives.

22. C. Joseph Nuesse, *The Catholic University of America: A Centennial History* (Washington, DC: Catholic University of America Press, 1990), 110–11, 195.

23. Ibid., 213–14.

24. Ibid., 222–23, 242, 244.

religion, language, and social life. [25] By way of such formulations, Considine's thesis embodied many elements that inspired his view of the peoples of the world and the church's mission to them throughout his life. I will suggest that what unifies the entire thesis and much of Considine's career is a focus on mission methods, and I shall return to those themes presently.

In the middle of Considine's thesis is a section on St. Ramon Lull and the Jews. The section is remarkable for the positive treatment accorded to the Jews. Such positive treatment offers an indication of what Maria Mazzenga has described as a certain strain of Americanism that had survived the 1899 Vatican condemnation and was very much alive at Catholic University in the 1920s. What follows is a brief description of how Considine portrayed Ramon Lull's treatment of the Jews, along with an exploration of the context of Catholic University in the 1920s.

Lull was sixty-six years old when he returned from the Near East, and he would soon depart to North Africa a second time. The year was 1302. Considine explained:

> During his visit to Majorca, after his return from the East, Ramon worked among the Jews. It is worthy of note that for several short periods during his life, Ramon thus engaged himself on his native island. Several writers have called attention to his charity toward the Jews in face of the general attitude of the times, particularly in Spain. (p. 43)

Considine described the religious and political situation of the times—Jews had benefited from Muslim rule in Spain, and so Jews fought with Muslims against Catholic Spain.

> This linking of the Jew with the Moslem may have been a contributing cause in Spain, at least[,] for the cruel persecution of the Israelite at the beginning of the first Crusades. (p. 44)

Considine reviewed the situation of popular hatred on the part of Catholics toward Jews in thirteenth century, but noted the fact that Ramon had a significantly more favorable view of Jews:

> The Fourth Council of the Lateran (1215) prescribed a Jew badge and popes and kings legislated against them, though the popes often willingly acted on appeal to mitigate the attacks against the race. . . . Ramon was not a partisan to this attitude. Besides . . . his ministe-

---

25. John Joseph Considine, "Blessed Ramon Lull: A Thirteenth Century Missioner" (Licentiate in Sacred Theology dissertation, Catholic University of America, 1924), 13.

rial activity for their conversion, he wrote for them several books notably "Liber contra Judaeos," "Liber de Reformatione Hebraica," and "Liber de Adventu Messiae." Majorca contained many of the race after the reconquest. (p. 44)

The section is only a couple of pages in an eighty-page document, but it invites a consideration of the academic, ecclesial, and theological context in which Considine was writing.[26] Do these remarks tell us something about the academic, ecclesial and theological climate of Catholic University in the 1920s? Similarly, what sort of an impact did the intellectual climate of Catholic University have on John Considine?

Mazzenga has argued that Catholic University in this period reflected a particular resolution of the Americanist and modernist crises; at issue was religious liberty, which is enshrined in the First Amendment of the U.S. Constitution. The problem was that Catholics were to believe that they belonged to the one, true religion; in the church's eyes at that time, a Catholic who admitted the desirability of religious liberty seemed to be endorsing the idea that all religions are equally good.

Although the debate within Catholicism on the acceptability of religious liberty did not gain widespread attention until after the Second World War, the roots of the debate are found in the 1890s Americanist controversy. At that time, the liberal position advocated that Catholics could move in the direction of greater acceptance of U.S. institutions and democratic ideals, which included religious liberty and church–state separation. In 1899, however, Pope Leo XIII, in *Testem Benevolentiae Nostrae*, condemned the liberal position. Nonetheless, because of religious pluralism and the ideal of religious liberty in the United States, the liberal view did not simply disappear. Mazzenga notes that after *Testem*, "American Church authorities took the formal position that religious liberty was unacceptable," while those same church authorities "were compelled to grapple with the fact of the plurality of faiths in American life . . . despite the doctrinal position."[27]

Msgr. John A. Ryan at Catholic University was one of the strongest proponents of this Americanist way of living the faith in the context of U.S. life

---

26. In contrast, the 1912 edition of the *Catholic Encyclopedia,* while offering a good deal of historical context on Judaism, nonetheless argued that Judaism was corrupted after the destruction of the Second Temple, and also called Jews "enemies" of Christ. Francis Gigot, "Jews and Judaism," in *Catholic Encyclopedia,* ed. Charles G. Herbermann, Edward A. Pace, Conde B. Pallen, Thomas J. Shahan, John J. Wynne et al., vol. 8, (New York: Robert Appleton Company, 1910), 402–3.

27. Maria Mazzenga, "Toward an American Catholic Response to the Holocaust: Catholic Americanism and Kristallnacht," in eadem, *American Religious Responses to Kristallnacht* (New York: Palgrave Macmillan, 2009), 86–87.

and institutions. Mazzenga points out that, by the late 1930s, two strains of thought could be identified as having emerged from the Americanist controversy. John Ryan represented one strain, which tried to reconcile Roman Catholicism with U.S. ideals of religious liberty; Fr. Charles Coughlin represented the other strain, a defensive and anticommunist Catholicism that understood the faith as being persecuted by "leftists." John Ryan would speak about the Jewishness of Christ and emphasize that hatred of the Jews by Catholics was wrong.[28] Coughlin would use his radio pulpit to decry what he believed was an international Jewish conspiracy behind communism, and he would grow more vehement in his anti-Semitism as the years progressed[29] until he was silenced by church authorities in 1942.[30]

The passages of Considine's thesis that treat of St. Ramon Lull and the Jews can be understood as a window on the climate of Catholic thought during the 1920s at Catholic University. If John Ryan's position is an indication, then the years that followed the Americanist and the modernist crises in the church did not produce at Catholic University an ultramontanism that failed to take into account the church's desire to have an impact on U.S. institutions and ideals. Formal acceptance of papal teaching was the norm, but the project of relating the life of the church to its U.S. context, even in interreligious affairs, was carried forward at Catholic University by Msgr. John Ryan and many other faculty.

Missioners do not always face serious scrutiny over doctrinal questions. Because they are committed to sharing the gospel and expanding the church's influence, missioners are frequently seen as upholders of traditional orthodoxy. As Considine wrote his thesis and developed his mission ideas, he was probably favored by a general disposition on the part of church authorities to give missioners the benefit of the doubt. But Considine's treatment of the Jews in his thesis makes clear that a particular ambience at Catholic University in the 1920s allowed him to continue to develop his mission thinking in an atmosphere that featured sympathy for culture and a justification of the church's engagement with modern concepts and institutions.

Considine's Concept of Methods

Fr. Considine had a great concern for missionary methods—for example, the mission conference he organized for the Maryknoll Fathers in 1954 was dubbed the Lima Methods Conference.[31] His main concern was that

---

28. Ibid., 90.

29. Ibid., 89.

30. Leslie Woodcock Tentler, *Seasons of Grace: A History of the Catholic Archdiocese of Detroit* (Detroit: Wayne State University Press, 1990), 338–42.

31. See chapter 8.

mission methods—the practical and strategic actions of mission—have two features: they should flow from the church's orthodoxy, and they should take seriously the cultures and beliefs of the people of the world.

In his licentiate dissertation on St. Ramon Lull, Considine makes explicit this importance of attention to the customs and beliefs of people whom the missionary addresses with the message of Christ:

> It is to be noted that through all Ramon's works runs the belief that of the two faculties will and understanding, understanding is the superior in bringing men to God. This trust in the understanding seems to be the foundation for his whole policy in presenting the faith to the infidel.[32]

> Besides general training of mind and acquisition of the instrument of address the missioner, Ramon teaches, should study the temper and the customs of the people among whom he is to work, but especially their beliefs that by a proper use of the science of comparative religions he may strike the happy mean between the wholesale condemnation of native tenets and any disastrous compromise of Christianity.[33]

Thus, Considine's focus on methods was quite definitely not a focus on practicalities only. His perspective followed that of missionary ethnologist Fr. Wilhelm Schmidt, and Schmidt's student, Friedrich Schwager, whom Considine met at Catholic University.[34] This perspective included a faithfulness to the magisterium but also the use of the social sciences. Considine's formulation can also be understood as falling within the norm of pastoral consideration that Pope John XXIII would express at the Second Vatican Council: the truth of the faith is one thing—not to be disputed—but the expression of it is another thing—open for pastoral discussion.[35]

Priestly Ordination in 1923; Off to Rome in 1924
Considine was ordained to the priesthood on May 26, 1923, in the Cathedral of the Fall River Diocese, St. Mary of the Assumption. He and his classmate William Fletcher joined fifteen other men being ordained to the diocesan priesthood that day.[36] In the fall of 1923, Considine returned to Catholic University to continue his graduate studies.

---

32. Considine, "Blessed Ramon Lull," 73.

33. Ibid., 81.

34. John Considine, Washington, to James A. Walsh, Ossining, NY, December 5, 1923. MMA, Considine Papers, 2:1.

35. John XXIII, Opening Discourse of the Second Vatican Council, October 11, 1962.

36. Before 1930, Maryknoll ordinations at times took place in dioceses around the

Beginning in October 1923, in his correspondence with Maryknoll co-founder James A. Walsh, Considine began relating the details of the upcoming Vatican Mission Exposition, to be held in Rome throughout the 1925 Holy Year.[37] Considine appears to have learned about the Exposition through Fr. Schwager.[38] The substance of the correspondence between Walsh and Considine for the next year centered on the importance of the Exposition, and then on the details of arranging for a Maryknoll exhibit to appear in the event.

The tenor of the letters is a window on Considine's organizational capabilities. Ever so diplomatically, he first had to give his superior the news that there would be such an event and then convince him of its importance for mission. Once that was done, he needed to suggest that Maryknoll have an exhibit and then be ready for the push-back from the superior on the costs that would be incurred by the fledgling mission group. On that point, Considine responded to Walsh that Maryknoll could not afford not to be there, that a Maryknoll exhibit would raise the mission group's profile among the many U.S. Catholics who were expected to visit the Exposition. Additionally, Considine would see if he could raise some funds through his family to help.

Later, the content and size of the exhibit—which in the end became two exhibits—had to be determined, so Considine contacted the event's organizers in Rome and submitted a plan for Walsh to review. Next he explored the possibility of a Maryknoller accompanying the exhibits to Rome, so that they would be properly assembled. Of course he volunteered to be that Maryknoller, and once again assured Walsh that his family would cover his travel costs. Although Considine was not the only talented Maryknoller at Catholic University who had heard of the Exposition, he had championed its cause. Walsh agreed to send Considine to the Exposition, and Considine made his plans for travel to Rome.

Prior to continuing the narrative, a word about Considine's operative missiology is in order—how did Considine understand the goals and the scope of the worldwide mission of the church?

---

country. Although many vocations from the Fall River Diocese continued to come to Maryknoll throughout the twentieth century, when Considine and Fletcher were ordained in 1923, it marked the last time a Maryknoller would be ordained to the priesthood in that particular diocesan cathedral.

37. John Considine, Washington, to James A. Walsh, Ossining, NY, October 13, 1923. MMA, Considine Papers, 2:1.

38. John Considine, Washington, to James A. Walsh, Ossining, NY, December 5, 1923. MMA, Considine Papers, 2:1.

Plantatio Ecclesiae

In missiology, Considine was not an innovator of new theories but rather one who could start with a traditional idea of mission and then, in most creative fashion, call attention to the abundant logical and practical conclusions that needed to be drawn from that idea. While he was never averse to new ideas, the main idea underpinning his mission thought throughout his career was *plantatio ecclesiae*, the implantation of the church. In a strict sense, *plantatio ecclesiae* as a missiological concept refers to the church being established in a new context. Thus, the goal of missionary work is not just the religious conversion of individuals to the gospel (*conversio animarum*), but rather the foundation of churches. In *World Christianity* (1945), Considine expanded the concept of *plantatio ecclesiae*. He started with the fact that the church sends out missioners to establish churches. Why are they sent out? In imitation of the missions of the Son and the Holy Spirit. He thus connected the action of mission today to the identity of the Godhead.

For what purpose do the Son and the Holy Spirit go out, and for what purpose do missioners go out today? So that all might believe. Once again, he connected mission to its roots in the words of Jesus. From there, he went on to define who "all" are, which led him to the concept of universality—the definition of the word 'catholic.' From this same point he would argue for the unity of the human race.

Already Considine had identified the activity of mission vertically by tying this activity of the church to a true understanding of who God is and horizontally by emphasizing that this mission directs itself toward all peoples of the world through their histories and in their cultures. He then employed "missiography" to expand the horizontal and the vertical dimensions; in Considine's formulation, missiography is

- The study of the world's peoples (making use of anthropology, sociology, historical studies and even economics for a comprehensive picture)
- The study of the church's opportunities to be in mission to the world's peoples (drawing on biblical studies and church history)

What meanings did *plantatio ecclesiae* carry for Considine? In addition to being his fundamental missiology, the goal of establishing the church had theological, sociological, and anthropological implications.

In *World Christianity*, the theological implications of *plantatio ecclesiae* were based in trinitarian theology. Considine used Jesus' farewell discourse in John to illustrate a parallel between the sending of the Son and the Holy Spirit and the sending of missioners ("As the Father has sent me, so I send you").[39] *Plantatio ecclesiae* therefore has a firm foundation in discipleship, in the definition of what a Christian is. The logical conclusion that Considine will make is that all Christians are called to either become missioners themselves or to support the sending of missioners.

A sociological implication is that the concept of *plantatio ecclesiae* as used by Considine always referred to a community of believers being established. Like many others, Considine could embrace the solitary witness of Charles de Foucauld in his Saharan hermitage, but even that example is given a communal focus in Considine's writings. He asked: "Was de Foucauld a mere pessimist? Quite the contrary. He called the Sahara Desert his parish, and the ten thousand Tuaregs of its oases his missionary flock."[40] Mission always carries a sense of a community, and even the current religious affiliation of the community is a secondary matter.

Anthropologically, Considine understood mission and the establishment of the church as offering an important qualification to the definition of the human—the human is that being who is open to the reception of the divine message of Christ. There must therefore be for all Christian believers a permanent sense of the unity of the entire human race. All people are called to receive the gospel and take part in Christ's church.

The concept of *plantatio ecclesiae* has been somewhat eclipsed by that of the *missio Dei* (the mission of God) and the theology of the local church, but not completely. At its heart *missio Dei* was a correction, a correction that brought about a change within the evangelizers—to see the church not as an end in itself but as a servant of God's mission in the world. This change did not necessarily alter the identity of the missioner—the missioner is still, humanly speaking, an agent of the church—nor the actual tasks a missioner engaged in, which would still have to do with establishing the church as a community in the service of God's mission.

Similarly, a focus on local theologies does not undo the idea of *plantatio ecclesiae* but rather refines it by asking if the church that is being established in a given context is culturally recognizable in that context or if instead it is foreign to its context, an outpost of some other local church—often the church of origin of the missioners who established it.

Thus, while twenty-first-century missiologists have not given much attention to *plantatio ecclesiae*, it is clear that this concept maintains a certain usefulness for understanding the missionary activity of the church. Considine's unique contribution will be the ways he applies this basic formulation to mission contexts around the world and to the mission support efforts of sending churches. Considine will ask in context after context

---

39. John J. Considine, *World Christianity* (Milwaukee: Bruce, 1945), 23.
40. Considine and Kernan, *Across a World*, 364.

the following question: if God has indeed established a unity of all human beings and the church is God's instrument to make that unity an active reality, what do we need to do to be faithful collaborators in achieving that unity in Christ?

A Young Man Grown Up

As this portion of the narrative closes, Considine has finished his studies and been ordained. Before continuing the story, a short description of Considine as an adult person is in order.

If you were a colleague who saw him regularly, Fr. Considine had noticeable mannerisms. He worked a lot, putting in long hours on whatever pressing enterprise he was involved in. This sometimes made him seem like a loner to some observers; at the same time, the pages of his diaries speak of how he valued being on good terms with his fellows and mention several close friendships.

We have already noted his friendship with Maryknoller Francis Ford; other Maryknoll friends included James Keller, Edward McGurkin, Alonso Escalante, Al Nevins, and Miguel D'Escoto, all of whom, like Ford, went on to distinguished careers in the church or in Maryknoll.[41] Outside Maryknoll two friends stand out—his colleague Msgr. Unzalu, the Spanish-language editor at Fides, and Fr. Fred McGuire, C.M., with whom he worked on the U.S. Mission Secretariat in the 1950s and at the NCWC/USCC in Washington during the 1960s. McGuire and Considine also roomed at the NCEA house in Northwest Washington 1960–1963.

Fr. Considine had an indirect way of accomplishing his goals; typically, he would get others to suggest his ideas. Many years after the fact, he described the 1927 founding of Fides as taking place when he could get Msgr. Quinn to suggest the idea to the Superior Council of the Pontifical Mission Societies.[42] Fr. Thomas V. Kiernan, who served with Considine on

---

41. Keller was the founder of the Christophers. McGurkin became the founding bishop of the Diocese of Shinyanga, Tanganyika, in 1956. Escalante was consecrated a bishop when he became the founding vicar apostolic of the Apostolic Vicariate of the Pando, Bolivia, in 1943, and he went on to found the Mexican Foreign Mission Society, known as the Misioneros Guadalupanos in 1949. Nevins, ordained in 1942, worked under Considine at *Maryknoll-The Field Afar* and then succeeded him as editor in 1960. D'Escoto, ordained in 1961, became the founding publisher of Orbis Books in 1971. D'Escoto is also well known for his leadership in the government of Nicaragua; following the Sandinista Revolution in 1979 he served eleven years as Foreign Minister of Nicaragua and from 2006 to 2010 as the Nicaraguan ambassador to the United Nations. He was also elected president of the U.N. General Assembly and served in that capacity from September 2008 to September 2009. During his service as Foreign Minister, the Vatican suspended his exercise of priestly ministry, a suspension that has not yet been lifted.

42. John J. Considine, "For the Revelation of Events," *Worldmission* 23 (Summer 1972):

the General Council of the Maryknoll Society from 1936 to 1946, commented that Considine did not take a position on an issue until he understood how everybody else was going to vote.[43]

He was not a man of marked devotion to the spiritual life; generally speaking, he rarely offered advice on how to grow spiritually. As a priest, he celebrated Mass every day (usually in the company of one altar server, but also alone when necessary), but his diary entries on the subject of spirituality betray an awkwardness about his own lack of constancy in regard to prayer and spiritual exercises.[44] Though he did serve a number of years as chaplain to the Maryknoll Sisters' Cloister, he commented in his diary how helpful he found that task for his own spiritual well-being.[45]

John's family was important to him throughout his life; for many years he wrote a letter to his mother every Sunday, and he visited the family a few times each year when he was living in the United States. Even when away, news from home was always something he valued. As was noted in chapter 1, Considine also had great personal closeness with his brothers throughout his life. He most often stayed with his youngest brother, George, when home in the New Bedford area.

Considine was extremely diplomatic and rarely exhibited a strong temper; he might have appeared as nerdy or even aloof, but students in his classes reported that he was ever approachable. His students, in addition to recalling his brilliant lectures on world affairs and mission, reported also a nervous space-filling laugh or expression, "Well—ah, ha, ha . . ." In spite of the fact that from 1935 to 1968 he spoke regularly to large audiences in the United States, his diary entries after a speaking engagement reveal much self-doubt about his ability as a public speaker. He was clearly more comfortable as a writer.

Considine was a man frequently on the go. Whether it was the short trip from Ossining to New York City to meet a visiting bishop or Vatican diplomat upon arrival from overseas, or his mission study tours that were months long, Considine was at ease with moving about any distance. He was also astutely sensitive to the feelings of others and eager to host visiting dignitaries at the Maryknoll headquarters. During one month in the late

---

30–33. Msgr. Quinn was the U.S. National Director of the Society for the Propagation of the Faith at the time.

43. "He never committed until he knew what the rest of us were thinking. . . . We never knew how John was going to vote until it was clear what the majority of the rest of us thought and John (laughing) was always with the majority" (Thomas V. Kiernan, interview by Laurence Murphy, December 1982. Maryknoll Society Oral History Project, Maryknoll Fathers and Brothers, Ossining, NY. Transcript p. 10).

44. CD, June 23, 1949; February 13, 1947.

45. CD, February 13, 1947.

spring of 1943 he hosted first General Peñaranda, the president of Bolivia, and then Mrs. Arroyo del Río, the first lady of Ecuador. In his public relations work at Maryknoll he strove to inculcate in his colleagues the importance for mission of maintaining warm and cordial relationships with just about everyone.

Considine was also very organized. Since he traveled frequently, he had a knack for setting up his office on a train, a boat, and, later, in an airline seat. He was always a journalist, and so being able to work while on the road was key to his task.

To the Eternal City
In Considine's letters to Maryknoll co-founder and Father Superior James A. Walsh during the late summer and fall of 1924, Considine kept Walsh updated on the assembly of materials for the exhibits and then on the effort to get them to Rome. The correspondence reveals Considine busy with many things yet ever tactful and respectful with his superior.

Father O'Neill[46] writes that he has attended a meeting held recently at which the assignment of exhibit space was discussed. At the date he wrote, October 15, no decision had been made finally. The tentative plan, which he said was to be changed, was much below what we requested and were told we could count on. Whatever we get we shall make the most of, of course. It has been somewhat of a gamble deciding what was wanted of us as you know. We waited as long as it was advisable gathering the best information available but even now there are gaps in the data. I am going to Rome prepared to be surprised at nothing in the adjustments which may be necessary. Father O'Neill cabled November 1 that our goods had reached Naples and that I should come soon.[47]

On November 12, 1924, Considine found himself on board the RMS *Mauretania* headed for Southampton. An entirely new chapter in his life was about to open.

---

46. Fr. O'Neill was a Paulist stationed in Rome who was assisting Maryknoll with arrangements for the Exposition.

47. John J. Considine, New York, to James A. Walsh, Ossining, NY, November 10, 1924. MMA, Considine Papers, 2:1 (Correspondence with James A. Walsh 1916–1935).

CHAPTER 5

An Enterprising Man in an Enterprising Town Rome, 1924–1930

WHEN FR. CONSIDINE traveled to Rome in November 1924, Maryknoll Society Superior and co-founder Fr. James A. Walsh understood a basic plan: Considine was going to Rome "to prepare the exhibit of his society and then he is going to China."[1] Instead of just getting into the Exposition and then moving on to a mission assignment, Considine stayed in Rome for ten years. He worked as a Vatican insider—albeit one who founded a world mission press service—and established there a permanent Maryknoll community with official representation to the Vatican. How did an unknown priest, barely ordained a year, come to establish himself and his new American mission Society in Rome of the 1920s?

This chapter explores precisely that question, because establish himself he did. In Rome Considine's life quickly became a real whirlwind. After setting up the two Maryknoll displays at the 1925 Vatican Mission Exposition, he became an English-speaking guide at the Exposition, and then a priest-secretary to Archbishop Francesco Marchetti Selvaggiani (1871–1951). Marchetti at the time was both the president of the Exposition and secretary of the Sacred Congregation of Propaganda Fide (SCPF). From mid-1925 Considine coordinated significant portions of a world survey of Catholic missions, which was to become the descriptive and statistical manual *Missiones Catholicae* (1930). In 1927 Considine became the founding director of Fides Service. He was responsible for weekly news

---

1. Considine's translation of the words of introduction used by Archbishop Marchetti when he presented Considine to Pope Pius XI on January 5, 1925. It was, in fact, the second time Marchetti presented Considine to the pope (John J. Considine, Rome, to James A. Walsh, Ossining, NY, January 11, 1925. MMA, Rome House Correspondence, 2:2).

dispatches of fifteen to twenty articles in English, Italian, German, Spanish, and French,[2] articles that were drawn from submissions from a network of nearly two hundred correspondents and delivered to newspapers and other distribution networks. By 1928, he was also father superior for the seven members of the Maryknoll community and the landlord for another eight priest boarders at Collegio Maryknoll. In 1928 he was officially appointed procurator general of the Maryknoll Society, and in that capacity oversaw public relations and hospitality to visiting bishops and other dignitaries; there were times when he slept on a couch in order to offer his room to an unexpected guest.

He also enjoyed two special Vatican assignments: he made his first trip to Africa in 1929, when Pius XI appointed him secretary of the Pontifical Mission to the Court of the Sovereigns of Ethiopia, and in 1931 he was called upon to make the official English translation of the papal encyclical *Casti Connubii*.

But he was really no worse for the wear; his health had been good, and John Considine in Rome was quite at home. Rome represented for him the center of world Christianity. Like most Catholics, he had a certain spiritual admiration for the Eternal City. But on another level, life at the center meant the opportunity to engage in very meaningful work—work that could help the mission enterprise of the church in far-flung areas of the globe. John Considine was an enterprising man in an enterprising town.

To understand the narrative of Considine's activities during the first years of his sojourn in Rome, I first tell the story of the mentor who opened many ecclesiastical doors for him, Archbishop (later, Cardinal) Francesco Marchetti Selvaggiani. Then I explore the prominent place that missions held during the papacy of Pius XI (pope 1922–1939). This will be followed by the narrative of Considine's life and work in Rome from 1924 to 1930, years in which he founded Fides Service. These were also years that were most formative for the young Maryknoll priest.

While Considine was very active during this period in Rome, he also quickly became ubiquitous—whenever and wherever significant events related to Catholic missions took place, Considine was not far away. I close the chapter by recounting two such incidents—the founding of the Missionary Ethnological Museum in 1927 and the 1929 Pontifical Mission to the Court of the Sovereigns of Ethiopia. In these events, Considine's role was not that of leadership, but nonetheless he was closely associated with those churchmen who were working on momentous issues—for example, the relationship of religion and science, and, later, the Italo-Ethiopian conflict, considered by some to be the beginning of World War II. Considine

---

2. For a brief time at the beginning, Fides also published a Polish-language edition.

was the kind of priest the pope and the leadership at the SCPF trusted to be part of a team charged with carrying out the church's plans. Additionally, Considine's is the voice on these matters that is still heard, even as the official records have been lost or concealed.

Considine traveled to Rome with Harold Dahill, a high school classmate from New Bedford.[3] The trip was exciting and memorable: a seven-day passage on RMS *Mauretania*, a London–Paris plane ride, and a twenty-eight-hour luxury train journey from Paris to Rome. "Harold paid the extras for the trip as of course Father Walsh would be provoked at my extravagance had I spent the money."[4] The pair arrived in Rome the evening of Tuesday, November 25, and the very next day Considine reported to the Vatican Mission Exposition. Harold stayed on in Rome for a week before returning to the United States.

A Mentor and Ally: Archbishop Francesco Marchetti Selvaggiani

That first day that Considine arrived at the grounds of the Vatican Mission Exposition in November 1924, he met the man who was soon to become key in his life and work in Rome: "'Maryknoll' sent in on a card brought Msgr. Marchetti to the gate . . . and immediately we began activities."[5] Archbishop (later Cardinal) Francesco Marchetti Selvaggiani, president of the Exposition and secretary of the SCPF, soon arranged for Considine to work as an English-speaking guide at the Exposition, and thus began their long and close association.

The exact circumstances of Considine's being hired as priest-secretary to Archbishop Marchetti are not known, though practically from the moment they met Considine was aware of the favorable treatment that Marchetti had granted him.[6] Marchetti had served under Archbishop (later Cardinal) Falconio in the Apostolic Delegation to the United States from 1899 to 1905 and had finished a term as nuncio first in Venezuela and then in Austria.

Marchetti was one of the most highly valued Vatican diplomats of his day. Originally from Rome, he studied philosophy and theology at the

---

3. John J. Considine, Rome, to James A. Walsh, Ossining, NY, 11 January 1925. MMA, Rome House Correspondence, 2:2.

4. John J. Considine, Paris, to Alice Considine, New Bedford, MA, November 23, 1924. Considine Family Archives.

5. John J. Considine, Rome, to James A. Walsh, Ossining, NY, November 26, 1924. MMA, Rome House Correspondence, 2:2.

6. Considine described to James A. Walsh how Archbishop Marchetti personally showed him around the Exposition, explaining the highlights, and how Marchetti even had a pillar removed that was obstructing the Maryknoll booth space. "Father Gubbels, the Franciscan in immediate charge of the halls, said it was a triumph" (John J. Considine, Rome, to James A. Walsh, Ossining, NY, December 14, 1924. MMA, Rome House Correspondence, 2:2).

prestigious Capranica College and was ordained in 1895. He continued his studies at the Gregorian University, where Eugenio Pacelli—the future Pius XII—was a classmate and friend. During these years, he began work at the Vatican Secretariat of State.

Before he was consecrated archbishop in 1918, Marchetti had been given postings in Switzerland during World War I with the explicit assignment from Benedict XV to bring representatives of the belligerent powers together.[7] Though he was not successful in setting up a peace conference, he was nonetheless the pope's man in this sensitive negotiation. Later, he served as apostolic nuncio to Venezuela (1918–1920) and then Austria, from 1920 until he took up duties as secretary of Propaganda Fide in 1922. In the mid-1930s when he was cardinal vicar of Rome, Marchetti formed part of a faction in the Roman Curia with Secretary of State Cardinal Eugenio Pacelli that was intent on minimizing any antagonism on the part of the Vatican toward the Nazi government of Germany.[8] How much of a role Marchetti played at the Vatican in 1936 to scuttle condemnations by the Holy Office of two Nazi measures against the Jews approved at the September 1935 Nuremburg Party Rally is a matter of current and intense scholarly debate.[9]

At one point Marchetti moved to center stage in this fateful drama. In November 1936, the cardinals of the Holy Office met to consider a twenty-five point document that would condemn National Socialism in Germany for its racism and for the abusive limitations placed on Catholic schools, presses, associations, and clergy.[10] At the meeting, Marchetti argued persistently that the condemnations be passed over in silence or, at the most, that the pope issue a general letter to warn or enlighten workers.[11]

Peter Godman believes that the blame for Vatican "silence" during the Nazi regime has been misplaced; the inaction of the Vatican cannot be understood as coming exclusively from Secretary of State Cardinal Pacelli, who later became Pius XII. Godman instead argues that the problem seems

---

7. Brendan A. Finn, *Twenty-Four American Cardinals Biographical Sketches of Those Princes of the Catholic Church Who Either Were Born in America or Served There at Some Time* (Boston: Humphries, 1947), 358–59.

8. Peter Godman, *Hitler and the Vatican: Inside the Secret Archives That Reveal the New Story of the Nazis and the Church* (New York: Free Press, 2004), 128; Alois Hudal, *Römische Tagebücher: Lebensbeichte eines alten Bischofs* (Graz: Stocker, 1976), 121.

9. Frank J. Coppa, "Between Anti-Judaism and Anti-Semitism, Pius XI's Response to the Nazi Persecution of the Jews: Precursor to Pius XII's 'Silence'?" *Journal of Church and State* 47, no. 1 (Winter 2005): 63–89. The Vatican Secret Archives opened the records of the papacy of Pius XI to scholarly consultation in the fall of 2006, and research on this important period is ongoing.

10. Godman, *Hitler and the Vatican,* 105.

11. Ibid., 128.

to have been a real lack of political or spiritual unity within the Vatican for confronting the Nazis.[12] This episode shows that Marchetti was one of the actors in that drama; Godman discusses several other Vatican officials who also were important figures in other episodes.

Considine, of course, returned to Maryknoll headquarters in New York from Rome at the end of 1934; he thus met and worked for Archbishop Marchetti before the deliberations on Nazism at the Holy Office came to pass. Nonetheless, it would be hard to believe that Considine was unaware of the tremendous tensions that were brewing between the Vatican, Italy, and Germany in the 1930s. He later returned to Rome for the coronation of Pius XII in early 1939 and experienced the sense of relief felt by some at the Vatican at that time—when Pius XI died, a faction of Vatican officials that had feared that the late pope was trying to enter into a confrontation with the Nazis and the Italian fascists breathed a sigh of relief.[13] After meeting a former colleague in Rome, Considine wrote in his diary: "I was particularly pleased with his buoyant and hopeful outlook, so different from that of many of the carping pessimists among the priests here who insist on seeing no good angle to the Fascist efforts."[14]

High curial officials like Archbishop Marchetti usually had young priests working as private secretaries; often, the priest would live in the apartment of the official. Such a job would entail assisting a given church official with correspondence, in addition to accompanying him to official functions, on walks and other outings, and on visits to religious orders sponsored by the archbishop. In many ways, the job was part secretary and part butler or valet; an accoutrement of curial culture, this sort of service was embedded in a respect for hierarchy and authority.[15]

However, Considine never lived in Archbishop Marchetti's apartment.[16] In contrast to the usual relationship of a curial official to a priest secretary, Marchetti's relationship to Considine was much more that of a mentor, a guide, and a faithful ally. Archbishop Marchetti taught Considine the ropes

---

12. Ibid., 170–71.

13. Emma Fattorini and Carl Ipsen, *Hitler, Mussolini and the Vatican: Pope Pius XI and the Speech That Was Never Made* (Cambridge: Polity Press, 2011), 14.

14. CD, March 14, 1939.

15. Joseph McCabe, Rome, interview with author, June 8, 2011, and Arthur Dwyer, Los Altos, CA, telephone interview with author, August 24, 2011.

16. In fact, the opposite came to pass, when in 1930 Marchetti unexpectedly announced that he would be moving into Collegio Maryknoll after he was elevated to the College of Cardinals (John J. Considine, Rome, to James A. Walsh, Ossining, NY, June 8 and 10, 1930. MMA, Rome House Correspondence, 3:1). There is little doubt that the move was always temporary for Marchetti, who in fact moved out in 1937 when he acquired his own villa in Monte Mario, Rome (Edward McGurkin, Rome, to John J. Considine, Ossining, NY, February 23, 1937. MMA, Considine Papers, 2:7).

of working in the Curia and early on gave him responsibilities in the Pontifical Mission Societies, located within the Congregation of Propaganda Fide, leading to his 1927 appointment as the founding director of Fides. Considering that Considine was only twenty-nine at the time, the Fides appointment was truly extraordinary.

For Considine's part, he was eager to learn and to be given a chance to use his talents in Rome in the service of Catholic missions. Indeed, he would certainly have found the usual duties of a priest-secretary to be too mundane, perhaps even a waste of time. Conversely, Considine provided for the archbishop a link to the church in the United States. In particular, an early instance at the Exposition reveals how U.S. ascendancy in the world seemed to impact their relationship. The Maryknollers had been promised seven meters of frontage for their exhibits, but when Considine arrived he found that the space had been reduced to three. Considine was able to speak with Archbishop Marchetti about this:

> I began very placidly the task of gaining more frontage. I took pencil and paper to show that we had a definite plan. I think the argument that the many American travelers will expect to see a respectable display for the only American mission society will be the clincher in holding for us the seven [meters] frontage which is ours by last report.[17]

Considine also commented that he was "quite tickled to find—and concerned as well—that 'American' and 'Maryknoll' are words to conjure with at the Exposition grounds."[18]

Marchetti seemed to understand that Maryknoll and the U.S. church had great potential to make an impact on Catholic missions; he also recognized leadership qualities in Considine. Thus, while he indeed "used" Considine's services as a priest-secretary, he also took great care to promote Considine slowly in the curial bureaucracy and to educate the young Maryknoller on how to position Maryknoll and U.S. missions for growth vis-à-vis the Vatican.[19] Working in the employ of Archbishop Marchetti became Considine's

---

17. John J. Considine, Rome, to James A. Walsh, Ossining, NY, November 26, 1924. MMA, Rome House Correspondence, 2:2.

18. Ibid.

19. Through Considine's auspices Marchetti also gave particular attention to the Maryknoll Society constitutions, which from 1926 to 1929 moved through stages of modification toward approval by Propaganda. Marchetti gave the document a "searching examination," spending three successive Sunday mornings going over them (James A. Walsh, "Preliminary Address." MMA, General Chapter I & II, Box 1, Folder 2 [I - 1929 Report + Working Papers - photos]).

ticket to a front-row seat at the spectacle of mission activities that characterized the papacy of Pius XI.

Missions and the Papacy of Pius XI

If Considine's 1924–1934 stint in Rome was characterized by extraordinary official awareness of missions, the table was set for such an awareness in the previous decade, which saw the founding of the Missionary Union of the Clergy by Fr. Paolo Manna in 1916. The previous pope, Benedict XV, in 1919 published his encyclical letter *Maximum Illud,* which called for an indigenization of the clergy and hierarchy in mission areas, an end to nationalism in missions, and for the scientific study of missions.[20]

Pius XI succeeded Benedict XV in 1922, and in the first four years of his pontificate he continued to carry out a vigorous mission agenda: relocating the Society for the Propagation of the Faith from Lyons, France, to Rome in 1923; convoking the Vatican Mission Exposition during the 1925 Holy Year; commissioning works on mission statistics in several languages; and, at the close of the Exposition, calling for the establishment of a permanent Missionary Ethnological Museum that would continue to display in Rome the more outstanding objects from the Exposition.[21]

Pius XI was responsible for many other mission initiatives: the establishment of the Mission Library, first at the Vatican and then next to the new Missionary Ethnological Museum at the Lateran; the ordination in Rome

---

20. The goal of establishing a native clergy and hierarchy in mission areas was a remarkable change from the mission policies of Leo XIII, which had basically understood the European colonial apparatus, particularly the colonial settlement, as an excellent vehicle for evangelization; indigenous clergy was not an important component of such a framework (Claude Prudhomme, *Stratégie missionnaire du Saint-Siège sous Léon XIII [1878–1903]: centralisation romaine et défis culturels* [Rome: Ecole française de Rome, 1994], 392–99). Of course, a world war had occurred during the intervening years between the papacy of Leo XIII and Benedict's *Maximum Illud.* During the war, missioners were drafted into European armies, and in some cases the missioners of one colonial nationality were expelled, arrested, or had to operate under a cloud of suspicion when the territory in which they were working was taken over by another colonial power. A 1929 memo from SCPF prefect Willem Cardinal Van Rossum to the apostolic delegate to Germany, Archbishop Pacelli (later Pope Pius XII) details the expulsions during the war of missioners in Africa and Oceania. German missioners were expelled and their property was handed over to trustees. The Holy See had confirmed this situation by reassigning these territories and the mission property to non-German missioners, and the biggest beneficiaries were French mission societies (Cardinal Van Rossum, Rome, to Archbishop Pacelli, Berlin, July 9, 1929. ASPF Rubrica 81, Sottorubrica 4, Nuova Serie 1101, Foglio 558–564). For both Benedict XV and Pius XI, the war had proven that a mission strategy based on colonialism was simply too fragile; working to indigenize the clergy and the hierarchy became the wisest strategy.

21. His Holiness Pope Pius XI, *Rerum Ecclesiae*, nos. 3–4, http://www.vatican.va/holy_father/pius_xi/encyclicals/documents/hf_p-xi_enc_28021926_rerum-ecclesiae_en.html (accessed June 28, 2011).

of the first Chinese, Japanese, and Vietnamese bishops; and *Rerum Ecclesiae*, a 1926 encyclical on missions that emphasized the indigenization of church leadership.[22]

If Benedict XV had already taken up the issue of the indigenization of church leadership in 1919, why did Pius XI take up the same topic again just seven years later in *Rerum Ecclesiae*? In today's parlance, racism and colonialism appear to have contributed to a slowness with which mission-ers took up the work of indigenization. Two assumptions that were held by many missioners of that time had to be addressed: an understanding that the "civilizing" work of mission involves (a) a belief in the superiority of European cultures to all others and (b) a belief that mission needed the material assistance—or at least the acquiescence—of colonial governments. In *Rerum Ecclesiae*, Pius XI countered both of these assumptions. Racism or discrimination against indigenous clergy is not to be accepted in mission work; the pope in fact turned that issue around in a practical way with this word to missioners: "On the contrary, you should prefer the native priests to all others, for it is they who will one day govern the churches and Cath-olic communities founded by your sweat and labor."[23]

Regarding colonialism, Pius XI is prescient about the need for the church to establish itself with a native clergy, precisely because colonial governments were unstable:

> Let us suppose, for example, that either because of the fortunes of war, or because of certain political happenings in a mission field, the ruling government is changed in that territory and that the new gov-ernment decrees or requests that the missionaries of a certain nation-ality be expelled; or let us suppose—something which rarely, if ever, occurs—that the inhabitants of a particular territory, having reached a fairly high degree of civilization and at the same time a correspond-ing development in civic and social life, and desiring to become free and independent, should drive away from their country the gover-nor, the soldiers, the missionaries of the foreign nation to whose rule they are subject. All this, of course, cannot be done without violence. Everyone can see what great harm would accrue to the Church in that land in the circumstances, unless a native clergy had been spread beforehand throughout the country like a network and were, by consequence, in a position to provide adequately for the population which had been converted to Christ.[24]

---

22. In an encyclical that contained a total of thirty-four paragraphs, nine paragraphs dealt directly with the issue of indigenization.

23. Pius XI, *Rerum Ecclesiae*, no. 26.

24. Ibid., no. 22.

Challenging the assumption of European cultural superiority or the usefulness of colonialism was not simply a change in mission policy. At a philosophical level, the popes were convinced of the unity of the human race. Recalling the initial reaction of Pius XI to news of the Italian racial laws in 1938, Emma Fattorini notes that it is a sense of the universality of Catholicism—a theme that is fundamental to mission—that was at the heart of the pope's reaction to laws that discriminate based on race:

> He referred to "having on that very day received an item of great seriousness," one that took on the form of a "true apostasy." "It is no longer a question of this or that idea that is in error, but rather the whole spirit of the doctrine is contrary to the faith in Christ": "'Catholic' means 'universal': there is no other possible translation. . . ."[25]

Throughout his papacy, Pius XI carried out a very active agenda that promoted the church's mission work. Did that agenda bring with it a perceptible impact on the pope's policies in other areas?

At a practical level, Pius's perspective in *Rerum Ecclesiae* was that of keeping the church's mission focused on its goal of preaching the gospel and making the institutions of the church available to all the world's peoples, a goal that must ever be pursued independently of the particular interests of any nation or government or organization or church institute. Moreover, if necessary, he pledged to use his authority to keep the pressure on missioners who did not share that perspective.[26]

In the latter years of the pontificate of Pius XI, the pope worked diligently to resolve the centuries-old cultural conflict concerning the Christian faith and the Chinese Rites, which was officially resolved in the first months of the pontificate of his successor, Pius XII, in 1939. Pius XI also settled the "Roman Question" with the signing of the 1929 Lateran Treaty with Italy. This accord had a far-reaching impact on church-state relations throughout the world; with the ratification of the treaty, the pope's claims on the territory of the former Papal States officially

---

25. Fattorini and Ipsen, *Hitler, Mussolini and the Vatican,* 158.

26. In *Rerum Ecclesiae*, Pius XI put those in charge of the church's missionary organizations on notice that he, as pope,

> without hesitation and whenever it shall appear to be either necessary, more opportune, or useful for the larger growth of the Catholic Church, shall transfer the mission territory of one Institute to another Institute; We shall also divide and subdivide a mission territory and shall confide it to the care of native priests or shall assign new Vicariates and new Apostolic Prefectures of other religious Congregations than those occupying the original territory (no. 33).

came to an end.[27] This in turn ushered in a new era in which the Holy See would enjoy greater independence and moral esteem in its spiritual, pastoral, and humanitarian efforts. In the same year, Pius XI sent a Delegation of the Holy See to the Court of the Sovereigns of Ethiopia; Fr. Considine was a member of this delegation, which worked toward the establishment of formal diplomatic ties with this noncolonized African nation.

All of these developments were significant for the church's worldwide mission. Agostino Giovagnoli has argued that what was consistent in Pius's approach to both the rise of fascism and the process of indigenization in missions worldwide was the single-minded purpose of maintaining the independence of the church from the state or from any other power.[28]

Additionally, the impact of missions on Pius XI can be perceived in his embrace of the work of missionary ethnologist Fr. Wilhelm Schmidt, S.V.D.[29] As will presently be discussed, the pope was not totally convinced of the value of modern science; nonetheless, Pius XI invited Schmidt to take charge of two ethnology pavilions in the Vatican Mission Exposition, and at the end of 1925 the pope asked Schmidt to convert the exhibits of the Exposition into a permanent museum.[30] This was a significant turnabout of events. Schmidt first came to Rome in 1911 to propose the founding of an ethnological museum in the Eternal City but met only resistance

---

27. In spite of the fact that in the 1929 concordat Pius XI made peace with modern Italy, Fattorini makes the case that Pius XI's acceptance of Mussolini was always tentative, and that ultimately the pope repudiated Mussolini's fascism (*Hitler, Mussolini and the Vatican,* 180–87).

28. Agostino Giovagnoli, "Il Vaticano di fronte al colonialismo fascista." In *Le guerre coloniali del fascismo,* ed. Angelo Del Boca (Rome: Editori Laterza, 1991), 112–31, here 113.

29. Fr. Wilhelm Schmidt of the Society of the Divine Word, was, together with Frederic Bouvier, S.J., the organizer of the Semaine d'Ethnologie held at Louvain in 1912 and 1913. Having trained in linguistics at the University of Berlin, Schmidt brought an ethnological approach to his teaching duties at St. Gabriel Seminary in Mödling, Austria, where he involved his students and collaborators in the collection of field data and published widely on the languages of New Guinea, Oceania, and Southeast Asia. In 1906, ten years after joining the St. Gabriel faculty, the priest-ethnologist founded *Anthropos International Review of Ethnology,* and later, in 1932, he founded the Anthropos Institute. Schmidt was perhaps the first Roman Catholic to make use of modern social science in the service of mission, ever concerned that a rigorous and academically credible ethnological approach to humanity would be of the most service to the church's mission. This insight worked the other way as well—Schmidt believed that missioners, because of their knowledge of local language, their usually long-term presence among a group of people, and the confidence extended to them by people, often make better ethnological field workers than academics who spend shorter periods of time among the groups they study (Louis J. Luzbetak, "Wilhelm Schmidt, S.V.D., 1868–1954: Priest, Linguist, Ethnologist," in *Mission Legacies: Biographical Studies of Leaders of the Modern Missionary Movement,* ed. Gerald H. Anderson, Robert T. Coote, Norman A. Horner, and James M. Phillips [Maryknoll, NY: Orbis Books, 1994], 475–85).

30. An Vandenberghe, "Entre mission et science: La recherche ethnologique du père Wilhelm Schmidt SVD et le Vatican (1900–1939)," *Le fait missionnaire* 19 (2006): 15–36.

from curial officials. The antimodernist climate during the papacy of Pius X did not favor the founding of such a museum.

Fourteen years later Schmidt was back in Rome, invited by Pius XI. What had happened? The founding of the Missionary Ethnological Museum at the Lateran marked an extraordinary change in behavior at the Vatican. The contours of this behavioral change can be outlined as follows: rather than immediately condemn what was perceived as different from or outside the church's tradition, by 1925 the leadership of the church had adopted a stance in which, in regard to the way missioners were to approach non-Western cultures, it was possible to suspend judgment and gather information. A more circumspect attitude to human cultures had been adopted, and this change had immense theological and missiological consequences. It seems clear that the missionary engagement of the popes was a significant factor in this change.

A final influential factor in the climate of Rome that Considine encountered in the 1920s was the beginnings of an internationalization of the Curia. For example, the prefect of Propaganda, Cardinal Willem Van Rossum, was the first Dutchman elevated to the College of Cardinals since the Reformation. In turn, moves to internationalize the Curia in the second decade of the twentieth century had their roots in the reforms of the Curia undertaken by Leo XIII and Pius X, reforms that eliminated the aristocratic element from the College of Cardinals; a new focus for church administrators would be a sense of duty to the church.[31]

A Roman Career?

The basic dynamic of a career in the Roman Curia is to work so as to gain greater and greater recognition throughout life. Was Considine himself attracted to a career in the Roman Curia, to that particular pathway of advancement?

While this is an important question, it is one that is decidedly difficult to answer; Considine's diaries and other writings of the period reveal neither inclination nor disinclination to such a career path.[32] What is manifestly clear is that Considine was pleased when his stay in Rome was prolonged so that he could take on responsibilities at Propaganda. The tone of his correspondence with Maryknoll co-founder and superior general Fr. James A. Walsh often portrayed a great enthusiasm for what he was able to accomplish for Maryknoll and mission in Rome. The 1920s was also a time when

---

31. Giuseppe M. Croce, "Regards sur la Curie romaine de 1895 à 1932," *Trajecta* [Leuven] (2010–2011): 53–65.

32. On the other hand, in the late 1940s and during the 1950s there were indications that he demurred from being recruited to return to the Roman Curia or to join the Vatican diplomatic corps. See chapter 8.

many religious orders were establishing either Generalates or Procures in Rome, a trend Considine mentioned to James A. Walsh.[33] In short, being Maryknoll's man-in-Rome certainly agreed with him.

Additionally, he had the right combination of perspectives for working in the Curia in the 1920s and 1930s. For Catholics from the United States, a general ultramontanist sense—characterized by a reverence for the pope as the arbiter of all Catholic matters and a respect for the church's hierarchical order—could be found in seminaries and religious houses of formation, and also among the Catholic faithful in the United States at the turn of the twentieth century. Considine had been exposed to this sort of ultramontanism during his upbringing and academic training[34] and had developed an abiding sense of the ability of the papacy and the Vatican to understand what was best for the entire Body of Christ. To this mix of perspectives and convictions on the church as an institution, we can add two qualities held by Considine: his profound curiosity about and devotion to world mission, and a diplomatic temperament.

He also had sufficient political sense for working effectively in the Roman Curia. For example, prior to his appointment as director of Fides, he employed a woman as a secretary, but, were that to have become known, he could have become suspect. With the Fides appointment, he had to find a male secretary. At that time Considine wrote to Maryknoll co-founder Fr. James A. Walsh:

> You will easily understand that there will be problems aplenty in launching an American idea in the lap of a Roman Congregation. My program consists mainly for the next few months in convincing everybody of my conservatism and in doing everything that is not conservative under cover.[35]

What he still lacked, however, was an experience of foreign mission. Yet, since he was only twenty-seven when he arrived in Rome, he believed there would be still be time later for mission service. Nonetheless, this Maryknoll missioner, who had not served in a foreign mission, found the work in Rome to be a cross-cultural challenge. In addition to working every day in Italian, French, and English, he also approached his environ-

---

33. Considine reported that Archbishop Marchetti had been urging Maryknoll to purchase a house in Rome (John Considine, Rome, to James A. Walsh, Ossining, NY, June 12, 1927. MMA, Considine Papers, 3:7).

34. See chapter 4 on the intellectual climate of the Catholic University of America in the 1920s.

35. John Considine, Rome, to James A. Walsh, Ossining, NY, April 27, 1927. MMA, Considine Papers, 3:7.

ment with the same sort of sympathetic understanding that he had found so attractive in the writings of Blessed Ramon Lull—with, of course, one rather large difference. Unlike Ramon's work among Muslims, in his situation of learning about and adapting to the culture of the Roman Curia, Considine did not have to guard against a sympathy for the native that might lead to doctrinal error.

The Vatican Mission Exposition

Having arrived in Rome in late 1924 with the Maryknoll Exhibits, Considine attended orientation meetings on the Exposition and was recruited to work as an English-speaking guide once the Exposition opened on December 21, 1924. The Exposition was not just a collection of mission artifacts but rather a year-long event that combined ritual moments (numerous canonizations and beatifications of missioners and converts to Christianity)[36] with educational moments, and publications with scholarly conferences. The Exposition brought together some of the brightest minds who were at work on the church's mission concerns at the time and served as the catalyst for the establishment of permanent mission institutions: the Vatican Missionary Library was founded to continue the work of the Exposition Library, and the Missionary Ethnological Museum at the Lateran was proposed by Pope Pius XI as a way to keep open to all Catholics the lessons of the Exposition exhibits.

At the Exposition meetings, Considine would meet people he had previously only read about, such as Cardinal Willem Van Rossum, the prefect of Propaganda Fide. Also in Rome to work on the Exposition were the well-known bibliographer of missions, Fr. Robert Streit, O.M.I., and missionary ethnologist Fr. Wilhelm Schmidt, S.V.D. Fr. Streit was charged with the Exposition Library, and Fr. Schmidt organized the two ethnology pavilions at the Exposition.[37] There was also a young Msgr. Angelo Roncalli—the future Pope John XXIII—who, as head of the Society for the Propagation of the Faith in Italy, served on the Commission for the Exposition.[38]

---

36. St. Thérèse of Lisieux was one of the many canonizations of 1925, and two years later she was proclaimed co-patroness of missions—along with St. Francis Xavier. Carlo Salotti, *I Santi ed I Beati proclamati nell'Anno santo 1925. Panegirici tenuti in Roma in occasione dei Tridui solenni* (Turin: Soc. Ed. Internaz., 1927).

37. Ester Maria Console, "Incontri tra culture nelle collezioni del Museo Missionario Etnologico," in *I Musei Vaticani nell'80° anniversario della firma dei Patti Lateranensi 1929–2009*, ed. Antonio Paolucci and Cristina Pantanella (Vatican City: Edizioni Musei Vaticani, 2009), 168–77, esp. 169.

38. *Revue illustrée de l'Exposition Missionaire Vaticane: publication officielle.* Bergamo: [s.n.], (March 31, 1925), 263–64. In 1961, when called to an audience with Pope John XXIII, Considine in his diary recalls having spoken with then Msgr. Roncalli and Archbishop Marchetti in 1925 on a street in Rome (CD, March 22, 1961. MMA, Considine Papers, 7:1).

The Exposition featured the extraordinary personal involvement of Pius XI; he visited the pavilions on several occasions and held countless audiences with Exposition officials and visitors alike. Pius very much participated in the papal tradition of using his personal charisma to enchant audiences, but with an important mission-minded twist: he spoke frequently to groups about mission as a high priority for the church.

The Exposition also included Ethnology Week, held in Milan during September 1925. This was the fourth time that Fr. Wilhelm Schmidt had organized this week-long set of workshops for missioners and mission superiors on the topic of what ethnology could teach missioners. Additionally, the Exposition published twenty-six semi-monthly issues of an illustrated review in French and Italian.[39] The pages were large and the subject matter of the articles was related to exhibits in the Exposition. However, the articles were not so much an explanation of the exhibits but rather were meant to offer plentiful background on the context of the missions from which exhibits came; Considine wrote several articles for the French edition.

Collaboration on Mission Statistics, 1925–1934

While serving in Rome, Considine collaborated closely with Fr. Robert Streit, O.M.I., on the *Little Atlas of Catholic Missions* (1926) and *Catholic Missions in Figures and Symbols* (1927).[40] He also contributed much statistical work on a voluminous manual covering official surveys of Catholic missions around the world: *Missiones Catholicae* (1930). Statistics was an area where he understood practical matters as having a large influence on the enterprise of Christianity. Compiling mission statistics, no matter how great the drudgery, was for Considine a concrete service to mission, as statistics form part of a body of knowledge on missions that is not only useful to missioners but also vital for the church's own self-understanding. Along with Maryknoll Fr. Edward McGurkin, Considine also worked on an updated version of *Missiones*, another thick volume of statistics and descriptions of mission work published in 1934, *Guida delle Missioni Cattoliche.*[41]

---

39. *Revue illustrée de l'Exposition Missionaire Vaticane: publication officielle* (Bergamo: [s.n.], 1924). Esposizione Missionaria Vaticana, *Rivista illustrata della Esposizione Missionaria Vaticana: pubblicazione ufficiale* (Rome: [s.n.], 1924).

40. Considine's name does not appear in either text, but he wrote of doing statistical work in correspondence with his mother (John J. Considine, Rome, to Alice Considine, New Bedford, MA, November 15, 1925. Considine Family Archives).

41. Catholic Church, *Missiones catholicae* (Vatican City: Typis Polyglottis Vaticanis, 1930). The lead researcher on this project was at first Fr. Robert Streit, O.M.I., whose premature illness and death prevented him from seeing it to completion. Considine is not mentioned in the printed volume, but the diary of the Maryknoll procure in Rome offers some insight into the production of the volume: "'Missiones Catholicae,' new official survey of the foreign

Fides International Service, 1927–1934

The official Vatican version of the founding of Fides Service, like all such Roman institutional innovations, highlights the role of Congregation officials and puts Considine in a passive role: the Cardinal Prefect of Propaganda Fide was the founder, and Considine was the first director of the agency.[42] Of course, that would leave out a large part of the story; Fides was an idea that Considine came up with and advocated for, and when it was established he developed it into a flourishing international press bureau of Catholic missions.

Considine understood that Fides, by providing news from far-flung areas of Asia, Africa, Latin America, and Oceania, would be the right vehicle to exploit a certain opening in both the secular and Catholic press. He knew secular editors would reject anything that smacked of propaganda, but he also knew how hungry they were for news. Therefore, if Fides could provide "information of genuine news value prepared in the proper newspaper style," editors would not be so ready to reject such news simply because it came from Propaganda Fide in Rome.[43]

Fr. Considine recruited the U.S. national director of the Society for the Propagation of the Faith (SPF), Msgr. Quinn, to present the idea to the annual meeting in Rome of the Superior Council of the Pontifical Mission Societies in April 1927. The idea that the Pontifical Mission Societies in Rome should begin a mission publication was not new; Considine had been lobbying Archbishop Marchetti on the idea for a couple of years. At the 1927 meeting the time was right, and the proposal was approved by the council, Cardinal Van Rossum, and the pope.[44] Considine became the first director of Agentia Fides, as it was known in Latin.

Between the founding of Fides in April 1927 and the first English edi-

---

missions of the church came off the press today. This large volume of well coordinated statistics has claimed Father Considine's every spare moment for months past. Father Skelly and Brother Leo spent many a weary hour over adding machines and the like—in fact we all had our hands in the making of the index. Hence there was great rejoicing in our little circle on the appearance of this latest census of the mission world" (Rome House Diary, February 6, 1930. MMA, Rome House, Box 1, Folder 2; *Guida delle Missioni Cattoliche*, ed. Sacra Congregazione di Propaganda Fide [Rome: Unione Missionaria del Clero in Italia, 1934], vii–x, here ix). Both Considine and McGurkin are credited for their research assistance in the preface to the volume by Cardinal Fumasoni Biondi.

42. In the Minutes of the Superior Council, no founder is listed; once the council created Fides, it was entrusted to Considine (*Acta Pontificii Operis a Propagatione Fidei: Cura Consilii Superioris Generalis* vol. I, no. 7 [September 30, 1927]: 265).

43. "Fides Service: Second Annual Report," April 1, 1929, p. 7. MMA, Considine Papers, 3:7.

44. John J. Considine, "For the Revelation of Events," *Worldmission* 23 (Summer 1972): 32.

tion in December of that year, Considine was busy with the organization of the press service. He initially sought advice from SPF and curial officials, not all of which he found helpful:

> As to the actual working out of things no one has any suggestions. — Msgr. Quinn says take carte blanche; Msgr. [Marchetti] says do your best but make sure Missiones Catholicae does not suffer (in other words make a go of both): Msgr. Nogara wants to buy me a type-writer and suggests the news copy go out in Latin(!). I am my own boss with the one limitation that I must extricate myself from all such embarrassing proposals.[45]

The service almost immediately grew a network of nearly three hundred active correspondents in Asia, Africa, Latin America, and Oceania;[46] the correspondents were missioners themselves who were already stationed in those regions of the world. Reports from the correspondents were drafted by a small staff in Rome into press releases in five languages and distributed weekly to newspapers and to the national offices of the Society for the Propagation of the Faith; the United States, France, Italy, England, Ireland, and India were the countries with the largest distribution networks.[47] Dispatches from Rome were also sent to Vatican diplomats posted around the world.

News from Fides Service had a very long trajectory: correspondents sent their dispatches to the central office in Rome; the dispatches were then selected, edited, and translated, and then sent off to the subscribers.[48] The subscribing presses, in turn, could use the materials at their own discretion. Thus, whether it was the story of a convert family being devoured by a lion in northern Rhodesia[49] or the first announcement of the 1929 Barcelona Missionary Exposition,[50] the long road began with a mission correspondent who sent in a dispatch to Rome. The dispatch then passed through and was edited by the central office in Rome before being sent to a newspaper or publication and then on to readers of those publications, mainly in Europe, North America, and parts of Asia and Oceania—and all in a matter of weeks.

---

45. John Considine, Rome, to James A. Walsh, Ossining, NY, April 7, 1927. MMA, Considine Papers, 3:7.

46. See "How to Be a Missiographer."

47. "Fides Service: Second Annual Report," April 1, 1929, pp. 8–11. MMA, Considine Papers, 3:7.

48. Considine, "For the Revelation of Events," 30–33.

49. *Agenzia Fides* No. 2, March 22, 1928.

50. *Agenzia Fides*, May 1, 1928.

This Is Fides Service

The first English edition of Fides was released on December 20, 1927, and the Italian edition debuted in March 1928. Fides quickly became a happening in the world of the Catholic press—a reliable and useful source of international news and analysis on missions, mission organizations, and, most particularly, the social, political, and religious context of the "Outerworld"[51] countries—what today is often referred to as the Global South—where most Catholic missions operated at the time.

Fides Service aimed from the beginning to be a journalistic undertaking. The usual distinction between journalism and propaganda hinges on impartiality as the dividing line between the two. Stuart Price has suggested that it is more precise to speak of issues of control and power, that propaganda is characterized by coercive techniques to control information as an exercise of power by the powerful.[52] Already it has been noted that the Vatican under Pius XI inherited the social context of modern Europe, a context within which for some hundreds of years the Roman Curia and the popes had felt a loss of power—in modern Europe, the church was no longer the sole regulator and guide for its members, as its members were also citizens of states that, like the church, demanded allegiance. In such a situation, the founding of a more or less independent press within the Vatican—even though the Pontifical Society for the Propagation of the Faith was responsible for Fides—seemed counterintuitive. If the Vatican felt besieged by modernity, why would it adopt an independent press rather than an official mouthpiece or other form of propaganda in order to make sure its views were correctly communicated?

It appears that the notion of Fides as a tool for educating Catholics and the public about missions was what carried the day. Every mission organization believed more people needed to know about the value of their work, and the SCPF was no different in this regard. It also helped that Considine, as the founding director, seemed to be a loyal collaborator. Indeed, Considine was cautious about pushing the envelope; he carefully chose the areas in which the character of Fides Service as an independent voice would distinguish itself: comparative religions, countering prejudice, and science and missions.

Comparative Religions

Twenty-first century readers may be surprised to learn that even in 1927 Fides was operating from a comparative religions perspective, running an article on the effectiveness of Muslim schools for promoting conversion to

51. The Fides masthead in the late 1920s had a subheading: "Outerworld Catholic News via Propaganda Fide, 1-Rome, Italy."

52. Stuart Price, *Media Studies* (Harlow: Longman, 1998), 88.

Islam in Italian Somaliland.[53] It was a perspective that would mark Fides as a credible source of information on the socioreligious context of missions. In March 1928, a headline that read "100,000 Pound Moslem Mosque for London" carried wording that treated this news as a normal event:

> The desire to erect a fitting Moslem temple in London is understandable when it is recalled that of the world's 220,000,000 Moslems, almost 100,000,000 are in the British Empire. Moslems of Morocco recently opened a beautiful mosque in Paris.[54]

This same dispassionate perspective was found in many other articles on world religions during the early years of Fides under Considine's directorship. For example, Fides carried stories from India on theosophy[55] and on Catholic converts who had returned to the practice of Hinduism;[56] an article on Japan reported a noticeable increase in pilgrimages to Buddhist shrines.[57]

There were also articles in Fides that displayed mission boosterism and a sense of Catholic triumphalism; articles about the pope and missions carried the customary reverential tone in regard to the Roman pontiff. But the articles on non-Christian religions were notable for a clear style that presented these faiths in a sympathetic light.

Countering Prejudice

Fides was less than a month old when it ran its first feature aimed at countering racial prejudice; the piece carried a provocative headline, "But He Is Unclean and Smells Bad." Originally written by an unnamed missionary correspondent in the Volta (modern-day Burkina Faso and northern Ghana), the piece begins by stating racist assertions about a distaste for carrying out missionary work among African blacks, in order to refute them with facts. In the racist view, Africans were held to be lazy, mean, thieving, and filthy. Fides responded:

> We begin patiently to disabuse the poor deluded creature who has given vent to the above outburst. We describe the life of our blacks on the Volta, a life similar to that of many other parts of West Africa.

---

53. "Moslems Winning Red Sea Converts by Their Schools," *Fides Service* NE 16 (December 24, 1927).

54. *Fides Service* #24 — NE:175 (March 6, 1928).

55. "Indian Theosophy Now Has 'World Mother,'" *Fides Service* #47 — NE:283 (June 6, 1928).

56. "Catholic Press Differs in Attitude toward India Apostasies," *Fides Service* #39 — NE:248 — NE:249 (May 16, 1928).

57. "Evidences of Attachment to Buddhism by Japanese Masses," *Fides Service* #191 — NE:82/30 (April 3, 1930).

We convince him that many an African Missionary of Lyons has con-
fided to us that he loves and admires the tribes to whom he adminis-
ters and that he respects even many of the pagans for the qualities he
discovers in them.[58]

The article displays a strategy of countering prejudice that Considine
would practice over and over again throughout his career. The author will
go on to refute each of the racist assertions, but from a very particular
angle: that of introducing Africans to readers through the words of missionaries who have grown in empathy and respect for them.

The author makes use of cultural relativism, taking pains to emphasize the
comprehensible logic of the African ways of organizing home and village life
that are described in the article. Furthermore, the religious identity of the
missionary author serves as a bridge between the two groups discussed—
Africans and their racist detractors. The supposition is that the missioner is
someone well known and trusted by both. In this way, the value of the work
of the missionary is affirmed in a new way. That is, rather than presenting the
missionary as the key to the African's salvation or uplift, the missionary functions, in the name of Christ, to bring together those separated by prejudice
or distance. It is thus an approach that is at the same time traditional—bringing together in Christ people of every race, nation, and tongue—and innova-
tive—aimed squarely at twentieth-century white prejudice.

Fides under Considine also countered prejudice by exploring the perspective of populations that were discriminated against by whites. Under
the pseudonym Peter Cosmon, Considine penned a commentary on the
state of race relations in Africa and in the African diaspora around the
world, which began with a quotation from W. E. B. Du Bois, and was
quickly followed by Considine's acknowledgment of black resentment:

Burghardt Dubois, a leader of some of America's Negro citizens,
wrote in 1925, "The nations and races of color will not suffer the
treatment they are forced to bear from the white race any longer than
they must. Then they will make war and the war of color will surpass
in inhuman savagery all past wars. For men of color have many things
to remember and they do not forget."

All Negroes, it is safe to say, do not share in such ugly menaces. Yet
regardless of the degree of resentment, most of them must feel that
their race has a history of mistreatment which surpasses that of every
other.[59]

---

58. "But He Is Unclean and Smells Bad," *Fides Service* NE:73i — 73k (January 6, 1928).
59. Peter Cosmon, "They Do Not Forget," *Fides Service* #195 — NE:106/30 —
NE:107/30 (May 1, 1930).

Fides took a variety of approaches to the task of countering prejudice. The article "'Negro,' 'Native' Not Acceptable in Africa; Term 'African' Preferred" quoted a Catholic editor in Uganda in 1930 in regard to the African desire to define the terms with which they themselves are described.[60] Another strategy was to report Catholic participation in racial reconciliation initiatives.[61]

Science and Missions

Science in relation to missions was another topic frequently reported on in Fides; a May 1928 article covered a recent conference on ethnology and the soul, given by Fr. Wilhelm Schmidt. Fr. Schmidt's remarks, quoted at length in the piece, disputed the evolutionism of those times by making comprehensible the worldview of so-called primitive peoples. According to Schmidt,

> these ancient men whom we know are already in possession of a human reasoning fully active, of a sentiment and of a love truly human and of a will morally orientated and directed, that by means of this reasoning and of this will they know how to master life and to understand the world; that, further, they know how to comprehend the great fact of the existence of the world and to make the fact ascend causally to a supreme personal creator. . . .[62]

Here again, Fides displayed a sympathetic mission perspective; ethnology was a science that made the so-called primitive world comprehensible to modern readers.

The Establishment of Collegio Maryknoll, 1928

From the beginning of his time in Rome, Fr. Considine was called upon to transact Maryknoll Society business with the Roman Curia—usually with Propaganda Fide. A large matter of Society business was the Maryknoll Constitutions. The Maryknoll Society had been allowed by Propaganda to use a provisional constitution from 1915 to 1926, and so from 1926 until the Society's First General Chapter in 1929, Considine was involved in a series of consultations on behalf of the Society with Propaganda in regard to the Maryknoll constitutions.

---

60. *Fides Service* #205 — NE:181/30 (July 10, 1930). *Fides Service* #145 — NE:703 (May 9, 1929).

61. "Priests in Conference Seeking White-Black Peace in South Africa," *Fides Service* #145 — NE:703 (May 9, 1929).

62. "Science Belies Evolution of Soul Asserts Savant," *Fides Service* #43 — NE:267 — NE:268 (May 28, 1928).

During these years, the Maryknoll community in Rome had been growing to include newly ordained priests who were earning graduate degrees as preparation for years of teaching in Maryknoll houses of training; Bro. Leo Shields had also come in late 1927 at Considine's request to work at Fides. In the early years when Considine was alone in Rome, he simply lodged at boarding houses that catered to priests, such as the Collegio Leonino; the first Maryknoll priests to join him in Rome took rooms in the same establishments with him. However, when a seminarian was sent to study in Rome in the fall of 1926 and it was not possible to house him at a boarding house for priests, Considine rented a block of rooms at the Collegio della Misericordia near the Borghese Gardens. Meanwhile, Archbishop Marchetti had been encouraging the Maryknollers to purchase a permanent residence in Rome. In 1928 a three-floor palazzo was secured on Via Sardegna, off the Via Veneto and not far from the Palazzo di Propaganda on the Piazza di Spagna.

It was a step up from rented lodgings and an expense that was justified only by its utility to the Society in terms of a stable place for the Maryknoll student community, the income that would be generated from priest boarders, and a place in Rome from which to conduct public relations on behalf of Maryknoll. Over the years, Collegio Maryknoll has always had a steady stream of visitors who know and support Maryknoll and has been able to cultivate the favor of bishops from the United States and elsewhere by offering them hospitality.

With a permanent residence, Considine received a permanent assignment as Maryknoll's procurator general. Prior to this appointment he was the Maryknoll superior in Rome. The appointment did not change his work load—after the appointment, as before, he continued to transact Society business and represent Maryknoll in Rome—but now he was able to navigate the status-conscious curial culture of Rome with a proper title.

One other element of his role as Maryknoll's representative in Rome was being recognized as something of a Catholic U.S. foreign service officer or perhaps chaplain to those looking after U.S. international interests while in Rome. For example, he met and carried on a ten-year friendship with Charles R. Crane, a wealthy former ambassador to China and advisor to presidents on the Middle East, Russia, Eastern Europe, and China. The occasion for their meeting was the 1929 wedding of Crane's son John Oliver to a member of a Roman noble family. Another example involved the Kennedy family—when Considine returned to Rome in 1939 for the coronation of Pius XII, he used his Vatican connections to make sure the Joseph Kennedy family was seated properly at the ceremony. Considine took great care with these relationships, and clearly relished his role as an unofficial U.S. Catholic priest representative at the Vatican.

While serving in Rome Considine also assisted Kenneth Scott Latourette, professor of mission history at Yale, to gain access to the mission
library and archives of Propaganda Fide. The two had met at Maryknoll in
the 1920s, and their decades-long friendship is a clear example of Considine's ecumenical missionary spirit.[63]

Busy as Considine was at Propaganda and with Maryknoll business,
there were also opportunities in those years to connect with family
and friends from afar. In 1926 he met his mother and brothers Ray and
George in Ireland and then brought them to Rome for a visit. He visited
the United States twice—accompanying Archbishop Marchetti on a semi-
official trip in 1927 and then by himself to the first Maryknoll General
Chapter in August 1929. At the end of 1928, he also hosted Maryknoll co-
founder Fr. James A. Walsh and Frs. Francis Ford and Francis Winslow in
Rome. Ford had traveled from China and the other two from New York
for this meeting, which was arranged to put the finishing touches on the
Society constitutions.

At the same time, Considine sensed tentativeness on the part of the
Maryknoll Society leadership about his initiatives in Rome. The basic situation was that Maryknoll co-founder and father superior James A. Walsh
favored the Rome initiative, but Walsh did not have the support of Frs.
Byrne, Drought, and Lane, who were members of the General Council. It
may have been that during the 1929 Chapter Considine noticed this attitude in those three priests.[64]

As Considine understood it, Maryknoll had no fixed policy on operations in Rome; however, this was not a source of concern, as the absence of
a defined policy could be interpreted positively. Namely, it meant a lack of
restrictions on the development of his mission initiatives in Rome.[65]

While Considine's years in Rome included significant initiatives such as
Fides Service, during these years he also became a trusted Vatican insider
who could be called upon to assist in initiatives of the Holy Father. Two
such initiatives were the 1927 founding of the Missionary Ethnological
Museum at the Lateran and the 1929 Pontifical Mission to the Court of
the Sovereigns of Ethiopia. Moreover, in both initiatives, the official records
have been lost or concealed. Therefore, Fr. Considine's records have become
key to understanding the events.

---

63. See Excursus II, "Considine, Ecumenism, and Interreligious Dialogue," below
following chapter 8.

64. John J. Considine, China Sea, to Edward McGurkin, Rome, September 1, 1932.
MMA, Considine Papers, 2:6.

65. John J. Considine, Fushun, Manchuria, to Edward McGurkin, Rome, July 16, 1932.
MMA, Considine Papers, 2:6.

A Drubbing That Seemed Necessary to Administer:
The Beginnings of the Missionary Ethnological Museum[66]

John Considine served on two advisory commissions for the new Missionary Ethnological Museum at the Lateran during the spring of 1927, and these circumstances inserted him straightaway into a religion and science controversy. Briefly, the founding of the Missionary Ethnological Museum at the Lateran at the close of the Vatican Mission Exposition is often mentioned as a high point in the Catholic Church's embrace of ethnology in its mission work. More particularly, An Vandenberghe describes it as a triumph for missionary ethnologist Fr. Wilhelm Schmidt, S.V.D. As has already been seen, Schmidt attempted to found such a museum in Rome in 1911, but with the Curia in the throes of the modernist crisis, his efforts were unsuccessful. Vandenberghe then gives credit to the partnership of Pius XI and Schmidt for making the museum a reality at the end of 1927.[67]

Unnoted by Vandenberghe was the mini-crisis produced in the spring of 1927 around the pope's concern that Schmidt was overemphasizing ethnology to the detriment of missiology; in Fr. Considine's correspondence of the time, however, there is a narrative of the controversy. It was the second advisory commission[68] that had the strictly defined charge of enforcing the pope's desire that an emphasis on missiology not be sacrificed to ethnology in the Missionary Ethnological Museum. This was a smaller commission (Considine, Henri Dubois, and Henricus Pierre Gubbels), and it had the "unpleasant"[69] task of bringing Fr. Schmidt into line.

The earliest indication of a controversy emerged in the report of the

---

66. The author would like to express his appreciation to Fr. Nicola Mapelli, P.I.M.E., curator of the Museo Missionario Etnologico at the Vatican, and to Dot.ssa Nadia Fiussello, also of the Museo Missionario Etnologico, for her devoted assistance with research in the museum archives.

67. Vandenberghe, "Entre mission et science," 15–36.

68. At the end of 1926, Pius XI himself called for the formation of a Commission that would be a consultative body on the operations of the Museum ("Motu Proprio," November 12, 1926; *Acta apostolicae sedis* 1926: 478–79). The two already mentioned commissions met before any such permanent body was established. The first consultation—on the parts of the museum that were to be dedicated to missions and missiology—was a three-day meeting, held April 20–22, 1927, at the Lateran Palace. Taking part were eight priests, all of whom were well known in the world of Catholic missions and missiology: Considine, Joseph Schmidlin, Robert Streit, O.M.I., Gubbels, Dubois, Bernard Arens, S.J., Fr. Pancratius, O.F.M., and Michele Schulein, S.V.D. Msgr. Pietro Ercole, the administrator of the Lateran Museums, also made a presentation ("Risoluzzioni accolte dalla riunione dei Missiologi convocati per discutere sull'istallazione della parte missionaria del Pontificio Museo Missionario-Etnologico, Roma, Palazzo Laterano 20–22 Aprile 1927." Archives of Museo Missionario Etnologico, Busta 27, 1927).

69. John J. Considine, Rome, to James A. Walsh, Ossining, NY, June 12, 1927. MMA, Considine Papers, 3:7.

first commission, which had been charged with assisting Fr. Schmidt to present missions and missiology in the new museum. The report captured many practical points and proposed some solutions regarding logistics and organizational tasks. Among the tasks recommended was the necessity of making an appeal to all missionary vicars apostolic and prefects apostolic to provide the museum with more missionary objects to display. However, the first sentence of the report went a step further, making a bold statement about what the overall museum should be: "Missions should be given the dominant place in the Missionary Ethnological Museum."[70]

This could not have been easy for Fr. Schmidt to hear. He had spent his entire career focusing on ethnology as a science,[71] and for many years he also strove to keep ethnology and mission work functionally and theoretically separate, precisely so that his study of ethnology could be credible as science. He also believed his formulation worked in the opposite direction, to the benefit of the church and mission. By engaging Catholic missioners in ethnology in a scientifically credible way, such engagement allowed the church to be involved in a scientific enterprise that did not sacrifice key doctrinal elements, such as the historicity of divine revelation.

However, Schmidt was not unconcerned about mission as such. According to Fr. Considine's correspondence from the spring of 1927, he and Fr. Schmidt had been talking over the idea of a Pontifical Academy of Mission Studies.

> [The] Academy . . . would be a society of from 40 to 200 choicely selected mission leaders of the world who would meet once a year at the Lateran Palace for a congress. A small executive committee of 7 would do the real work, a couple of whom would be located permanently at the Lateran. Besides special projects, the Academy would aid in improving the Museum, library of missions, statistics archives, would conduct a scholarly mission quarterly, and a world mission press service.[72]

---

70. The rest of the report did not refer to the museum as a whole but rather limited itself to the task of how to best organize the representations in the missiological part of the museum. "Risoluzzioni accolte dalla riunione dei Missiologi convocati per discutere sull'istallazione della parte missionaria del Pontificio Museo Missionario-Etnologico, Roma, Palazzo Laterano 20–22 Aprile 1927." Archives of Museo Missionario Etnologico, Busta 27, 1927.

71. Schmidt had developed his own brand of ethnology, the culture-circle school. For Schmidt, ethnology was principally an inquiry into the history of religions. Ethnology as Schmidt practiced it was science in the continental, not Anglo-American, sense of the term: the sustained inquiry into a particular subject (Ernest Brandewie, *When Giants Walked the Earth: The Life and Times of Wilhelm Schmidt, SVD* [Fribourg: University Press, 1990], 102ff.).

72. John J. Considine, Rome, to James A. Walsh, Ossining, NY, April 2, 1927. MMA, Considine Papers, Box 3, Folder 7.

Although the academy based at the Lateran that Considine and Schmidt discussed never was established, the world mission press service became a reality with the founding of Fides Service.[73]

What happened next is not clear;[74] perhaps the first sentence of the first commission's report became a rallying point for some against the designs that Fr. Schmidt had for showcasing the importance of ethnology in the museum. In any case, according to Fr. Considine's correspondence, in the time between the end of the consultation and April 26, Considine was informed by Archbishop Marchetti of a second series of gatherings to discuss the Museum. Considine, Dubois, and Gubbels[75] were to be appointed to the smaller, second commission,[76] and the members together with Schmidt had an audience with the Holy Father on May 1.[77] Shortly after the first meeting of the commission in May, the agenda before this body came into sharp focus for Considine. In a letter of May 17, 1927, to Maryknoll superior and co-founder Fr. James A. Walsh, Considine expressed his dismay at discovering the real purpose of the second commission:

> For your edification I am sending the official appointment to the Museum Commission. The details behind the scene are not so edifying. We are part of the machinery to put the screws to poor Father Schmidt because the suggestion has gotten abroad that he is slighting missiology for ethnology and acting a little stubbornly in holding his position. There is basis to the charge in this that unconsciously he is emphasizing the subject he knows best and can most easily place. But he is too good a man to get the drubbing that it seemed necessary to administer.[78]

---

73. *Acta Pontificii Operis a Propagatione Fidei; Cura Consilii Superioris Generalis* I, no. 7 (September 30, 1927): 265. Considine, "For the Revelation of Events," 30–33.

74. Research in the Archives of the Museo Missionario Etnologico to date have yielded information only on the April 1927 consultation and the subsequent call to mission vicars and prefects apostolic to send in mission objects for display; the records of the smaller subsequent commission have not been located.

75. Gubbels, from Belgium, had served many years in China, and Dubois, from France, had served more than twenty years in Madagascar. Considine considered himself a little too young and inexperienced to be placed in this distinguished group: "It will be interesting to see how long this game will last—my hanging out with all these old warriors. I was the only youngster at the congress" (John J. Considine, Rome, to James A. Walsh, Ossining, NY, April 26, 1927. MMA, Considine Papers, 3:7).

76. John J. Considine, Rome, to James A. Walsh, Ossining, NY, April 26, 1927. MMA, Considine Papers, 3:7.

77. CD, May 1, 1927. MMA, Considine Papers, 4:2.

78. John J. Considine, Rome, to James A. Walsh, Ossining, NY, May 17, 1927. MMA, Considine Papers, 3:7.

In another letter to Fr. Walsh, Considine described the deliberations of the commission in regard to Fr. Schmidt's views on mission and ethnology as "a very unpleasant affair."[79] His correspondence reveals his distaste for the operation, yet he is also resigned to taking part. As will be seen,[80] in matters of ecclesiastical authority Considine made use of a realism—to work in the church one must accept that those in authority are responsible for the church as an institution and therefore have prerogatives to take action.

Considine claimed to have kept a copy of the letter the pope sent to Schmidt "at the height of the excitement over his failure to give missions equal place with ethnology."[81] The final meeting of the commission was held on May 27,[82] and a preliminary report was sent to the Holy Father in early June of 1927.

The Museum opened on December 21, 1927. The coverage offered by Fides Service approvingly noted that the exhibits reflected a solid relationship of ethnology and mission; the article likened the new Museum to "a trumpet call to the world that the goal of the Church of Rome is world unity, the gathering of all men to a brotherhood under the Cross." If mission is truly universal, reaching "all men," ethnology is a missionary tool. Thus, a museum on mission must pay attention to ethnology.[83] When the museum opened, could any slant favoring ethnology over missiology be perceived in the way the exhibits were displayed? The same article from Fides indicated that of twenty-six halls and seven galleries in the new Museum, only three were dedicated to ethnology, while approximately twenty halls contained exhibits from the contemporary missions of the church in Asia, Africa, Latin America, and Oceania. Additionally, the halls of the section on mission history were not near completion.[84]

What may have appeared as a persistent favoring of ethnology over missiology could have been noticed in the way the displays in the individual halls on contemporary missions were arranged. The description of the Hall of India, cited as similar in plan to the other halls, seemed to indicate that the displays on mission activities were not as extensive as the displays on culture and religion.[85]

79. John J. Considine, Rome, to James A. Walsh, Ossining, NY, June 12, 1927. MMA, Considine Papers, 3:7.

80. See chapter 7.

81. John J. Considine, Rome, to James A. Walsh, Ossining, NY, April 26, 1927. MMA, Considine Papers, 3:7; the pope's letter is yet to be found.

82. CD, May 27, 1927. MMA, Considine Papers, 4:2.

83. "A Monument to World Unity: The Papal Mission Museum," Fides Service, December 20, 1927, p. 9k.

84. Ibid., p. 9l.

85. From the Fides description of the Hall of India:

The Museum Archives contain further evidence that the dispute between Schmidt and the pope over ethnology continued even after the museum was inaugurated in December 1927. An appeal to all missionary vicars apostolic and prefects apostolic to provide the museum with more missionary objects was sent on October 4, 1928, in the form of a memo signed by both Schmidt and Archbishop Marchetti. The memo contained the following statements:

> For if in the Museum, as it is constituted today, the ethnographic part is nothing short of amazing, the missionary part on the other hand needs to be further developed.
>
> Given the purpose of the Museum, the second part of the program is unquestionably the most important.[86]

These remarks would seem to indicate that the museum opened on December 21, 1927, on the basis of some sort of a compromise in regard to the question of how much to emphasize ethnology vis-à-vis missiology. During 1927, did Schmidt and the second commission arrive at an agreement to emphasize ethnology at first with a view to making the above appeal for missionary objects in 1928? Or were the statements from the October 1928 memorial indicative of the lack of resolution of this issue?

Facing us, on the opposite wall is mission data with St. Francis Xavier's statue in heroic size in the center. On the right is Indian life—the classes, the castes, clothes, implements, arms, a wealth of detail but a triumph of order, great features drawing to climax points the stories to which the individual specimens lead. The salon of an Indian home, for instance, and its family of occupants, puts in the concrete the multiplicity of objects which relate to the home and family.

On the other side of the hall are the Indian religions, again with hundreds of individual specimens for the student and great gripping features for the untrained visitors. Most striking is the carved teak piece collection of wood, marble and porcelain Hindu gods. Beautiful new steel cases of latest style hold the displays. There are 200 of them in the museum, some, as in the 1st hall of China, easily eight yards long by three yards of glass face high.

("A Monument to World Unity: The Papal Mission Museum," *Fides Service,* December 20, 1927, p. 9l).

86. My translation. The memo limited itself to requesting only objects that had some actual link to Catholic missionary work and not ethnological objects that would help create understanding of a people's culture or religion (if other than Christian). However, under the rubric of missionary objects that were requested was a wide range of items. The request included a heavy emphasis on the need for objects that were indigenous expressions of Christian life—for example, any native artistic renderings of Holy Scripture (Francesco Marchetti Selvaggiani and Guglielmo Schmidt, Rome, to Révérendissimes Ordinaires et autres Supérieurs des Missions, October 4, 1928. Archives of Museo Missionario Etnologico, Busta 27, 1927).

Should the records of the second commission itself be located, further research on these questions is needed.

I have called this episode a "mini-crisis" because the museum opened seemingly on schedule in December 1927, with Schmidt as the curator, and he remained at that post through 1939.[87] Whatever happened in the course of the activities of the commission, it appears that the matter was eventually brought to a satisfactory conclusion. However, thanks to Fr. Considine's correspondence, a window has opened on this early religion and science controversy involving a scholarly pope and a scientist.

The 1929 Pontifical Mission to the Court of the Sovereigns[88] of Ethiopia

On Sunday, November 3, 1929, Fr. Considine was banging away on his Smith Corona typewriter—while he lived in Rome, most Sunday afternoons he wrote a letter to his mother. The seminarians and priests in the house were accustomed to hearing Considine at his typewriter, and the letter to his mother was a well-known routine most Sunday afternoons. But almost as soon as the typewriter stopped clacking, Considine was hurrying down the stairs and then out the door. He returned several hours later with unusual news—he had been at the Vatican for an audience with the Holy Father. But that was not all. He told them he would soon be leaving for one month on a secret mission. [89]

Evidently, it was not necessary to keep the mission a secret from his mother, for he had already told her about it and about his papal audience in the letter he wrote just before leaving for the Vatican. The Holy Father would be sending Archbishop Marchetti, Considine's boss, as a special envoy to the Court of the Sovereigns of Ethiopia, and Considine had been selected to be one of three in the Archbishop's entourage, along with Msgr. Eugene Tisserant of the Vatican Library and Fr. Paulus Yupin, a recently ordained priest who was teaching at the Urban College. In the letter to his mother, Considine commented on the composition of the entourage:

> The second after the archbishop is a Monsignor Tisserant of the Vatican Library, then comes yours truly, and the fourth is Father Yupin, a Chinese priest who is a professor at the College of Propaganda. As Monsignor Tisserant is French, this makes each member of the

---

87. Brandewie, *When Giants Walked the Earth,* 182–83; Console, "Incontri tra culture nelle collezioni del Museo Missionario Etnologico," 170.

88. In 1929 Ras Tafari Makonnen was Regent and shared power with Empress Zauditu.

89. Maryknoll Rome House Diary, November 3, 1929. MMA, Rome House Diaries 1926–1967, 1:1.

papal mission of a different nationality, the precise desire of the Holy Father.[90]

Considine understood the Holy Father's choices in the composition of the entourage as highlighting the truly international character of the church. The Pontiff wanted the Emperor and his court to understand that the church ". . . was independent of all government."[91]

Msgr. Eugène-Gabriel-Gervais-Laurent Tisserant had a long career in the Roman Curia; he was later an archbishop, then elevated to cardinal. He participated in the Conclave of 1939 and served as dean of the College of Cardinals in the 1958 and 1963 Conclaves. He was also a Council Father at Vatican II. Still newly ordained, Fr. Paulus Yupin was later appointed archbishop of Nanjing. Like Tisserant, he was elevated to the College of Cardinals and was a Council Father at Vatican II. Considine was therefore making the six-week trip to Ethiopia in the company of three future cardinals—Marchetti would be elevated to the cardinalate in June 1930.

As personal secretary to Archbishop Marchetti, Fr. Considine already had a close working relationship with the archbishop at the time of the mission. From that fact it can be surmised that his role was to assist Archbishop Marchetti with any difficulty encountered on the mission. Additionally, as secretary of the delegation, Considine was responsible for any correspondence or reports generated during the mission.[92]

---

90. John J. Considine, Rome, to Alice Considine, New Bedford, MA, November 3, 1929. Considine Family Archive.

91. John J. Considine, "Ethiopia," *The Commonweal* 22 (May 3, 1935): 5–6.

92. Unfortunately, the Vatican records of the writings of this firsthand observer remain off-limits to scholarly investigation; the official records of this Mission of the Holy See are apparently sealed in the archive of the Sostituto per gli Affari Generali of the Vatican Secretariat of State, and the mission was not reported in the *New York Times*. Considine wrote several accounts—the above-cited 1935 article published in *Commonweal*, and he wrote a series of nine letters to his family during the trip, dated from November 3 to December 22, 1929. Additionally, there are two other accounts by him, published in the Italian edition of *Fides* (December 11, 1929) and in *L'Osservatore Romano* (December 15, 1929), the latter being practically identical to the former. The account published in *La Civiltà Cattolica* (80, no. 4 [1929]: 547–48) is apparently based on the account found in *L'Osservatore Romano*. An independent account of the mission is found in Edoardo Borra, *La carovana di Blass: Padre Gaudenzio Barlassina : ricordi di un medico* (Bologna: Missionaria Italiana, 1977), 153–56. The following two sources discuss the mission in the context of church and colonialism in Ethiopia: Giovagnoli, "Il Vaticano di fronte al colonialismo fascista," 112–31; Cesare Marongiu Buonaiuti, *Politica e religioni nel colonialismo italiano (1882–1941)* (Milan: Giuffrè, 1982). Finally, Lucia Ceci, "Chiesa e questione coloniale: Guerra e missione nell'impresa d'Etiopia," *Italia Contemporanea* 233 (2003): 618–36, is a good source on the Consolata Missioners of Turin and their enthusiastic support of the Italian colonization of Ethiopia (though the 1929 mission is not mentioned in this essay). For a book-length assessment of Italy's colonial relationship with Ethiopia written after the Vatican Secret Archives opened

The trip was to be mainly a diplomatic exercise.[93] Ras Tafari Makonnen (1892–1975), the future Emperor Haile Selassie I, had toured Europe
in 1924 and had made an official visit to the Vatican; Pius XI desired to
repay the visit of the Ethiopian Negus (regent), and Archbishop Marchetti
had been selected as Papal envoy. Yet, given the tense political and religious
climate of Ethiopia in 1929, Pius XI must have understood that his delegation would have to be skillful in navigating the many conflicting interests that were in play. Ethiopia was one of only three independent African
nations,[94] and was the sole African member of the League of Nations. The
pope's envoy was to show respect for the Ethiopian monarchs, and doing
so in fact produced a complaint from the Italian Governor of Eritrea, who
wondered why Archbishop Marchetti had recalled "the glorious Emperor
Menelik II";[95] in 1896, Menelik II had defeated invading Italian forces at
Adowa.[96] Archbishop Marchetti's diplomatic efforts could not escape the
charged political atmosphere of an independent Ethiopia that was attempting to keep colonial powers in check.[97]

---

the records of the papacy of Pius XI for consultation in 2006, see also Lucia Ceci, *Il papa non
deve parlare: Chiesa, fascismo e guerra d'Etiopia* (Rome: Laterza, 2010). Though Ceci discusses
the 1929 Pontifical Mission in this book, this comprehensive work sheds no new light on
that mission, most likely due to the unavailability of records in the various Vatican Archives.

93. Many years later, Tisserant described the 1929 Pontifical Mission as "strictly
diplomatic"; Eugène Tisserant and Sever Pop, *Recueil cardinal Eugène Tisserant: «Ab Oriente
et Occidente»* (Louvain: Centre international de dialectologie générale, 1955), 804. Similarly,
Considine's accounts of the mission portray it as a pro-forma diplomatic exercise.

94. Liberia and Egypt were the other two noncolonized African nations.

95. Giovagnoli, "Il Vaticano di fronte al colonialismo fascista," 121.

96. Haggai Erlich, "Adwa, battle of," in *Encyclopaedia Aethiopica,* ed. Siegbert Uhlig
(Wiesbaden: Harrassowitz, 2003).

97. In 1929 it was openly known that Italy wanted to colonize Ethiopia. Numerous
attempts to gain access to Ethiopian resources had taken place between the defeat of the
Italians by the Ethiopian forces at Adowa in 1896 and the beginning of the 1935 Italian
invasion (George W. Baer, *The Coming of the Italian-Ethiopian War* [Cambridge: Harvard
University Press, 1967], 6–20). Ras Tafari Makonnen clearly desired modernization as a
national security strategy; he was convinced that, given the presence of military threats from
the colonial powers surrounding Ethiopia—in particular from the Italians—the country
could not hope to be favored with any sort of tranquil isolation. He thus spent his energies
trying to bring about changes to Ethiopian society that favored modernization as a way of
strengthening his military, and he worked to achieve international cooperation to check the
superior military power of his colonial neighbors. In effect, colonial nations had Ethiopia
surrounded. The French had colonized the strategic port of Djibouti on the Gulf of Aden.
The British had colonized British Somaliland to the east of Djibouti, farther along the
African coast on the Gulf of Aden; the British were also in Kenya, directly to the south of
Ethiopia and, in a power-sharing arrangement with Egypt, occupied parts of the Anglo-
Egyptian Sudan on the western border of Ethiopia. The Italians occupied two colonies:

The religious tensions were equally difficult to navigate. For centuries, Ethiopia had been a Christian country; its population was majority Coptic Christian.[98] The Pontifical Mission therefore tried to show respect to a Christian ruler and at the same time not rankle the sensitivities of the Ethiopian Coptic Church, which surely would have been suspicious of the pope's motives in sending the mission.[99] Pius XI's strategy with the Coptic Church was twofold: he sought the larger goal of finding a way to reunite that Christian body with Rome[100] while also pursuing a smaller goal of establishing indigenous Catholic leadership in an official Ethiopian rite.[101] To accomplish these goals, the pope also had to be sympathetic to the good works of Roman Catholic missioners in Ethiopia,[102] while distancing him-

---

Eritrea, on the Red Sea coast to the north and west of Djibouti, and Italian Somaliland, which extended from the tip of the Horn of Africa southwest to the Kenya border.

98. Ethiopia claims a biblical heritage as the home country of the Queen of Sheba, who had called upon King Solomon in Jerusalem (1 Kgs. 10:1–13). From New Testament times, Christians in Ethiopia cite the story of the Ethiopian eunuch, baptized by Philip, as evidence of the beginnings of the Christianity in their country (Acts 8:26–39). Additionally, the fourth-century St. Frumentius is credited with establishing the church in Ethiopia. Since the fifth-century Council of Chalcedon, the Ethiopian Coptic Orthodox Church, like the Coptic Orthodox Church in Egypt on which it depended, forms part of the Monophysite churches.

99. The Coptic Orthodox bishop, Abuna Cyril (Qerəllos), was not present in Addis Ababa during the visit of the mission. Upon the mission's departure he went in person to see the Negus to make sure that Ras Tafari Makonnen had not betrayed Coptic Orthodoxy with his visitors from Rome (Borra, *La carovana di Blass,* 156). Given his own conservative Orthodox base of power, Ras Tafari Makonnen himself was not in a position to make any real commitment to new Catholic projects with the Papal envoy (Marongiu Buonaiuti, *Politica e religioni nel colonialismo italiano,* 167).

100. Giovagnoli reports that, under Pius XI in the 1920s, a fresh approach was being taken to propose a "return to Rome." Though this approach did not shorten the path of return—converts would still undergo evangelization and a second baptism—it did amount to a recognition by the Holy See of some validity in the Christian faith held by Ethiopian Copts ("Il Vaticano di fronte al colonialismo fascista," 120).

101. There are indications that an additional task of the mission was to test the waters for the establishment of a Catholic university and an astronomical observatory in Ethiopia. The index of the Vatican Secret Archives refers to correspondence in March 1930 regarding Vatican interest in constructing a church and an astronomical observatory in Addis Ababa; Marongiu Buonaiuti (*Politica e religioni nel colonialismo italiano,* 168) cites Bernoville to say that a Catholic university was also contemplated.

102. The Roman Catholic religious or missionary activities in Ethiopia ranged from evangelization work aimed at the conversion of Muslims and the practitioners of African Traditional Religions, to the operation of schools and hospitals, to efforts to bring Orthodox Coptic Christians into communion with Rome. Jesuit missioners had been working in the country since the sixteenth century. In 1839, the prefecture apostolic of Abyssinia was

self from those missioners seeking to convert Coptic Christians to Roman Catholicism. [103]

In the end, the mission seemed to produce two concrete results beyond its stated diplomatic and goodwill agenda. The first result was Marchetti's elevation to the College of Cardinals in June of 1930; a year later he was given the influential post of cardinal vicar of Rome. It seems reasonable to assume that the pope in the end gave little credence to the complaints received about Marchetti as a result of the mission; had Pius XI any serious concerns about Marchetti's performance as his envoy, he probably would not have promoted him so soon after the mission.

The second result was the appointment of the first Catholic bishop of the Ethiopian rite in July 1930; by appointing Chidané Mariam Cassà to become ordinary of Ethiopian Rite Catholics in Eritrea,[104] Pius XI underscored his interests in indigenous Catholic leadership of the church. Additionally, by locating the see for the new bishop in Eritrea rather than Addis Ababa, the pope showed respect for Coptic sensibilities while keeping the new bishop a bit more insulated from Catholic missioners hostile to Ethiopian Christianity.

For Considine personally, the trip was highly significant. In addition to handling the extensive responsibilities of secretary of the Pontifical Mission, it was his first trip to a non-Western country. Many of his Maryknoll

---

erected, and its see was the new capital of Addis Ababa. In 1847, the prefecture apostolic of Galla was established in the southeastern part of the country.

103. Some Catholic missioners were trying to convert Ethiopian Coptic Christians to Roman Catholicism. The basic missionary idea was to point out the alleged defects of Coptic Orthodox Christianity (according to this view, it was superstitious, its liturgy made use of a dead language, and it perpetuated a discontinuity between faith and life) to show that it was uncivilized or at least outmoded, and to propose Roman Catholicism as a modern alternative. These missioners, many of them Italians, basically denigrated Coptic practice. For many Italian missioners in Ethiopia, this civilizing mission could not be separated from the colonial designs that their home country held on Ethiopia. Like contemporary citizens of other European powers, they understood colonial government as an excellent way to facilitate the evangelization of a primitive people, even one in which the majority was already Christian. Italians who held this civilizing and colonial perspective tended to look down on the creation of an Ethiopian rite or on any rapprochement with the Coptic Orthodox. Thus, the Italian fascist government in 1930 greeted the news of the appointment of Bishop Cassà as the first Ethiopian rite bishop rather negatively. At the Italian Embassy to the Holy See, Ambassador De Vecchi di Val Cismon was quite explicit: "the provision of such high dignity to an Eritrean will help diminish their healthy sense of inferiority to Europeans" (Giovagnoli, "Il fronte al colonialismo fascista," 122). De Vecchi di Val Cismon was a former governor of Eritrea. Additionally, the Consolata missioners present in Addis Ababa would later complain of Marchetti's critical attitude toward them (Borra, *La carovana di Blass,* 154; Marongiu Buonaiuti, *Politica e religioni nel colonialismo italiano,* 167).

104. Marongiu Buonaiuti, *Politica e religioni nel colonialismo italiano,* 187.

classmates had by this time put in several years of work in China; at last Considine would set foot in a world quite different from the West he had always known. Even though it was his third ocean-going trip since coming to Rome, this trip was called a "mission," and so for Considine that term represented travel with a very special purpose.

Every mission begins with a journey; Archbishop Marchetti, Considine, and their two companions traveled first to Marseilles by train and then boarded the *Azay-le-Rideau*,[105] an Asia-bound ocean liner that would take them to Port Said, then through the Suez Canal, and then down the Red Sea and on to Djibouti at the west end of the Gulf of Aden. On board also were thirty-seven missioners headed to assignments in Asia; among them was Archbishop Eugène Mederlet of Madras.[106] Considine felt right at home on the eleven-day journey by ship.

Once ashore in Djibouti, the group of four on the mission boarded a special train sent by Ras Tafari for them for a three-day journey to Addis Ababa. The Fides Service reporting on the mission described local officials, and its portrayal of the surrounding area read like a *National Geographic* piece of the period.

> The first night was spent at Dire-Daoua, a growing commercial center, where the envoy and party were quartered and offered a dinner by the Governor of the City. The Governor, Baashahwarad Habtwold, is a graduate of Ohio State University and is one of the only two Ethiopians to have completed their education in the United States.
>
> The second day's journey was through bush country made interesting by frequent sighting of wild game and birds strange to Europeans. Herds of camels, sheep and goats were at pasture. The night was passed at Aouache, a primitive post where accommodations, though comfortable were not those of Europe.[107]

In a letter to his brother Frank, Considine spoke of travel conditions on the train and observations on the surrounding countryside.

> The train is quite European as the railroad was constructed by the French. It is the only piece of line in this country which, being extremely mountainous and primitive, has poor communications. As

105. Compagnie des Messageries Maritimes.

106. John J. Considine, Gibuti, to Alice Considine, New Bedford, MA, November 17, 1929. Considine Family Archives.

107. "Cordial Reception Tendered Papal Mission to Ethiopia throughout Journey," *Fides Service* #180 — NE:962–963 (January 9, 1930).

secretary of the envoy I have been using my machine quite freely and have a little room set apart where I have been able to work quite comfortably though the shifting of the train accounts for frequent miscuing in striking the keys. There has been a great deal to note. . . . During the last few hours we have entered into the real Abyssinia with rich farm lands and fat herds of cattle. Except for the houses, and the long spears in the hands of the shepherd boys, it suggests certain parts of France and now higher up it is like the farm districts of Switzerland.[108]

The trip prepared Considine and whetted his appetite for his fourteen-month mission study tour, which he initiated two years later. During a long voyage and a ten-day visit to Addis Ababa, he tried out the practicalities of working while in transit and began to understand the usefulness of such travels for his work at Fides.

On the return trip, the party took a side-trip to Cairo, and there occurred a most remarkable moment for Considine—his first real encounter with religious diversity. He observed the devotion of those coming to pray; the following passage in a letter to his mother carries a feeling of having his open-minded views in regard to world religions ratified, as if almost to say, "Now I have seen it for myself."

In the afternoon we visited a couple of the more famous mosques of Cairo which is a great Moslem center. At the door of each we had sandals tied on our feet as we are not allowed to tread a Moslem house of prayer in our shoes and had a Moslem guide to explain everything to us. Much as one reads about in books, we saw believers enter, take off their shoes, wash their hands, face and feet and procede [sic] to pray very simply and very earnestly.[109]

The stock market crashed just prior to his departure, and so half-way through the journey Considine's letters to his family begin to express some concern for the family's welfare. Postal communications of the time precluded him from receiving any word from home about this major event until early December when he reached Port Said on the return trip. The news on the severity of the financial crisis, both from home and from the media, would trickle in over the next few months. Considine's family took losses as a result of the crisis but did not become destitute—his mother was

---

108. John J. Considine, aboard Gibuti-Addis Ababa train, to Frank Considine, New Bedford, MA, November 20, 1929. Considine Family Archives.

109. John J. Considine, aboard ship in the Mediterranean, to Alice Considine, New Bedford, MA, December 8, 1929. Considine Family Archives.

able to manage the family's funds and real estate so that the younger Considine brothers could finish their college educations during the 1930s.

A report on the mission beat the delegation back to Rome, appearing in the Italian edition of Fides Service on December 11, 1929. Probably Considine had sent the dispatch via air mail or wire service from a port stop while en route for Marseilles. On December 13, their boat docked at Marseilles, and the delegation took the train back to Rome, arriving on December 15.

As Considine returned, he wrote his mother about what the coming Christmas holidays would mean for the small Maryknoll community in Rome; his mind turned to concern for his fellow Maryknollers.

> As soon as I arrive we must begin preparing the holiday celebrating for the seminarians who, away from home and in such a small group, require special care at such times. If we are able to make things as enjoyable this year as last we can feel very satisfied.[110]

The Christmas holiday was extra special that year, as Mother Mary Joseph Rogers, foundress of the Maryknoll Sisters, would visit the Maryknollers on Via Sardegna with two companion sisters for Christmas Eve; Mother Mary Joseph was in Rome seeking information on missions before a visit to East Asia.[111] And Considine would also have the opportunity to join a small party of Vatican officials that accompanied Pius XI to the Basilica of St. John Lateran and to the Missionary Ethnological Museum on December 20. The visit was historic for two reasons: it was the first trip a pope had made outside the Vatican since the Papal States came to an end in 1870, and the occasion was the celebration of the pope's fiftieth anniversary of priestly ordination.[112] Once again, Archbishop Marchetti had been the doorway for Considine's access to such an event, and, because it was kept from the press, Considine's published account was a complete scoop.[113]

Conclusion

During the years 1924–1930, Considine established himself and Maryknoll in Rome. It was a formative time for the young Maryknoll priest—Catholic missions were given great prominence by Pope Pius XI. In Considine's

110. John J. Considine, Genoa, to Alice Considine, New Bedford, MA, December 14, 1929. Considine Family Archives.

111. Ibid.; and John J. Considine, Rome, to Alice Considine, New Bedford, MA, December 22, 1929. Considine Family Archives.

112. Ibid.

113. "The Pope Comes Forth to the World," *Fides Service* #181— NE:974–976 (December 20, 1929).

view, Rome itself became an essential part of how mission is to function in the modern world, a vital center for the church's far-flung mission enterprises. These were years when Considine exercised significant leadership at Fides Service, but also years during which he became a reliable collaborator for the pope and the leadership at the SCPF, affording him opportunities to be present as key events unfolded. Additionally, the experience of his first years in Rome laid the groundwork for more extensive travel to and study of the church's missions during his final years in Rome.

Archbishop Marchetti had helped Considine to gain his footing in Rome; he had been like a patron to the young Maryknoller. Now that Marchetti was moving out of Propaganda (but also moving into Collegio Maryknoll), maneuvering the Vatican bureaucracy would not be quite as easy for Considine as it was before.

CHAPTER 6

A Window on the World
1931–1934

As Archbishop Marchetti was elevated to the College of Cardinals in 1930, Considine could look back on the previous six years of their association and note that a great deal had been accomplished. Fides Service was established, and Considine was a recognized Vatican insider—not a decision-maker such as a secretary or prefect but a reliable and influential mid-level manager who was also a well-known expert on Catholic missions. He could also note that the Maryknoll community—seminarians and priests—had grown in their permanent home on Via Sardegna, and he took particular satisfaction in the fact that the community featured some of the Society's best and brightest, men like Frs. Eugene Higgins, Edward McGurkin, and Fred Dietz. These men became Considine's closest friends during these years.

In the coming years, Considine would consolidate his organizational and journalistic service to missions by taking a fourteen-month mission study tour to the Near East, Asia, and Africa. He would also, however, come to the decision that it was more important for him to support Maryknoll in the United States than to continue to work on behalf of Catholic missions in Rome. There were nuances of the decision to return to the United States in 1934 that had to do with leadership changes at the Sacred Congregation of Propaganda Fide (SCPF), but perhaps the most important factor was the needs of Maryknoll, given the declining health of Maryknoll co-founder and superior general Fr. James A. Walsh.

In addition to other activities undertaken by Considine during 1930–1934, the 1931–1933 mission study tour is given special attention in this chapter—how he conceived and planned it, the story of the journey, and how it opened up new horizons for him and confirmed his particular vocation as a journalist in service to mission.

Mission Study Tour, 1931–1933

Fr. Considine's first mission study tour of Asia and Africa began in November 1931 and ended in January 1933. The mission study tour was taken up out of a concern he felt about his own lack of mission experience; ordained for Maryknoll in 1923, he had lived his entire priesthood first as a graduate student at the Catholic University of America, and then in Rome. If he was going to take on a larger role in an expanded Fides, he needed direct experience of missions. Feeling that he was getting no younger, he proposed a fourteen-month mission study tour of the Near East, Asia, and Africa.

It was the proposed expansion of Fides to establish a mission studies department and a quarterly journal that prompted Considine to undertake his journey to the Orient and Africa at the end of 1931. Archbishop Carlo Salotti became the secretary general of Propaganda Fide when Marchetti was elevated to the cardinalate in June of 1930. Considine's relationship with Salotti was never as cordial as it was with Marchetti, but neither were there significant problems, and it was Salotti who approved an expansion of Fides in July 1931.

Considine's main concern in 1931 was his own lack of mission experience—he was already ordained eight years, but apart from the brief trip to Ethiopia in 1929, he had never set foot in a mission. In August 1931 he traveled to Paris for a meeting of the Missionary Union of the Clergy, and after consulting colleagues there, he began to formulate plans for a year's mission study tour.

> While in Paris some 10 days ago Père Robert mentioned in conversation the value of a personal contact with the missions for my work. I remarked that undoubtedly I would be better off if I had 10 years' experience in the field. Père R. said this was not necessary; for my work a year . . . and a half of travel would perhaps be better than experience at a single station.
>
> This is an old idea, born some years ago when it became evident that I was to remain some time in Rome and to work for missions with Fides Service. It is interesting to recall that Maryknoll's Father General anticipated, if anything, my own resolve to seek this form of general preparation for the work in Rome, mentioning several times that I should look forward to visiting the Orient. Naturally it did not occur to him to mention Africa since he has never had interests there. I have discussed the idea with Cardinal Marchetti and had his

approval for a journey to be made sometime in the future when he was Sec. of Prop.[1]

But could he get away from Fides with all the plans there for an expanded area of work, and from the bustling Maryknoll community of students? The more he thought about it, the more the moment seemed opportune. He recalled the July meeting at Fides in which Archbishop Salotti approved the expansion of Fides:

> After the splendid conference of July between Mons. Salotti, Drago, Don Caselli [and] I it will be best to have the year before entering on the new program. With the passing of time it becomes increasingly urgent that there be someone in the office who has seen the missions, both for the efficiency of our work and for our prestige with missionaries and with the press. At Collegio Maryknoll there will be no new students this coming year so I believe Fr. McGurkin can successfully serve as superior.[2]

In the very next line he outlined a preliminary budget. A week later, after having received a cool reaction to his study tour plan from Archbishop Salotti, he expressed a sense of urgency about his proposal.

> I shall go ahead with the plans without further hesitation, and since Salotti did not seem enthusiastic I am decided on the Asia-Africa plan. My situation is summed up in the words 'Now or never;' I must see any opportunities of future extensive travels as remote.[3]

This was a key moment in his vocation as a missioner. While all that has been said about his faith in the Roman dicasteries to be of service to missioners is true, it is also true that Considine harbored a serious concern that his own lack of real experience in missions would hobble his efforts in Rome.

Before he could undertake such a journey, Considine had to seek approval for the trip from the cardinal prefect of Propaganda, Willem Van Rossum. What would become of Fides in his absence, the cardinal asked him? Considine's colleague, Fr. Bernardino Caselli, was prepared to take it over in his absence, and the expansion of the work of Fides would be postponed until his return—or so he thought. The cardinal found those

1. CD, August 26, 1931. MMA, Considine Papers, 4:2.
2. CD, August 26, 1931. MMA, Considine Papers, 4:2.
3. CD, September 3, 1931. MMA, Considine Papers, 4:2.

arrangements satisfactory and went on to encourage Considine to take great care to not overplan his journey. Considine recorded the cardinal's advice in his diary: "I should advance only when I had seen well the missions upon which I stood. He was satisfied, he said, if I took even two years but I should come back with a good knowledge of the ground I covered."[4]

Heeding this advice, Considine was to embark on a study tour that would do him a world of good. For most of his life his health had suffered under fatigue, probably due to his penchant to work without taking proper rest. But on the road, he was constantly energized; the journey clearly agreed with Considine. He read volumes of history and anthropology as he traveled, and he wrote prolifically of his journey; he filled up diary after diary with observations and recollections of conversations. The diaries were the raw material for a series of articles entitled "Other Men's Lands," which were a special feature Fides produced and sold to newspapers and mission agencies.[5] Later on, many of these stories were gathered into a book, *Across a World*.[6]

Considine spent two months in India, more than a month in French Indochina, three months in China, a month and a half in Manchuria, Korea, and Japan, and he also visited Palestine, Beirut, Damascus, Iraq, Burma (Myanmar), and Siam (Thailand) for shorter periods of time. On his westbound return, he briefly visited the Philippines, Singapore, Ceylon (Sri Lanka), and the Seychelles; he also spent nine days in the Dutch East Indies (Indonesia). He reached Mombasa, Kenya, on October 15, 1932,[7] and from there for the next seven and a half weeks Considine traveled overland, crossing the African continent. He made visits to missions in Kenya, Tanganyika (Tanzania), Uganda, and the Belgian Congo. On December 6, he reached Matadi, the port city of the Belgian Congo, and took a ship up the west coast of Africa to Douala, Cameroon, with stops in Point Noire, Port Gentil, and Libreville.[8]

Considine was, at this point of his journey, needing to hurry on, as his time away from Fides Service would be up at the end of January 1933. In order not to have to wait two weeks for a ship to Dakar, Senegal, he abandoned the idea of sailing around West Africa and through the Strait of

---

4. CD, September 21, 1931. MMA, Considine Papers, 4:2.

5. Considine financed the trip from three sources: money he had saved from his ordination gifts, his salary at Fides, and the sale of articles (CD, August 26, 1931. MMA, Considine Papers, 4:2).

6. John Joseph Considine and Thomas Kernan, *Across a World* (New York: Longmans, Green & Co., 1943).

7. CD, October 15, 1932. MMA, Considine Papers, 4:4.

8. John J. Considine, Enroute Matadi–Douala, to Alice Considine, New Bedford, MA, December 11, 1932. Considine Family Archives.

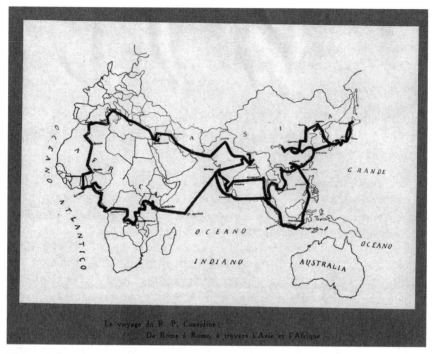

Figure 1 shows Fr. Considine's first mission study tour,
November 1931–January 1933.

Gibraltar for his return to Rome. Instead, he would make his way inland,
and cross the Sahara overland to Algeria. In order to head inland, at Douala
he caught another ship for Lagos, arriving December 16.[9] He stayed in
Nigeria for the next ten days, moving from there on to Accra, Dahomey
(Abomey, Benin), Togo,[10] Kumasi, and Tamale in present-day Ghana, and
then Ouagadougou[11] in present-day Burkina Faso. He finally reached Gao,
French Sudan (Mali), on January 15, 1933.

Early on Saturday, January 16, he departed from Gao for Algeria, traveling with the Transsaharan Company for the next six days to Colomb
Beshar, Algeria.[12] From there he took a train to Oran and then on to

9. John J. Considine, Lagos, Nigeria, to Alice Considine, New Bedford, MA, December
18, 1932. Considine Family Archives.

10. John J. Considine, Accra, Gold Coast, to Alice Considine, New Bedford, MA, January
1, 1933. Considine Family Archives.

11. John J. Considine, Ouagadougou, French West Africa, to Alice Considine, New
Bedford, MA, January 8, 1933. Considine Family Archives.

12. John J. Considine, Reggan, South Oran, North Africa, to Alice Considine, New
Bedford, MA, January 17, 1933; John J. Considine, Algiers, Algeria, to Alice Considine, New
Bedford, MA, January 22, 1933. Considine Family Archives. See Appendix.

Algiers. He visited the White Fathers' Generalate, the Maison Carree, and on January 26 caught a hydroplane to the Roman port of Ostia, bringing his fourteen-month journey to a close.

On the road, Considine found that, wherever he was meeting Catholic officials or missioners, the doors swung open wide for a Roman visitor. It helped that Considine was an adventurous traveler, as it was not all smooth sailing. While trying to get from Accra to Dahomey (Benin) in late December 1932, Considine missed a connection, which meant waiting all day for the next thing going—at 9:00 P.M.

> With another priest I made the lagoons in a launch, sleeping in a canvas chair with no question of taking off any clothes. I shaved the next morning with help of a glass of water begged from the French customs boat.[13]

He talked mainly with missioners and other church officials on this lengthy trip; in his writings, it is the voices of missioners, rather than local people, that are heard. But not everything said by a missioner was worth repeating in print; it was the voices of missioners who were sympathetic to their people and hopeful for bringing more of them into Christ's church that prevail. For example, in his diary Considine recorded a conversation with missioners in Kenya who at length disparaged the "native dances" as an occasion of sexual immorality and licentiousness;[14] Considine left these comments out of his published writings and approached native customs in a more circumspect manner. For example, in the few places he mentions African dancing, he merely reports it as a cultural phenomenon, does not condemn it in any way, and then quickly moves on to other subjects.[15]

During this trip, Considine also found himself in the role of trouble-shooter of practical mission problems, most especially those of personnel,[16] but his diary also records encounters with missioners that had him rethinking how Propaganda Fide could offer improved service to the mission

---

13. John J. Considine, Accra, Gold Coast, to Alice Considine, New Bedford, MA, January 1, 1933. Considine Family Archives.

14. CD, October 18, 1932. MMA, Considine Papers, 4:4.

15. African dances are mentioned in only two photo captions in *Across a World* (photos are between pp. 288 and 289).

16. A memorable troubleshooting moment for the Maryknoll Society was Considine's confidential memo of October 14, 1932, to James A. Walsh suggesting the official establishment of a Maryknoll mission in the Philippines with an unofficial but useful purpose—as an assignment for those missioners who, because of difficulty with language-learning or some other difficulty, were unable to be successful in the Maryknoll missions in China, Manchuria, and Korea (John J. Considine, en route Bombay–Mombasa, to James A. Walsh, Ossining, NY, October 14, 1932, MMA, Rome House Correspondence, 3:3. See chapter 7).

cause. For example, in Jakarta he spoke with a consultor for Propaganda Fide who complained that Propaganda is not open enough to input from the missions, and Considine's diary then became a drawing board for thinking through such a problem at length: Shouldn't Propaganda officials try to visit missions more often? Or would it be better if Propaganda filled its ranks from employees of the Apostolic Delegations in Asia and Africa?[17]

This led him to launch into a reflection on the deeper issues of missionary morale, in reference to what he observed among the Maryknollers in China, Manchuria, and Korea:

> Now that I have left our missions, I reflect that what almost all need is a warming up from the center. First of all, financial aid, not because the men have a right to it but as a bond of union. Most of the fellows have no idea how things ought to work [and] feel they simply have been betrayed by being thrown into the field by MK[Maryknoll] [and] no provision made to put them to use. I figure the Dept. of Income should work for Common Houses on basis of duty [and] for Missions on basis of charity and good feeling. The Dept. of Income should take the attitude [with] the individual pastor, "What can we do for you?", set out [and] work its level best to bring aid regardless of how many ask, make known regularly what it is doing, and express regret to the individual for all it cannot land. . . . Most certainly my heart goes out to these devils whose souls have been seered by coldness, not intentional in the least but this does not help much. I should say we must set about to rebuild the battered structure of good feeling.[18]

Considine communicated regularly with his Maryknoll superior and with Propaganda Fide, giving them accurate information about concerns and problems he noted during his journey. He saw it as his role to help those with responsibility for missions to deepen their understanding of mission conditions. When in Algiers, he also visited the superior general of the White Fathers, giving him an in-person report of his mission visits in Africa.[19] In Rome, he had a private audience with Pius XI and also met with the superior general of the Jesuits.

When the fourteen-month trip was over, Considine calculated that he had traveled fifty-two thousand miles on this study tour and had spoken with officials and representatives of hundreds of mission dioceses, vicariates, and prefectures.

---

17. CD, September 21, 1932. MMA, Considine Papers, 4:4.

18. CD, September 21, 1932. MMA, Considine Papers, 4:4.

19. Joseph P. Carney, "The History of the Functional Structure of the Maryknoll Mission in Musoma and Shinyanga, Tanzania" (Ph.D. dissertation, St. John's University, New York, 1973), 54.

In particular, the trip proved to be useful to Maryknoll as that Society considered the opening of missions in Africa in the late 1930s. Considine spent more than three months visiting Catholic missions in Sub-Saharan Africa; he was therefore the only Maryknoller to have set foot in the region prior to the opening of the Tanganyika mission in 1946. The records of Considine's tenure on the General Council of the Maryknoll Society (1934–1946) indicate that his firsthand and in-depth knowledge of Catholic missions in Sub-Saharan Africa was essential for guiding the process in which Maryknoll was selected by Propaganda Fide to work in Musoma, Tanganyika.[20]

Considine's first mission study tour had done two things for him: first, he had found a very useful way to be directly involved in the mission cause, serving it as a journalist capable of interpreting its struggles and successes of mission to a wide audience; second, it established him as an authority on Catholic missions.

Professor of Missiography, 1933–1934

In November 1933, Considine stepped into the classroom again, but this time as the professor of a course in missiography-geography at the Urban College's brand new Istituto Pontificio Missionale Scientifico (IPMS).[21] As he looked out on the group of nine students, he saw a cross-section of the church's missionary effort in the early 1930s. They were all priests of missionary orders, and though they were all European, they hailed from diverse countries on the Continent: France, Germany, the Netherlands, Italy, Poland, and Yugoslavia. According to Institute records, the majority of these were headed to Africa, India, or China, and some were most likely destined to become seminary professors in the houses of study run by their orders.[22]

Teaching agreed with Considine. As will be discussed presently, the hoped-for expansion of Fides did not occur after the 1933 conclusion of Considine's mission study tour. As he stepped into the role of professor, it can be asked if the work of teaching missioners opened his eyes to a new way to contribute to the cause of mission. In future years he went on to teach versions of his missiography course to seminarians at Maryknoll and

---

20. See chapter 7.

21. Although the IPMS was inaugurated in November 1932, it enrolled its first full cohort of students in the fall of 1933 ("Nuntia. Instituti Missionalis Scientifici," December 1, 1934. Archivio Storico di Propaganda Fide [ASPF], Nuova Serie 1343, Foglio 6).

22. The records indicate areas of specialization exams selected. Most were for languages, but several elected to take exams in mission bibliography ("Nuntia. Instituti Missionalis Scientifici," December 1, 1934. Archivio Storico di Propaganda Fide [ASPF], Nuova Serie 1343, Foglio 6).

to give numerous talks and conferences in the United States; he would fully develop his ideas on mission and the unity of the human race while teaching a summer course at Notre Dame in 1960.

Hong Kong, September 1932

Changes at the top had taken place in Propaganda Fide. Archbishop Marchetti was elevated to the College of Cardinals in June 1930 and was transferred out of Propaganda; he was replaced as secretary general of Propaganda by Archbishop Carlo Salotti. In late August 1932, Cardinal Van Rossum passed away, and in early 1933 Cardinal Pietro Fumasoni Biondi replaced him as cardinal prefect of Propaganda.

Considine had departed for his mission study tour in November 1931, and he returned to Rome in January 1933. In the meantime, changes were also afoot among the leadership of Maryknoll. In April 1932, the Maryknoll Society General Council was preparing to send one of its members, Fr. Raymond Lane, to Manchuria, where he would become the apostolic prefect of Fushun. Seeking to appoint a replacement on the Council for Fr. Lane, Fr. James A. Walsh and his Council focused on Fr. Considine.

In the summer of 1932, Lane departed for Japan, and he and Considine ran into each other in Tokyo on August 25. When Lane told Considine that he was being considered for appointment to the General Council, Considine was taken aback and explained to Lane that a suitable replacement for him at Fides was not "on the horizon." Lane agreed to cable the superior general, advising him to consult with Considine before appointing him to the Council.[23] But it was too late, and by only hours—on August 23, the Council had unanimously elected Considine as its newest member.[24]

In September 1932, Considine was making a stopover in Hong Kong. It was supposed to be simply a chance to visit again with Maryknollers before making connections to a ship in the direction of Africa and eventually back to Rome, the next major legs of Fr. Considine's mission study tour. Instead, when Considine arrived in Hong Kong, telegrams awaited that informed him he had been appointed to the Maryknoll Society's General Council. He was directed to make plans to leave his work at Fides Service in Rome to take up residence at the Maryknoll headquarters in Ossining, New York. The idea of leaving his work at Fides, just when that work was about to expand in new directions, was profoundly distressing for Considine. The stopover that was supposed to be a happy reunion turned into an infuriating headache.

The Council had acted on reports from Maryknoll Society vicar gen-

23. CD, August 25, 1932. MMA, Considine Papers, 4:4.

24. General Council Minutes, August 23, 1932 (222). MMA, Council Meetings Minutes 1912–37, 3:4 (Minutes 1929–33).

eral Fr. James M. Drought, who had spent most of April and May 1932 in Rome. The General Council had cabled Fr. Drought to inquire in Rome if Propaganda would object to Maryknoll recalling Considine to serve in the Society's leadership.[25] Drought made those inquiries and reported back that "no objections whatever" to the move came from Archbishop Salotti and Cardinal Van Rossum.[26]

In Considine's mind, this was an incredible diplomatic blunder, one that led Drought to an erroneous conclusion about Considine's work at Fides.

> Father Drought of Maryknoll visited Rome recently and asked someone at Propaganda (I suppose either the Cardinal, Mons. Salotti, or Mons. Carminati, the only three who could speak legitimately) if Propaganda would object if I were withdrawn to Maryknoll. Naturally, the Holy See could hardly say that a youngster such as I was indispensable and this was interpreted as . . . proof that all would be quite satisfied if I were withdrawn.[27]

Considine was especially distraught because this move had come just as the proposed expansion of Fides was about to take place. In July 1931, Archbishop Salotti, the secretary general of Propaganda Fide, approved a reorganization of Fides so that mission studies could be tackled more purposefully. It was a move that Considine had angled for since Fides was founded. A quarterly journal would be set up, Considine would become the director of special studies, and his colleague Fr. Caselli would become editor-in-chief of Fides Service. In this new configuration, Considine understood the original Fides mission press service as "but the first step in the development of something very appreciable."[28]

The expansion contemplated was rather modest in comparison with what Considine had envisioned; together with Fr. Wilhelm Schmidt, S.V.D., he had been advocating at the time of the founding of Fides in 1927 for the establishment of a "Pontifical Academy of Mission Studies." Such an academy would not only run a world press service but would also gather annually from forty to two hundred Catholic mission leaders, publish a journal, and help to improve existing Roman mission institutions

25. General Council Minutes, May 3, 1932 (216). MMA, Council Meetings Minutes 1912–37, 3:4 (Minutes 1929–33).

26. General Council Minutes, May 11, 1932 (217) and June 7, 1932 (219). MMA, Council Meetings Minutes 1912–37, 3:4 (Minutes 1929–33).

27. John J. Considine, en route Hong Kong–Manila, to Bernardino Caselli, Rome, September 6, 1932. MMA, Considine Papers, 3:4.

28. Ibid.

such as the Missionary Ethnological Museum at the Lateran and the Mission Library.[29]

The inspiration for such ideas came from Considine's knowledge of Protestant mission publicity agencies, such as the Missionary Education Movement based in New York, but with an important nuance—a Catholic institution of this kind had to be based in Rome and had to have the backing of the Holy See.[30]

In September 1932, Considine realized that if he were assigned back to the United States, all these hopes, ideas, and plans would most certainly founder, and this was for him a source of great consternation. He wrote to his colleague Fr. Caselli:

> I have been thinking during these past two days of the magnificent struggle which these five years have represented for us; no one knows what you and I have put into this proposition. Another five years and we would have our idea sufficiently consolidated that its future would be assured.[31]

Thus, everything seemed to be put in doubt. The mission study tour had opened up for him the world of mission in a way that was ever fresh and surprising to him. In conversations with missionaries, natives, and church officials along the way, and in his writings, he took full advantage of these opportunities to make comprehensible the scope of the tasks the church was assuming as it attempted to share the gospel message and invite the peoples of the earth to participate in Christ's church. Ever an expansive thinker and creative organizer on behalf of mission, he felt dejected as he contemplated a premature end to his efforts in Rome.

But all was not lost—Considine successfully negotiated the revocation of his appointment to Maryknoll's General Council. He continued his study tour, traveling three and a half months in East, Central, and West Africa and Algeria in North Africa. Later on, at the end of 1934, he was elected again to Maryknoll's General Council, replacing Fr. Patrick Byrne who became the superior of Maryknoll's new mission in Kyoto, Japan. This time, however, his election was different; in 1933 Maryknoll co-founder James A. Walsh was appointed a titular bishop, and his consecration was held in Rome. During that visit and during another visit to Germany for medical treatment in the summer of 1934, he and Considine spent a good deal

29. John J. Considine, Rome, to James A. Walsh, Ossining, NY, April 2, 1927. MMA, Considine Papers, 3:7.

30. John J. Considine, en route Hong Kong–Manila, to Bernardino Caselli, Rome, September 6, 1932. MMA, Considine Papers, 3:4.

31. Ibid.

of time together. Walsh was sixty-seven in 1934 and not in strong health, things Considine could not ignore as they traveled. As he contemplated the ailing co-founder of Maryknoll and discussed the work of the group with him, he had the opportunity to understand a role for himself back at the Maryknoll headquarters. Considine's election to the Council in 1934, therefore, did not come as a surprise; he accepted his election, resigned from Fides, and arrived at the Maryknoll headquarters in Ossining, New York, just before Christmas, 1934.

On a personal level, his departure from Rome on December 8, 1934, came just eighteen days after his brother, Fr. Raymond Considine, had arrived for a one-year program of studies in missiology. Fr. Ray had been appointed director of the Society for the Propagation of the Faith in the Fall River Diocese and was sent by his bishop to take the study program before assuming his duties. Of course, John Considine had helped to arrange things for him in Rome, and Fr. Ray stayed at Collegio Maryknoll during his study program. Ray and John Considine were close—while John Considine was in Rome, Ray wrote him a weekly letter with news of home. It was probably hard for John Considine to let go of a hoped-for year together with his brother in Rome; however, he knew it was time to return to the United States.

In terms of his work at Fides, Considine's ambitious proposals for expansion of the enterprise were not realized. It is intriguing to note that the founding of the Service of Documentation and Study of Global Mission (SEDOS) in the 1960s brought two of the three parts of Considine's plan to reality—an annual assembly of mission thinkers and leaders, and a scholarly journal. But the third part—obtaining the full backing of the Holy See, so that the organization would operate fully resourced and with authority—has never been attained.

What Was Gained

When Cardinal Marchetti passed away in 1951, Considine wrote in his diary that "his passing brings memories of the greatest single experience of my life."[32] There can be no doubt that the ten years Considine spent in Rome were truly a formative period, a time that shaped who he was in a significant way. Working in Rome and having a close association with Marchetti gave Considine a sense of gaining access to a large and living missionary tradition, and such access allowed him to think long about deep and practical questions—questions that would motivate later work.

What were the criteria for opening a mission? What were the best ways to ensure a successful start in a mission? What did Maryknoll need to do

---

32. CD, January 15, 1951. MMA, Considine Papers, 5:4.

to form young people from the United States into missioners who would truly advance the church's mission program? How best to confront the situation of missioners who fail at language-learning or at some other aspect of adapting to a foreign culture? What were the most helpful suggestions for keeping missioners and indigenous clergy and religious working together harmoniously? What to do when bandits hold a missioner hostage? What to do about maintaining the health and morale of missioners? Certainly he was thinking about the sometimes harsh conditions of missions, but also about how to prepare young people for the hardships that may possibly come.

The questions for Considine were often many and varied, but he frequently found answers that made him think. On the subject of seminary formation, Considine wrote out a memo in 1926 that captured his recollections of a conversation with Marchetti during one of their outings to the Roman suburb of Frascati; Considine's memo reads:

> The faculty should really know the men. Notorious [were] the errors made in the colleges in Rome and in other parts of the world from time to time due to snap judgments and the absence of means of contacts. The system in some Irish sems and in some American ones is to be deplored by which professors are put high up on a pedestal where the students are expected to gaze from afar in awe but who instead often look with misunderstanding, dislike and contempt. The character forming influence of the faculty in such cases is minimized.
>
> The practice of giving different food to the faculty than to the students is a very important source of discontent. I mentioned that this was avoided at Maryknoll. He said many [seminaries] began that way but got away from it. It is quite the natural thing for the cooks to give greater care to the faculty and if care is lacking with the student dishes the directors are seldom the wiser.[33]

The remarks from Marchetti recorded by Considine display an unexpected sense of understanding formation for ministry as an interpersonal process; the remarks are almost devoid of a task orientation or goal-centeredness—that is, seminarians are required to demonstrate that they have learned things so that they can ascend from the lowly stage of seminarian to a place in the hierarchical priesthood. Indeed, Marchetti seemed to suggest that it is the duty of faculty to not create a distinction between the

---

33. Although the use of the first person in the second paragraph indicates Fr. Considine was the author, the item as found in the Maryknoll Mission Archives was entitled "Memo from Marchetti to Considine: *Seminary faculty and student body.*" 14 November 1926. MMA, Maryknoll Fathers and Brothers General Council Correspondence, Box 10, Folder "Marchetti".

ordained and those who aspire to orders. Considine's own formation in Maryknoll had been marked by a "family" atmosphere; was it surprising for Considine to hear a validation of that experience from a respected figure like Marchetti?

Considine relished such insights, and as soon as he could he sat down and wrote a memo about them and then sent that memo to Fr. Superior back at Maryknoll. It was a time when Considine's expansive mind tackled question after question of mission life and found answers that were helpful for carrying on the mission cause.

Writing in a Certain Voice

In the process of learning the ropes of the Roman Curia, Considine also positioned himself as an interpreter of Rome's mission concerns for U.S. Catholics. The Holy Year and the Exposition were only half over when Considine completed *The Vatican Mission Exposition: A Window on the World* (1925).[34] The book featured descriptions of exhibits, stories from the mission fields from which the exhibits came, and beautiful black-and-white photographs. The main message was that Catholic foreign missions, though a relatively new concept for U.S. Catholics, were a vital and thriving enterprise. The universal church's head and members were actively involved in sending missioners to call the world's peoples to Christ and his church. Mission was an activity for the whole church, from the pope to the Curia to the bishops to parishes to Catholics in their homes in many lands. *The Vatican Mission Exposition* received strong reviews and sold well; it also launched Considine's publishing career in a particular key or voice.

Three aspects of Considine's voice in print can be discerned. He was an interpreter of the "big picture" of Catholic mission concerns, connecting today's missions with Christ and the Bible:

> The Vatican Mission Exposition does not begin its lessons with the portrayal of the present-day apostolate. . . . If we would have its pro-oemium we must take ourselves back to the cradle days of Christianity, when Jesus of Nazareth walked in Palestine. . . . Hence, as we begin our tour of the Exposition, the first hall before us is the Hall of the Holy Land.
>
> I entered the hall the other morning to stare and be curious. I left, as all others near me seemed to leave, with the traits of the idle sight-seer sloughed off; I had been moved to the depths with the magnitude of a thought which even I, a missioner, had heretofore not sufficiently appreciated: *Palestine was the home of a missionary Savior.*[35]

---

34. New York: Macmillan, 1925.
35. Considine, *Vatican Mission Exposition,* 36.

The second aspect of Considine's voice in print is that of an interpreter of official Catholic mission teaching and programs; Considine will strive to show how all the institutions of Catholic missions, from the pope in Rome to the humblest missioner or mission supporter, were working together to gather all people into Christ's church. There is a familiar story that Considine used in several places about a discussion he once observed at Propaganda Fide. The discussion centered on the Andaman Islands:

"What seems to be the problem?" I asked.

One of the priests smiled. "We are considering the merits of some muddled records," he said. "We must decide for the Holy Father whether the Archbishop of Calcutta or the Bishop of Rangoon has responsibility for the Andaman Islands. You might say, 'For heaven's sake, give them to one or the other and be done with it.' In a way you would be right. But by a very beautiful tradition here in Rome, the assignment of responsibility for the souls in any territory in any part of the world is regarded as akin to a sacred trust and is never treated lightly."

"It is striking to recall," he continued, "that every square mile on the face of the earth is charted here in Rome, and responsibility for the care of souls, Christian or non-Christian, within every area has been carefully determined. With the Holy See there is no forgotten man."[36]

As he left Rome for the United States in 1934, Considine was uniquely positioned as an interpreter for U.S. Catholics of the church's universal mission efforts; he was especially able at explaining the workings of the Holy See and the teachings of the popes in relation to the Catholic mission cause around the world.

An ability to explain mission situations that would otherwise be strange or foreign to audiences is a third aspect found in Considine's writing. In a passage on Shintoism in Japan, Considine first described the participants and the "grace and artistry" with which ceremonies take place at a shrine. He gives an accurate account of offerings of rice, fruit, vegetables, and fish, and even includes a drawing of a "Typical Temple Plan." Then he offers these words on the practitioners he observed:

At this temple in the heart of Nagasaki, it was impressive to see so many making an early morning visit before going to their work of the day. Professional men with brief cases, and business men as well

---

36. Considine and Kernan, *Across a World*, xiii.

as family folk, entered, evidently through an urge to do the proper thing. They remained but a moment. They clapped their hands three times, as is their custom, tossed a coin into the large offertory box, bowed the head, and uttered a brief prayer. Then they were gone.[37]

In short, he wrote clearly and with sympathy for the peoples and situations he described, able to introduce foreign situations in a way that captured the human dimensions with which his audience could identify. He had become a missiographer—one well versed in the study of the earth's peoples and the study of the church's opportunities to be in mission to them.

Considine's Particular Place in the Cause of Mission

In addition to establishing himself as a mission journalist and an authority on Catholic missions, Considine's first mission study tour also accomplished a more personal goal—he had established a dynamic connection between himself, a missionary priest dedicated to research and writing, and the actual mission enterprises of the church. His good friend Fr. Francis Ford had written to him from China, over and over, about how much mission changes a person. While Considine understood his path as not that of a missioner in the field, after the study tour he could rightly feel he had helped missioners by first understanding their struggles and their contexts and then sharing what he learned with a large audience. In addition, the trip itself allowed him something of the experience of being changed by mission, of feeling himself on foreign terrain in order to seek there the ways that the missioners will attempt to gather into Christ's church people of many cultures.

In what ways was he changed? He had gained a missioners-eye view of the missions. *Across a World*, Considine's book-length treatment of his journey, reads in some parts like a travelogue or an orientation to the geography and history of the Middle East, Asia, and Africa. But the mission story is never far away. The text delivers an assessment of the contemporary difficulties of the missionary task. In India, Catholic missionaries staff fine schools that are attended by the children of prominent Hindus and Muslims; the students "know as much Catholic teaching as do the Catholics." Nonetheless, powerful family and social pressures circumvent the desire a young person may have to take the step of becoming Christian.[38]

The same volume recounts a lengthy conversation with Bishop Rouchouse, apostolic vicar of Chengtu, China, who gave Considine a real-

---

37. Ibid., 231.
38. Ibid., 58–64.

istic idea of what it would take, at a minimum, to bring about the much hoped-for conversion of China. He described the pace of conversions in his own vicariate as "modest" but going steadily forward. He then goes on to explain a "matter of mathematics." Specifically, there were one hundred thousand converts per year in China, but at that rate, four hundred million Chinese would not be converted without one of two kinds of miracles— a saint anointed by God to motivate a greater increase, or else a dramatic increase in the number of missioners.[39] Such straight talk from a China veteran surely helped Considine to temper his missionary optimism.

Considine would go on to make four more lengthy mission study tours: to Latin America in 1945, to Africa and Asia in 1953, to South America in 1954, and to the Caribbean and Central America in 1955. Similar to the pattern of his first mission study tour, he would take extensive notes and later turn his observations into books and articles.

Conclusion

During his ten years in Rome, Considine gained a deeper understanding of the cause of mission as a whole, and greater clarity about his own particular mission within that enterprise. He managed to become an effective Vatican insider, even though he did not gain a foothold on the pathway of advancement in the hierarchy. Moreover, it seems doubtful that he ever sought such a path; it is clear that when he was needed by Maryknoll he set aside further work in Rome. As he moved into a leadership role in the Maryknoll Society, what continued to attract him was the building up of institutions that would advance the church's global mission.

39. Ibid., 139–40.

How to Be a Missiographer

Msgr. Marchetti says one reason he approves the news service is its value to replace by genuine news of wide scope the flood of appeal letters of individual missioners which constitutes almost the only food the Catholic people are getting on missions.

—John J. Considine to James A. Walsh, 1927[1]

JUST LIKE THAT, in April 1927, Fides Service was given the order to transform missioners pleading for funds into reporters and international correspondents capable of educating the Catholic public on missions. It is not clear that Considine was able to turn back the tide of mission appeal letters, but he did manage to organize Fides into a capable international news organization in just eight months—the inaugural edition of Fides Service was published on December 20, 1927.

In chapter 5 we have already discussed the editorial and distribution arrangements at Agenzia Fides in Rome. But how did Considine recruit and train the nearly three hundred correspondents accredited to the organization in its first two years of operation? More importantly, how did those correspondents learn to write as reporters?

The short answer is that we do not know. Fides regularly published material that was obviously transmitted by correspondents from points around the world to the central office in Rome, but it is also clear that the central office had the final say about content. Without access to drafts of the dispatches from correspondents and feedback on them from the Fides Rome office,[2] it is hard to understand the state of the reporting skills of the mis-

---

1. John Considine, Rome, to James A. Walsh, Ossining, NY, April 27, 1927. MMA, Considine Papers, 3:7.
2. Due to the Fides Service Interim Director being away, requests during May and June of 2011 for access to the Fides Archives in the Opera Pontificia della Propagazione della Fede in Rome were not granted.

sioners recruited to work as correspondents. It is also clear that no training of correspondents in the field was carried out. Until Considine undertook his mission study tour at the end of 1931, Fides staff from Rome did no traveling to mission territories in Asia, Africa, Latin America, and Oceania.

Documents from 1927, however, provide a window on what Considine was asking of Fides correspondents; the documents also illuminate the purpose of Fides Service. Two of these documents—the announcement of the founding of Fides Service and "Instructions to Service Correspondents"—were produced in the five original languages of Fides Service—English, French, German, Italian, and Spanish.[3] Ecclesiastical ordinaries and the apostolic delegates of mission territories received the multilingual announcement and a cover letter in Italian that requested that he appoint a correspondent from his territory.[4] Propaganda secretary general Archbishop Marchetti suggested threatening to reduce mission subsidies to those mission vicariates, prefectures, and dioceses that did not appoint a correspondent, but such a threat is not explicit in the cover letter.[5]

How to Do It

In particular, the "Instructions" offered a mini-handbook for what Considine later called missiography: the study of the world's peoples, and the study of the church's efforts to share the gospel of Christ with those peoples.[6] Though the document does not bear Considine's name, its June 1927 date indicates that it was produced when the only Fides staff person was Considine himself.

In terms of the types of material requested from correspondents, the document first makes a distinction between two broad areas that are to be covered: news and studies of mission conditions. Considine defined news mainly by its timeliness—new correspondents needed to understand that old news is of no value, and that if Fides hoped to make Catholic missions

---

3. "Announcing Fides Service." ASPF, Nuova Serie, Vol. 974, Fogl. 807–808. "Instructions to Service Correspondents." ASPF, Nuova Serie, Vol. 974, Fogl. 815–816.

4. Willem Van Rossum, Rome, to mission bishops [circular letter], June 4, 1927. ASPF, Nuova Serie, Vol. 948, Fogl. 78–79.

5. John J. Considine, Rome, to James A. Walsh, Ossining, NY, April 7, 1927. MMA, Considine Papers, 3:7. With no other correspondent recruitment plan—and no funds available for such a plan—the results were understandably uneven. The Fides second Annual Report noted that there was sometimes great quality in the dispatches, but also that out of 353 enrolled correspondents a little more than half were listed as active, and that the central office needed to provide "directives to Correspondents which will secure more valuable material." ("Fides Service: Second Annual Report," April 1, 1929. MMA, Considine Papers, 3:7, pp. 2–3, 7).

6. John J. Considine and Peter L. Blake, *An Outline of Missiography* (New York: Society for the Propagation of the Faith, 1927).

a news item, all Fides dispatches would need to conform to the standards of journalism, especially in regard to timeliness and accuracy. In regard to studies of mission conditions, timeliness may not be as important, but the document noted that it would be helpful to select topics that have some currency among Western readers. Material should satisfy the heart and the head—he mentioned a need for "anecdotes and incidents" that arouse human interest. Additionally, correspondents were free to engage local writers in order to produce attractive copy. No budget was offered to correspondents; however, those feeling overburdened by expenditures were free to make their situation known to the Fides central office in Rome.

The document then gives detailed instructions on what correspondents should look for—what are the areas and subject matters that will open up for both the correspondent and his or her readers an accurate view of mission conditions or news from a mission? What, in effect, would constitute news for Fides? What followed was a comprehensive list of possible subjects to be covered by correspondents; the list was divided into three main areas: the mission territory, the people, and the mission itself. By "mission territory," the document meant the physical environment, its geographical description, flora and fauna, minerals and mines, and agricultural products, along with several "human" factors: population, healthfulness, and communication and transportation. This was the shortest of the three main areas. Under "The People," the document suggests eighty-nine topics, which were listed under ten subheadings: race; social life; economic life; education; history; art; sciences; literature, writing, and thought; law and government; and religious and moral life. The subheading with the largest number of topics was religion (twenty-one), followed by economic life (fifteen) and law and government (twelve). The final main heading, "The Missions," suggested sixty-two different topics that could be covered, which were listed under nine subheadings: history; mission organization and administration; personnel; training of personnel; church institutions; Catholic people; financial conditions; non-Catholic religious activity; and general. "Catholic people" was the subheading that had the highest number of topics (thirteen), and the list portrays a depth of curiosity that was asked of the correspondents:

- Population movements
- Information throwing light on the quality of Catholicity
- Frequency of Mass and the sacraments
- Devotion to the Eucharist
- Religious education
- Religious sodalities
- Catholic home life
- Intellectual conditions of Catholics

- Social conditions of Catholics
- Economic conditions of Catholics
- Observance of feasts
- Funerals
- Support of the church

Probably it was not the case that someone could read the "Instructions" and on that basis alone become a correspondent capable of writing newsworthy dispatches for Fides. But it was the case that Considine understood the Catholic background and the relatively high level of educational attainment of missionary priests; he knew that he was not starting from scratch. He also understood that there were ways to properly motivate missioners to become correspondents, and the key to providing that motivation was the clear statements of the purpose of Fides that were contained in the "Instructions." According to the document, three main points stand out.

Moving missions into the world of the press. Fides was founded for the purpose of getting news about Catholic missions into the Catholic and secular press worldwide. Considine acknowledged that newspaper editors would be cautious of missioners (and anyone else) who sought to use their pages as free advertising. At the same time, he was aware of the hunger for news in the competitive world of newspaper publishing, and so Fides was meant to create news copy that would conform to journalistic canons and provide attractive news copy from far-flung places. Inviting correspondents to tell the stories of their missions to a wider audience was certainly a way to motivate their curiosity and creativity.

Promoting the cause of mission. Yet Fides also acknowledged that its overall purpose was to promote the cause of mission in indirect ways. In the "Instructions," the submission of photographs is encouraged, and a note was added that a single photograph had recently inspired several mission vocations and generated more than $10,000 in support.

Countering prejudice. The document placed particular importance on an accurate portrayal of people and mission situations:

Undoubtedly it is the out-of-the-ordinary features of the mission world that catch attention in the West but in justice to the peoples to whom we are bringing the Word of God let us take care that we do not present them in a false light by dwelling with unwarranted force on the curious, the ridiculous, the gross, the bizarre, on the extremes in poverty, in ignorance, in cruelty, and the like. Prudence as well as charity counsels that we write nothing for Western consumption that we would not wish the indigenous peoples to read.

Portraying people and situations accurately was a way to advance an important editorial aim of Fides—spreading the message of the unity of the human race.

While using to an ordinate degree the points of difference between mission peoples and Westerners, at the same time let our goal be to impress Catholic peoples with the similarity of the human family in the possession of those gifts of God which give them an equal right with the most learned of the earth to the blessings of Christianity.

The final item on long the list of topics was an open-ended invitation to think like a journalist: "Beyond these, any other subject." The unstated expectation was that correspondents were to remain curious, ever interested in how the study of the people among whom they worked and the study of mission might not only help them to write good news copy but also would improve their ability to share the gospel with the people to whom they were sent.

CHAPTER 7

The Mission Executive: Service on the Maryknoll Society General Council, 1934–1946

The Big Apple

> On 1:21 to N.Y., to Al Roon's. Met George for supper. . . . He + Steve his companion + I to Wedgewood Room at Waldorf Astoria for very pleasant dinner + entertainment. Home on 10:40.
> —John Considine Diary, October 22, 1942

WHEN FR. CONSIDINE returned from Rome at the end of 1934 he took up residence at the Maryknoll headquarters near Ossining, New York, just a short, one-hour train ride from New York City, and he remained in residence there until 1960. His diaries from the late 1930s forward record frequent visits to Manhattan to conduct Maryknoll Society business but also to take in the city's cultural attractions, visits that increased after 1938 when Maryknoll purchased a residence on East 39th Street, just three blocks from Grand Central Station; Considine had successfully lobbied his colleagues on the General Council for its purchase.[1] The "New York Procure" was home to the Maryknoll priests doing promotion work in the New York area, a group that included Fr. Considine's longtime friend Fr. James Keller. However, owing to the fact that it was a large residence, over the years the policy on the use of the house evolved to offer lodging to larger constituencies: Maryknollers on official business in New York, Maryknollers coming and going from overseas missions, visiting bishops and dignitaries, and so on.

---

1. Minutes, February 3, 1938. MMA, Council Meetings Minutes 1937–1944, 4:1 (Minutes 1937–1938).

On a personal level, Considine simply enjoyed being able to come and go to this important world city. He frequented the theater and took in concerts, browsed the bookstores, and when he wasn't writing a book, he would go on a jag where he took in as many as five movies a week. At times he would meet up with his brothers, usually George or Ray, and at other times enjoy a meal followed by a show or a concert with Maryknoll friends such as Fr. Keller or Bishop Escalante. For a time in the early 1940s, Considine was a regular at Al Roon's Health Club on the Upper West Side.

He was probably able to afford this lifestyle in the 1930s and 1940s through a combination of his meager personal allowance from Maryknoll,[2] Mass stipends, help from his family, and reimbursable expenses. Considine, after all, had a long list of official business undertakings he conducted in New York City: meetings with visiting Vatican dignitaries and bishops from around the world, research at the New York Public Library, and meetings with publishers, printers, and church officials.

The transition from life in Rome to life in the United States appears to have been eased for him by the proximity of the city and all its cultural resources. Considine was not a snob, but his cultural "cruising altitude" was high, and he delighted in the world that was New York. Moreover, by the 1960s, he had committed the ultimate treason for a Massachusetts native— he had become a Yankees fan.

The Mission Executive
The term "mission executive" refers to one who is charged with the administration of missions. In the Anglo-American cultural context, it is often the case that administrative roles are undervalued as (worst case) bureaucratic or (happier case) simply instrumental or supportive of the real work of organizations, which can be accomplished only by those on the front lines—missioners themselves, in this case.

However, in Protestant mission agencies in North America and Great Britain, the role of the mission executive is indispensable. Frequently, Protestant mission executives, regardless of whether they are the actual founder of a mission organization, are routinely called upon to do the leadership work of founders by inviting and inspiring new missioners, new mission contacts in local churches where the missioners will work, and new supporters of mission in the home church. They also have a major role in shaping and articulating the mission visions and strategies with and for the organization.

In short, the mission executive has to embody the missionary aspirations

---

2. A statement from 1963 showed his personal allowance at $35 per month; probably it was lower in the 1930s and 1940s.

of the organization, ever challenging missioners, supporters, and church officials to act on the urgency of the mission work. Skill sets among mission executives have to include a strong combination of most of the following: the human relations skills of persuasiveness and consensus building, an extensive knowledge of mission contexts, mission and the Bible, and/or knowledge of mission and ecclesiology. Sometimes mission executives have missionary experience themselves, but often that is not a requirement.[3]

Apart from the reverence in which Catholics hold the founders of their missionary organizations, Catholics do not generally make use either of the term "mission executive" or of the mystique around the role that is often found in Protestant missionary agencies. For Catholics, the leadership's main role is not to get in the way of the real work, which is mission and is accomplished by missioners.

Fr. Considine saw things differently. While he always had a great deal of sympathy for missioners in the field, he understood that it is faithfulness to Christ's purposes that defines the missioner, not the spot on the globe that the missioner occupies. Considine understood that faithfulness to Christ's mission meant a lot more than just serving in a mission field—it meant understanding and living a global vision of Christ's mission in the world today.

Especially after returning from Rome in 1934, Considine had adopted an articulate global vision of mission, and he very much embodied the qualities of a mission executive. These qualities marked his years of service on the Maryknoll Society's General Council, 1934–1946. There was much administrative and personnel work during these years but also considerable deliberation and action on mission strategy—how could Maryknoll work in such a way as actually to make Christ better known and the church more available to the world's peoples?

Prior to this period, Considine would routinely consult with Maryknoll co-founder James A. Walsh and the Maryknoll Society leadership through visits and correspondence; he also understood the pages of Fides Service as a bully pulpit for making known his views on mission strategies to those

---

3. A recent example of an Evangelical mission executive was the late Rev. John Stott (1921–2011), founder of Langham Partnerships (known as John Stott Ministries in the United States). He had led an Evangelical revival in Britain and is understood as the framer of the 1974 Lausanne Covenant. Stott's ministry does not recruit and send out missioners but rather sponsors students from the Global South to get advanced degrees in theology so that they can teach in their own countries. Stott authored many popular books on Christian faith and then used the royalties to set up trusts that financed the advanced theological education of gifted students. Mark A. Noll commented that Stott became "a patron, mentor, friend and encourager of thousands of pastors, students and laypeople from the newer Christian parts of the world" (Wolfgang Saxon, "Rev. John Stott, Major Evangelical Figure, Dies at 90," New York Times, July 27, 2011).

responsible for the sending out of Catholic missioners. As he took up duties as part of the Maryknoll leadership, his consultations on mission became more frequent, thinking and speaking about mission strategy for Maryknoll and the church on a daily basis.

Returning from Rome in 1934

When Fr. Considine returned to Maryknoll headquarters from Rome in December 1934, he found a setting that had changed significantly during the ten years of his Roman sojourn. Because he had been in frequent contact with the Maryknoll Society leadership while serving in Rome, and because he had made one visit to Maryknoll in 1929 to attend the Society's first General Chapter, he had been aware of many of the changes as they occurred. Even so, there must have been many adjustments for Considine as he settled into his new environment.

The size of the Maryknoll family had continued to grow, to well over a total of 1,001 priests, brothers, sisters, and students in 1935. Approximately 40 percent of this number were priests, students, sisters, and brothers located on the twin properties near Ossining, New York.[4] Similarly, this growing population was no longer housed in a collection of farm buildings—a large stone building had been erected as the seminary, and a large brick building served as the motherhouse for the Maryknoll Sisters.

Perhaps the biggest change was in the one person who, through that time, had seemed to embody the Maryknoll movement, co-founder Bishop James A. Walsh.[5] When Considine returned to Maryknoll for Christmas 1934, Bishop Walsh's health was such that soon after Considine's arrival, Walsh left for an extended convalescence in Florida.

Certainly with a view to the continued growth and life of the Maryknoll Society beyond the life of the co-founder, some formalities by then had been put in place to govern the Society. At the first General Chapter in 1929, then Fr. Walsh was elected for the first and only time to the office of superior general of the Maryknoll Society. According to the Society's constitutions, which had been approved by Rome in 1928,[6] Chapters were to gather representative delegates from among the membership, to elect

---

4. The Maryknoll Sisters (officially known at that time as the Foreign Mission Sisters of St. Dominic) had purchased a property across Pinesbridge Road from the Maryknoll Society property in 1928 ("The Sisters' Mother-House," *Field Afar* 22, no. 7 [July–Aug 1928]: 199–200).

5. James A. Walsh had been consecrated bishop in Rome on June 29, 1933. Cardinal Fumasoni Biondi, prefect of the Sacred Congregation of Propaganda Fide, was principal consecrator.

6. See Chapter 6.

leadership, and to deal with other matters that might improve the life and work of the Society.

Also elected in 1929 was a cadre of young Maryknollers who served as the General Council to Bishop James A. Walsh: vicar general Fr. Patrick Byrne and Frs. James M. Drought, William O'Shea, and Raymond Lane. Fr. Lane had departed in 1932 to become prefect of Fushun in Manchuria, and he was replaced by Fr. Francis Winslow, a classmate of Considine. Fr. Patrick Byrne was soon to depart for Japan, and Considine had been appointed to take his place on the Council. [7] A reshuffling of responsibilities took place when Considine joined the Council. Fr. Drought was made vicar general and treasurer and, over the next two years, was to exercise considerable power within the governing structure of the Society as the health of Bishop James A. Walsh declined. Considine was made secretary general, director of propaganda, and assistant treasurer.

If there was any lingering tension between Considine and Drought over the latter's role in trying to bring Considine onto the General Council in 1932, no record can be found of that in Considine's diaries. As will be discussed presently, however, dealing with the volatility of Fr. Drought's personality would become a regular feature of Considine's work on the General Council.

As director of propaganda for Maryknoll, Considine's responsibilities included fundraising and public relations—often called "promotion" within Maryknoll. He also ran the day-to-day operations for publishing *The Field Afar*, though he did not become editor until 1936. [8] Considine's office diary of the years 1934–1937 does not give abundant detail on the situation he inherited in the Propaganda Department. From his recent mission study tour, he had become convinced that missioners in the field should have greater material support from the Society Center. What was the state of fundraising as he assumed his duties in early 1935? Did he encounter a serious state of disorganized effort which he began to organize and manage, or did he simply wish to build a stronger institutional structure around fundraising and outreach activities that were already working fairly well? The fact that it was the middle of the Great Depression may argue for the former idea; conversely, the correspondence of Maryknoll Fr. Charles McCarthy with the General Council seems to show that this other

---

7. Fr. Winslow elected to the Council to replace Fr. Lane (MMA, Council Meeting Minutes 1912–1937, January 13, 1933, p. 230; Box 3, Folder 4 "Minutes 1929–1933"); Fr. Considine elected to the Council to replace Fr. Byrne (MMA, Council Meeting Minutes 1912–1937, December 26, 1934, p. 275; Box 3, Folder 5 "Minutes 1934–1937").

8. Considine served on the editorial staff of *The Field Afar* from 1934 to 1960 and exercised editorial leadership during the entire period, even though he did not always have the title of editor.

Maryknoller had already been managing the Society's promotional efforts for a number of years.

Considine's diary entries in 1935 and early 1936 considered a wide-ranging set of issues related to his new work: decisions to make motion pictures about mission and manage their distribution and use;[9] how to fundraise effectively while maintaining good relations with the national Society of the Propagation of the Faith (SPF) along with bishops, priests, and parishes;[10] managing the public image of the group when some members complained that the group's budget priorities did not sufficiently support missioners in the field;[11] and intraoffice personnel issues.

Beyond the organizational and public relations problems, what was consistently on Considine's mind was the question of what were the best ways to be in mission? This was a continuing concern, as we have already seen. Considine's comparison of Maryknoll and the Jesuits made prior to joining Maryknoll, his lengthy study of Ramon Lull's mission program, the notes he made in 1932 during his mission study tour on issues of morale experienced by Maryknoll personnel in Asia—all of these represented his continued and growing concern for finding the best ways to be in mission with the available human and material resources. As a mission executive, he would be concerned about many matters: the meaning and purpose of mission, mission strategies, and the formation of new missioners. Organizational matters such as public relations and fundraising would be his special area of responsibility in Maryknoll for many years, but Considine never stopped thinking about the big picture and how all the various elements of the mission enterprise were part of that picture.

A Sea Change: The Death of Bishop James A. Walsh

The death of Maryknoll co-founder Bishop James A. Walsh in April 1936 occasioned an important transition for the entire Maryknoll family. The only superior general that the membership had known was gone, and the following summer in Hong Kong the Second General Chapter was held

---

9. John J. Considine, "FA Office Diary," January 6, 1935, and March 19, 1936. MMA, Considine Papers, 5:1.

10. Considine records a conversation with Archbishop McNicholas of Cincinnati: "possibly a dozen bishops are thoroughly sold to Maryknoll as he himself is, while possibly there is another little group at the other end which is ill disposed. The great majority of the bishops of the country are quite satisfied with us but if some charge were brought against us such as this one, that Maryknoll had horned in on SPF control, many of the bishops in the middle of the path might be influenced" (John J. Considine, "FA Office Diary," February 28, 1935. MMA, Considine Papers, 5:1).

11. John J. Considine, "FA Office Diary," January 26, 1935. MMA, Considine Papers, 5:1.

to elect new leadership, which would serve a ten-year term, 1936–1946. This new General Council, led by superior general Bishop James E. Walsh (no relation to the Maryknoll co-founder), would, in 1942, send the first Maryknollers to Latin America and would also lay the groundwork for the sending of the first Maryknollers to Africa in 1946.

The Second General Chapter's voting on the Council membership reflected continuity with the previous Council: reelected were Fr. Drought as vicar general, and Frs. O'Shea and Considine as second and third assistants general. The fourth assistant general, Fr. Thomas Kiernan, had been laboring in a South China mission at the time of his election.[12]

How did this Council organize itself in the wake of the death of the Society's co-founder? What were the major tensions that surfaced, and how did this leadership group tackle those challenges? What were the main accomplishments of this Council?

Power Struggles among the New Leadership
When Bishop James E. Walsh was elected superior general in 1936, he promised to spend one year in every three of his term in visitations to Maryknoll missions. Presumably his policy was a response to center–periphery tensions felt in the growing Society at the time, and a reflection of what he thought was most important in the life and work of Mary-knoll—that is, the missioners working in the field themselves.

Yet, when he departed in May 1938 for his first year-long mission visitation, the strength of the Society's fairly new institutions—a constitution rather than the person of the co-founder as the authority for the group—would be greatly tested. Added to the mix was continued growth in membership, which, for the sake of an ordered common life in Society residences, meant that more of an institutional rather than a family atmosphere would begin to characterize the group.[13]

The basic problem at that time was that there was little precedent for interpreting the Society constitutions. It could probably be said that the constitutions, adopted in 1928, while technically in place since that time, were not actually needed while Maryknoll co-founder James A. Walsh was still alive. As was the case with many Catholic societies or religious orders of the time, in most matters almost full authority was accorded to the superior general, who, in the case of Maryknoll, was the co-founder

12. Charles McCarthy, Ossining, NY, to SPF Directors, July 22, 1936. MMA, J.E. Walsh collection, 3:3.
13. Memo, James E. Walsh, Ossining, NY, to Society and Local Superiors, June 1, 1939. MMA, Superior General Papers (Correspondence) 1920–1989, 3:3. The memo to superiors emphasized the importance of following policies and regulations, "If we are to operate as a harmonious unit. . . ."

and enjoyed unrivaled authority. How were decisions made at that time? Simply by consulting Bishop James A. Walsh.

Thus, it was only after the death of Bishop James A. Walsh in 1936 that the entire membership of the Society in general and the superior general and his Council in particular would have to learn to interpret and rely on their constitutions as an authoritative guide for making decisions. It was therefore not surprising that the interaction between Bishop James E. Walsh and his Council members would become quite rancorous during his first year-long absence for a mission visitation from May 1938 to May 1939. While Bishop James E. Walsh was in Asia, telegrams and letters were flying across the Pacific in which the superior general, on the one hand, and the Council members, on the other, quoted relevant passages of the Society constitutions to rule each other out of order.

The first dispute ran from August to October 1938 and had to do with the assignment of Maryknoll Sisters to the Maryknoll mission in Korea. In early September, Walsh simply informed the Council that he was taking care of this matter "as an Executive," in effect telling them not to interfere with his decisions.[14] Fr. Drought's response was sent in a telegram:

COUNCIL DISAPPROVES YOUR VARIOUS RECALL ORDERS
WITHOUT ANTECEDENT CONSULTATION [STOP] FREQUENCY
THREATENS SPIRIT OF STABILITY [STOP] CONSTITUTION
REQUIRES VOTE / COUNCIL[15]

The Council sought guidance from a canon lawyer in Rome, Msgr. Bartocetti, who was a consultor for the Sacred Congregation of Propaganda Fide (SCPF). He mentioned that amendments to the constitutions on the authority of the vicar general in the absence of the superior general could be made, due to the fact that such absences are likely to recur. At the same time he urged that the matter be thoroughly researched and discussed before any amendments were proposed to the SCPF.[16]

The second dispute came after the death of Pius XI in February 1939; at that time, the Council unanimously urged Bishop James E. Walsh to end his mission visitation early and go to Rome for the coronation of the pope

---

14. James E. Walsh, Pyongyang, to James M. Drought, Ossining, NY, September 10, 1938. MMA, Superior General Papers (Correspondence) 1920–1989, 3:2.

15. Telegram, James M. Drought, Ossining, NY, to James E. Walsh, Hong Kong, October 25, 1938. MMA, Superior General Papers (Correspondence) 1920–1989, 3:3.

16. Memo, Msgr. Bartocetti, December 14, 1938. MMA, Superior General Papers (Correspondence) 1920–1989, 3:2.

who was to be elected (Pius XII).[17] Bishop Walsh refused,[18] and the matter was settled when Walsh agreed to authorize Fr. Considine to represent the Society at the coronation and to conduct the Society's business in Rome.[19]

In early 1939, the General Council minutes cease to be a source of information on these controversies, as the Council did not meet for lack of a quorum between February 23 and May 2, 1939. Considine had traveled to Rome to represent Maryknoll at the coronation of Pius XII; Bishop James E. Walsh was still away; and William O'Shea had resigned from the Council in the summer of 1938 with a view to becoming the apostolic vicar of Pyongyang, Korea.

In the disputes, there was a united opposition of the Council members—Frs. Drought, Considine, and Kiernan—to positions taken by Bishop James E. Walsh. However, in the written record, the most heated rhetoric against Bishop Walsh emanated primarily from Fr. Drought and secondarily from Fr. Kiernan. Fr. Considine, while agreeing with his two colleagues on the Council, remained ever diplomatic. In fact, he endeavored to urge Fr. Drought to adopt a more civil tone:

When a man like the Bishop has different views from ourselves . . . , there is a note of stability in the Church which militates against the idea that he can be eliminated and someone put in his place. He is there and the choice lies between trying to make him go along with what we regard [as] sound views, or of quarreling with him and ruining the chances of having either his views or ours prevail; there is a danger of nullifying everything.

Quarreling with him will do harm throughout our Society, for some will take his side and some ours and the result will be division and bitterness on what will be believed by most to be a personal issue.

Better to push along despite his unpleasantness, accepting the minor thwarting that will come, reminding him plainly but verbally and secretly of what it is we do not like. . . .[20]

---

17. Telegram, James M. Drought, Ossining, NY, to James E. Walsh, Hong Kong, February 10, 1939. MMA, Superior General Papers (Correspondence) 1920–1989, 3:3.

18. Telegram, James E. Walsh, Hong Kong, to James M. Drought, Ossining, NY, March 2, 1939. MMA, Superior General Papers (Correspondence) 1920–1989, 3:3.

19. Telegram, James E. Walsh, Hong Kong, to James M. Drought, Ossining, NY, March 2, 1939. MMA, Superior General Papers (Correspondence) 1920–1989, 3:3.

20. John J. Considine, New Orleans, to James M. Drought, Ossining, NY, October 22, 1938. MMA, Superior General Papers (Correspondence) 1920–1989, 3:2.

Four aspects of Fr. Considine's strategy for conflict management can be noted. First, at the time of this writing, Considine was not willing to change his views, but at the same time he understood that the proper way forward included recognition of the authority of the person with whom he disagreed. Second, there was also recognition of his own relationship to the person in authority. Third, discretion must characterize the way one advanced one's views with those in authority. Fourth, though here he did not make explicit mention of it, it is also useful to keep in mind Fr. Considine's general sense for achieving a sympathetic understanding of others as part of his conflict-management strategy.

Two additional facts are important. First, subsequent to the return of superior general Bishop James E. Walsh in May 1939, such conflicts between the bishop and his council are not repeated in the General Council records. Second, Bishop Walsh continued to make lengthy mission visitations through the end of his term in 1946. These facts support the suggestion that, once Bishop James E. Walsh had returned in May 1939, the bishop and his Council were able to arrive at a satisfactory working arrangement for conducting the Society's affairs even when the superior general was absent from the Maryknoll headquarters for prolonged periods of time. In other words, this leadership group learned how to get along with each other.

On Consideration of This Special Relationship: The Maryknoll Sisters and the Society after the Death of Bishop James A. Walsh

When Father General (our first Fr. General) was alive, he, of course, was our Father Founder, and he had for us the tender love and solicitude of a father, the same as towards his students and his priests.

Father General always valued our advice and acted upon any suggestion of ours whenever he saw any good in it. There, again, he was our father. Now we are only working with our brothers and there is every difference in the world.[21]

The comments of Maryknoll Sisters foundress Mother Mary Joseph Rogers sum up another side of the impact of the death of Bishop James A. Walsh. Nearly four years after his death, Mother Mary Joseph spoke to the Maryknoll Sisters with a sense of loss and also an awareness of changes

21. Mother Mary Joseph, March 15, 1940; Mary Josephine Rogers, *Discourses of Mother Mary Joseph Rogers, Foundress, Maryknoll*, vol. III, compiled by Mother Mary Coleman and Archives Staff, 1982, pp. 1183–84. The author is grateful to Sister Camilla Kennedy, M.M., for pointing out this reference.

that were in the wind. As we shall see, her remarks were not merely melancholic—later in the talk she rallied the Sisters to a sense of purpose in the changes that had taken place and the changes that were sure to come as both Maryknoll groups continued to experience dramatic growth and as the nations of the earth headed toward the violent conflagration of World War II.

Amid many types of pressures, 1938–1940 was a time when the relationship between the two groups would falter in significant ways. Mistakes were surely made, and as part of the General Council of the Maryknoll Society, Fr. Considine had his share of responsibility[22] for what turned into a near total collapse in communication between the leadership of the two groups. But in the end, Considine would be a voice that urged both groups to return to a sense of their common purpose.

At the outset, it is important to recognize that Maryknoll superior general Bishop James E. Walsh actually began his tenure by gaining the respect of the Maryknoll Sisters. When in 1937 he was asked to address their Third General Chapter, Walsh invited the Sisters to ask themselves if they were "merely auxiliaries" or if instead they were "full fledged missioners in their own right?" He concluded by asking them to keep focused on mission work, "because you are apostles, and God calls you to that."[23]

So what happened between 1937 and 1940? Tensions had been growing among the leadership of both groups over finances. Both groups were in debt as they struggled through the Depression to erect buildings to house their growing numbers of missioners-in-training, and of course those debts could be paid off only slowly as the income of each group had to be used to feed, clothe, and educate new recruits at the two Maryknoll headquarters as well as to maintain those missioners already sent to mission areas. By 1940, the total number of Maryknoll priests, brothers, sisters, and students had grown to 1,253, and in 1946 it would climb to 1,839.

There was also an institutional issue that was unresolved. In fact, it had

22. Since several of the disputes between the Society and the Sisters had to do with fundraising and public relations and since those were Fr. Considine's areas of responsibility on the General Council through 1939 when Fr. Charles McCarthy took them over, it would logically follow that Considine's day-to-day concerns about how the separate fundraising efforts of the two groups could be coordinated were driving some of the Society's lack of satisfaction with the way the Sisters did fundraising. However, the documented record does not allow such a conclusion, as Fr. Charles McCarthy, not Considine, was the author of the memos and correspondence on the fundraising problems that the Society's Council perceived were caused by the Sisters.

23. James E. Walsh, July 13, 1937. MMA, MKS 3rd General Chapter 1935, MSA / GENERAL / CHAPTERS / ASSEMBLIES / 3RD GENERAL CHAPTER – 1937 / TALKS, Box 4, Folder 7. The author is grateful to Sister Ellen McDonald, M.M., for pointing out this reference.

been unresolved almost from the beginning of the Maryknoll enterprise, and it very well may be unresolved even today. The church structures that were in place at the time of the founding of Maryknoll mandated that men's and women's groupings be completely independent.[24] When two independent groups with an important shared history both lay claim to the name and spirit of Maryknoll, on any given day who gets to define what Maryknoll is?

Paradoxically, financial matters also allowed for the shared history of the two groups to continue. During Fr. Considine's terms on the Society General Council from 1934 to 1946, Maryknoll Sisters were employed by the Maryknoll Society at their headquarters in a variety of tasks: production and distribution of *The Field Afar*, secretarial work and letter writing to donors, cooking and other kitchen duties, laundry, and other tasks.[25] In terms of purpose—what men and women joined Maryknoll to do—the same ideal was shared by both groups. U.S. Catholics were for the first time in an organized way joining in the church's worldwide efforts to call all people to Christ and his church, and both the Society and the Congregation recognized the importance of that cause.

Nonetheless, in terms of how that foreign mission effort would be organized and the allotment of resources, there were considerable opportunities for resentments to set in as the unresolved institutional question exacerbated financial matters. The Maryknoll operation subsisted on fundraising income, augmented by investment income. So, when people made a donation, subscribed to *The Field Afar*, purchased an annuity or made a bequest from an estate, which of the two independent groups would control that income? During Fr. Considine's years on the General Council, a general pattern had been inherited from co-founder Bishop James A. Walsh. On the one hand, the Society was in charge of the income from *The Field Afar* and carried on a number of other fundraising activities, and, on the other hand, the Society had the obligation to assist the Sisters' Congregation financially as much as possible.

But a further tension was much discussed by the General Council in the years 1936–1940, and that was keeping a unified or coordinated fundraising image of Maryknoll before the public. In particular, the Society leadership during this time complained that Maryknoll Sisters' fundraising efforts were not coordinated with the efforts of the Society. The solution proposed by the Society's General Council was to codify the obligations of

---

24. Thus, the Maryknoll men adopted the canonical structure of a Society of Apostolic Life, as in the Catholic Foreign Mission Society of America. The Maryknoll women became a religious congregation and from 1920 to 1954 were officially known as the Foreign Mission Sisters of St. Dominic—thereafter as the Maryknoll Sisters of St. Dominic.

25. Between 1932 and 1939 the Society paid $254,000 in salaries to Maryknoll Sisters (Minutes, November 2, 1939 [p. 687]. MMA, Council Meetings Minutes 1937–1944, 4:2).

both groups to each other in an agreement or contract. To codify the terms of a relationship in a written agreement was undoubtedly a big step away from the old "family spirit" of common purpose at Maryknoll and a step toward greater institutionalization. Consequently, the agreements between the two groups during this period produced a testing of the relationship of the two entities and certainly reflected the inevitable confusion over the unresolved institutional question.

The first agreement was proposed by the Society to the Congregation on February 3, 1938, and it was accepted by the Sisters' leadership on April 5, 1938. The Society leadership continued to note problems in the coordination of fundraising between the two groups even after the first agreement, and so a second agreement was proposed by the Society on January 5, 1940.[26] It was never approved by either group. In fact, this latter proposal was the immediate antecedent for the March 15, 1940, remarks of Mother Mary Joseph quoted at the beginning of this section.

Both agreements contained similar provisions on several matters;[27] however, the two agreements differed sharply in tone (see fig. 1). The 1938 agreement carried a diplomatic and collegial tone. It began by stating that the basis for the relationship rested on the three mission aims of the Maryknoll Sisters: to work as auxiliaries of the Maryknoll Society, to make the foreign mission vocation available to American women, and to devote themselves to evangelization. The agreement went on to express how "compatible" such aims were for the Society and, at the end, took pains to explain why a proviso[28] that may be viewed as intrusive by the Maryknoll Sisters was not intended as such.

---

26. The Society's General Council minutes record discussion of problems the Society was experiencing with the promotional activities of the Maryknoll Sisters on several occasions during the period between the proposals of the first and second agreements between the two groups: February 3, 1938 (first proposed agreement is also recorded on this date), November 2, 1939, December 13, 1939, and January 9, 1940 (second proposed agreement is also recorded on this date).

27. The Society would employ Sisters in sufficient numbers to enable the Sisters to service their outstanding debt; support was to be paid by the Society through either the principal of a portion of annuities received (1938) or through a direct grant (1940); the Society would offer securities for one of the Sisters' outstanding loans; there would be coordination of fundraising activities; the Sisters would have two pages of space per issue in *The Field Afar* for their own news and appeals to benefactors (the Society rejected the idea of a larger insert run by the Sisters).

28. The proviso had two parts: that the Sisters submit to the Society leadership for approval any new activities, works, and assignment of personnel that would make a direct or indirect impact on expenditures, and that the Sisters send quarterly financial statements to the superior general of Maryknoll (Minutes, February 3, 1938 [p. 430]. MMA Council Meetings Minutes 1937–1944, 4:1). Interestingly, the proviso of the 1938 agreement was not included by the Society in its proposed 1940 agreement.

FIGURE 1

1938

The basis of mutual relationship thus established and agreed upon was essentially as follows: (1) that the aim of the Maryknoll Sisters is to fulfill the role of (a) auxiliaries to the Maryknoll Fathers, (b) national organization for vocations of American women to the foreign mission apostolate, (c) missioners devoted to evangelization in all its phases, with the preference for direct mission work, and (2) that the direction, tendency, emphasis and development of the Sisters be gauged with said aims in view.

On consideration of this special relationship, the Maryknoll Council feels that it is entirely compatible with its own direct responsibilities to its own Society to assume a portion of the burden in assisting the Sisters in any problems connected with their providential development, and particularly at the present time in the alleviation of their financial problem, which is their greatest necessity.

Accordingly, the Council adopted [a] plan . . . as a proposal to be offered to the Sisters, with a view to cooperating with them in the solution of their present financial difficulty. In moving the proposal, however, the Council felt obliged to add a proviso which will be noted as an addendum to the plan. The purpose of this proviso will be apparent. It is not intended to assert any measure of control over the affairs of the Sisters as such. It is the usual and necessary provision that accompanies all proposals of this character, namely, such as involve the allocation of large sums of money to needs for which no direct responsibility exists.

1940

Canonically, the Sisters are a distinct and independent organization, subject only to the authority of their own canonical superiors.

It is recognized that the Maryknoll Fathers have no authority, nor do they presume to impose any particular religious character or special relationship upon the Sisters. If the Sisters and their Superiors desire the maintenance of a completely separate character, in fact as well as law, the Fathers would in no way question such a decision, and the procedure of interrelationship could be readily and satisfactorily established on this basis.

But if the Sisters officially declare it to be their aim to fulfill the role of: (1) auxiliaries to the Maryknoll Fathers, (2) national organization for vocations of American women to the foreign mission apostolate, (3) missioners devoted to evangelization with a preference for direct mission work in the Maryknoll territories, then the direction, tendency, emphasis and development of the Sisters will be worked out according to the above aims and in particular as follows.

As regards to their external activities, the Sisters will be, by virtue of their official aim to help Maryknoll, in a subordinate position to the Maryknoll Fathers, who make the plans of Maryknoll.

Maryknoll is the Maryknoll Fathers. Its plans are made by the Maryknoll Council. Maryknoll in practice is the Maryknoll Council in operation.

The 1940 agreement, on the other hand, carried a tone that was legalistic or perhaps defensive. The first paragraph recognized the Maryknoll Sisters as independent of the Society, and the second paragraph launched into a hypothetical case, noting that if the Sisters desired greater independence, "the Fathers would in no way question such a decision." The proposed agreement then reviewed the three aims of the Maryknoll Sisters and offered sharp definitions of the Society leadership as the ones who "make the plans of Maryknoll." The Sisters, "by virtue of their official aim to help Maryknoll," are "in a subordinate position."

Mother Mary Joseph took a few weeks to respond, but when she did, she was very direct:

> We wish to go on record as stating that there has been no time when we have not been auxiliaries of Maryknoll, nor have we entertained any other thought than giving the Maryknoll Fathers preferential service. It is your Society that is making an issue of it, and I feel that anyone reading your letters to us would conclude we have been annoying and harmful to the general good of the Catholic Foreign Mission Society.
>
> This seems hardly fair. . . . We have not intruded ourselves on the public nor jeopardized the fair name of Maryknoll.
>
> We appreciate the grant or loans so far given, but we feel it is better not to continue receiving them. We shall find other means of reducing our debts.[29]

Mother Mary Joseph's letter went on to engage the proposed agreement point by point, and at the end referred to reaching a "finished agreement." She also suggested that a term of three years be set for the agreement.[30] But for some months, she received no reply from the Society.

---

29. Mary Joseph Rogers, Ossining, NY, to James E. Walsh, Ossining, NY, January 29, 1940. Minutes, January 31, 1940 (pp. 726–27). MMA, Council Meetings Minutes 1937–1944, 4:3.

30. Mother Mary Joseph's letter also responded to a rather strongly worded suggestion contained in the Society's proposal as to how the Sisters were to speak publicly about their support. On this point, the Society's proposed agreement read, "When Bishops or Pastors ask the Sisters why they do not appeal for collections or similar questions, the Sisters will reply that they are working for Maryknoll and that Maryknoll provides the substance of their needs." (Minutes, January 9, 1940 [p. 719]. MMA, Council Meetings Minutes 1937–1944, 4:3). Mother Mary Joseph responded: "We can hardly reply as you suggest. If such questions arise we can simply say it is not our policy to collect at the moment" (Mary Joseph Rogers, Ossining, NY, to James E. Walsh, Ossining, NY, January 29, 1940. Minutes, January 31, 1940 [p. 728]. MMA, Council Meetings Minutes 1937–1944, 4:3).

The seminary kitchen was another matter that created tension between the Sisters and

As was noted at the beginning of this section, it was in March 1940 that Mother Mary Joseph spoke to the Sisters about changes in Maryknoll after the death of co-founder Bishop James A. Walsh. But her remarks were also a strong urging of the Sisters to carry on amid changes, for changes remain a necessary part of living, and certainly part of the life of a missioner.

> The degree in which we suffer is the degree in which God intends to work out our sanctification in us, and if we are not able to meet that suffering, then that is where we are losing spiritually souls depending on us, and who are losing great graces on account of us. So, Sisters, I beg you, as I have begged you before, to meet any changes with alacrity. Welcome them and do not start in, the minute they are proposed, with objections. There are some people who always pride themselves on being able to see what is wrong with everything. That is a very poor kind of intelligence.[31]

There is no record in the General Council minutes of the agreement with the Maryknoll Sisters being discussed after receiving the letter from Mother Mary Joseph. A note in the minutes of the April 26, 1940, meeting simply concluded:

> Feeling that no further progress can be made at this time and under the present circumstances, the Council decided to advise the Sisters that all former agreements between the two Communities are hereby cancelled and that their Congregation will henceforth be considered entirely independent and separate, with full freedom of action, from the C.F.M.S. of A.[32]

---

the Society in the immediate aftermath of the debacle over the 1940 proposed agreement. At that time, the seminary kitchen was staffed by Maryknoll Sisters who were employees of the Society. At the same meeting in January 1940 at which the proposed agreement was recorded, the Council decided to hire a chef (Minutes, January 9, 1940. MMA, Council Meetings Minutes 1937–1944, 4:3). In June, the superior of the Sisters in the kitchen informed the Society that the Sisters will no longer do scrubbing work (Minutes, June 24, 1940. MMA, Council Meetings Minutes 1937–1944, 4:3). The following year, the Sisters made the decision no longer to do the dishwashing at the seminary; that matter was finally settled in correspondence between Bishop James E. Walsh and Mother Mary Joseph in December 1941, and the Society hired laywomen to do the dishwashing (James E. Walsh, Ossining, NY, to Mary Joseph Rogers, Ossining, NY, December 2, 1941. MMA, MFBA Maryknoll Sisters Csp. 1936–1941, Box 2, Folder 8 [Correspondence 1941] and Mary Joseph Rogers, Ossining, NY, to James E. Walsh, Ossining, NY, December 4, 1941. MMA, MFBA Maryknoll Sisters Csp. 1936–1941, Box 2, Folder 8 [Correspondence 1941]).

31. Mary Josephine Rogers, *Discourses of Mother Mary Joseph Rogers,* 1183–84.

32. Minutes, April 26, 1940. MMA, Council Meetings Minutes 1937–1944, 4:3.

Following the death of Fr. James M. Drought in May 1943, Fr. Considine was appointed the Society's vicar general, the number two position after that of the superior general. During the Second World War, Maryknollers in East Asia attempted to carry on. Fr. Considine reported at the end of 1943 that, of the almost five hundred Maryknoll priests, brothers, and sisters working in the Pacific and in East Asia at the time of the attack on Pearl Harbor, approximately one-third had been repatriated, more than half were at their posts in unoccupied China and in the Hawaiian Islands, and there were even five Maryknollers who had received special permission to carry on their ministries within the Empire of Japan. The rest were presumed to be interned in the Philippines.[33]

In the dark and uncertain days of December 1943, Fr. Considine attempted to revisit the relationship of the Society and the Sisters. He penned the following statement and proposed to Bishop Walsh that this declaration or an amended version be sent to Mother Mary Joseph for her approval, so that the leaders of both communities might share it with their communities at Christmas. It was something of a joint declaration of purpose:

> The profound experience which has been the common lot of so many Maryknoll Fathers and Maryknoll Sisters during these past two years that our country has been at war prompts our two communities to mark this Christmas of 1943 by a declaration of mutual dedication to the purposes for which both Societies were founded.
>
> While recognizing the substantially different role which the Church's long tradition has assigned to communities of priests and Brothers as distinct from communities of Sisters, both of our organizations feel that in their close common origin and in the use by both of the name "Maryknoll" they constitute parts of a single movement devoted to the Church's world missions.
>
> The spiritual achievements of this Maryknoll movement will depend much on the joint efforts of the two communities, each according to the course which God designs for it. Each, therefore, asks its members to labor and pray ceaselessly that perfect harmony and unity of ideal may characterize all the relations between the Maryknoll Fathers and the Maryknoll Sisters. Whether it is in the mission field, or in the homeland, the things of God are the sole and exclusive goal of both communities, in the spirit of Christ the Great Missioner—"That they all may be one, as thou, Father, in me, and I in

---

33. John J. Considine, "A note to Maryknollers on the Gripsholm regarding publicity," November 10, 1943. MMA, GC Reports and Memos 1936–1983, Box 1, Folder 5 (Memos 1942–1943).

thee; that they also may be one in us; that the world may believe that thou hast sent me." (Jn. 17:21)[34]

Unfortunately, this joint declaration was not made; the Society's General Council postponed any action on it until after April 1, 1944. In late January 1945, Considine again urged Bishop Walsh on this issue, suggesting that the twenty-fifth anniversary of the foundation of the Maryknoll Sisters on February 14, 1945, should be recognized, but no action was taken on that either.

Finally, near the end of his term in February 1946, Fr. Considine wrote Bishop Walsh a longer memo on the need for an agreement between the Society and the Sisters Congregation, noting that the lack of any agreement had been a principal cause of disharmony between the two groups. The memo is remarkable for the depth of acquaintance with church practice over time that is displayed. For example, Considine mentions that the Holy See is opposed to "arrangements such as existed in past centuries whereby a community of Sisters is made subject to a community or priests." He goes on to say that the experience of four other missionary groups that have both masculine and feminine communities suggests "that things go best when the Fathers avoid the tendency (which is, as we know, a general tendency among priests everywhere) to impose their will on the Sisters." [35]

Apparently, no action was taken by Bishop Walsh on this suggestion either—although the relationship between the Society and the Maryknoll Sisters was put on the agenda for the Society's Third General Chapter in August 1946. Considine served on the Chapter Committee on the Maryknoll Sisters, which proposed a new agreement between the Society and the Maryknoll Sisters. The agreement was adopted by the Chapter and recommended to the new General Council for implementation in consultation with the Maryknoll Sisters. Considine must have felt his persistent efforts to maintain a strong working relationship between the two groups had finally paid off.

The breakdown in communication mainly existed between Bishop Walsh and Mother Mary Joseph. For example, information about the welfare of Maryknollers in the Asian war zones was shared between the two organizations, and many Maryknoll Sisters continued to be employed by the Maryknoll Society. However, change was in the wind on that score as well. A memo from Considine in December 1944 described a conversation he had with Mother Mary Joseph about Sisters doing kitchen work

34. John J. Considine, "A Declaration," December 6, 1943. MMA, GC Reports and Memos 1936–1983, Box 1, Folder 5 (Memos 1942–1943).

35. John Considine to James E. Walsh, Memo, February 27, 1946. MMA, GC Reports and Memos 1936–1983, Box 1, Folder 6 (Memos 1944–1946).

for the Society; Mother Mary Joseph was not in favor of further commitments to such work and expressed concern that such assignments would "harm vocations by branding the community as engaging in too much non-mission-field work at home."[36]

Considine was convinced that the Maryknoll Sisters were a key component of the Maryknoll mission effort. When visiting China in 1932, he had the chance to observe the key role that the Maryknoll Sisters were playing in the evangelization of Chinese women. Once again it was a logic of mission that drove Considine's thinking—reaching Chinese women was a task that could not be put off in the belief that women would become Christian in the degree that their husbands or fathers were converted to the faith. Rather, it was important to dedicate concerted effort to reach Chinese women so that they too could become evangelizers to their children and families. And if Chinese women were to be reached for Christ, it had to be accomplished through the efforts of women.

On the home front, Considine worked closely with Maryknoll Sister educators to set up the Maryknoll Mission Education Bureau. The same logic of mission drove this decision—if students and children were to be reached for the mission cause, women with teaching experience were the experts at reaching them. Maryknoll Sisters were recruited by Considine to staff the Mission Education Bureau within the Propaganda Department of Maryknoll. The creative work accomplished by this bureau is an example of the way Considine sought out the most qualified people to reach his targeted audience—Catholic school students, in this case.

Inside the Mission Education Bureau was the Schools Section, which was charged with developing mission education materials for Catholic schools. The idea was not to create materials on the topic of Catholic missions that would be taught as a separate subject in the curriculum, but rather to integrate mission perspectives into religion, geography, and social studies textbooks. The School Section staff included Sisters Juliana Bedier, Chaminade Dreisoerner, Alma Erhard, Mary Just David, and Grace Marian Martel. Sister Louise (Maria Giovanni) Trevisan rounded out the staff as a capable illustrator. In the late 1940s and early 1950s, they created a K–12 series on geography built around the concept of neighbors.[37] The basic inspiration of the series was Considine's "Catholic sense" of geogra-

---

36. John Considine, Memo to Council, December 19, 1944. MMA, GC Reports and Memos 1936–1983, Box 1, Folder 6 (Memos 1944–1946).

37. Examples in the series authored by Sister Juliana Bedier included *Neighbors Across the World: Eastern Hemisphere*; *Neighbors in Eurasia*; *Southern Neighbors: South America — Africa — Australia — Oceania: Geography for the Air Age*; *Neighbors in One World*. Sister Mary Just David was responsible for the high school geography series: *Our Neighbors of the Andes*; *Our Neighbors the Chinese*; *Our Neighbors the Koreans*; *Our Neighbors the Japanese*.

phy helping us to understand, respect, and love our neighbors around the world.[38] The books were amply illustrated with photos and maps, and with charts that were adequate for each grade level.

Never content to be successful in just one area, the Mission Education Bureau had four other highly active sections:[39] press, reference and research services, literature, and entertainment and lectures. The press service and the reference and research services were something of a smaller-scale duplication of what Considine had set up at Fides Service in Rome. The press service aimed to supply mission photos and articles to newspapers and magazines, thus promoting mission news to presses that were hungry for news. By providing written and photographic resources on a consistent basis and by packaging them with a human interest angle, Considine was able to cultivate press outlets and increase the exposure of Catholic missions before the reading public.

The literature section of the bureau concerned itself with the publication of books on mission, but Considine eschewed the idea of Maryknoll having its own press in favor of reaching a wider audience by publishing with established commercial presses: McGraw-Hill, Charles Scribner's Sons, Dodd Mead and Company, and Longmans, Green, and Company. Considine and Maryknoll Sister Alma Erhard, who went by the pen name of Marie Fischer, wrote the first two books for the literature section. In *Grey Dawns and Red*, Sister Alma told the life story of Blessed (now Saint) Theophane Venard, and in *When the Sorghum Was High*, Considine profiled Fr. Gerard Donovan, a Maryknoller who had been killed by bandits in Manchuria. There was lighter fare as well. Over the next fifteen years the literature section was able to get dozens of books on mission published.

Some of the activities of the entertainment and lecture section of the bureau had been in place before Considine started the Mission Education Bureau in 1937. Since 1922 Maryknoll had developed a lecture series that included stereopticon slide show presentations on missions, and the first Maryknoll film had been produced in 1923. Considine had the entertainment section and the schools section collaborate to develop World Horizon Films, productions that were aimed at school-age audiences. As with the geography series, the purpose was to introduce young people to the peoples of the world.

But the Entertainment and Lectures Section was not limited to films. Sister Immaculata Brennan wrote more than twenty-five plays, complete with sheet music and indications for costuming and staging. Sister Immac-

<hr>

38. See the introduction to this book.
39. A longer summary of the activities of the Mission Education Bureau can be found in Jean-Paul Wiest, *Maryknoll in China: A History, 1918–1955* (Armonk, NY: M. E. Sharpe, 1988), 415–22.

ulata's plays were for all different ages, from primary school to college to adults. Before joining the Mission Education Bureau, she had worked with Sister Alma Erhard on the staff of the *Maryknoll Junior* and *Maryknoll Pioneers*, publications that were aimed at young people.

Fr. Considine continued to be the point person for the Society in relation to the Maryknoll Sisters, even after his term on the General Council ended in 1946. Bishop Raymond Lane succeeded Bishop Walsh as Maryknoll superior general in 1946. When he was asked in 1952 to address the Maryknoll Sisters Chapter, he turned to Fr. Considine to draft his message. The draft that Considine submitted to Lane reprised many of the themes of collaboration that Considine had raised with Bishop Walsh during the previous Council but also included a lengthy section on the importance for mission of the work of the Sister educators of the Mission Education Bureau.[40]

Four New Missions Are Not Undertaken

Between 1936 and 1940, the new Council would explore undertaking four different missions outside of Asia. In each case, the explorations afforded superior general Bishop James E. Walsh and his Council opportunities to reflect on the nature and purpose of Maryknoll, about the populations to be served, and about the way such particular mission possibilities fit into the overall mission of the church. Since Considine was secretary general of the Council, he was the author of many of the memos that today serve as a guide to the group's deliberations on these four possibilities.

One possibility was a "home mission" opportunity—for mission work within the United States—and three were foreign mission opportunities, two in Latin America and one in Africa. The home mission opportunity—mission work among African Americans—was proposed at the second General Chapter in 1936 but would be rejected by the SCPF.[41] Though in the end none of these mission opportunities was adopted by Maryknoll

40. John Considine, "Very Reverend Mother and Sister Delegates," draft of text for Bishop Lane, June 28, 1952. MMA, Lane Papers, 1:4.

41. Chapter motion 47 instructed ". . . the General Council, contingent upon the approval of the Holy See, to seek to obtain mission work in the United States among colored classes, preferably among the Negroes. . . ." ("Acts and Motions of the Chapter, Hong Kong, 1936," MMA, General Chapter II, 2:3). Thomas Kiernan in a 1982 interview said that a 1936 Chapter resolution petitioned the Holy See to take up work "among the Negroes, Indians and the Spanish Americans in the Southwest"; however, the latter two groups are not mentioned in the Acts and Motions. Fr. Kiernan appears to conflate the Council's subsequent search for an "outlet" for those missioners not well adapted to Asian missions with the Chapter resolution—see below (Thomas Kiernan, interview by Laurence Murphy, December 1982, Maryknoll Society Oral History Project, Ossining, NY, pp. 23, 25). On the decision of the SCPF against Maryknoll taking missions among African

during this period, the discussions with Propaganda Fide in Rome provided the General Council with a learning experience on how to negotiate effectively with church authorities.

One of the three foreign missions—a mission in Africa—began as an initiative of Maryknoll, but as negotiations with the Vatican continued, Propaganda Fide took the initiative and invited Maryknoll to take up a mission in northern Nigeria. The proposals for Latin American missions—a mission among Chinese immigrants in Lima, Peru, and a mission in Brazil among Japanese immigrants—came at the initiative of Propaganda Fide. In each case, the initiatives of Propaganda Fide came as something of a surprise to the Council and were the subject of considerable deliberations before they were ultimately shelved.

The negative decision of Propaganda Fide on work among African Americans in the United States came first, and was followed by the proposals for work in South America with Asian immigrants; the negotiations on Africa closed out this period during 1939–1940.

The South American proposals were first made known to the Council in a July 1938 letter from the Propaganda prefect Cardinal Fumasoni Biondi.[42] In the fall of 1938, Society superior general Bishop James E. Walsh traveled to Rome on the first leg of his year-long visitation of Maryknoll missions. After he met with Cardinal Fumasoni Biondi, he came away thinking that the cardinal was not serious about the invitation. The cardinal had given Walsh his approval for Maryknoll to begin mission work in the Philippines, but he did not persuade Walsh to take his suggestion of work in South America as urgent.[43]

Bishop Walsh left Rome for East Asia, but the matter of "Oriental work in South America" was not settled. As was discussed above, when Pius XI died in February 1939, the Council urged Bishop Walsh to interrupt his mission visitation and proceed to Rome for the coronation of the new pope. In the end Walsh did not go but authorized Fr. Considine to go and to transact Society business in Rome. This meant another meeting with Cardinal Fumasoni Biondi, so the Council deliberated on how to respond to his request in regard to South America. The decision was to decline the invitation, but such a deflection of an invitation from the SCPF would have to be done properly. The Council came up with this reason for not wanting to accept the invitation:

Americans in the United States, Considine met with SCPF cardinal prefect Fumasoni Biondi and acknowledged the decision (CD, March 27, 1939).

42. General Council Minutes, July 19, 1939.

43. James E. Walsh, Rome, to James Drought, Ossining, NY, September 14, 1938. MMA, Superior General Papers (Correspondence) 1920–1989, 3:2.

We are inclined to believe that as Americans we could serve better the good of religion in South America by working among the
natives rather than among foreigners. By giving parochial assistance,
we might relieve a South American priest for work among the Ori-
entals in Brazil and Peru.[44]

It was a reason based on the perception of a possible pastoral need of the
local population—Asian and South American. The minority Asian group
may already be isolated from the rest of the Catholic population. If local
priests work with the Asian population, there is a better chance that the
isolation would lessen than if foreign priests were to take up responsibilities among them. Considine met with Cardinal Fumasoni Biondi in March
1939, and that was the last action of the General Council before December
1941 in relation to Maryknoll taking up mission work in South America.[45]

The German invasion of Poland in September 1939 marked the beginning of the Second World War and occasioned for the Maryknoll Society
General Council a process of reflection in regard to missions in Africa. Up
to this point, Maryknoll Society missions were concentrated in East Asia,
along with a handful of works among Asian immigrant groups in Hawaii
and the United States. From his work at Propaganda Fide in Rome and his
mission study tour in 1931–1933, Considine had a great interest in Africa.
The Council of Maryknoll superior general Bishop James E. Walsh was
indeed interested in opening a mission in Africa as soon as sufficient personnel were to become available.

The Council began work on a policy that would guide Maryknoll as it
sought a new mission in Africa. In 1939, it was clear that another five years
or more would be needed to be able to commit to a new mission in Africa
while maintaining current levels of missionary staffing in East Asia. However, the outbreak of hostilities in Europe became the occasion for reflection on a different, more limited African mission plan. Although Maryknoll
could not yet commit to staffing a full mission in Africa, it could instead
volunteer to send Maryknoll priests to existing missions where, because
of the new European war, the missionary personnel of one country had
been detained or expelled by the colonial authorities of another country.
Maryknoll would also use the occasion to state to the SCPF its interest
in an eventual mission in Africa and to talk about the criteria the Society
would employ in the search for an African mission field.

The policy developed in the fall of 1939 had two distinctive features—
the desire to break the popular image of Maryknoll as a mission society at

44. General Council Minutes, February 17, 1939.
45. CD, March 27, 1939.

work only in East Asia, and the innovation of receiving African American men as candidates for the priesthood in Maryknoll on an equal basis with white candidates. The Council believed that receiving African American candidates into Maryknoll might stimulate other Catholic religious groups "to greater effort for the conversion of the Negro population of our own country."[46]

In July 1939, Fr. William O'Shea was appointed vicar apostolic of Pyongyang, Korea, and he was invited to be one of twelve men consecrated bishop by the pope in Rome in October of the same year. The Council decided to send Fr. Thomas Kiernan with O'Shea to Rome to open a conversation with Propaganda Fide about Maryknoll taking up mission work in Africa. When Kiernan met with Cardinal Fumasoni Biondi, the cardinal suggested that Maryknoll work in northern Nigeria.

The suggestion that Maryknoll consider a mission in northern Nigeria in late 1939 and early 1940 was unexpected, but it allowed the Society an opportunity to make its situation better known to the SCPF. Considine typed up the diary notes from his visits to northern Nigeria in December 1932 and January 1933 and circulated them to his colleagues on the Council. He even furnished them with a copy of the hand-drawn map he had made of the area.

In the end, there was no urgency of acting on the SCPF suggestion of northern Nigeria; Maryknoll had already stated that for the next five years the Society would not be ready to accept the full responsibility of building up a new mission territory. But since the suggestion was made by the Propaganda Fide, Maryknoll would have Fr. Frederick Dietz, its procurator general in Rome, carry on further conversations with Propaganda Fide prefect Cardinal Fumasoni Biondi in the spring of 1940. The Council met again and developed a refinement of the policy on accepting a mission in Africa.

The subsequent iteration of the policy had three distinctive features: it cited the ignorance of U.S. Catholics in regard to Africa as a reason why Maryknoll should preferentially be given an area in the "belt of conversions" in Sub-Saharan Africa, so that Maryknoll's first mission on the continent could have a reasonable opportunity to be successful. The "conversion belt" comprised areas where strong responses to Catholic mission efforts were taking place, roughly south of the 14th parallel in the northern hemisphere and north of the Tropic of Capricorn. At that time, these areas were also characterized by a relatively weak Muslim presence. Once Maryknoll had had some success in both the actual mission work in Africa and in

---

46. General Council Minutes, October 31, 1939. MMA, Council Meetings Minutes 1937–1944, Box 4, Folder 2, pp. 686–87.

educating U.S. Catholics on the church of that continent, then Maryknoll would be in a position to accept other, more difficult mission areas in Africa. The second feature was a certain insistence on the Lake Victoria area of Tanganyika. Such insistence, communicated ever so diplomatically, was meant to put the SCPF on notice of Maryknoll's desire to be in line for a mission territory there whenever one should open up. The third distinctive feature was a moving up of the start date for a Maryknoll mission in Africa; the document mentions being able to make a modest beginning with the assignment of four priests in the summer of 1941. While such numbers would be truly modest for a large mission territory (such as the one suggested by SCPF in northern Nigeria), the moving up of the date was most likely a signal to the SCPF that Maryknoll was serious about going to work in Africa.

There was also an interesting subtext in this policy—it notes an anticipated reticence among some Maryknoll missioners about accepting a mission in Africa while so much work remains undone in the existing Maryknoll missions in East Asia. The policy notes that these men will have to be reminded that growth in those areas "must come slowly if it is to be solid."[47] Why was this mentioned at that particular time? Joseph P. Carney has suggested that Maryknoll may have been trying diplomatically to remind the SCPF that the Society had been a good sport in accepting and remaining faithful to missions in China that were considered "barren" in terms of the prospects of making large amounts of converts to Catholicism.[48]

Something not mentioned in the 1939 and 1940 policy memos on Africa was Considine's desire that Maryknoll begin its work in Africa under the tutelage of an established missionary group on the continent. This would provide the Maryknollers who had no experience of Africa with an apprenticeship in mission methods adequate for the African context. But this would be a delicate negotiating point with the SCPF—it might easily be seen as a desire to take over successful mission efforts begun by other groups rather than building one's own mission enterprise in Africa from the ground up.[49]

Nothing further happened in 1940 in regard to Maryknoll being assigned by the SCPF to a mission territory in Africa; the suggestion that

---

47. John Considine, "Council policy regarding a Mission in Africa," Confidential Memorandum, March 7, 1940. MMA, General Council Meeting Minutes, 4:2.

48. Joseph P. Carney, "The History of the Functional Structure of the Maryknoll Mission in Musoma and Shinyanga, Tanzania" (Ph.D. dissertation, St. John's University, New York, 1973), 79.

49. Thomas Kiernan, Rome, to James E. Walsh, Ossining, NY, December 15, 1939. MMA, Rome House Correspondence, 4:6.

Maryknoll take a mission in northern Nigeria was successfully deflected. In March 1940, word came from Fr. Dietz that the Lyons African Mission Society would turn over the northern Nigeria territory in question to another unit of their own society.[50] However, the groundwork had been laid for a strong policy on how to begin Maryknoll missions in Africa, and the policy was implemented when Maryknoll did assume responsibility for its first missions in Africa in 1946.

Thus, even though none of these four opportunities panned out, the consideration of each brought the leadership of the Maryknoll Society two types of experience in mission strategizing: (1) the assessment of their own resources, the needs of the church, and the actual evangelization possibilities of a proposed mission context, and (2) seeking the input of church mission authorities on such an assessment and then effectively negotiating with those same authorities an implementation of the chosen mission strategy. In both kinds of experiences in the years 1936–1940, Fr. Considine's input played an important role as the General Council considered these four opportunities.

1942—Mission to Latin America

At present it looks as if our missions [in Latin America] will within the next four or five years form a second unit of action very similar to the missions of the Far East. Of course from the point of view of pagan souls, they are in no way comparable in importance.

—John J. Considine to Cardinal Fumasoni Biondi, June 5, 1942[51]

The event that is taking place today reflects not only our policy but that of the Holy See. We could not send our missioners to Bolivia without the commission of the Holy Father, and it is due to his act in assigning this mission territory to Maryknoll that our priests are proceeding to take up this work at this time. A foreign mission society may be defined as an army that is trained and held in readiness to answer the calls of the Holy See. . . .

—Bishop James Edward Walsh, M.M.,
Departure Day Talk, September 6, 1942[52]

---

50. Thomas Kiernan, Ossining, NY, to James E. Walsh, March 4, 1940. MMA, Superior General Papers (Correspondence) 1920–1989, 3:4.

51. John J. Considine, Ossining, NY, to Cardinal Pietro Fumasoni Biondi, Rome, June 5, 1942. MMA, General Council-Sacred Congregation for the Propagation of the Faith, Box 2, Folder 2 (1940–1945).

52. MMA, Superior General Papers 1920–1989, Box 1, Folder 4.

It is abundantly clear that the Catholic Foreign Mission Society of America before 1942 had defined the mission vocation of its members as concerned almost exclusively with what was then known as "conversion work"[53]—proclaiming Jesus Christ to those who do not know or accept him and helping new converts to Christianity to develop their faith within the structures of the Catholic Church. On that September day of 1942, Bishop Walsh presided over a departure of missioners to Bolivia, a country nestled in the heart of a continent that was predominantly Catholic. How did the new definition of mission he proposed that day come about?

Though in other parts of his talk Bishop Walsh mentioned World War II, he avoided numbering the bombing of Pearl Harbor among the reasons stated for sending new missioners to Latin America. There is no doubt, however, that the U.S. entrance into the conflict had created a restricted field of action for Maryknoll. Because of the war, the work in East Asia and the Pacific would be shut down in some areas or carried on with great difficulty in others, and with transatlantic travel unsafe, the planning for a new mission in Africa had to be put on hold. What is clear is that the plan to send missioners to Latin America was developed very quickly—in less than a month. Here is the chronology of this decision.

Pearl Harbor was attacked by the Japanese on December 7, 1941, and the United States entered World War II the following day. Two very critical issues occupied the attention of the Maryknoll Society's General Council, which met three times before Christmas: how to ascertain the whereabouts of and offer assistance to Maryknoll missioners in East Asia and the Pacific, and where to assign personnel in the coming months.[54] On December 9, 1941, the Council discussed the cutting off of communications with missions that had occurred in East Asia due to the U.S. entrance into the war,[55] and the topic of Maryknollers serving as military chaplains was tabled. On December 15, the Council met again to discuss the conditions for mission since the U.S. entrance into the war. On December 22, the Council met again and proposed that new missions be opened in Brazil and Chile.

On December 23, Bishop James E. Walsh sent a letter to Archbishop Cicognani, apostolic delegate to the United States, requesting an appoint-

---

53. The Maryknoll missions in the Philippines and Hawaii, both of which were small in 1942, were the exceptions. Nonetheless, the work in Hawaii also included efforts to evangelize non-Christian Asians, and there was at times a focus on working among the Chinese in the Philippines.

54. John Considine, "Some Points on Our Changed Mission Situation," Memo, January 10, 1942. MMA, Superior General Papers 1920–1989, Box 3, Folder 4.

55. The Council cabled Rome to ask the Holy See to help ascertain the condition of Maryknollers stationed in East Asia.

ment in the near future to discuss new missions in Brazil or Chile, as "the world wide war has temporarily closed the African and Oriental mission fields to us." He also mentioned the desirability of implementing a new policy that would prohibit Maryknollers from serving as military chaplains, since the foreign missionary vocation is "not to be interfered with by the call for military chaplains." Under normal circumstances, the Maryknoll Society leadership would have communicated directly with Propaganda Fide in Rome, but the war had cut off those channels of communication. It was therefore necessary to ask the apostolic delegate to relay Maryknoll's request to Propaganda.[56]

On January 2, 1942, Bishop Walsh and Fr. Considine met with Archbishop Cicognani in Washington, and in that meeting the decision was made to request that Propaganda Fide assign to Maryknoll a new mission in South America.[57] Only twenty-six days had passed since Pearl Harbor, and new Maryknoll missions were being sought in a new part of the world.

The initial plan was to seek approval from Propaganda Fide in Rome, and then Fr. Considine would travel to Latin America to investigate possible mission areas for Maryknoll.[58] However, on February 11, 1942, the Society was presented with a fait accompli—a letter from Archbishop Cicognani informed Bishop Walsh that Propaganda had assigned to Maryknoll the new apostolic vicariate of the Pando, Bolivia.[59] Considine scrapped his travel plans.

Of the five members of the General Council, only Fr. Drought had been to Latin America before;[60] when they wrote to Archbishop Cicognani, they

56. James Walsh, Ossining, NY, to Amleto Cicognani, Washington, December 23, 1942. MMA, General Council Correspondence with Organizations, Box 17, Folder 9 (USA.D. 1941–1943).

57. Considine's memo of January 10, 1942, "Some Points on Our Changed Mission Situation," revealed that the plan was already set—the Maryknoll Society was seeking an assignment in Latin America from Propaganda and the apostolic delegate was facilitating communication. The rest of the memo simply explored the logistics (how many missioners to assign to Latin America, and where to gain training in Spanish) and the question of how to introduce this new idea to the membership in a way that would avoid injury to morale. At the meeting, Archbishop Cicognani suggested that the Maryknollers seek a mission field in Brazil, so as to avoid giving the impression of being part of the U.S. Government's Good Neighbor Policy with Spanish-speaking countries (James E. Walsh, Memo, January 5, 1942. MMA, General Council Correspondence with Organizations, Box 17, Folder 9 [USA.D. 1941–1943]).

58. James E. Walsh, Memo, January 5, 1942. MMA, General Council Correspondence with Organizations, Box 17, Folder 9 (USA.D. 1941–1943).

59. Amleto Cicognani, Washington, to James E. Walsh, Ossining, NY, February 11, 1942. MMA, General Council Correspondence with Organizations, Box 17, Folder 9 (USA.D. 1941–1943).

60. As treasurer, Fr. Drought had traveled to Venezuela and Brazil to conduct business

used the French spelling of a country name as they sought "a field situated in Central Chili or Southern Brazil."[61] Maryknoll was entering a totally new area of the world.

These events unfolded rapidly, and there is no evidence in the record that Maryknoll's missiology could keep pace during the month in which the decision to open missions in Latin America was made. In early January 1942, the strongest reason for accepting missions in Latin America was framed in terms of a personnel concern. Considine estimated that over the following three years there would be sixty new missioners to be placed overseas as soon as they were ordained,[62] and he emphasized the importance of safeguarding the mission vocations of the young Maryknollers through the provision for them of a foreign mission in which to work. However, for Considine, this was indeed a strong reason for accepting new missions, and a missiological one as well. Keeping missioners engaged in activities organized by missioners was clearly a better alternative than having them join the military chaplain corps or work in U.S. dioceses, where, in either case, they could be distracted from the aims of missionary work by pressing pastoral concerns.

In terms of the church's missiology, Propaganda Fide in 1934 had published a definition of mission that included the sort of work that Maryknoll was about to assume in Latin America. The SCPF understood mission as taking place in three different contexts: (1) among non-Christians; (2) among non-Catholic Christians; and (3) among Catholics in those churches where normal parish life was not established or which were not self-sustaining.[63] Mission work among Catholics in Latin America was understood as part of the third context as defined by the SCPF.

Therefore, in 1942 the redefinition of mission that Maryknoll was undertaking was an "in-house" problem, not a theological or missiological problem. The new work in Latin America was clearly understood as mission by Propaganda Fide, but for Maryknoll, prior to 1942, so attached was the group to the idea that their mission work should be exclusively dedicated to the first context, that Considine wrote about introducing this new idea to the membership in a way that would "avoid injury to

there; the Maryknoll Society had invested in businesses in those two countries during the late 1930s.

61. James E. Walsh, Ossining, NY, to Amleto Cicognani, Washington, DC, December 23, 1941. MMA, General Council Correspondence with Organizations, Box 17, Folder 9 (USA.D. 1941–1943).

62. Considine, "Some Points on Our Changed Mission Situation," January 10, 1942.

63. *Guida delle missioni cattoliche* (Rome: Unione Missionaria del Clero in Italia, 1934), 57.

morale."[64] Considine would much later note that even the Society's constitutions seemed to require a narrow interpretation of mission, as the
document described Maryknoll's mission as among "the heathen." Nonetheless, Considine also argued that it was not the intention of those who
drafted the constitutions "to rigidly exclude any accepted interpretation
of the term missions."[65]

In the confused period at the beginning of the war, it is clear that the
concern of keeping Maryknoll missioners in missions and focused on
mission was the first reason offered by the Society General Council for
seeking and accepting missions in Latin America. Later on, other missiological justifications of the work in Latin America would emerge, but in
the beginning the issue was keeping the missioners on task. Moreover, the
idea of keeping missioners focused on their special vocation dovetailed
with another personnel concern, that of finding an "outlet" for men who
cannot adjust well to service in a foreign mission.[66] For example, one plan
under consideration as the work in Latin America began was to accept an
invitation to work among the Mexican American Catholic population in
the Texas Diocese of Corpus Christi. Considine suggested that the work in
Corpus Christi would serve as "a training ground for work among Latins
and eventually as a 'cushion' for men going to South America and elsewhere who do not make good."[67] That plan was never implemented, but
the idea of an "outlet" was one that the Council had been working on for
some time;[68] possible "outlets" under consideration were the development
of Maryknoll works among the following groups in the forty-eight states

64. Considine, "Some Points on Our Changed Mission Situation," January 10, 1942.

65. Lima Methods Conference of the Maryknoll Fathers, *Proceedings of the Lima Methods Conference of the Maryknoll Fathers, Maryknoll House, Lima, Peru, August 23–28, 1954* (Maryknoll, NY: Maryknoll Fathers, 1955), 236–37.

66. This concept was also referred to as "a 'farm' for less successful members" (John J. Considine, "Considerations on a Maryknoll Mission among Mexicans," Memo, November 2, 1941. MMA, General Council Reports and Memos 1936–1983, 1:4).

67. Considine, "Some Points on Our Changed Mission Situation," January 10, 1942.

68. Considine first wrote to Maryknoll co-founder Fr. James A. Walsh on this topic in 1932 in regard to the Philippines as an outlet for those Maryknollers who could not adapt to mission life in South China. (John J. Considine, aboard SS. Kenya Bombay-Mombasa, Confidential Memo to General Council, Ossining, NY, October 14, 1932. MMA, Rome House, Box 3, Folder 3.) The theme had been thoroughly negotiated by Superior General James E. Walsh and his Council with the SCPF in regard to the Philippines and Hawaii during 1937–1939 (James E. Walsh, Rome, to James Drought, Ossining, NY, September 14, 1938. MMA, Superior General Papers [Correspondence], 1920–1983, 3:2). Considine's memo of November 2, 1941, carried the further consideration of an outlet within the forty-eight United States.

and Hawaii: Chinese, Japanese, Mexicans, and white Catholics in parishes that are not self-supporting.[69]

The search for "outlets" for missioners who were not able to adapt well to foreign missions needs to be understood as a human issue within the overall enterprise of mission. It may be that the public will want to support missioners who are successful in their mission work; Maryknoll publications certainly carried a strong gung-ho mission rhetoric as standard fare during this period.[70] Yet every mission group also knew that the difficulties of cross-cultural mission are such that not everyone can be successful; Considine advocated that the group had an obligation to such members: "placing these men is an integral part of our Society life."[71]

The search for "outlets" is pertinent because it was more than an administrative or personnel question; it became instead a question of the legitimacy of Maryknoll's mission work in Latin America, the Philippines, and Hawaii. The dynamic is as follows: if "outlets" are accepted, then the Maryknoll Society is not being faithful to its original inspiration, which was a preference for the context of doing conversion work with non-Christians and establishing the church in those areas. Accepting "outlets" would also mean that pluriformity within Maryknoll was acceptable—not all Maryknollers would be doing the same things (i.e., conversion work), and were therefore not held accountable in a fair and equal fashion. This sets up the expected discussions among the membership about who the "real" missioners are, with appeal being made to the group's original inspiration as a way to establish legitimacy.[72]

---

69. John J. Considine, "Considerations on Placing Maryknoll Priests Who Cannot Work Overseas," Memo, November 2, 1941. MMA, General Council Reports Memos 1936–1983, 1:4.

70. John Joseph Considine, *When the Sorghum Was High* (New York: Longmans, Green and Co., 1940), 38–39.

71. John J. Considine, "Considerations on a Maryknoll Mission among Mexicans," Memo, November 2, 1941. MMA, General Council Reports Memos 1936–1983, 1:4.

72. There is significant evidence that the decision to accept missions in Latin America for many years drove an uneasiness among the membership over what constituted "real" mission for Maryknollers. Even though the matter was resolved at an official level by the General Council of superior general Bishop James E. Walsh and the decision was subsequently discussed and then ratified by the Third General Chapter in 1946, at the Lima Methods Conference in 1954 the issue was taken up again by delegates from Maryknoll missions in South America. Some of those delegates by that time had worked in Latin America for twelve years, yet the question of the legitimacy of the mission was still very much on their minds (Lima Methods Conference of the Maryknoll Fathers, *Proceedings of the Lima Methods Conference of the Maryknoll Fathers,* 236–37). Fr. Thomas V. Kiernan, who served from 1936 to 1946 on the General Council of Bishop Walsh, commented in a 1982 interview that, outside of the Pando vicariate in Bolivia (a mission territory assigned

If outlets are rejected, the opposite is true. There is no perception of moving away from or otherwise altering the group's original inspiration, and all missioners are called on to do the same things. The difficulties would arise in view of the high bar that is set for missioners—everyone would be expected to move well with the many cross-cultural, linguistic, economic, and climate challenges of missions in rural Asian outposts in the first half of the twentieth century. The fact of the matter was that Maryknoll from very early on experienced what Considine referred to as "wash-outs"—those who just could not adapt to "the hard task in China."[73]

It is important to keep in mind that the "outlets" were not conceived as a place to assign problematic individuals. In a distinction made early on in the discussion of "outlets," Bishop James E. Walsh clarified to Propaganda Fide that Maryknoll did not seek to establish "outlets" in the Philippines as a place for Maryknollers who were unfit for ministry. Walsh was concerned that Propaganda prefect Cardinal Fumasoni Biondi understood an outlet

> as referring only to actual misfits, whereas I carefully explained to him, both by word and in the written memorandum, that the outlet we sought was not for men who were misfits in any essential sense, but only for that class of zealous and worthy priests who were hampered in their mission work by health, temperament, or some other similar disability.[74]

In addition to having personnel that could not adapt well to mission conditions, it was also becoming evident that it was not credible to believe that all Maryknoll missioners were doing the same things or were subject to the same hardships. Geography itself was a factor, as Manchuria, Japan, and Korea (Maryknoll's original "Northern Group" of missions in East Asia) had a different climate from South China. In the popular mind of missioners, the climate differences between the northern and southern group sort of canceled each other out (harsh winters vs. the harshness of the tropics),

---

by Propaganda to Maryknoll), the work in Latin America was supposed to have been temporary, not permanent (Thomas Kiernan, interview by Laurence Murphy, December 1982, Maryknoll Society Oral History Project, Ossining, NY, p. 25).

73. The shorthand on why some were washing out was "for whatever reason," but clearly the reasons were several: some required "a place in the field to save their honor when they prove failures at the hard task in China," indicating difficulties with language learning and cultural adaptation, and with the climate and physical conditions of rural South China; some suffered from health problems, behavioral problems, and disaffection from Maryknoll or from mission (John Considine, "Confidential Memo," October 14, 1932. MMA, Rome House Correspondence, 3:3).

74. James E. Walsh, Rome, to James Drought, Ossining, NY, September 14, 1938. MMA, Superior General Papers (Correspondence), 1920–1983, 3:2.

but the reality was that it could not be expected that such equations would exist anywhere the church needed to call on Maryknoll missioners.

Whether considered in terms of a search for "outlets" for personnel or in terms of opening missions in Catholic Latin America, Considine was not only aware that these moves would require an adjustment to Maryknoll's definition of mission as only to the nonbaptized, but something he welcomed and advocated for. Even in 1931, as Considine reflected on taking his first mission study tour, he included Africa in his study plan even though he knew that Maryknoll co-founder Fr. James A. Walsh "had no interests there."[75] It was an instance in which Considine knew what the recognized authority in his own Society wanted—or did not want, in this case—yet he knew that missions in Africa were crucial for the future of the church, so he pressed ahead with his plan. Similarly, we have already noted how Considine persuasively argued at the 1954 Lima Methods Conference that the framers of Maryknoll's constitutions were not trying to uphold a rigid interpretation of mission as being only to the nonbeliever. In these ways, Considine pushed for the ideas he believed to be most important for the church's worldwide mission.

It is also clear that he could recognize when the time was right for such initiatives; these were certainly not initiatives that Considine somehow rammed through an approval process, simply by force of personality. What the record from superior general Bishop James E. Walsh's tenure of 1936–1946 shows is that the Council sought consensus among themselves and among the membership of the Society as they established missions in Latin America and sought outlets for Maryknoll Society personnel, and in that way they assisted the group to own a new definition of the group's purpose.

Even with all that, the Third General Chapter in 1946 proved to be a moment when the Chapter delegates at least initially pushed back on the opening of missions in Latin America and formed a committee within the Chapter to scrutinize the decisions of Bishop Walsh on the matter. However, it is to the credit of all concerned that, while the committee was not satisfied with the nuance of the process of opening the Latin American missions, the Chapter called for no changes of direction in regard to Maryknoll missions in Latin America, and in fact the work of the Society in that region of the world continued to grow under the leadership of Bishop Raymond Lane, who was elected by the Third General Chapter to succeed Bishop Walsh as superior general.

The Third General Chapter became one more moment in which Considine was able to build consensus on issues like the Latin American missions. As has been noted, it did not settle the issue for everyone once and

75. CD, August 26, 1931.

for all, but the Chapter was nonetheless another moment of building a con-sciousness of how the universal church was looking at mission. By accept-ing missions in the Philippines, Hawaii, Latin America, and subsequently in East Africa, the Society implemented a de facto policy of accepting wide differences in mission conditions, more or less eliminating the need for "outlets" run by Maryknoll in the forty-eight contiguous United States. A tacit acceptance of the development of the group's understanding of the original vision to include Propaganda's third category of mission took place. This development allowed for the expansion of the original mission inspiration of the Society based on what had been learned in the actual conditions of mission.

The chronology of events notwithstanding, I am not suggesting that Maryknoll's decision to go to Latin America in 1942 was bereft of a mis-siological basis. What was going on was that the circumstances in which the Society carried out its mission work changed so dramatically in such a short period of time following the attack on Pearl Harbor that the Society's leadership had to make decisions very quickly and let the missiology come later. This produced a situation in which missiology was done on one's feet—the Maryknoll Society was an example of a mission group of the church that sought to be faithful to the gospel in extremely difficult cir-cumstances. And when that group needed a nimble missiology in the midst of such dire circumstances, two voices were available that could point to the church's mission tradition and a careful analysis of the human situations of mission: Fr. Considine and Fr. James Drought.

Prior to December 1941, Considine was plainly not focused on Latin America as a mission possibility for Maryknoll. Had he understood Latin America as an important part of the Maryknoll mission strategy, surely he would have said so when the Lima and Brazil initiatives from Propa-ganda Fide were entertained in 1938 and 1939. Fr. Considine's preference for a new mission field outside Asia was Africa; we have already seen his efforts in the years 1939–1940 to develop criteria for the Society to use in eventually accepting a mission territory in Africa. It therefore seems that Pearl Harbor occasioned a significant change of policy for Considine, but once he had made the shift, he was in all the way. Just as prior to the war he had helped shape the ideas around an outlet for Maryknoll missioners who cannot work overseas, in the immediate aftermath of Pearl Harbor, Fr. Considine played a significant role in the elaboration of a missiology for Maryknoll in Latin America, leading to the new definition of mission pro-nounced by Bishop Walsh at the departure ceremony in September 1942. Considine was tapped by Bishop James E. Walsh to accompany him to meet with Archbishop Cicognani on January 2, 1942, and was the author of the memo of January 10, 1942, "Some Points on Our Changed Mission

Situation," which laid the framework for the next steps in the process of accepting missions in Latin America. In 1945, Considine would make a mission study tour of Latin America, and when he returned from that trip he proposed a ten-year Maryknoll personnel plan for the region and published his first volume on the church in Latin America, *Call for Forty Thousand*. Especially after the death of Fr. Drought in 1943, Considine became the Maryknoll "go-to" man on Latin America.

Maryknoll vicar general Fr. James M. Drought also played a significant role in Maryknoll's move to Latin America. In a memo in August 1942, he urged superior general Bishop James E. Walsh to approach work in Latin America wholeheartedly, not just sending missioners to territories assigned by the Holy See. In the spring of 1942, Bishop James E. Walsh traveled to more than ten countries in Latin America, and Drought excitedly described the importance of the trip:

> [The] Superior General has served practically, though not by official designation, as the legate of a new policy of the Holy See. He has visited the Papal Nuncios and Delegates, and many of the Bishops in Mexico, Guatemala, Panama, Colombia, Ecuador, Peru, Bolivia, Chile, Brazil, Uruguay, Argentina. I think it would be perfectly correct to say, and it is remarkable, that our Superior General has been the first ecclesiastic in the history of the hemisphere to go to these countries, not as a visitor, not even as an ambassador of good-will, but as the founder to inaugurate the missionary cooperation of the Catholic United States with the Latin Americas. [76]

It is important to keep in mind, however, that several U.S. mission groups had preceded Maryknoll to Latin America, and one by nearly fifty years.[77] Considine's *Call for Forty Thousand* (1946) included in-depth reports on missions run by U.S. church personnel in Latin America, most of whom began work in Latin America prior to Maryknoll.[78]

---

76. James M. Drought, Ossining, NY, to Reverend and Dear Father, August 8, 1942 (p. 3). MMA, SG Papers 1920–1989, Box 1, Folder 8 (Letters to All, 1939–1968).

77. The New England Jesuits began work in Jamaica in 1894 (Considine, *Call for Forty Thousand*, 251).

78. *Call for Forty Thousand* (pp. 305–6) offers a table on U.S. missioners in Latin America at the time, and in the text of that volume some information on these other groups can be found: Haiti—New England Oblates of Mary Immaculate (n.d., but presumably before 1940 [*Call for Forty Thousand*, 235]); Manaus, Brazil—St. Louis (now Denver Province) Redemptorists (n.d., but presumably before 1944 [p. 22]; Jamaica—New England Jesuits (1894 [p. 251]). OTHERS: the Immaculate Heart Sisters of Pennsylvania, who founded a school in Lima in 1923 (http://www.ihm.com.pe); the Marianists arrived in Peru in 1939 (http://perlegrino.marianistas.org/historia-marianistas-peru/); and the Redemptorists

As will begin to become clearer at the 1946 Society Chapter (and in *Call for Forty Thousand*, and at the Lima Methods Conference), a new definition of missioners would be put forward by Considine and James E. Walsh, that of a force or corps available for the urgencies designated by the church. Considine would not hesitate to tie the work in Latin America to the more "traditional" conversion work among nonbelievers, as the idea was that building up the church in any place enabled the church to be stronger and so able to send out missioners to those who did not know Christ or his church.[79] On a more specific plane, Considine, like Drought, would hook the Maryknoll initiatives in Latin America to the Holy See's concerns for building up the church in the region, something that would get strong official backing with the foundation of the Pontifical Commission for Latin America (CAL) in Rome in 1958.

1946—Mission to Africa

After all the deliberations during 1939–1940 on the subject of Maryknoll opening a mission in Africa, the story of the actual assignment to Maryknoll in 1946 of the Musoma section of the apostolic vicariate of Mwanza, Tanganyika, is relatively brief. In early 1946, Propaganda Fide informed Maryknoll that Musoma, Tanganyika, was available and inquired if Maryknoll still wanted a mission in that area. The Society promptly answered in the affirmative. The offer included an apprenticeship of several years with the White Fathers, an arrangement Considine had deeply desired. Carney's history of Maryknoll in Tanzania notes that the Society's work in East Africa had been successful, and that that success could be linked to the policy that Considine, together with the General Council, wrote in 1939 and revised in 1940.

On the Home Front

Among significant personal events during these years, there was a singular family reunion in 1935. Shortly after Considine's close friend Francis Ford was consecrated bishop in 1935, the two friends traveled to New Bedford to celebrate Alice Considine's sixty-fifth birthday. A Solemn High Mass was offered by the three priests among the Considine brothers—John, Ray, and Arthur—along with Bishop Ford and the local pastor.[80] It was also the

---

(Baltimore Province): Puerto Rico (1902), Campo Grande, Brazil (1929), and Paraguay (1935) (http://www.redemptorists.net/our-history.cfm).

79. John Considine, Washington, to Edward McGurkin, Ossining, NY, January 9, 1968. MMA, Considine Papers, 3:2.

80. "Three Sons Honor Mrs. Considine by Singing Birthday High Mass," *New Bedford Standard-Times*, September 30, 1935, p. 1.

first time all the Considine brothers were together since John Considine returned from Rome in December 1934. Although John Considine had visited New Bedford since his return from Rome, his brother Ray had spent the 1934–1935 academic year in Rome studying missiology and had only recently returned prior to their mother's birthday.

Considine's mother died at the end of July 1941; she was seventy at the time of her death. John Considine joined his five brothers and their families at funeral services in New Bedford. However, during the years that Considine served on the Maryknoll General Council, he did not go home to New Bedford for holidays; often it was the case that his diary for Thanksgiving Day or Christmas recorded a day of quiet work at the office. Why was he absent from significant moments of family celebration? No evidence of conflict in the family at this time has been found; not going home for holidays may have been part of duty within Maryknoll—Maryknollers were encouraged to think of Maryknoll as their family.

After Alice's death, the house at 46 Pearl Street in New Bedford passed to Considine's brother Frank and his growing family; it stayed in his family until 2002.

On the Road Again

At the end of June 1945, John Considine found himself on an unexpected three-day layover in Miami. He was headed south to Panama and then on to Chile, the first legs of what would be a seven-month mission study tour of Latin America. After twelve years, Considine was on the road again to visit Catholic missions.

Miami was apparently not a bad place to be stuck waiting for a seat on a flight south. He stayed at a local hotel, studied Spanish at the local Berlitz School, visited Miami Beach, and celebrated Mass daily at a local church. Then in the wee hours of Sunday, June 24, he boarded a Pan American flight for Balboa, Panama.

The diary entry from his first day in Panama spoke of the purpose of his journey:

> Began the main theme of my journey by discussion all day on get-
> ting the faith to the people here, with strong emphasis on the need
> of a true Catholic social philosophy as basis for all solid development.
> Archdiocese of Panama has 40 priests for 600,000.

These were the two main themes on Latin America that Considine would work on for the rest of his life—how to share Catholic social thinking in a way that will improve the faith life of Latin American Catholics, and the unfavorable priest-to-Catholic-faithful ratio that he would encounter in nearly every Latin American context of his visits.

The latter point—the unfavorable priest-to-Catholic-faithful ratio in Latin America—came home to Considine during the first weeks of his journey and led to the title of the book he would write on the study tour, *Call for Forty Thousand*. Considine was visiting Bishop Manuel Larraín in the Diocese of Talca, Chile, when he suddenly put two and two together to come up with a way to understand the clergy shortage in Latin America. The "call for forty thousand" referred to a need for forty thousand more priests to care for the Catholic population of Latin America at that time.

> I began working up more figures. "If we allow not one thousand but two thousand souls for each priest, the present clergy could care for something like forty-five million. Non-Catholics in Latin America, then, probably number from five to ten million. Subtracting these from the main body, which numbers one hundred and forty million, it would appear that eighty million Catholics in Latin America are living today without adequate priestly care."
>
> I stopped for a moment, amazed at my own figures, appalled by what they indicated. "Were these Catholics to be supplied with priests at the rate of one per two thousand souls, the Latin American world would need forty thousand new priests!"[81]

Numerical formulations were a rhetorical device that Considine enjoyed. The whole calculation of the problem gave him a story to tell about a large and important issue in the church—how to strengthen a Latin American church that had been reeling in most of the republics since the early nineteenth century independence period. It was a problem that Considine quickly judged deserving of his attention—if the 130 million Catholics of Latin America were to assume their rightful roles in the church, the forces for mission and for a full living of Catholic faith in the world would be greatly improved.

Considine noted that under recent popes, the church's teaching was forward-looking; priests were to be the progressive champions of the poor, upholders of human dignity, proponents of the equality of all peoples.[82] As Considine saw it, these characteristics gave the church a real advantage with the people of Latin America.

> If the Church can only find a minimum of priestly leaders to make her social philosophy known and felt in Latin America, she would carry the continent by storm even in the field of social action. For the Latin American finds something inherently commendable in being

---

81. Considine, *Call for Forty Thousand*, 9–10.
82. Ibid., 112.

rebelde. Almost every political party he forms contains the adjective "revolutionary."[83]

While this was something of an oversimplification, we will see that nearly ten years later on his next mission study tour in Latin America, and certainly during his years at the Latin America Bureau (1960–1968), the idea of the church playing a key part in Latin American social revolutions was one that consistently appealed to Considine.

Conclusion

At the Third General Chapter in 1946, Considine served on two committees: the Committee on Business concerning the Maryknoll Sisters, and the Committee on the Mexican Seminary. The former committee produced a new agreement to be proposed to the Maryknoll Sisters' leadership, and once again the conciliatory tone of the 1938 agreement was heard. Their motion for a new agreement was approved by the Chapter. The Mexican Seminary Committee was appointed to study a proposal from the Mexican hierarchy that Maryknoll assist them to establish a Mexican Foreign Mission Seminary. For Considine, it represented the wave of the future—U.S. missioners could assist to build up the church in Latin America so that that local church could take up its own responsibilities in the church's worldwide mission. On his most recent trip to Latin America, Considine had met personally in Mexico City with Archbishop Márquez of Puebla, who was also president of the Mexican Missionary Union of the Clergy, to discuss the proposal.

The proposal to offer personnel assistance for a period of years to the initiative was adopted by the Chapter, and a few years later the Instituto Santa María de Guadalupe para las Misiones Extranjeras, popularly known as the Misioneros Guadalupanos, was established. Today their members are at work in Asia, Africa, Latin America, and also in the United States.

It was a formative time for the still-young Maryknoll Society, a time in which the seeds of future commitments to Latin America and Africa were sown, and a time in which the new leadership attempted to carry on in the tradition of the founders, even as it adapted to new conditions.

---

83. Ibid.

CHAPTER 8

Teaching and Organizing for Mission 1946–1960

THE THIRD GENERAL Chapter in 1946 not only reviewed the previous ten years of the Maryknoll Society's work, it also elected leadership. The prospect of Bishop James E. Walsh not being reelected superior general initially came as a complete surprise to Considine, though he quickly adjusted to this new political reality within the group. Evidently, he had expected the group to vote for continuity as it had at the previous two chapters.

> Keller tells me Lane seems choice for new General. Aside from rather bizarre shifting from one General to another, this would be O.K.[1]
>
> Bishop Lane postulated on the 2nd ballot; 24 votes. . . . Bishop Walsh seemed a bit puzzled and possibly dismayed that he received so small a vote. The main group is set on having a complete new Council, all missioners.[2]

With this changing of the guard, Considine actually did not find himself out of a job. He was no longer on the General Council, which meant that personnel and administrative matters over the range of the Society's world-wide missionary operations were no longer part of his responsibility. But the new Council moved to keep him and fellow former Council member Fr. Charles McCarthy in place in the Promotion Department. This was certainly a vote of confidence—over the previous ten years, Considine and McCarthy had worked hard to develop a successful fundraising and public relations apparatus for Maryknoll. Nobody wanted to upset the goose that was laying golden eggs.

---

1. CD, July 31, 1946.
2. CD, August 5, 1946.

It was also a sign of an increased institutionalization as the Maryknoll Society grew. Prior to the death of Maryknoll co-founder Bishop James A. Walsh, Council members were also heads of various departments, such as Treasury and Promotion, and James A. Walsh himself served as both superior general and editor of *The Field Afar*. In those times, decisions on editorial content for each issue were discussed by the General Council. His successor, Bishop James E. Walsh, delegated that work to a committee, and now the work would be delegated on an ongoing basis to the Promotion Department—in reality, the work began to fall more and more to the magazine's editor, Considine, rather than to the committee.

There was therefore no indication that Considine took this moment as his chance to finally take an overseas assignment in a Maryknoll mission. His former colleagues—Bishop James E. Walsh and Frs. Tom Kiernan and Tom Malone—soon took their leave of the Maryknoll headquarters and returned to China, but the coming years for Considine were to have the opposite effect on him—his service to mission would become more closely bound up with U.S.-based support work for foreign missions and would include research, writing, speaking, and teaching.

This chapter has two parts. In the first part I will tell the story of how Considine was being recruited for high ecclesiastical office, a prospect he ultimately resisted, and then I follow a roughly chronological orientation of his several new initiatives and collaborative efforts aimed at intensifying the U.S. Catholic mission effort. I then backtrack a few years in the second part in order to review Considine's writings from 1942 to 1962. These were the years in which Considine produced some of his strongest statements on Christian mission and the unity of the human race, in addition to the theme of using sound Catholic theology to confront racial prejudice in a systematic way.

PART I: VATICAN INSIDER AND U.S. MISSION INNOVATOR

Considered for High Office in the Vatican Diplomatic Service

As was discussed in chapter 5, there is very little data available on Considine's feelings about his own prospects for high office in the church. But what seems clear is that in 1947 he was considered to become the apostolic delegate in one of three East Asian countries—China, Indochina, and Japan—and again in 1953 he was considered to become an apostolic delegate in Africa.

The story emerges from a 1953 letter from Archbishop David Mathew, apostolic delegate in East Africa, to Maryknoll superior general Bishop Raymond Lane. After Considine visited Mathew in Mombasa, Kenya, in early 1953 during the Africa leg of that year's mission study tour, the archbishop was genuinely impressed with Considine's knowledge of Africa and African mission concerns. Archbishop Mathew wrote to Bishop Lane:

> I have just received a visit from Father Considine and have been much impressed by his penetrating comments on the problems of the mission field. . . . I have proposed to Rome that this Apostolic Delegation should be divided. I feel that the political developments in the Gold Coast and Nigeria require a resident representative of the Holy See and I favor the nomination of an American since these countries look to the United States for financial and technical assistance. I have mentioned among other possibilities the name of Father Considine for this post in letters to Propaganda and the Secretariat of State. I have also suggested that if Rome is not prepared to divide the delegation at present, Father Considine might be considered among other candidates for Mombasa.[3]

That summer, Bishop Lane wrote to the prefect of Propaganda, Cardinal Fumasoni Biondi, asking for his assistance to take Considine out of consideration for an apostolic delegation in Africa. While admitting his pleasure that Fr. Considine's qualifications for such a post had been recognized, Lane began the letter by saying that he, Lane, had been "considerably alarmed" by this possibility. The letter goes on to state that, since the death of Maryknoll co-founder James A. Walsh in 1936, "Father Considine has done more . . . to educate Catholics to the mission idea than any other priest in America." Lane made the case that Africa's gain would be the universal church's loss by limiting Fr. Considine's scope of action to a single geographic area.[4]

Lane then spoke of Fr. Considine himself not being disposed to accept higher office and noted that this has not been the first time that Considine was considered for a Vatican posting:

> I know that Father Considine is quite happy in his present duties and would be greatly disappointed in any limitation of his scope. Your Eminence will recall that some six years ago a similar proposal was being considered by the Sacred Congregation of the Propaganda. When this was broached to Father Considine he was considerably upset and very definitely declared that he preferred to continue his

---

3. David Mathew, Mombasa, Kenya Colony, to Raymond Lane, Ossining, NY, March 20, 1953. MMA, Considine Papers, 2:4.

4. Raymond Lane, Ossining, NY, to Pietro Fumasoni Biondi, Rome, July 14, 1953. MMA, MFBA GC SCPF, 2:4 (Folder: MFBA GC SCPF 1949–1956).

present capacity, which he considered of more far-reaching importance to the missions as a whole.[5]

Considine's diary for the same day records his response to the news; the
response offers some clues to the offices for which he was considered in
1947:

Bishop Lane told me today that Arch. Mathew has written twice
explaining his plan to propose me as his successor. This adds a fourth
to China, Japan and Indochina. Council has instructed [Maryknoll
procurator general Fr. Fred] Heinzmann to see that Fumasoni leave
me on the job here.[6]

Did Lane correctly represent Considine's feelings on being considered
for high office? While Bishop Lane's letter does not exclude the interpretation that he, Lane, took these measures against Fr. Considine's desires, the
fact that the diaries contain no other reference to these incidents[7] and
that Considine's single entry on the subject contains no sense of disappointment would seem to support the contention that Lane had in fact
described Considine's sentiments accurately to Cardinal Fumasoni Biondi.

While serving as vicar general of Maryknoll from 1943 to 1946, Considine temporarily assumed the title of Monsignor. He was in fact made
a Monsignor by papal appointment on April 14, 1961, though this event
passes without remark in Considine's diaries. Was it just a formality to be
carried out before he could be named a consultor to Propaganda Fide in
1963? No written record has been found from any time after his official
appointment as a Monsignor in which he called himself by that title or
others used it to address him. He remained simply Fr. Considine. At the
very least, Considine's lack of interest when he was made a Monsignor
indicated an attitude that would seem consistent with the similar lack of
interest displayed in his 1953 diary at the prospect of being considered for
appointment as an apostolic delegate. Considine's mature view of his role
in the church did not include promotion to high office in the church.

One more set of clues on how Considine himself viewed the prospect
of higher office came to light when he was in Rome for the Second World

5. Ibid.

6. CD, July 14, 1953.

7. While no reference to Considine's being considered for higher office can be found
in his diaries for 1947, the fact that his diary entry of July 14, 1953, expands on Lane's
account of his being considered in 1947 by Propaganda for similar high office leads to the
reasonable assumption that he was aware that Propaganda was considering him in 1947 for
such a promotion but that he chose not to write about it in his diary.

Congress for the Apostolate of the Laity in October 1957. His diary records that Msgr. (later Bishop) Baldelli made the proposal that Considine stay in Rome to become the secretary general of the International Conference of Catholic Charities, but Considine simply explained that he was already busy and committed ("impegnato").[8]

A few days later Considine visited with a missiologist colleague, Fr. Johannes Dindinger, O.M.I., at the Generalate of the Oblates of Mary Immaculate. Fr. Dindinger and Considine commenced to discuss the state of mission, and agreed that "adaptation"—the adaptation of the church's life and practice to particular sets of cultural circumstances—was at the time very weak, and attributed this situation to an ignorance on the part of missioners of what Propaganda has consistently taught for centuries on the subject.[9] Their discussion on mission prompted Considine to make a diary entry that sharply evaluated the performance of Propaganda Cardinal Prefect Fumasoni Biondi.

> Dindinger tells me that Costantini[10] has written his memoirs but they are not to be published till he dies. Costantini was evidently guided by [Dindinger], if [Dindinger] has it properly sized up. Costantini has refused to buck Fumasoni but does not agree with [Fumasoni's] laissez aller ways. Fumasoni's satisfaction comes from having lived to be the second in line to hold his post over 25 years, hardly a great achievement in view of the absence of thinking that his regime has represented.[11]

Did this pessimistic view of the leadership of Propaganda influence Considine's desires not to work again in Rome or in some other part of the Vatican bureaucracy? The question brings to mind Considine's dashed hopes for an expansion of Fides Service in the early 1930s. At that time, returning to Maryknoll headquarters in the United States after ten years of trying unsuccessfully to create an effective mission think-tank seemed to be the best option. If one takes him at his word in 1957 about already being busy and committed, the intervening twenty-two years had proven to Considine that much fruitful work on behalf of the church's world-wide mission could be done within the United States. It seems logical to understand that his view of Fumasoni Biondi's leadership as lackluster over a long period of time provided one more reason why Considine was reluc-

---

8. CD, October 6, 1957.

9. CD, October 10, 1957.

10. Archbishop Celso Costantini, who at that time was serving as secretary general of Propaganda.

11. CD, October 10, 1957.

tant to reengage with the Roman Curia from the inside. Why would he trade more optimal work circumstances in the United States for a system that had rewarded Fumasoni Biondi's "absence of thinking"?

We will return to Considine's discussion with Frs. Dindinger and Perbal at the end of Part I. But to bring to a close the question of Considine's being recruited to high ecclesiastical office, two concurrent personal events from roughly 1947–1953 are considered.

Considine had a gall bladder operation in late June 1947 and was hospitalized for two weeks. He then spent two months recuperating at the home of his youngest brother George in North Dartmouth, Massachusetts, nearby to New Bedford. The diaries from these months present a different Considine—one who gardens, is fascinated by his brother's successful antique business, and is pretty much unplugged from Maryknoll and mission. The visit seemed to make an impression on him—afterward, he would visit home more frequently than in the past and would always stay with his brother George when visiting the New Bedford area.

When Considine went home for Thanksgiving that year, his diary description of that day is filled with real qualities of warmth and happiness. Many of those same qualities pervade his diary ruminations about his family from a certain point during his summer stay in North Dartmouth, and the tone continued for many months afterward. It is the tone of someone who has rekindled close ties. At Thanksgiving he also remarked that it was the first time all six brothers had been together on Thanksgiving since 1914. As was asked in chapter 7, was it a sense of duty to Maryknoll that kept him away from holiday celebrations with his family in the years 1935–1946? The diary entries on Thanksgiving or Christmas those years portray him alone at the Maryknoll headquarters near Ossining, New York.

The other notable personal event during this period was the death of his close friend Bishop Francis X. Ford, M.M. In 1949, Mao Zedong proclaimed the People's Republic of China, and over the next three years nearly all Maryknoll missioners withdrew from China. While these events rocked the world of all missioners with connections to China, in Considine's case it was a personal friend who was imprisoned by the new communist regime and then died in custody in February 1952.

Although Considine was not as close to Bishop James E. Walsh, M.M., the Maryknoll community around the world followed Walsh's fortunes closely as he elected to remain in post-revolutionary China. His activities were first restricted by the new regime, and then he was placed under house arrest in 1956 and finally imprisoned. He was released by the Chinese authorities into Hong Kong only in 1971 when he was in ill health.

Given the harsh realities for missioners in China, the tone of anti-communism among Maryknollers in the 1950s is noticeably subdued. As with most Catholics at the time, opposition to communism was understood almost as an article of faith. Yet the proceedings of the 1954 Lima Method Conference provide a window on how anti-communism did not inspire shrill rhetoric on the part of missioners but rather kept them focused on Catholic mission work as presenting a clear alternative to communism. As will be discussed later,[12] there can be no doubt that Considine viewed anti-communism as one of two big motivators for maintaining Catholic mission work in Latin America—the other motivation being that of checking the advance of Protestantism. It is indeed surprising to find such a coherent approach to communism so recently after the expulsion of missioners from China and the death of Bishop Ford.

1946–1960: Years of Teaching and Organizing

As editor of *Maryknoll—The Field Afar*, Considine collaborated closely during these years with Fr. Albert Nevins, the younger Maryknoll priest whom Considine had recruited for the mission magazine immediately after Nevins's ordination in 1942. Nevins had been a reporter for New York area newspapers prior to entering the seminary. Those who knew the two of them in this period remember how loudly they might argue over editorial matters, but then peacefully walk together from their offices back to the Maryknoll seminary building for lunch or supper.[13]

Considine and Nevins consistently gave attention to the content of Maryknoll publications, but also to their look and feel. In this regard, a large budget item over the years was photography—the two held to a policy of printing only excellent photographs that could communicate well the mission reality and ideal. When good photographs taken by actual missioners were not available, the magazine purchased photos taken by professionals. Both Considine and Nevins were active in the Catholic Press Association, from which *Maryknoll—The Field Afar* consistently received awards during this period.

After finishing his term on the General Council in 1946, Considine taught his missiography course sporadically at Maryknoll Seminary through 1960, and he went by the title of Professor of Contemporary World Affairs. He also became a mentor to lay mission groups such as the Grail and the Association for International Development. Under Considine's guidance, members of these groups would become affiliated with the Papal Volunteers for Latin America (PAVLA), which Considine would found in 1960. Additionally, throughout this period he was a regular contributor to the CSMC publication *The Shield*.

---

12. See chapters 9 and 10; discussion of other aspects of the Lima Methods Conference, which was organized by Considine, is found later in this chapter.

13. Joseph O'Neill, interview with author, August 26, 2009.

Considine was a joiner during these years—he joined the Council on Foreign Relations, became a representative of the International Conference of Catholic Charities for UNICEF, was co-chair of the Africa Committee of the Catholic Association for International Peace, and was a founding member of the African Studies Association (ASA)—one of only three clergy in that founding group. The late 1940s and the 1950s were thus times when Considine was involved in establishing or contributing to existing U.S.-based institutions that were concerned with the broader goals of world mission, international cooperation, and world peace. It is not as if today Considine is easily remembered outside of these organizations for what he did in any of them. Rather, what is remarkable—and what his students recall from his course on missions taught at Maryknoll Seminary during this period—is the way he understood the church's mission as connected to foreign affairs and to international organizations—Catholic and governmental—as well as to disciplines like African Studies. At the very least he tried to convey that it was in the interest of missioners to coordinate efforts and to study the problems of mission together, and to seek out those civil and academic organizations with which the church's missioners could be an important conversation partner.[14]

Considine was also chaplain of the Maryknoll Sisters Cloister from 1947 through the mid-1950s. In 1960, he published a large pamphlet or small book, *God So Loved the World*, which described the Cloister and explored the relationship of the contemplative life to mission.

Major events. In 1950, the U.S. Mission Secretariat began operations; it was created to be a consortium of U.S.-based mission-sending groups, allowing its members to pool some resources and coordinate missionary activities. Considine and Fr. Calvert Alexander, S.J., first discussed the founding of such a group in 1944, and later both of them, along with Robert Hunter, S.V.D., Mary Augustine Kerby, S.M.S.M., and Fred McGuire, C.M., were the founding board members.[15] *Worldmission* was created as the publication of the Secretariat. Considine finally had established more of the original Fides or Pontifical Academy of Mission Studies dream, but at a national level. Because the Mission Secretariat resided in Washington and answered to the U.S. Bishops Committee for Missions, it was a mission organization that was, at least nominally, invested with the authority of the U.S. hierarchy. The Mission Secretariat held an annual conference in September, and Considine was a regular presenter and participant at this event.[16]

---

14. Gerard McCrane, interview with author, November 13, 2008.

15. Angelyn Dries, *The Missionary Movement in American Catholic History* (Maryknoll, NY: Orbis Books, 1998), 152–54.

16. Additionally, Dries describes a conflict between Considine and Bishop Fulton J.

Considine was a close collaborator of anthropologist Fr. J. Franklin Ewing, S.J. (1905–1968), who in 1953 founded the Institute of Mission Studies at Fordham University—a six-week summer institute for missioners—and the Fordham Conference of Mission Specialists. Students in the Institute were required to take both missiology and an area course; the latter courses were taught by a social scientist who had worked in the area of the world to be studied.

In the Fordham Mission Institute, Considine and Ewing collaborated in an equivalent area course for students who did not have an assignment to a particular part of the world. Dubbed "Intercultural Human Relations," this course exemplified the thrust of the entire institute—making the social sciences available to missioners to aid them in their task of understanding and working among peoples of many cultures and nations. The course drew on missionary examples to outline the principal features of human social activity around the globe and also offered a review of the church's mission situations around the world.

Ewing had hoped to develop a master's degree for missioners. The idea was to prepare faculty and leaders for mission-sending organizations, but the proposed program was also meant to address a practical mission need that was felt in 1959:

> It is becoming increasingly necessary that the missionary be equipped with a degree or proof of being a specialist in some field, in order to be admitted to the mission country at all. This is the pattern in India, Burma and Indonesia. It has been predicted that this pattern will spread to other portions of the mission world, as nascent nationalism spreads.[17]

Ewing was concerned to keep missioners prepared to engage the peoples of the world as the independence movement continued to gather force

---

Sheen after Sheen became director of the national Society for the Propagation of the Faith in 1950. The framework of their conflict was postwar anti-communism. Both churchmen were committed anti-communists, but Sheen saw the struggle to oppose communism in terms of good versus evil and was ready to enlist missions and missioners to be the frontline in the worldwide struggle. Considine basically approached the same situation the other way around—if missioners are recruited, sent out, and funded as an essential part of the church's life, their worldwide focus and care for people as people will do much to stop the advance of communism. In Sheen's view, missions and missioners were useful to a particular struggle (i.e., against communism); in Considine's view, mission—proclaiming Christ in word and deed—is essential to the church and also has the benefit of checking the advance of communism (*Missionary Movement in American Catholic History,* 166–69).

17. Arthur A. North, William R. Frasca, J. Franklin Ewing, Ralph E. Lynch, "For a Better Missionary: The Institute of Mission Studies, and an M.A. Program for Missionaries," 1959. Fordham University Archives, J. Franklin Ewing, S.J. papers.

in Asia, Africa, and Oceania. The M.A. was offered by the Department of Sociology and Anthropology for a time in the late 1950s and early 1960s, and a student could earn it in a year and two summers. Evidently, the degree was discontinued sometime in the 1960s.

Considine took a second Asia/Africa mission study tour in 1953, and from that tour came *Africa: World of New Men*, which is reviewed later in this chapter. He took two more mission study tours to Latin America: in 1954 to South America, and in 1955 to the Caribbean and Central America. Based on his visits to Latin America he published *New Horizons in Latin America* in 1958.[18]

Throughout the 1950s Considine continued to teach his course on missiography at Maryknoll Seminary, served as editor of *Maryknoll—The Field Afar*, and was often called upon to speak on Catholic missions before Catholic and Protestant audiences. I turn now to a more in-depth exploration of an event that Considine organized in 1954: the Lima Methods Conference of the Maryknoll Fathers.

Lima Methods Conference

The Third General Chapter of the Maryknoll Society in 1946 urged that regional conferences "for the exchange of ideas on pertinent questions be held every five years."[19] The first and only such Maryknoll regional conference prior to the Second Vatican Council was the Lima Methods Conference, held August 23–28, 1954. Considine was the principal organizer of the conference, which convened the leadership of the Maryknoll Society in South America along with representatives from the Society's headquarters near Ossining, New York.

According to Bishop Raymond Lane, Superior General of the Maryknoll Society at the time, the purpose of the meeting was to review mission methods employed and tasks accomplished since the beginning of Maryknoll's work in Latin America in 1942, study the church's social philosophy, and make specific applications of the church's mission methods to local conditions.[20]

While it was clear that the Maryknoll Society had officially called for such a meeting, Considine was also aware of the need for Maryknoll missioners in South America to reflect on the experience of their first twelve years of work in the region and set a direction for the future that would

---

18. *New Horizons* is reviewed in chapter 10.

19. "Acts and Motions of the Third General Chapter," p. 27. MMA, General Chapter III, Box 3, Folder 8 (1946 - Third - Acts & Motions).

20. Lima Methods Conference of the Maryknoll Fathers, *Proceedings of the Lima Methods Conference of the Maryknoll Fathers, Maryknoll House, Lima Peru, August 23–28, 1954* (Maryknoll, NY: Maryknoll Fathers, 1955), xiv.

make use of Catholic social teaching to tie the work of the Maryknollers to pressing social concerns. In broad terms, this had been Considine's formula for Catholic mission in Latin America from his first journey to the region in 1945, and would continue to be his focus when he became the director of the U.S. bishops' Latin America Bureau in 1960. Additionally, because Maryknoll missions in the People's Republic of China were closed to new missioners in the early 1950s, Maryknoll's missions in Latin America were poised to grow as some of the group's largest ordination classes received their first mission assignments in the 1950s.

The 1954 Lima Methods Conference was therefore a significant moment of missionary reflection for Maryknoll, and the conference bore a Considine stamp in both its style and its substance. It was an example of the kind of patient educating and lobbying that had characterized Considine's work on the General Council (1934–1946). In effect, he was able to orga-nize the event, create a framework for selecting the participants, preside over the meeting itself without seeming to impose an agenda on his con-freres, guide the drafting of the *Proceedings,* and subsequently see the suc-cessful adoption of key points of the Lima Methods Conference program, such as the establishment of cooperatives and the organization of networks of catechists.[21]

Considine designed the conference to be a catalyst for change among South American Maryknollers. Therefore, rather than inviting a panel of experts to educate the missioners about social concerns or catechesis or vocations to the priesthood, Considine first invited key leaders of Mary-knoll's South American contingent and then asked nearly all of them to write a paper on a specific topic and present it. The combination of sev-eral elements—pent-up desire to reflect on the real mission problems they had been experiencing, thoughtful input from colleagues in leadership, and a schedule that permitted the gathering to process the information and come to conclusions—had the desired effect of producing an impulse for change in the work and outlook of the Maryknollers.

The selection of Maryknoll Fr. William Coleman as the first speaker at the conference showed Considine's desire to have the Lima Methods Con-ference build upon a significant Latin American church conference held just one year prior. In 1953, the Tercera Semana Interamericana de Acción Católica was held in Chimbote, Peru, and Fr. Coleman had taken part in that conference. The 1953 Catholic Action conference gave great attention to the place that the Catholic faith held for the average Latin American and issued an outcry that a general lack of frequent participation in church life

---

21. Ibid., 91–109, 252, 295–97, 300–301.

had produced a profound ignorance of church teaching. Though high percentages of people in all countries represented were baptized, their Catholicism tended to be "nominal."[22] Some years later, Considine would have Fr. Coleman's English translation of the documents of the Tercera Semana Interamericana published as one of Maryknoll's World Horizon Reports.[23]

At the conference, there was considerable debate as the participants attempted systematically to review early missionary experiences of the group in South America and set a direction. A great deal of energy was given at this meeting to matters of the particular work of religious instruction and parish life. Taking stock of the low economic conditions in which so many populations lived in Latin America, an undercurrent of debate on what should get the greater priority—social action or religious instruction—is found throughout the *Proceedings*. There is also little doubt that the problem they most wanted to address in South America, as they generally saw it, was the perception that Catholics in Latin America were not very observant of church teaching. To use the words of Fr. Robert Kearns, one of the participants, the goal they operated with was "the re-establishment of the Church."[24]

As the Maryknollers gathered in Lima focused on their work, they made note of the familiar challenges posed by communism and Protestantism in Latin America but did not spend much time on these issues. Regarding communism, the absence of a defensive attitude on the part of these Catholic missioners is somewhat surprising, given the fact that only two months prior President Jacobo Arbenz had been deposed in Guatemala in what has widely been understood to have been a CIA-planned coup to oust a left-leaning national leader. Additionally, the Maryknollers themselves could not have failed to recall how the 1949 inauguration of the Peoples Republic of China had effectively brought an end to the group's mission work in that country. Present at the conference also was Maryknoll Fr. Bernard Meyer, a member of the first group of Maryknollers sent to China in 1918 and a companion of Maryknoll Bishop Francis Ford, who had perished in a Chinese communist prison in 1952. Given the pain that the Maryknollers had recently been through in relation to communism, the lack of any shrillness at the conference in regard to communist activities in Latin America was remarkable.

The participants also took some time to think about themselves—what

---

22. Ibid., 9.

23. William J. Coleman, *Latin-American Catholicism: A Self-Evaluation* (Maryknoll, NY: Maryknoll Publications, 1958).

24. *Proceedings*, 236.

made them missioners, if they were not reaching out to non-Christians?[25] Considine was called upon to speak at length about Maryknoll's decision to go to Latin America, about the ratification of that decision at the Third General Chapter in 1946, and about how work among Catholics in churches that were not self-sustaining did indeed fit the church's official description of mission as defined by Propaganda Fide. As the discussion continued, Considine offered a definition of the role of the missioner:

> A practical interpretation of a mission society is that of a body of apostolic trouble-shooters who'll go anywhere where the Church has to be planted or replanted. That's the type of society the Church needs. Weak men let things get out of order; sectors of the Church go down hill continually. You have only two divisions of priestly workers in the Church. You've got those dedicated to the ministry to the faithful and you've got the missioners. There's no third group who are not missioners but who devote their lives to building the Church up again when it breaks down. In the life of the Church, it is the missioner who is sent in to do this job.[26]

The Lima Methods Conference accomplished many things—its reports and papers alone provide a window on South American mission work at mid-century.[27] Through that window is seen a group of U.S. missioners who were learning to be sympathetic to the Latin American population they had been sent to serve. The very format of the conference fostered a spirit of openness to the local scene in order to be more effective at sharing

---

25. Ibid., 236–38.

26. Ibid., 237–38.

27. In particular, the conference offered a sustained focus on missionary work among the indigenous peoples of the Andean highlands: Quechuas and Aymaras in Peru and Bolivia, and Mapuches in Chile. Since 1943, Maryknoll had been working among these groups, and elsewhere I have offered an analysis of that focus of the Lima Methods Conference ("What Happens When Church Elites Begin to Take Seriously the Perspective of Indigenous Peoples? John J. Considine, M.M., and the 1954 Lima Methods Conference of the Maryknoll Fathers" [paper given in the World Christianity Group at the Annual Meeting of the American Academy of Religion, Chicago, Illinois, November 3, 2008]). As may be expected, a great deal of energy was given at this meeting to the question of the indigenization of the church—the development of a local clergy to serve the church in South America (*Proceedings,* 188–205, 276–82); attention was also given to working with groups of Catholic Sisters and lay institutes (ibid., 206–19, 282–85). Additionally, matters of the particular work of religious instruction and parish life were discussed. The conference also focused on many other issues related to the Maryknollers' mission work, for example, the question of whether the Maryknollers should run Catholic schools (ibid., 110–19, 263–65) and how to orient newly arrived missioners to the mission work in South America (ibid., 248).

the gospel. Considine is to be credited for the design and execution of such a process.

Mission in the Middle of the Twentieth Century

Considine's diary from his 1957 trip to Rome recorded a conversation with two missiologist colleagues, Frs. Johannes Dindinger and Albert Perbal, both of whom were members of the Oblates of Mary Immaculate. Considine knew Dindinger best, having worked with him on the *Guida delle Missioni Cattoliche* (1934 and 1935), an encyclopedia on mission that offered both a survey of Catholic mission activity worldwide and a thorough summary of the church's missiology. Dindinger was also the successor to his fellow Oblate Fr. Robert Streit as editor of the *Bibliotheca Missionum*,[28] after the latter's untimely death in 1930. Considine had also been a colleague of Dindinger at the Pontifical Urbanian University in the early 1930s. As professor of mission history at the Istituto Pontificio Missionale Scientifico (IPMS) from 1932 to 1948, Dindinger taught an area parallel to the field of missiography that Considine had taught in 1933–1934. Albert Perbal had similarly served as professor of missiology at the IPMS from its founding in 1932 until his retirement in 1954;[29] in the 1940s he would reorganize the curriculum of the IPMS and also teach courses on Islam.[30]

The three mission thinkers discussed the bright light in missiology at the time, *La philosophie bantoue* (1949) by Fr. Placide Tempels (1906–1977). Tempels was a Franciscan missioner in the Belgian Congo who sketched a set of ideas that emerge from traditional African cultures: being is distinguishable from non-being by the presence of a vital force; persons do not think of themselves as individuals but as members of a family and a community; and so on, all of which Considine considered much more accurate than the assumption, commonly held by Westerners at that time, that the minds of Africans were as a tabula rasa.[31] Perbal and Considine concurred that the study was indeed helpful for missionary adaptation or accommodation.[32] But as Considine, Dindinger, and Perbal conversed, the bright missionary perspective of Tempels became juxtaposed with the serious obstacles the church's missioners faced at that time.

---

28. Willi Henkel, "The Legacy of Robet Streit, Johannes Dindinger, and Johannes Rommerskirchen," *International Bulletin of Missionary Research* 6, no. 1 (January 1982): 17.

29. "Nunitia. Instituti Missionalis Scientifici," December 1, 1934. ASPF, Nuova Serie 1343, Foglio 11.

30. Willi Henkel, "Perbal, Albert," in *Biographical Dictionary of Christian Missions*, ed. Gerald H. Anderson (New York: Macmillan Reference USA, 1998), 526.

31. John J. Considine, *Africa: World of New Men* (New York: Dodd, Mead & Co., 1954), 150.

32. CD, October 10, 1957.

In the mid-1950s, U.S. Catholic missioners had little reason to be pessimistic about the church's global mission enterprise. Membership in Catholic missionary orders was rising, and financial support from U.S. Catholics was forthcoming. In comparison to European missioners, U.S. missioners could think of themselves as less invested in colonial projects, which were at the time unraveling throughout the Global South. The outlook seemed bright indeed. But Considine, who preferred to look more deeply at the fortunes of the church's mission, had a different assessment, and after his 1957 conversation in Rome with Dindinger and Perbal, his diary displayed a fresh round of questioning about the effectiveness of Catholic missioners. At the beginning of this chapter, reference was made to the view that missioners were not taking the concept of adaptation seriously enough; additionally, Considine understood "the missionary attitude" as "rather inglorious in that in such great degree [missioners] have succumbed to the influence of colonial thinking."[33]

But the "colonial thinking" appears to have been of the ecclesiastical variety, an imposition on the peoples of Asia, Africa, Latin America, and Oceania of the forms of ecclesial life found in the home country of the missioner. Considine mentioned missiologist Albert Perbal's (1884–1971) concern that missioners "make European parishes in mission lands. Each nation brings its own spirituality and imposes it on the new peoples." Considine's diary noted that already there were signs that such an arrangement may not stand:

As yet Catholics in Africa have not broken with the Church but Protestant groups through dissatisfaction with Western ways have set up syncretisms in the French Congo, Ubanglii and Cameroun. Catholic groups sympathize. "We are whites and therefore have not understood the African," [Perbal] says they say.[34]

Considine cited Perbal to underscore his own concern that the problem was with missioners themselves.

[Perbal] like others leads a double life in that he is unhappy about missionary attitudes and yet considers it inadvisable to make a frontal criticism of these attitudes. "I bend my knee to the zeal and sacrifice of the missionaries but regret their methods. I regret the fact that they rebel against all criticism." This sums up Perbal.[35]

Considine believed that further education of missioners was needed, and he thought of writing a teaching manual for such education. "I'd com-

33. Ibid.
34. Ibid.
35. Ibid.

bine the principles of mission theory with Propaganda and Papal teaching and enliven the methodological exposition with examples of good mission practice."[36]

From the early days of his tenure at Propaganda in the mid-1920s, Rome was for Considine the unique place where Catholic missioners could think through the many problems and issues that came up in mission work throughout the world. Even if the effectiveness of Propaganda Fide had suffered some under lackluster leadership, Rome still was a gathering point for missioners and scholars and so remained vitally connected to churches and mission enterprises throughout the world. His 1957 reunion with colleagues in Rome was one more opportunity to savor the resources of first-rate scholars and to renew his faith in the way the church's structure in Rome could give the practical mission concerns of the whole world a hearing by the church's best mission minds.

Part II:
Published Works 1942–1962

Considine published several books and many articles in the years 1942–1962; it was a time in which his ideas on mission, the unity of the human race, and the importance of respect for the culture and faith experience of all peoples blossomed on both the printed page and in conferences given to various audiences. Space considerations will not allow us to review all his writings,[37] but I present here an introduction to six key Considine texts of the period.

---

36. Ibid.

37. *New Horizons in Latin America* is discussed in chapter 10. Considine also wrote or edited three books based on the 1964–1966 annual conferences of the Catholic Inter-American Cooperation Program (CICOP), and these are touched on in chapter 9 and listed in Appendix II.

A couple of years prior to this period, Considine authored two books that were written at least in part with a view to enhancing Maryknoll's promotional efforts: *When the Sorghum Was High* (1940) and *March into Tomorrow* (1942). *When the Sorghum Was High* tells the life story of Fr. Gerard Donovan, M.M., the first Maryknoll priest to die a violent death while serving in an overseas mission—Fr. Donovan was murdered by bandits in Manchuria in 1938. The book is written for young people and holds up Fr. Donovan's life as an example of an ordinary young man who decided to do extraordinary things by becoming a missionary priest. As can be expected, the missionary life is portrayed as a life with deep joys and satisfactions, but a life that demands the total gift of self. Fr. Donovan's death is held up as a heroic sacrifice which he made by choosing to serve the church in a dangerous time and place.

March into Tomorrow offers a profile of the work of Maryknoll missions as the decade of the 1940s was beginning. Nearly all of the missions described in the book were in East Asia, though space was also given to the beginning of Maryknoll's work in Bolivia. The book is

Christianity: The World Idea That Unifies

In chapter 6, it was noted that Considine wrote *Across a World* (1942) based on his fourteen-month mission study tour of the Near East, Asia, and Africa.[38] Yet inserted into the introduction to that work there was an idea that emerged some years after his early 1930s journey: Christianity is the "world idea" that could unite the planet. In order to argue that this was not simply a pious missionary notion but rather an urgently needed way of talking about the unity of the human race, Considine compared Christianity to three other great "world ideas" that were then in vogue: the communist materialism of Moscow, the racism of the Nazis, and modern power politics, the kind that had destroyed the good intentions of equality found in the League of Nations.

Considine assumed that the reader was familiar with the failures of each of these, and so he moved on to describe the worldwide shape of Christianity. Yes, Christians themselves are divided into Protestant and Catholic—the Orthodox being curiously omitted in this discussion—yet in the twentieth century a world consciousness among Protestants had been developing: the work of missions, of Bible societies, of the YMCA and the YWCA, in addition to the great international meetings[39] were cited by Considine as examples of this development. He noted that a sense of sadness over the divisions among Christians seemed to have replaced the partisan bitterness that was so prominent in other times.

Considine then described the structure of the Catholic Church in relation to the peoples of the world, highlighting the work of the Holy See:

> The Center in Rome from which the world missions of the Church
> are directed represents at once the traditions of centuries and the

---

eighty-seven pages in a large-page format and displays numerous photos of the missions profiled in its text.

Considine taught an intensive summer course at Notre Dame in the summer of 1960 and turned his lectures into a book, *Fundamental Catholic Teaching on the Human Race* (1961). Like *World Christianity* (1944), it is a theological proposal about the church's social vision of humanity. It is a fine statement but not terribly impressive—Considine was not a theologian by trade.

Please refer to the bibliography for a complete list of publications by Considine.

38. See the excursus "Considine, Ecumenism, and Interreligious Dialogue" for a discussion of the epilogue of *Across a World*.

39. For example, the 1910 Edinburgh Missionary Conference; the "Life and Work" conference held at Stockholm (1925); the "Faith and Order" conference held at Lausanne (1927); and the International Missionary Conference in Madras (1938).

vigor of a resilient spirit which, in some miraculous manner, has a way of constantly renewing itself.[40]

The text goes on to describe how Propaganda Fide is set up to carry out missions, which are described as "one of the Pope's special world tasks."[41] The text is not a work of apologetics, nor is it insistent in any way. Yet at every turn, Considine emphasized that the church had been set up in such a way as to allow those who guide it from Rome to be in touch with the faith, culture, and even geography of the peoples of the entire globe.

The introduction concluded with an invitation to reconsider the concept of universality—was it possible that a true unity of the human race could come about by political force, or was world unity fundamentally a venture of the spirit, a venture made possible through the workings of a living body, the church?

> In no figurative but in a very literal sense, the Church goes to the world. . . . The good tradition of the Popes carries on through the ages. Christianity is by divine command, by organization, by its world mission action, the earth's great spiritual universalism.[42]

In a time of great conflict, Considine proposed that Christianity was a solid alternative to communism, racist nationalism, and power politics precisely because it was a spiritual idea.

Some of the elements of *Across a World* have already been described in chapter 6, but many other features are remarkable. It was at once a travelogue and an introduction for the English-speaking reader to the church in many non-Western contexts. At the same time, the report on the church was mainly presented by the church's missioners—not many voices of local laypeople are heard in its pages. The book tackled substantive mission matters, is framed in Considine's comparative religions perspective, and contains a surprisingly ecumenical appeal at the end.[43]

Combating Racism

In the summer of 1938 "The Manifesto of Racist Scientists" was published in Italy, one more step on the way to Mussolini's promulgation of anti-Jewish laws that same year. Pius XI, who had published both *Mit Brennender Sorge* (With Burning Concern) to condemn Nazi abuses in 1937 and a

---

40. Considine, *Across a World,* xiii.
41. Ibid., xiv.
42. Ibid., xvi.
43. See the excursus "Considine, Ecumenism, and Interreligious Dialogue."

syllabus condemning racist errors in April 1938, would again in the summer of 1938 resolve to write a new encyclical condemning racism and anti-Semitism.[44] Indeed, his first reaction to the Manifesto was to describe it as a "true apostasy."[45]

Yet it is now widely understood that Pius XI's opposition to the advent of racial laws in Fascist Italy did not produce a tide of support within the church for the pope's position. Indeed, a prominent Italian Jesuit, Angelo Brucculeri, wrote at the time in a national journal that he had no objections to racism.[46] Although from a post-Shoah perspective it may be difficult for Catholics to accept, in 1938 the church was not of one mind on anti-Semitism. Indeed, until the outbreak of the Second World War, within the Vatican there was intense debate about what to do about Nazi abuses in regard to the Jews, Pius XI's views from the late 1930s notwithstanding.[47]

In the early 1940s, the war had already wreaked havoc on large areas of the earth. By that time, voices were heard within Catholicism that more clearly denounced the murderous practices of the Third Reich and the Axis powers. One such voice was that of Jacques Maritain, who unleashed a lightning bolt on the pages of *Commonweal* in June 1943.[48] Maritain presented a well-reasoned yet horrifying description, denunciation, and analysis of the Nazi extermination of the Jews. The article was originally a talk he gave in French in January 1943. For U.S. Catholic readers, this was the strongest official confirmation of the many rumors that had been circulating about the systematic murder of Jews, homosexuals, dissidents, and those deemed by the regime to be physically or mentally defective. The article is well remembered by Jews and others for its unequivocal denunciation of Nazi state terror against defenseless populations.

In 1944, Considine was called upon to write *An Outline of Missiography* (1944) for *The Missionary Academia,* a journal published for Catholic seminarians as a joint effort of the U.S. Society for the Propagation of the Faith and the Missionary Union of the Clergy. Seemingly because of the war and because of the clarity of Maritain's outcry, a couple of new topics had to be inserted into the section on the study of the world's peoples: an analysis of physical racial differences—they exist, but they are negligible—and a doc-

---

44. The encyclical was never published; it vanished from the desk of Pius XI at the moment of his death in February 1939. See Emma Fattorini and Carl Ipsen, *Hitler, Mussolini and the Vatican: Pope Pius XI and the Speech That Was Never Made* (Cambridge: Polity Press, 2011), 152–57; and Frank J. Coppa, "Between Morality and Diplomacy: The Vatican's 'Silence' during the Holocaust," *Journal of Church and State* 50, no. 3 (Summer 2008): 553–56.

45. Fattorini, *Hitler, Mussolini and the Vatican,* 158.

46. Ibid.

47. See chapter 5.

48. Jacques Maritain, "Racist Law and the True Meaning of Racism," *The Commonweal* 38, no. 7 (June 4, 1943): 181–88.

trinal statement condemning political and philosophical concepts of racial differences as heretical to Catholic teaching. Considine reproduced in this section the text of Pius XI's April 1938 syllabus condemning racial theories; the text had been supplied in Maritain's article.[49]

The previous year, Considine had reread J. H. Oldham's *Christianity and the Race Problem* (1924) and remarked in his diary, "Feel now that I have found what I want."[50] Apparently what he wanted it for was *Outline,* and its arguments against racism;[51] Considine cites Oldham's work four times.

Outline was a comprehensive presentation of missiography.[52] As was already discussed, Considine consistently understood missiography as the study of the world's peoples accompanied by the study of the church's efforts to be in mission to those peoples.[53] In regard to the latter aspect of missiography, *Outline* offered an analysis of the church's growth over the whole world, an overview of the work of the church in twenty mission areas, and concludes with a chapter on the church's mission personnel focusing principally on the development of indigenous vocations to religious life as well as an indigenous clergy and hierarchy:

> It is paramount to the establishment of the faith over the earth that [the] element of "one's-own-ness" be given to the life and leadership of the Church in each land. It is in the genius of Roman Christianity to make the faith at home among every people through giving it pride and love for its union with Christ's Vicar in Rome. This it does through unbending firmness as regards essentials of doctrine and practice but through encouragement of local forms and customs, local architecture and art, and, above all, in the building up of strong local spiritual leadership in the way of well-trained native-born priests, Brothers and Sisters.[54]

Making "the faith at home" in all cultures clearly anticipated the later concept of the inculturation of the faith. Considine understood the process as necessarily calling on the church to respect both the native-born persons who will lead the church and their points of view on what the world is and how to live in it.

---

49. John J. Considine, *An Outline of Missiography* (New York: Society for the Propagation of the Faith, 1944), 19; Maritain, "Racist Law," 182.

50. CD, April 4, 1943, referring to Joseph Houldsworth Oldham, *Christianity and the Race Problem* (New York: George H. Doran Co., 1924).

51. Considine, *Outline,* 16.

52. *The Missionary Academia* usually featured a single lengthy article; *Outline* contained ten chapters in forty-four pages, in addition to a page of study questions.

53. See chapter 5 and the excursus "How to Be a Missiographer."

54. Considine, *Outline,* 43.

World Christianity[55]

During 1945, Considine published a short meditation on the universality of Christ and the church, *World Christianity*. As in *Across a World* and *Outline*, the question of how the church can respond to the crisis brought about by World War II influenced Considine's work. He became convinced that a new universal view of humanity—always theoretically asserted, but before the twentieth century almost impossible for average people to approximate in any practical way—was becoming not only possible but also necessary for human life on the planet.

> Because of the profound outlook wrought by war, this world view promises to be more pronounced in days to come than ever before in the history of the Church. Single families have had members in the armed forces scattered among peoples on every continent of the globe. Civil governments, armies, learned societies, schools, popular movements of many varieties, have advocated greater understanding of our fellow men over the globe.[56]

Considine therefore endeavored to show how the universality of humanity has always been a part of the church's life and tradition, most especially in its missionary tradition. The book briefly reviews the main points of Catholic doctrine—Christ, God, the Church, faith, the human condition, human society—and offers suggestions for understanding all of these in the new context of a world that has managed to interconnect previously far-flung peoples.

For example, when speaking of the nature of God, the list of God's attributes—infinity, unity, simplicity—led Considine to the conclusion that there is an essential universality to such claims, necessitating a universal religion, one that is accessible to all. He concludes the point by citing Pius XI's arguments against a national god or the god of a single race in *Mit Brennender Sorge*.[57]

I will return to *World Christianity* in the conclusion of this chapter. Considine's next book touched on his new interest in the church in Latin America.

Latin America

Call for Forty Thousand (1946) was the book Considine published after his 1945–1946 mission study tour of Latin America. The work marked three

---

55. For a discussion of Considine's trinitarian view of mission as found in *World Christianity*, see chapter 4 above.

56. John J. Considine, *World Christianity* (Milwaukee: Bruce, 1945), xiv.

57. Ibid., 19–20.

significant shifts for Considine: it covered mission in a "Catholic" continent; it contained more material on local people; and it was published much more quickly following his tour. The basic themes of *Call* were discussed at the end of chapter 7.

The style of *Call* was similar to *Across a World*, which Considine wrote on the basis of his first mission study tour. *Call* therefore introduced the English-speaking reader to the Catholic Church in Latin America by speaking with local church leaders, missioners, and Latin American intellectuals. *Call* is above all missiography, concerned with the health of the church's life in Latin America, but it is also part geography and travelogue—visits to Machu Picchu and other sites of general interest are recorded in its pages.

But if in *Across a World* the voice of missioners and bishops was primarily heard, in the pages of *Call* a wide variety of voices concerned with Catholic life in Latin America come alive, such as an interview with local historian Dr. Placido Molina in Santa Cruz, Bolivia.[58] He also met with prominent national intellectuals, such as Peruvian Dr. Víctor Andrés Belaúnde. During the 1920s, José Carlos Belaúnde, Mariátegui, and Victor Raúl Haya de la Torre each proposed different ideas on the integration of Andean peoples into Peruvian Society, representing respectively the Peruvian right, left, and center-left.

Call became a Catholic best-seller. It was probably the urgency that Considine felt about mission work in Latin America that led him to finish the book within months of his return from his Latin American mission study tour. Though it is not possible to draw a line of causation from *Call* to the Vatican, in 1948—two years after its publication—Pius XII suggested to Richard Cardinal Cushing a Latin American expansion of the Cardinal's "lend-lease" program of sending Boston priests to dioceses in the United States that did not have sufficient clergy.[59]

Significant portions of Latin America had been under the purview of Propaganda Fide for hundreds of years prior to the 1940s, but it was principally European missioners who were involved in those mission efforts. This began to change slowly around the beginning of the twentieth century when the first U.S. missionary groups took up work in Latin America. With U.S. groups like Maryknoll taking up responsibilities in the region during World War II, the idea of sending greater numbers of U.S. missioners to the region had been gaining traction in Rome. *Call* therefore should

---

58. John J. Considine, *Call for Forty Thousand* (New York: Longmans, Green & Co., 1946), 57–58.

59. James F. Garneau, "Commandos for Christ: The Foundation of the Missionary Society of St. James the Apostle and the 'Americanism' of the 1950s and 1960s" (Ph.D. dissertation, Catholic University of America, 2000), 94–95.

be understood as part of this process, albeit one that gathered a lot of attention for a U.S.-based mission effort in Latin America.

The Revolutionary Tenor of the Times

The 1957 discussion on mission that Considine had with Dindinger and Perbal (mentioned above) seemed to lack a political sense—Considine's comments included the mention of only two actors, the church's missioners and indigenous peoples. Meanwhile, the 1950s were, of course, times of tremendous political change, as European colonial projects around the world began to unravel.

In his published writings, however, Considine showed a keen awareness of political developments. He visited Africa in 1953, and from that study tour came *Africa: World of New Men* (1954). As a commentary on the church's mission in contemporary Africa, *Africa: World of New Men* is attentive to the political climate. The text describes the postwar assimilationist policies that gave French West Africans citizenship and parliamentary representation in Paris and also the forms of self-government that were being set up in the Gold Coast during this period. But it was the deeply problematic beginnings of apartheid in South Africa that called forth a different kind of text from Considine, different from what he had usually written on his mission study tours.

The violence of Southern Africa is poignant in this text; Considine made no attempt to hide it, and it is not easy to read about it. For example, he described the stoning to death and dismemberment of an Irish nun at Duncan Village, on the outskirts of East London, and one can easily feel trapped in the violence of the narrative. Considine is evenhanded about the main cause of violence—apartheid—but notably absent in much of the texts on South Africa is the characteristic Considine optimism. In his writings from South Africa, Considine did not try to make sense out of a hopeless political situation.

If in *Across a World* Considine provided the testimony of missioners scattered across the Near East, Asia, and Africa, and then in *Call for Forty Thousand* he drew Latin American experts into the discussion, in *Afria: World of New Men,* Considine acquaints the reader with the discourse of Africans themselves. Some of this is fairly customary mission lore—in Dakar, Senegal, Considine describes the wedding of Mark Monet and Angelique Mendy, two upwardly mobile urban young people who were both of the Wolof tribe, and, in another spot, he describes the story of Margherite, who attempted unsuccessfully to avoid an arranged marriage to a non-Catholic polygamist in the Middle Congo.

But again it is in South Africa that Considine records the voice of a black African's view of apartheid and the economic hardship of his country.

The chapter is called "Mr. Cheap," which was how George Maruku, his Basutoland informant, named the value that black African labor had for the economy of South Africa: cheap labor to keep the mines and industry humming.

"As a man learns his job, does he get a raise in pay?" I asked.
"Very little!" said George. "That's the key to the whole labor problem. You have heard that gold is the most precious thing in South Africa. But the real wealth of the country is cheap labor. . . . The great commandment of the mine owners is, 'Thou shalt employ only cheap migrant labor.' Each of us Africans has a big tag tied to him, or better, a brand on his hide. It reads CHEAP. Every African is named 'Mr. Cheap.' By any other name, no employer wants him."[60]

In the Congo and in Rwanda, Considine is complimentary about the Belgian colonial administration, which, in his view, was doing things correctly on two scores: it had adopted an indigenizing policy to train Congolese and Rwandans for service in colonial administration and enterprises, and the church was given ample room and resources to carry out its mission.

After the 1994 Rwanda genocide, the place of religion in the history of tension between Hutus and Tutsis became the object of much scholarly scrutiny. Gerard Prunier, for example, has pointed out the role played by church officials during the earliest years of Belgian colonial administration to encourage a favored status for the minority Tutsis.[61] It would be a mistake to use postcolonial insights to judge Considine's views on Central Africa in the 1950s. Nonetheless, like many non-African commentators of those years, Considine was aware of the social divide between the Hutu majority and the Tutsis, but he did not grasp the tragic consequences that this situation would engender.[62]

Considine cared deeply about the welfare and future of the peoples of Asia, Africa, Latin America, and Oceania, and worked tirelessly to keep the church in step with their needs. But the late 1950s were a great challenge to such a keeping in step; it was a time when independence movements advanced in much of Asia, Africa, and Oceania, and, in Latin America, revolutionary solutions to entrenched social problems were contemplated. The pace of social change was picking up.

---

60. Considine, *Africa: World of New Men,* 220. An excerpt from this chapter is found in the appendix below.
61. Gerard Prunier, *The Rwanda Crisis: History of a Genocide* (New York: Columbia University Press, 1995), 26.
62. Considine, *Africa: World of New Men,* 164.

Mission and Development

The 1955 Bandung Conference marked the early beginnings of the Non-Aligned Movement. With the nations of the globe distributed into so-called "worlds"—First World Western industrial powers under the leadership of the United States and Western Europe, Second World nations in the socialist bloc led by the former Soviet Union—at Bandung, many leaders of the so-called Third World nations of Asia, Africa, Latin America, and Oceania formed an alliance from which to negotiate with the First and Second World powers. Their basic stance was "yes" to economic development but a pronounced hesitancy to embrace political alliances with the nations of the First or Second World.

Development was therefore a concept that was very much in vogue in the mid-1950s. In 1958, Considine served as host at the Maryknoll headquarters for the Fordham Rural Life Socio-Economic Conference; the conference had been organized by Fr. J. Franklin Ewing, S.J., from Fordham and Msgr. Luigi Ligutti of the Catholic Rural Life Conference. The event gathered forty social science scholars, administrators of international and governmental development agencies, missioners, and church personnel to discuss socioeconomic development. Considine later wrote a summary of the conference papers and discussions and published them as *The Missionary's Role in Socio-Economic Betterment* (1960).

Considine noted that the conference began with an overview of Catholic socioeconomic development approaches and proposed the role of the missionary as a catalyst for change. Then the framework of community development, cultural anthropology, and the phenomenon of cultural change were discussed. This was the first day of the four-day conference. A remarkable breadth of twelve socioeconomic development topics followed over the next three days, and a chapter in the book is dedicated to each topic.

By twenty-first century standards, the conference may have seemed unrepresentative, featuring a heavy contingent of white males. In its moment, however, it was something of a first. Approximately one-half of the participants were missioners, and the rest were specialists in various social science and other fields that focused on problems of socioeconomic change and development. Therefore, the main purpose of the conference was for these two groups to become better aware of the role each played in social change in the developing world. The missioners came to understand better how the people they serve could benefit from an academic analysis of their problems, and the academics came to understand better how missioners, if given some academic orientation, could play a pivotal role in processes of socioeconomic change in the developing world.

On hand were some notable figures: Fr. Joseph Fitzpatrick, S.J., dean,

School of Sociology, Fordham University; Dr. João Gonçalves de Souza, Organization of American States; Dr. August H. Groeschel, director, New York Hospital-Cornell Medical Center; Msgr. George Higgins, director, Department of Social Action of the NCWC; Fr. Ronan Hoffman, O.F.M.Conv., professor of missiology, Catholic University; Msgr. Ivan Illich, vice-rector of the Catholic University of Puerto Rico; Msgr. Luigi Ligutti, founder of the International Rural Life Movement; Louis Miniclier, chief of the Community Development Division of the International Cooperation Administration.

The Missioner of the Future

Already in 1962 Considine was speaking about the appearance of a new center of gravity in missions, one that is properly defined by a coalescence of Christianity in non-European cultures. Such coalescences were occurring in Asia, Africa, and Latin America, and Considine referred to them as "break-throughs." He was convinced that "modest islands of . . . authentically coalesced Christian society" in Asia and Africa were positioned for significant growth.

In the past, examples of Christian society taking root outside Europe were quite limited and faced insurmountable obstacles. Considine cited the example of India.

> In India, the St. Thomas Christians along the Malabar Coast represent the most notable example in the world of the thorough acclimatization of Christianity to non-Western society. This Church, which reached India through the Persian Gulf, and which never during long centuries was other than faithful to Rome though for centuries out of touch with Rome, was discovered by the Portuguese to possess tens of thousands of families congregated in hundreds of villages. Ironically, rather than rejoicing in this Church's substantial harmony with Indian culture, Portuguese officers and clergy sought to Latinize it. Rather than encouraging the building of Christianity on this Church as a possible agency for Indian penetration, a Western Latinism was introduced.[63]

In Africa, the Philippines, and Indochina, other churches were manifesting their own vitality, some with a longer history than others. What was the greatest danger faced by these new churches? Interestingly, Considine cited

---

63. John J. Considine, "The Church's Global Mission and the Future," in *Global Mission of the Church: Proceedings of the Fordham University Conference of Mission Specialists, Tenth Annual Meeting, January 19–20, 1962,* ed. J. Franklin Ewing (New York: Institute of Mission Studies, Fordham University, 1962), IX-1.

Arnold Toynbee's argument that Western expansion since 1600 had been characterized by the absence of religion. Toynbee contended that the wars of religion in Europe had led the governments of Europe to eliminate religion from the purview of the state, precisely at the moment when Europe was exporting its civilization around the world. This led Considine to ask if this pattern, which had been imported to new states in Asia and Africa, might prevent emerging Catholic churches from becoming thoroughly at home in non-Western lands.

Considine noted further signs of hope: a rejuvenated church in Latin America that would contribute to the strength of the church in the world and a more active Catholic laity throughout the world represented "a vast untapped reservoir of apostolic strength and achievement."[64] He also found hope for growth, as perspectives such as the right to an education, the right to health care in one's community, and the right to just wages and working conditions and collective bargaining were gaining universal acceptance. In terms of the world economy and the situation of poverty, which two-thirds of humanity then experienced, Considine spoke of a new philosophy that had societies seeking to alleviate that situation with "preventive, protective and remedial measures." The point was not that poverty could be wiped out by the end of the twentieth century, but certainly by that time the "cynical acceptance of poverty as the normal lot of the other fellow" could be removed. All of these perspectives, he noted, were "eminently Christian in their spirit."[65] Considine also noted as signs of hope the subsiding of Western ethnocentrism and arrogance and the gaining of acceptance of the notion of the equality of all peoples. The enfranchising of international law over greater and greater areas of human activity was another encouraging sign.

In short, the new center of gravity about which Considine spoke had everything to do with a church that was more and more at home in many cultures—as we have seen, a persistent theme for Considine throughout this period—and was aided by rejuvenated regions such as Latin America and by a more mature laity. This church was called upon to act in a world that held greater esteem for individual and collective rights and showed signs of appropriating a universal common good.

Considine's conclusion is that the missioner of the future is neither a technical specialist nor an ambassador who invites people to membership in a modern superstructure. The missioner of the future needs to embody a concern for all people and must know how to perceive and share a vision of Christ and the church that is adequate to the aspirations of the age. This missioner must be a theoretician, one who

---

64. Ibid., IX-4.
65. Ibid., IX-5.

should, it is true, be au courant with modern techniques but more than ever he needs to be able to imbue local Christian leaders of the younger segments of the world Church with the timeless social and ecclesiological principles of Augustine and Francisco de Vitoria. In short, he must provide the practical and social framework for the world-embracing charity of Christ.[66]

It has not been possible to consider all the works that Considine wrote during the years 1942–1962, but the six works discussed here represent several strong themes that Considine emphasized throughout his career: indigenization of the church understood as both indigenous leadership and indigenous categories of thought, the need to confront racism, the universality of the church and the human race, the role of the church in socioeconomic development and in political revolution, and concern for the fullest development of all the resources of the church. For example, whole regions of the world such as Latin America and entire categories of people such as the laity represented to him important resources to be developed for the church's mission. Above all, the entire group of writings is testimony to the high regard in which Considine held the emerging churches of Asia, Africa, Latin America, and Oceania, and his view that their growth was making and will make the church become more and more catholic. Equally important for him was the key function mission has as a catalyst for the growth of the entire church.

Conclusion

An eloquent repartee occurred when Fr. Considine was in Rome in October 1957 for the Second World Congress for the Lay Apostolate. One of the keynotes was given by John C. H. Wu, one of the principal authors of the Nationalist Chinese Constitution, a law professor, and a convert to Catholicism in 1937. He had served as representative of Nationalist China to the Holy See in the years 1947–1949 and had become acquainted with Jacques Maritain. He was the author of *Beyond East and West*, a work that argued for a Christianity that rises above both East and West, allowing its spiritual orientation to be at home in all cultures.[67]

Considine listened to Wu's address, and his diary that day records a string of ideas harvested from Wu's presentation:

Dr. John Wu spoke and . . . contained some good material. . . . The need of anthropological concepts of [the] right sort: "To convert a pagan is not to lead him away from himself but to help him find

---

66. Ibid., IX-7.
67. Jingxiong [John C. H.]Wu, *Beyond East and West* (New York: Sheed & Ward, 1951).

himself." Two questions if we would call others: 1- Are we sufficiently informed about the Kingdom of God? 2- Do we have at least a basic knowledge of the people whom we would call? Let not the apostle destroy whatever is genuinely good, true, beautiful. The true East and the true West are to be found only in Christ. Reference for recognizing the pastoral truth in Eastern thinkers: Paul Tsi: *From Confucius to Christ.*[68]

Considine was three days from his sixtieth birthday, and his curiosity about the nature of the encounter of the peoples of the world with God was still vibrant and growing. His diary notes seem almost as intense as the memos he wrote to James Anthony Walsh thirty years prior as he digested question after question on the church's mission while working in Rome.

But he was also at the top of his game; he was at this time a key player in the church's efforts to be at home in non-European cultures. In his address, Wu gave a prominent place to an excerpt from Considine's *World Christianity* that proposed the proper attitude toward nonbelievers for mission-minded Catholics. The text from which Wu quoted is given in its entirety:

It is inadvisable to study the errors in Protestant sects, in Buddhism, or in Mohammadanism, if we do so only to prove that we are right and all others are wrong. The spirit of the forward-looking Catholic is to grasp the elements which, when presented to those outside, will lead them to see the beauty of the true Church and to enter it with rejoicing. Although the mission-minded Catholic is firm and courageous, he always respects the dignity of those outside the Faith and conducts himself with an elevation and nobility of spirit such as Christ Himself would exercise.[69]

For Considine, listening to a Chinese Catholic give a keynote at a congress in Rome must have been another moment when he felt that the church really was becoming a global institution. Similarly, hearing his own words quoted by Wu was probably yet another confirmation that his efforts to articulate a vision of World Christianity had been aimed in the right direction.

---

68. CD, October 6, 1957.
69. Considine, *World Christianity,* 8.

Considine, Ecumenism, and Interreligious Dialogue

IN THE EPILOGUE to *Across a World* (1942), Considine takes a surprising geographic turn. In almost four hundred pages of text, *Across a World* retraced the steps of Considine's first mission study tour of the Near East, Asia, and Africa. With his usual journalistic flare, Considine introduced the English-speaking world to the front lines of the expansion of Catholicism in many non-Western venues, making comprehensible to the faraway reader the nature of the work of Catholic missions as Considine observed them in the years 1931–1933.

The epilogue is only five pages, but two of those pages have a different geographic center—the United Kingdom. Subtitled "A Program of World Christianity," the epilogue in those two pages described a statement of the Joint Committee of English Catholics and Protestants of May 28, 1942. The statement focused on three points: the obligations of all Christian people to maintain the Christian heritage and to enhance its influence on social problems; the existence of a "large area of common ground" for all Christians that is not affected by church order or doctrinal questions and allows for full cooperation between Christians; and that the freedom to worship according to conscience is an essential freedom.[1] Surprising as it is to find a focus on Catholic–Protestant cooperation at the end of this lengthy text—Considine had only alluded to this matter as he told the story of his journey across Asia and Africa—it was not the first time that Considine had focused on the importance of improving Catholic–Protestant relations for the church's worldwide mission. Indeed, Considine had made this point in many writings prior to and after 1942.

---

1. John J. Considine and Thomas Dickenson Kernan, *Across a World* (New York: Longmans, Green & Co., 1942), 374.

This excursus provides a few brief highlights in regard to how John Considine reflected on, wrote about, and often taught on both ecumenism and interreligious dialogue as key components of a vision of World Christianity. Throughout his career he had a significant friendship for many years with Yale historian of missions Kenneth Scott Latourette, as well as with other Protestant leaders. Additionally, Considine charted a strategy of engagement for the Catholic Church with both other Christian churches and other religions that remains a model for today.

A Warm Friend

Kenneth Scott Latourette (1884-1968) was for nearly half a century professor of missions at Yale Divinity School and was the author of more than thirty-five major works on the topics of history of missions and of Asia, in addition to general works on the history of Christianity. The occasion that brought Latourette and Considine together was the former's 1929 work *A History of Christian Missions in China.* The work was comprehensive, covering the mission work of Protestant, Roman Catholic, and Russian Orthodox churches.[2] Latourette had visited the Maryknoll headquarters as part of his research for that book, and when this 930-page volume was published, it was read in its entirety to the student body at Maryknoll Seminary during meal times.

In *A History of Christian Missions in China,* Latourette had endeavored to be both fair and irenic and was thus able to gain the confidence of Catholic mission experts. Considine was one of the Catholic mission experts who appreciated Latourette's openness; the same tone in regard to Protestant missions pervaded Considine's own correspondence with Father (later Bishop) Francis Ford and his 1928 article on Protestantism in China.[3]

In his autobiography, Latourette later described Considine fondly:

> John J. Considine . . . was an early acquaintance who became a warm friend. . . . in many ways, I am deeply indebted to him. A priest of complete commitment to Christ, asking nothing for himself, possessed of an amazing knowledge of missions, with wide-ranging vision and great wisdom, few if any of his generation have made greater contributions to the foreign missions of the American branch of his church.[4]

---

2. Kenneth Scott Latourette, *A History of Christian Missions in China* (New York: Macmillan, 1929); see idem, *Beyond the Ranges: An Autobiography* (Grand Rapids: William B. Eerdmans, 1967), 56.

3. See chapter 4.

4. Latourette, *Beyond the Ranges,* 78–79.

From the beginning the two were kindred missionary souls, both men very much taken up with study of the church's worldwide outreach, expansion, and growth in the past and the present, both men convinced that their own work of scholarship was in service to that growth. The two would consult each other about specific research questions and frequently comment on each other's published writings. While Considine was stationed at the Maryknoll headquarters near Ossining, New York, 1934–1960, Latourette would come to visit almost every year, and Considine too would find occasions to visit Latourette at Yale. Latourette also made several donations to Maryknoll, which were gratefully acknowledged by Considine.

There was a quality of warmth and admiration to their communication, as exemplified in this excerpt from a 1936 letter from Considine to Latourette, written after Considine had returned from Maryknoll's Second General Chapter in Hong Kong:

> You will be interested . . . to hear that I made a contact with you through my roommate on the President Grant. He was a lawyer of Memphis, Tennessee who spent several pleasant days reading your history of China. He spoke frequently of the enjoyment and benefit he received from it. I felt very happy to be able to tell him that I was acquainted with you.[5]

Their long association resulted in the opening of doors in a mutually beneficial way. Subsequent to the publication of *A History of Christian Missions in China,* Considine and Latourette met in Rome, where Considine was able to help facilitate access to the Archives of Propaganda Fide for him. Latourette's autobiography recalls times spent with Maryknollers and others in Rome, including a papal audience in which he presented Pius XI with a copy of *History.* Considine also arranged for Latourette to speak at the inaugural Fordham Conference of Mission Specialists in 1953. In 1949, Considine also published a review of the progress of Catholic missions in the *International Review of Mission,* the main Protestant scholarly publication on mission at the time.[6]

The Reason

Why was Considine so interested in ecumenical and interreligious cooperation? Of course there is the usual lament that a divided Christianity makes the work of the Christian missioner more difficult. Among peoples for

5. John J. Considine, Ossining, NY, to Kenneth Scott Latourette, New Haven, CT, September 17, 1936. Box 52, Kenneth Scott Latourette Papers (RG 3). Special Collections, Yale Divinity School Library.

6. John J. Considine, "Missions of the Catholic Church: 1948," *International Review of Mission* 38 (1949): 165–80.

whom Christianity is unfamiliar, it becomes an extra task to explain to those trying to learn about the faith why Christians have divided themselves into different camps. However, that does not appear to be the main reason.

Considine was a student of history, and as he studied history he had gained a sense that the world had changed. The disputes of the sixteenth century that had so divided Christianity at that time were actually losing their sway to two new challenges—the challenge of making sure that Christianity could free itself from its Western cultural moorings in order to be up to the task of becoming at home in all the world's cultures, and the challenge of being ready to counter the forces of anti-religion.

Much has already been said above about the first challenge, that of indigenization and contextualization. Considine was ever concerned that the church and its missioners be equipped to invite the peoples of the world into a communion of faith in Christ that allows them to be who they are and have their own leadership yet also makes them one with all other peoples who are disciples of Jesus.[7]

Interestingly, the concept of contextualization itself can be employed to mitigate the force of historical disputes among Christian churches over doctrine and questions of church order. To a certain extent, could not the doctrinal disputes be understood as contextual, as helping Christians of previous times and places appropriate their faith according to the dictates of their conscience? Could not the churches at least ask if those disputes might best be understood as appropriate to those contexts? If the question could be asked, there was then a way to ask further contextual questions about avoiding cultural impositions in missionary work in non-Western cultures, namely, what were the ways that the peoples of Asia, Africa, Latin America, and Oceania might try to live faith in Christ according to the dictates of their consciences?

Thus, a missionary strategy of contextualization could permit a diffusing of the tension of the historical disputes between Christian churches. And if, then, the historical tension between Christians were no longer to be the main focus of attention, what should occupy the attention of Christian missioners? Considine suggested that a program of World Christianity was the only way to effectively meet the challenge of anti-religion.

Today as always, mankind divides into two camps: those who recognize the spiritual element in life, and those who ignore it or fight against it. In India, China, Japan, even among the tribes of Africa, this division is found. However crude and false in concept a religion may

---

7. John J. Considine, "Protestantism and Self-Government in China," *Ecclesiastical Review* 79 (Summer 1928): 301–4.

be, it is better than anti-religion; and, certainly, world Christianity has an ally for its journey into men's hearts in the existence of men of religion everywhere over the globe.[8]

The program of World Christianity was broadly conceived and included all of the following: cooperation among people of all faiths in favor of the advancement of religion everywhere; consistent and prayerful efforts toward "the union of Christendom"; and a global effort to bring all people "in personal sanctity and corporate religious life" into the church of Jesus Christ as members of that church.

Did that third part of the program of World Christianity in some way lock Considine into a colonialist, paternalist, or imperialist view of mission? In the final analysis, was he convinced of the superiority of Christianity to all other faiths? His comment was that this program was "threefold." In other words, Considine would not conceive of the third part as being accomplished without the first and the second parts; the manner of bringing others to communion with the church must be of a piece with the kind of respect for difference that is found in the first two parts of the program. Considine was talking about a global evangelization effort that began and ended with respect for all people who would be invited to faith in Christ and participation in the church; he was talking about a new way of mission and a new way of being church, a church without ethnocentrism. Writing in 1925 of the Vatican Mission Exposition, Considine elaborated on the meaning of this definition of the church:

> The Exposition . . . was meant most of all as an instrument of interpretation for the Church. That curious twist of things that lets men picture a vista of Western World cities—European or American—with Western World houses of worship, Western World peoples, Western World priests and bishops, as the Kingdom of God on earth, and leads them to tack on, as anomalous appendages, the Catholic bodies of Asia and Africa, is an offspring of lopsidedness of mind—due to thoughtlessness perhaps, indifference perhaps, self-centeredness perhaps—that has led men to forget that the Faith is theirs by priority of time only, and not of right.[9]

The Strategy

Whether speaking of ecumenism or respect for all religions, Considine was to a great extent ahead of his time. The official position of Catholicism

---

8. Considine, *Across a World,* 373.

9. John J. Considine, *The Vatican Mission Exposition: A Window on the World* (New York: Macmillan, 1925), 165.

until the Second Vatican Council was that the Catholic Church professed the true faith, and that all other religions or faiths harbored some degree of error. Therefore, it was not a simple matter for a Catholic to speak of the usefulness of respect for Protestant and Orthodox Christian faith, much less of respect for religions that were not Christian.

In *World Christianity*, Considine proposed that respect for other faiths is simply good mission strategy.

> A basic principle in the approach to non-Catholic or non-Christian beliefs is to recognize whatever in them is good and true. Experienced missioners in almost every part of the world find in every religious system some elements of truth and many good people. Numerous adherents of even the crudest and most corrupt of religious systems are subjectively sincere.[10]

The statement is another iteration of Considine's preference for a sympathetic understanding of the peoples of the world. There is nothing un-Catholic about being sympathetic to people with whom you are hoping to share the gospel of Christ. In other words, a missioner avoids drawing the ire of those who zealously try to differentiate Catholic from Protestant or Christian from Buddhist, Hindu, Muslim or any other faith, simply because the missioner's overall intent is to share the gospel and work on the expansion of the membership of the church.

But there were two other pieces to Considine's ecumenical and interreligious strategy: make use of the most authoritative statements available, and push the boundaries on the issue. In the epilogue of *Across a World,* a good example of Considine's use of authoritative statements is found:

> Pope Pius XII, in his encyclical *Summi Pontificatus* . . . speaks feelingly of his gratitude for the good wishes and prayers of those "who do not belong to the visible framework of the Catholic Church." He is confident that, "in their generosity and honesty, they could not bring themselves to forget all those links which bind them to Us, our common love of Christ's person, our common belief in God." He delineates in this sentence the great common ground on which Catholics meet, can meet, and should meet, first with non-Catholic Christians and secondly with all non-Christians of the world.[11]

Considine was well aware that an institution as large as the Catholic Church had in place real policies for dealing respectfully with people who

---

10. Considine, *World Christianity,* 8–9. See also the end of chapter 7 above.

11. Considine, *Across a World,* 373–74.

were not members of the church or who related to the institution of the church out of a secular or at least nonsectarian framework. The church had in place protocols and policy statements for many tasks related to this dynamic, such as the sending of missioners to areas where Christianity is not widely professed. The Holy See also sent its diplomatic corps to countries where Christianity had no official standing with the government and received back ambassadors from those countries. An awareness of these long traditions within the Catholic Church gave Considine sources of authoritative Catholic statements on relations with non-Catholics and non-Christians.

But the other side of Considine's strategy was to always push the boundaries of the church's limits on ecumenical and interreligious matters. Of course, he would avail himself of the first two legs of the strategy to do so, making clear that, if he was talking about a Hindu practice or Candomblé rituals in Brazil, he was doing so out of a missionary concern to share Christ and would protect himself by citing authoritative Catholic statements. But he definitely understood it as his role to make a sympathetic perspective on the cultures of the worlds peoples more accepted within Catholicism.

In *New Horizons in Latin America*, Considine described his research on Candomblé in Bahia, Brazil. The chapter weaves data gathered in Angola and West Africa during his previous two trips there with a narrative of the religious situation of the Afro Brazilians of Bahia. Four pages of the chapter are an ethnography of a Candomblé *matança*, a ritual killing of hens, pigeons, or small animals in order to offer the libation of their blood to the gods.[12] It was 1954 and Considine was a Catholic priest in attendance at a Candomblé ritual, and he was in attendance precisely to write and publish about it. After *Nostra Aetate* was proclaimed by the Second Vatican Council, this type of research conducted by Catholic clergy would become more common, but in the 1950s only a handful of church people were involved in such matters. Considine's purpose in being there was in order to write about it from the perspective of comparative religions. Although the chapter closes with a customary disclaimer that called the experience "shattering" and recommended greater efforts at evangelization among Afro Brazilians, his purpose was clearly that of offering accurate religious information from a sympathetic viewpoint to all who would understand and relate to this group of people.

Whether the situation was ecumenical or interreligious, Considine's respectful and sympathetic approach to cultures and religions was a matter to which he applied considerable effort. In terms of Christian ecumenism, he cultivated friendships and professional ties. In his writings is found evidence of two things that characterized his concern in this area: a seri-

---

12. An excerpt of Considine's description of the *matança* can be found in the appendix.

ous reflection on the development of a Catholic theological framework for cooperation with people of other faiths, and also the trying out of strategies or practical ways for creating a sympathetic and respectful climate for such cooperation. As has been seen, quite early in his career Considine declared that one of his greatest achievements, the founding of Fides Service in Rome, was modeled after a New York-based Protestant mission publicity agency, the Missionary Education Movement. Learning from the work of Protestants along with ecumenical and interreligious relations was a long-standing concern which was first expressed by Considine in the early 1920s[13] and included ecumenical speaking engagements through the 1960s.[14]

Prior to Vatican II, these efforts could only be understood as pioneering, as a contribution toward ecumenical and inter-religious understanding offered from the perspective of the church's missionary activity. Blazing a new trail was probably a lonely task, but Considine clearly saw the definition of Christianity and Christian mission was at stake in these ventures.

---

13. See Chapter 4.

14. Considine's diaries record several engagements, among which were at talk at Yale on Catholic mission in Latin America (9 December 1959) and another engagement with an ecumenical group at Harvard on 4 February 1960. Also in 1960, Yorke Allen's comprehensive *Seminary Survey* commended Considine for calling for a reasonable attitude on the part of Catholics toward Protestants.

The Considine family, circa 1908. *Standing left to right:* Walter, John J., Frank; *seated left to right:* Raymond, John W., Arthur, Alice. (Considine Family Archives)

The cover of the November 1914 issue of *The Field Afar,* likely the first issue of Maryknoll's mission magazine that Considine ever read. (Maryknoll Mission Archives)

The first six Maryknoll graduate students sent to Catholic University in 1922 and Fr. Leopold Tibesar. *Standing left to right:* Tom O'Melia, Fr. Tibesar, Francis Winslow; *seated left to right:* John Considine, Joseph McGinn, Pat Cleary, Joseph Connors. (Considine Family Archives)

The newly ordained priest, May 1923. (Considine Family Archives)

Considine at Maryknoll headquarters preparing the Maryknoll exhibits for shipment to the Vatican Missionary Exposition in 1924. (MMA)

Mission Priests and Brothers at the Vatican Missionary Exposition in Rome, 1925. Fr. Considine is in the top row, one person over to the left from a shorter missioner with a beard on the right side of the photo. Archbishop Marchetti, President of the Exposition, is seated at center. (Considine Family Archives)

At the Collegio Maryknoll in Rome in November 1928. *Seated left to right:* Frs. Francis Winslow, Francis Ford, James A. Walsh, and John J. Considine. Four seminarians stand in the rear; Bro. Leo Shields stands at right. (Considine Family Archives)

The 1929 Pontifical Mission to the Court of the Sovereigns of Ethiopia after the presentation of credentials in Addis Ababa; Considine, Secretary to the mission, is on the far right. (© 1929 Biblioteca Apostolica Vaticana)

During his diplomatic mission to Ethiopia, Considine confers with a Coptic monk. (MMA)

In Egypt, on the return trip from diplomatic mission to Ethiopia. (MMA)

Considine, far right, in an audience with Pope Pius XI. (Considine Family Archives)

In Szechuan Province, China, May 1932. This was the farthest inland point of Considine's journey in China. (MMA)

With Apostolic Delegate Archbishop Mooney in Nikko, Japan, August 1932. (MMA)

In Rome, 1934. (MMA)

Hong Kong, 1936, the Maryknoll Society elects a new leadership after the death of co-founder Bishop James A. Walsh in 1936. *Left to right:* Fr. James Drought (Vicar General), Fr. Considine, new Maryknoll Superior General Bishop James E. Walsh, Fr. Thomas Kiernan, and Fr. William O'Shea. (MMA)

In the office of the Superior General James E. Walsh, 1937. (MMA)

At Maryknoll in 1939. (MMA)

Fr. Considine with Maryknollers and parishioners in Pando province, Bolivia, in 1945; Maryknollers began working in the Pando Vicariate in 1942. Considine was on his second mission study tour, his first visit to Latin America. (MMA)

During his 1953 mission study tour, Considine called on the Apostolic Vicar of Taeugu, Korea, Bishop John Baptist Choi Deok-hong. The bishop's secretary, standing second from left was Fr. Stephen Kim Sou-hwan, who in 1969 became the first Korean Cardinal. (MMA)

Fr. Considine received an honorary doctorate from Fordham University in 1955. Francis Cardinal Spellman, Archbishop of New York, looks on. (MMA)

At Maryknoll. (MMA)

A papal audience with John XXIII, March 22, 1961. At left is Archbishop Antonio Samorè, Vice President of the Pontifical Commission for Latin America. Later that same year, Pope John called on U.S. religious communities to send a tenth of their membership to serve the church in Latin America. (Considine Family Archives)

Fr. Considine in the 1970s at the Mission Research and Planning
Department at Maryknoll. (MMA)

CHAPTER 9

Coming to Grips with the Real Latin America 1960–1965

THE 1959 CUBAN revolution shifted U.S. public attention toward Latin America in a new way. The Cold War had first drawn the United States into the Korean conflict, and then into the arms race and the space race. When General Batista fled and Fidel Castro's band of rebels emerged victorious on New Year's Day in 1959, the U.S. populace began to understand Latin America as the next arena of contention with the world's other super power, the Soviet Union.

The Vatican was aware that this shift was taking place; it had, in fact, for some time been trying to get U.S. Catholics to pay attention to the needs of the church in Latin America, especially its lack of sufficient clergy to staff its many parishes and works. For Vatican officials, the twin threats of communism and Protestantism in Latin America could be effectively checked if a vigorous renewal of pastoral life could take place throughout the region. To achieve this renewal, more priests would have to be recruited for the church in Latin America. Pius XII and John XXIII sent pleas to various nations to share their clergy with Latin America, always with a view toward this being a temporary measure until sufficient new Latin American recruits could be trained and ordained in Latin America for service in their own church.

John Considine would be called upon to lead the effort to send more U.S. church personnel to serve in Latin America, an unprecedented effort of the church in one continent to aid the church in another. This chapter and the following explore Considine's work as director of the U.S. bishops' Latin America Bureau (LAB) in the years 1960–1968. Under his leadership, the number of U.S. missioners at work in Latin America doubled, even as the enterprise itself enjoyed only limited support from the U.S. bishops;

the lack of support was noticeable from as early as 1959. At the same time, Considine used every means at his disposal to consolidate support for the mission, only to be blamed later for its shortcomings.

The present chapter tells the story of the founding of the LAB through 1965 and gives particular attention to Considine's efforts to break down U.S. prejudice against Latin Americans as he worked to build up the U.S. Catholic mission to Latin America in the 1960s. The following chapter covers the subsequent years through Considine's retirement in 1968 at age seventy. That chapter also focuses on the controversy created by Ivan Illich's 1967 essay "The Seamy Side of Charity."

In order for a strategy of temporary assistance to the church in Latin America by U.S. priests to be implemented, church officials in Rome and in the United States were aware that North American apathy toward and ignorance of Latin America had to be addressed. Considine characterized the situation in this way:

> The truth is that most U.S. Catholics, like their fellow-citizens, possess an inadequate understanding of the 200 million Latin Americans with whom they share this hemisphere. In place of facts—historical, social and religious facts—we have too often cherished myths and stereotypes. "The Latins are backward," we hear it said. "They won't practice their religion." "They're lazy!" Such false though all too familiar impressions prevent our coming to grips with the real Latin America. Too often we lack an understanding of how each continent substantially influences the life of the other. This inhibits even our well-intentioned attempts to labor together with the Latin American peoples in resolving the common problems of our hemisphere.
>
> We must find our way out of this fog of misinformation and misunderstanding.[1]

While the Castro victory had made Latin America a battleground in the Cold War, it was not immediately apparent to U.S. Catholics in the 1960s that they should suddenly care about whether their impressions of Latin Americans were false or not. Yet this was precisely the point that Considine felt had to be made—any U.S. strategy to counter communism in Latin America that did not include creating real bonds of human respect between the peoples of the Americas would be woefully inadequate and certainly not worthy of endorsement by the church. For Considine, the communist threat provided an opportunity for the church to build impor-

---

1. John J. Considine, *The Church in the New Latin America* (Notre Dame, IN: Fides, 1964), 139.

tant bridges of understanding and respect between the Catholics of the Western Hemisphere.

> We owe it in charity to our Latin neighbors and to ourselves. Their destinies and ours are at stake; the future of our faith and the survival of our way of life are being decided now in Latin America.[2]

In late 1959, the National Catholic Welfare Conference (NCWC) created a Latin America Bureau (LAB), and in January 1960 Fr. John Considine accepted the U.S. bishops' offer to be its director. In this position from 1960 to 1968, Considine was charged by the bishops with organizing the sending of increased numbers of U.S. church personnel to aid the church in Latin America, working cooperatively with the bishops of Latin America.

U.S. influence in global affairs is generally understood to have been strong at the beginning of the 1960s. This influence came under sharp critique as the war in Vietnam escalated and new information concerning the abuse of human rights in the United States came to light during the civil rights movement. Latin Americans felt a particular betrayal by the United States in the mid-1960s when the United States invaded the Dominican Republic and the Alliance for Progress was transformed into an instrument of U.S. Cold War politics.

The story of the U.S. Catholic mission to Latin America has tended to follow this arc of decline in U.S. influence abroad: the mission worked well when U.S. influence was stronger in the years 1960–1964 but then faltered as skepticism and scrutiny of U.S. involvements overseas increased. However, that formulation is too simplistic and ignores the fact that, over time, missioners who stayed in Latin America began to mature, not decline, in their commitment to work in the region. Additionally, while it is true that in the past Christian mission has been criticized as too closely tied to the paternalistic interests of colonial nations, it is also true that the objectives of the church in its mission and the objectives of political powers are not identical, and that Catholic missions in the twentieth century began to operate from an indigenizing perspective which implied greater solidarity with the people among whom a missioner works.

As the U.S. bishops undertook in the 1960s to increase the number of U.S. church personnel working in Latin America, Considine understood his role at the LAB to be principally within the United States—his job would be to coordinate more involvement from the U.S. church, while the management of the mission work per se would be the responsibility of the bishops of Latin America. The basic goals of the LAB were to edu-

---

2. Ibid.

cate the church in the United States about the church in Latin America, to recruit new personnel and train them in the language and culture of their mission region; thereafter the supervision of their work would be the responsibility of the bishops of Latin America. Considine would, of course, meet with Latin American leaders frequently, either in Latin America or in Washington, and would remain in constant communication with them. He also devised a public forum—the Catholic Inter-American Cooperation Program (CICOP)—to educate the church in the United States on Latin American concerns.

At the Latin America Bureau 1960–1964

Though aware of a certain lack of enthusiasm for mission to Latin America among some members of the hierarchy, Considine seemed to have relished the opportunity to garner their support. Indeed, there was much about his new role that appealed to him. The LAB was understood as coming under the purview of the U.S. bishops, but was created through a request that the Vatican had made to the U.S. bishops at the 1959 Inter-American Bishops Conference. That configuration would afford Considine continuous use of one of his strongest mission strategies—aligning a project tightly to the aims and authority of the Holy See and bringing maximum benefit to the project from the higher-ups in Rome. It was a card that Considine would play over and over again with the U.S. bishops during his years at the LAB.

Considine also seemed game for the challenge of working with a new boss, the hierarchy of the United States. A missioner always has a particular axe to grind with the rest of the church. For the missioner, what he or she does—sharing the gospel with those who do not know it or supporting churches presently unable to sustain themselves—is a responsibility that should be assumed by all Christians. Working for the bishops would give Considine the opportunity as never before to tell diocesan priests, religious, and laity that they too could be missioners in Latin America, that their testimony and their communities were needed in this effort. It would no longer be a question of leaving mission to missioners but, rather, a matter of redefining Catholic life in the United States as actively in mission to Latin America.

As he hired a staff and established the offices of the LAB, he sought out collaborators with years of pastoral or intercultural experience. Chicago Msgr. William J. Quinn had been working as director for the bishops' Committee on Migrants when he was recruited by Considine to be LAB co-director in early 1962. Quinn was a veteran of Catholic Action and would soon serve as a peritus at Vatican II. As a seminarian, Quinn had been one of the protégés of Msgr. Reynold Hillenbrand at St. Mary of the Lake Seminary, several of whom were destined to have a large impact on the church in the United States: Msgr. John J. Egan, Msgr. George G. Higgins, Bishop Michael Dempsey, Msgr. Daniel Cantwell, and Bishop Alfred Abramowicz. Considine had hoped that Quinn would become his successor, but Quinn left the LAB at the beginning of 1967, apparently after a protracted conflict with Fr. Louis M. Colonnese, the LAB administrative director. Colonnese was a priest of the Diocese of Davenport and, in the end, was selected by the bishops to succeed Considine after the latter's retirement in 1968. Considine also tried to recruit Fr. (later Cardinal) Theodore McCarrick and Msgr. (later Bishop) James Shannon to join the LAB staff, but in each case their archbishops would not release them.[3]

The list of activities undertaken at the LAB gets long: Considine started and edited four LAB publications;[4] he worked with several international student initiatives, both for Latin American students in the United States and for sending U.S. students to Latin America for short-term educational trips; he met with leaders of Latin American trade unions; he established an NCWC Peace Corps Desk within the LAB;[5] and he coordinated an initiative to have the December 12 commemoration of Our Lady of Guadalupe raised to the category of a feast in the Western Hemisphere.[6] Considine also saw it as his responsibility to be an on-the-go ambassador of the North American Catholic mission to Latin America, and so he traveled to speaking engagements frequently—usually he had either more than one trip in a single week or more than one destination on a single trip. He spoke to clergy groups, lay associations of all sorts, to students and faculty at Catholic colleges and universities, and at the large annual conferences of Catholic organizations such as the National Catholic Education Association and Catholic Charities. He also met frequently in his office with visiting bishops and other officials from Latin America, as well as just about anyone who had an idea or suggestion to offer in reference to the church in Latin America.

The elements of the LAB program on which he concentrated the most were: CICOP; the Papal Volunteers for Latin America (PAVLA); fundraising and the annual allocations of funds to projects in Latin America; all kinds of recruitment activities for the mission; and the establishment of training centers in Latin America for the increased number of missioners

---

3. Considine's diaries describe the recruitment of both priests. McCarrick: 5 Nov 1962; 11, 18, and 22 Jan 1963; 13 Feb 1963. Shannon: 9 Feb 1962; 8 April 1963; 22 May 1963. Also on Shannon, the following correspondence: John Considine, Washington, to Leo Binz, St. Paul, MN, 10 May 1963. ACUA, NCWC General Secretary, Box 189, Folder 23.

4. *Latin America Calls; LAB Letter; Coordination Bulletin; Personnel Bulletin.*

5. CD, April 20, 1961.

6. John Considine, Washington, DC, to Karl Alter, Cincinnati, OH, May 23, 1962. ACUW, NCWC General Secretary, 189:6.

who were recruited to go there in the 1960s. During the years 1960–1963, the task of creating training centers in Latin America for new missioners occupied a good deal of Considine's time and attention. He turned first to Msgr. Ivan Illich, a Croatian by birth, who was trained in Rome and incardinated in the Archdiocese of New York. Illich had been running a successful Spanish-language and cultural training program during the summers in Ponce, Puerto Rico.

It was hard for people to be neutral about Illich—people were either enthralled by his ability to relate spirituality and theology to intercultural relations or were repelled by his caustic manner of speaking and teaching. Over the years of their association—Considine first met Illich at the Fordham Rural Life Conference in 1958—Considine experienced both polarities. Parts of the story of their relationship and conflicts are told below, but a larger description is contained in the following chapter.

It is clear that Considine admired Illich as someone who was very gifted at teaching important cultural intangibles to English-speaking students from the United States. Dom Helder Câmara had a Portuguese neologism for this cultural training process—*desgringalização*; Illich would later translate it as "de-Yankification."[7] But things did not go well between Considine and Illich—Considine criticized Illich's fiscal management of the Center of Intercultural Formation in Cuernavaca, Mexico, and also the sharpness of tone in Illich's "de-Yankification" methods. Considine enlisted Cardinal Cushing to write letters to rein in Illich on both matters,[8] seemingly without success—Illich was not someone to be controlled, and, as experienced as Illich was with the church's Roman bureaucracy, it would be surprising if he did not recognize Considine's hand in the Cardinal's missives. Finally, in August 1963, Considine established a second year-round training center in Ponce, Puerto Rico, to offer new missioners an alternative to Illich's program. Maryknoll Fr. James Stefaniak was recruited as the director of the new program.

Pope John's Call for Ten Percent
One of the first tasks on Considine's mind as he assumed the LAB directorship in 1960 was the creation of greater public awareness for the U.S. Catholic mission to Latin America by means of a "papal appeal." Indeed, the theme of envisioning all of the new LAB's efforts within a framework of

---

7. Francine du Plessix Gray, *Divine Disobedience: Profiles in Catholic Radicalism* (New York: Knopf, 1970), 253.

8. John J. Considine, Washington, to Richard Cushing, Boston, February 12, 1962. ACUA, NCWC General Secretary, Box 186, Folder 47. John J. Considine, Washington, to Richard Cushing, Boston, January 9, 1963. ACUA, NCWC General Secretary, Box 187, Folder 20.

the efforts of the Holy See pervades Considine's May 1960 draft "Outline of Functions for the LAB," which Considine developed for the NCWC. The document presents a comprehensive plan of action for the LAB and the NCWC as a response to the call of the Holy See to aid the church in Latin America. The Outline also made reference to a papal appeal.[9]

In the early summer of 1961 Considine learned that Archbishop Samorè, secretary of the Pontifical Commission for Latin America (CAL), had been given a spot on the agenda of the national meeting of Major Religious Superiors, to be held in August at the University of Notre Dame. Considine met with the U.S. apostolic delegate, Archbishop Vagnozzi, and several prominent superiors general of congregations of women religious on several occasions to confer about the kind of appeal that would have the greatest impact.

Due to the death of the Vatican's secretary of state, Cardinal Tardini, Archbishop Samorè could not come himself but sent Msgr. Agostino Casaroli to deliver the message of Pope John XXIII in regard to the church in Latin America. On the evening of August 17, 1961, Msgr. Casaroli delivered a clear call to U.S. religious communities to send a portion of their membership to serve in Latin America:

> This ideal is the following, namely, that each religious province aim to contribute to Latin America in the next ten years a tithe—ten per cent—of its present membership as of this current year. For example, if the present membership is 500, the ideal would be to contribute by the end of this decade fifty members for Latin America.
>
> Naturally, all will not be able to achieve this ideal. But it may be possible to reach at least ninety or eighty per cent of it.[10]

It is not entirely clear that Considine is the author of the "ten percent" formula. Although Considine's diary entry for the following day registered his strong satisfaction that his "set of notes of a couple of months ago become a reality in the name of the Holy See,"[11] the reference is ambiguous because Casaroli's talk covered many areas such as a thorough presentation of the Holy See's reasons for special concern for the church in Latin America, and a list of possible types of works to be taken up by U.S. religious in the region. It goes without saying, however, that the call to

---

9. This was Considine's second draft, composed after consultations with CAL in Rome. "Outline of Functions of Latin American Bureau, N.C.W.C." May 6, 1960. ACUA, Office of the General Secretary of the NCWC, Box 43, Folder 4. For the papal appeal, see p. 6.

10. Gerald M. Costello, *Mission to Latin America: The Successes and Failures of a Twentiety-Century Crusade* (Maryknoll, NY: Orbis Books, 1979), 281.

11. CD, August 18, 1961.

send ten percent of U.S. religious to Latin America was something Considine strongly supported. And the "ten percent" call, though never remotely
fulfilled numerically,[12] served the effective purpose of generating a great
deal of interest in the U.S. Catholic mission to Latin America. Religious
communities that had done no previous foreign missionary work were
approaching Considine and the LAB staff as never before for information
and orientation on how to best respond to the plea given by Msgr. Casaroli
on behalf of Pope John XXIII.

God Be Praised for This Day, Which Accomplished So Much Good[13]

On January 20, 1964, at the Edgewater Beach Hotel in Chicago, Considine witnessed two thousand people in attendance at the first Catholic
Inter-American Cooperation Program (CICOP). Such a strong turnout
certainly sparked feelings of thankfulness and considerable satisfaction in
him. Six cardinals—three from Latin America and three from the United
States—shared the presidency of CICOP, while fifty other Catholic leaders and specialists from Latin America were on hand as guests. Though U.S.
VIPs such as Senator Hubert Humphrey were also present, the main dyna-
mism that attracted so many people to the program was the opportunity
for U.S. Catholics to hear and learn about the church in Latin America
from Latin Americans themselves. Attending the meeting were representatives of dioceses and religious orders based in the United States that had
either made commitments to send people to Latin America or were con-
templating doing so.

To make CICOP happen, Considine had been able to count on the
capable assistance of the LAB staff, most notably the co-director, Msgr.
William J. Quinn of Chicago, a man who had nurtured and developed
the idea of CICOP for more than a year. Fr. Louis M. Colonnese assisted
on the LAB staff as its administrative director and conference secretary.
The idea of a big inter-American Catholic meeting had been brewing for
some time. In November 1961, Msgr. Ivan Illich proposed to Considine
the need for a "dialogue in depth meeting," but the two churchmen were
unable to agree on where such a meeting should be held and how it should
be called.[14] As we will see, such disagreements between Considine and
Illich were to become common in the 1960s, and in the planning stages of
CICOP the two churchmen would compete to become the organizer of

---

12. In 1967, Ivan Illich estimated that more than twenty thousand U.S. religious would
have to transfer to Latin America in order to fulfill the ten percent ideal ("The Seamy Side
of Charity" *America* [January 21, 1967]: 88).

13. CD, January 20, 1964.

14. CD, November 25 and 26, 1961.

an inter-American meeting. In May 1963, Illich proposed that Considine ask Illich's Center of Intercultural Formation (CIF) in Cuernavaca, Mexico, to organize a seminar for U.S. bishops at CIF, but Considine responded that the LAB was busy working on CICOP, and he requested that Illich join that effort.[15]

In May, Illich had also told Considine of a meeting of Latin American bishops and Canadian religious superiors at CIF, which he would be hosting in late May and early June, and he requested that Considine invite a couple of U.S. bishops and that LAB help pay for the meeting. Considine did not arrange for the LAB to support that meeting nor did he try to get any bishops to go.

It appears that not long after the CIF meeting, Considine was still inclined to the idea of having U.S. bishops and major superiors incorporate activities at CIF as part of an annual study journey.[16] However, sometime in the summer of 1963 Considine learned more about the CIF meeting and began to sour on Illich's plans, calling the conclusions of that meeting "unsatisfactory."[17]

In the fall of 1962, Msgr. Quinn was organizing on behalf of the LAB a large inter-American meeting to be held in January 1963. In November 1962, Considine convinced Quinn that such a meeting needed more preparation, and so it was postponed one year and given the name of CICOP. Illich came to the September 1963 CICOP planning meeting, but his participation provoked this reaction from Bill Quinn:

> Everyone seems quite interested in the meeting, and there should be a large turnout for the two days of "circus type" approach. Everyone, that is, except John Illich[18] who showed up briefly at the committee meeting in Washington two weeks ago and attempted to reroute the whole meeting. We managed to fend him off with a modicum of difficulty. I think this guy is becoming some kind of nut.[19]

---

15. Ivan Illich, Cuernavaca, Mexico, to John Considine, Washington, May 3, 1963; and John Considine, Washington, to Ivan Illich, Cuernavaca, Mexico, May 10, 1963. ACUA, NCWC General Secretary, 186:55.

16. John Considine, Washington, to Ivan Illich, Cuernavaca, Mexico, June 27, 1963. ACUA, NCWC General Secretary, 186:55.

17. John Considine, Washington, to Antonio Samorè, Rome, September 3, 1963. MMA, Considine Papers, 3:3.

18. That is, Ivan Illich; see Joseph P. Fitzpatrick, *The Stranger Is Our Own: Reflections on the Journey of Puerto Rican Migrants* (Kansas City, MO: Sheed & Ward, 1996), 17.

19. William Quinn, Chicago, to Leo Mahon, San Miguelito, Panama, September 17, 1963. UNDA, San Miguelito Papers, Box: 1; Folder: General Correspondence y Comienzos de la Obra; Jan., 1962–Dec., 1963.

CICOP and the LAB

The planning for the January 1964 first-ever CICOP progressed without Illich. By that time, Considine had been at the U.S. bishops' Latin America Bureau for three and a half years. Though he was in his sixties, the job had turned into a new mission for Considine—a new purpose in life. Between 1960 and 1968, he built the LAB up from scratch and into its catalyst role of promoting greater U.S. Catholic participation in missions to Latin America.

The first years had been filled with the usual fires to be put out as he sought to keep bishops in the United States and Latin America working cooperatively, all the while maintaining a good relationship with CAL in Rome. In addition to setting up the fundraising for his work and hiring a staff, Considine was also involved in allocating millions of dollars for projects in Latin America, establishing two training centers for new missioners, creating an inter-American lay mission movement, and recruiting about a thousand new missioners for work in Latin America. He was able to rely on CAL to provide a strong mission motivation for communities of religious men and women that were considering sending some of their members to serve in the church in Latin America.

However, the purpose of CICOP differed significantly from other LAB activities. Considine effectively used CICOP as a vehicle for addressing the intangibles in an effort to counter prejudice against Latin Americans and build a better relationship between the Americas, one geared toward ever more mutual respect among Catholics on both continents. It was one thing to do committee work with bishops and to run an office that focused on Catholic concerns in Latin America. It was quite another—and quite a tall order—to devise a plan to tip the scales of public opinion away from the prejudice against Latin Americans that, at the time, pervaded the outlook of U.S. Catholics.

It was the kind of challenge Considine thoroughly relished. He often asked himself what could be done to improve the quality of the relationship that Catholics of the Americas shared. CICOP was his answer, as it served as a forum that would foster dialogue between and amid the religious adherents of North and South America, as well as encourage an increased awareness of one group for the other. As he himself put it, in CICOP Considine had created

> . . . a program whereby the mass of Church members in the United States may as Christians achieve fuller understanding, friendship and concern for their fellow Christians of Latin America.
>
> It aims at mutual understanding and friendship based on the principle that, regardless of social or economic circumstances of life, Chris-

tian peoples, indeed all peoples should know and accept each other as people. The program is vital to the Church in the United States in its master plan to recognize its proper relations to the Church in Latin America.[20]

Dom Helder Câmara had put this problem on the agenda at the 1959 Georgetown meeting, calling for a change of "consciousness" in the developed world about the importance of the problems of the developing world.[21] When CICOP was launched in 1964, it aimed to be an explicit response to the challenge that the Brazilian bishop had laid down.

Future CICOPs —ten annual meetings were held each January from 1964 to 1973—would not feature the presence of as broad a group of Latin American and North American church leadership as was the case in 1964. Nonetheless, future meetings would consistently offer forums for reflections on the current state of Catholicism as practiced in the Western Hemisphere. Likewise, CICOP would continue to encourage conversation between the peoples of Latin America and North America. Nothing like this existed in any other Catholic setting, and perhaps not in civil society of the time either.

What is the place of CICOP in the history of inter-American Catholic relations? When we contemplate the late-twentieth- and early-twenty-first-century solidarity of U.S. Catholics with Latin America—the violent deaths of the four U.S. church women in El Salvador in 1980 or of Sister Dorothy Stang in Brazil in 2005 come to mind—it is important to understand that this north–south Catholic solidarity has many founders, and credit should be given where credit is due. For example, the Redemptorists were the first U.S. missioners to work in Latin America, beginning in Puerto Rico in 1899. Fr. John Burke, C.S.P., became a pioneer of inter-American Catholic relations when, in 1928, he assisted in the negotiations to end state persecution of the church in Mexico, effectively taking part in the first high-level inter-American discussions involving the U.S. hierarchy and a Latin American hierarchy.[22] Archbishop (later Cardinal) Ritter

---

20. John Joseph Considine, *The Church in the New Latin America* (Notre Dame, IN: Fides, 1964), 138–39.

21. James F. Garneau, "The First Inter-American Episcopal Conference November 2–4, 1959: Canada and the United States Called to the Rescue of Latin America," *Catholic Historical Review* 87, no. 4 (2001): 680–81. Dom Helder also spoke to Considine on this point in Washington: "[Dom Helder and] I . . . had a serious and perhaps a fruitful talk about Dom Helder's conviction that understanding between the peoples of the Americas is the major objective, above any question of personnel or money. We are committed both of us to seek to develop unofficially a committee to improve relations" (CD, October 22, 1961).

22. Though Fr. Burke was not a bishop himself, he was at the time representing the U.S. hierarchy as secretary general of the National Catholic Welfare Conference.

became the first U.S. bishop to found a diocesan mission in Latin America in 1956, and in 1955 the shared work of Frs. Ivan Illich and Joseph Fitzpatrick, S.J., assisted the U.S. church with the first systematic studies on religion and migration from Latin America to the U.S. mainland.

Some of Fr. Considine's Latin American "firsts" may seem bureaucratic—his office was in fact called a *bureau*, and his work was often behind the scenes. For example, the first U.S. bishops' committee dedicated to a region of the world was the Committee on the Church in Latin America. Considine did not set up this committee—it was put in place at the 1959 NCWC meeting—and in a technical sense, the committee was Considine's "boss." But Considine was always using his relationship with the bishops' Committee on Latin America to educate them on the church in Latin America and to expand the reach of the LAB. The fact of the matter was that, even though the U.S. bishops had started the Latin America Bureau at the request of the Vatican, they remained for the most part ambivalent—if not apathetic—about the importance of sending U.S. church personnel to Latin America.[23] Ever so diplomatically during the 1960s, Considine challenged their apathy and successfully set an ambitious agenda for the U.S. bishops on Latin America.

CICOP, of course, was an important first. Through CICOP, Considine set up the first broad-based inter-American Catholic consultation on the church's pastoral life, and, judging by the consistently high numbers of participants over its ten-year run, it was undoubtedly a needed forum. It was ever a venue that served its original purposes of creating greater ties and greater solidarity between Catholics of the Americas and served as an effective instrument for educating U.S. Catholics on Latin America.

Thus, in Considine the bishops had definitely hired the right man to lead the Latin American effort, one who was convinced of the importance of the U.S. Catholic mission to Latin America and who was able to convince them of its importance in turn. Considine set about to build institutions and to establish relationships among Catholic leaders in Latin and North America. He also created publications and an educational forum that served to introduce U.S. Catholics to their brothers and sisters in the faith south of the border. Thus, the first director of the Latin America Bureau succeeded in establishing fruitful relationships, ones that would engender a new north–south Catholic solidarity that would continue to grow strong

---

23. Archbishop Alter, chairman of the NCWC, spoke at the Georgetown Meeting of his opposition to sending U.S. religious to Latin America (Garneau, "First Inter-American Episcopal Conference," 675–76). At the 1959 NCWC meeting, Cardinal McIntyre imagined U.S. Catholic assistance to Latin America in terms of administration, of helping them to organize their chanceries (ibid., 684). See also below, the letter of January 27, 1960, from Cardinal Cushing to Bishop Comber.

for many years. Today we still have him to thank for his careful work of getting conversations going, conversations that launched many years of inter-American cooperation efforts.

The U.S. Bishops and Latin America 1928–1959

There were several historical antecedents in the U.S. church to the founding of the LAB in 1959, though none of these had as expansive a mission as the LAB would have post-1959. During the years 1929–1933, a Latin America Bureau did exist at the National Catholic Welfare Conference (NCWC);[24] it was led by Msgr. Ray McGowan of the Social Action Department. The purpose of the LAB at that time was "to help Catholics of Latin America and the United States to know one another and to become acquainted with one another's accomplishments and experiences particularly in Catholic action."[25] Just prior to this in 1928, the NCWC secretary general, Fr. John Burke, C.S.P., had been involved in the aforementioned negotiations to end the persecution of the church in Mexico;[26] the founding of a bureau to promote hemispheric understanding among Catholics may have emerged as a result of those efforts.

The USCCB Archives also list Richard Pattee as a part-time director of the "Latin America Bureau" at the NCWC from 1946 to 1950; Pattee produced several monographs on the Catholic Church in Latin America that highlight the progress of the church in that region, even in the face of tremendous obstacles.[27] Pattee's works aimed to educate Catholics in the United States on the church in Latin America, and in that respect foreshadowed the era of inter-American Catholic cooperation that the LAB would push so much under Considine's leadership in the 1960s.

Other initiatives were aimed at specific areas of cooperation or education. The Catholic Association for International Peace (CAIP) (1929–

---

24. A brief background on the nomenclature of the national organizations of the U.S. bishops: 1917–1919: National Catholic War Council (NCWC); 1919–1922: National Catholic Welfare Council (also NCWC); 1922–1966: National Catholic Welfare Conference (also NCWC); 1966–2001: twin organizations existed—the United States Catholic Conference (USCC) and the National Conference of Catholic Bishops (NCCB); 2001–present: U.S. Conference of Catholic Bishops (USCCB).

25. NCWC Press Release, 1931, cited in Angelyn Dries, *The Missionary Movement in American Catholic History* (Maryknoll, NY: Orbis Books, 1998), 97.

26. Mary M. McGlone, *Sharing Faith Across the Hemisphere* (Washington, DC: United States Catholic Conference, 1997), 61–62.

27. Richard Pattee, *Richard Pattee's Catholicism in Latin America* (Washington, DC: National Catholic Welfare Conference, 1945); idem, *Love Thy Neighbor: Is the Church Failing in the Americas?* (Huntington, IN: Our Sunday Visitor Press, 1930). The publication date of the latter work appears to be incorrect, as several parts of the text refer to events in 1948 (pp. 4; 5; 9).

1969)[28] was affiliated with the NCWC; its mission was to apply Catholic social teachings to international affairs. Latin America was the focus of the research and publications[29] of the CAIP on numerous occasions. Another initiative, inspired by the desire to make Catholic social teachings better known and to enable Catholics to participate meaningfully in the construction of a more just world order, were the Inter-American Social Action Seminars. Between 1942 and 1958, these seminars brought together a true inter-American grouping—the 1946 seminar counted eighty-seven participants from twenty-four different countries of the Western Hemisphere.[30] The Inter-American Rural Life Congresses throughout the 1950s were another forum for Catholic inter-American cooperation.[31]

Latin American Catholic Integration Initiatives

Meanwhile, a regional integration of Catholic leadership was launched in 1955: the Latin American Bishops' Conference (CELAM, for its Spanish and Portuguese initials) was founded in Rio de Janeiro, inaugurating solidarity among bishops of twenty-two Latin American countries. Through CELAM, the Latin American bishops began to speak with one voice. The bishops who would become Considine's principal Latin American partners all formed part of the early leadership of this group: Manuel Larraín, bishop of Talca, Chile; Helder Câmara, auxiliary bishop of Rio de Janeiro; and Msgr. Julián Mendoza, who would later become bishop of Buga, Colombia.

In 1958, Pope Pius XII inaugurated the Pontifical Commission for Latin America (CAL, for its initials in Italian, Latin, Portuguese, and Spanish), Rome's institutional answer to the question of what to do to aid the church in Latin America. The mission to aid the Latin American church permitted an almost unlimited scope of activities. Cardinal Mimmi of the Congregation of the Consistory headed the Commission, while Archbishop Antonio Samorè acted as its secretary and, later, vice president. Samorè had been

---

28. Over the years, the CAIP was led by Msgr. John A. Ryan, Msgr. Raymond McGowan, and Msgr. George Higgins. The CAIP disbanded in 1969 because the Office of International Affairs of the new USCC, along with LAB, had assumed many of the duties formerly accomplished by the CAIP (Thomas E. Quigley, "Notes on the History of the U.S. Bishops' Conference in Its Relations with the Church in Latin America" [unpublished manuscript], 3).

29. Catholic Association for International Peace, *Latin America and the United States; Preliminary Study Presented to the Catholic Association for International Peace* (New York: Paulist Press, 1929); Catholic Association for International Peace (U.S.) and Richard Pattee, *The Catholic Revival in Mexico* (Washington, DC: Catholic Association for International Peace, 1944).

30. Quigley, "Notes," 3–5.

31. Ibid., 5.

involved in the 1955 events in Rio de Janeiro, which, in addition to the creation of CELAM, also included an International Eucharistic Congress that had preceded the bishops' meeting.

The Georgetown Meeting

Throughout the 1950s Popes Pius XII and John XXIII issued calls for the church outside Latin America to send aid to that region.[32] CAL was greatly concerned to get the North American hierarchies involved, and so the Commission convoked an Inter-American Episcopal Conference, which was held at Georgetown University November 2–4, 1959.[33] Although in 1957 the U.S. bishops rejected a proposal to establish a bishops' committee on the church in Latin America, CAL called this inter-American meeting of bishops. What came to be called the 1959 Georgetown Meeting gathered six bishops from Latin America, six from the United States and six from Canada. A seventh U.S. prelate, Cardinal Cushing, was asked to chair the meeting, and Archbishop Antonio Samorè of CAL was present.

Although more than two thousand U.S. Catholic missioners were at work in Latin America at the time of the Georgetown meeting,[34] the U.S. Catholic hierarchy prior to that meeting had only had moments of contact with the church in Latin America; Catholic Relief Services had also sent aid to the region. At the Georgetown meeting, the Pontifical Commission for Latin America proposed a change in this state of affairs, challenging the bishops to become involved in the sending of personnel to aid the church in Latin America. This was a departure from previous mission practice; rather than leaving the organization of missions to the mission-sending groups such as Maryknoll, the Columbans, the Jesuits, the Medical Missionaries of Mary, or the Society of the Divine Word, the establishment of the Latin America Bureau meant that the relationship of bishops and mission-sending groups would be adjusted by two new concepts:

1. Anyone can be a foreign missioner. While most mission-sending groups always sought the support of the hierarchy in the United States for overseas mission work, Maryknoll had at the same time fostered a mystique of the foreign missioner as a special calling. But the picture within the church of who could be a foreign missioner was already changing in the 1950s. In 1956, the Archdiocese of St. Louis began sending diocesan priests to Bolivia to serve for a period of years,[35] and in 1958, Cardinal Cushing

---

32. *Acta apostolicae sedis,* 47 – Series II – Vol. XXII (June 29, 1955): 539–44.

33. Garneau, "First Inter-American Episcopal Conference," 662–82.

34. John J. Considine, *New Horizons in Latin America: Illustrated with Photographs* (New York: Dodd, Mead & Co., 1958), 337ff.

35. James F. Garneau, "Commandos for Christ: The Foundation of the Missionary

founded the Missionary Society of St. James the Apostle specifically to send English-speaking diocesan clergy to missions in South America for periods of five years.[36] The mission-sending groups had to understand that they would no longer have a monopoly on foreign mission work.

2. The U.S. bishops will organize foreign mission work. The bishops themselves, through the Latin America Bureau, in a sense became a mission-sending organization. Though they did not set up a total organization into which new missioners would be recruited, trained, and supervised, the bishops were themselves organizing the U.S. Catholic mission to Latin America at the request of the Vatican. They did so by recruiting dioceses and religious orders to train, send, and supervise their own members under the guidance of the Latin American bishops. The bishops therefore set up the Latin America Bureau as directly responsible to themselves, and through them to CAL. This was a departure from the bishops' previous practice of standing by and blessing the efforts of missionary groups. Those groups and many others would indeed be called upon in the mission effort, but the LAB's purpose was to coordinate the effort on behalf of the bishops. Thus, the bishops put their own prestige on the line in the organization of the mission effort. This was something that Considine no doubt found attractive—he was a firm believer in the principle that bishops are responsible for the church's mission;[37] the problem had always been getting them to be conscientious about their mission responsibilities.

With the Cuban revolution as a recent historical backdrop, the North American bishops at the Georgetown meeting were finally pushed to take action on sending personnel in addition to funds to aid the church in Latin America, and the LAB was created at the subsequent annual meeting of the NCWC that same November. James Garneau has asked whether the later problems of the U.S. Catholic mission to Latin America can be traced back to the Georgetown meeting. In Garneau's perspective, mutual incomprehension and a lack of agreement characterized the meeting's deliberations on the sending of U.S. Catholic personnel to aid the church in Latin America.[38] CAL was up-front about three big problems to be addressed in Latin America: a shortage of clergy, a need to counter the advances of communism, and a further need to counter Protestant growth. The "Indian problem" (see below) was also on the agenda but was given only scant attention. Yet just four years prior, a longer list of challenges to the church

---

Society of St. James the Apostle and the "Americanism" of the 1950s and 1960s" (Ph.D. dissertation, Catholic University of America, 2000), 99.

36. Ibid.
37. Pius XI, encyclical *Rerum Ecclesiae* 6, 34.
38. Garneau, "First Inter-American Episcopal Conference," 662–87.

in Latin America had been drafted by CELAM at their first general meeting in Rio de Janeiro, which, in addition to the three main problems on the agenda of the Georgetown meeting, also included the following:

1. The "Indian problem" in countries like Bolivia, Brazil, Colombia, Ecuador, Guatemala, Mexico, Panama, Paraguay, and Peru—the persistence of languages, forms of social organization, ritual, customs, etc. apart from the dominant culture was perceived by elites as a social problem, and certainly a theological and ecclesiological problem as well. The main pastoral question was, given the noticeably different characteristics of the religious practices of indigenous peoples and the infrequency of their attendance at Sunday Mass, to what degree could church authorities understand the Catholicism practiced by Indigenous peoples as Christian?[39]

2. In a similar way, the bishops viewed "Spiritism" at that time as a superstitious pagan practice to be countered by the church.[40]

3. The general situation of poverty in which a majority of Latin Americans lived at the time, including such problems as the lack of proper housing for rural and urban workers, whose situation was "anguished"; the bishops noted that a rapid process of industrialization was under way, adding that "Christian thinking" needs to be part of the process; in such circumstances, even though Christian charitable works are commendable, it was important to focus on the root causes of social ills.[41]

4. The laity is to be called upon to assist in the church's apostolic work; Catholic Action is given specific commendation.[42]

5. The church is to make use of modern methods of communication, such as radio and a Catholic press.[43]

6. The need for the church to do more for immigrants to Latin America; national parishes were encouraged.[44]

7. References to Masonry in the "Declaración" from the Rio de Janeiro conference are perhaps reminders of the rise of anti-clericalism and a consequent situation of political insecurity for the church in post-independence Latin American society.[45]

---

39. "Declaración de los cardenales, obispos y demás prelados representantes de la jerarquía de América Latina reunidos en la Conferencia episcopal de Río de Janeiro," August 4, 1955, IV; pp. 85–89.

40. Ibid., 75.

41. Ibid., 79–84.

42. Ibid., 42–45; 82.

43. Ibid., 61–68.

44. Ibid., 90–92.

45. Ibid., 76.

In addition to this list of church problems developed by the Latin American bishops, I would add three more:

1. Though not specifically mentioned, the "Declaración" from the Rio de Janeiro conference alluded to the post-independence period of the nineteenth century as the beginning of the clergy shortage, a shortage that delayed or derailed the activities of the church, though it also inspired great creativity among the laity in some places.
2. A situation in which many Latin American church leaders were eager to counter an image of the church as a chaplain to the dominant classes of society and as unconcerned about peasants and the poor.[46]
3. Another problem was noted by Considine in 1945: the general unevenness of evangelization or catechization outside of the metropolitan centers around the continent—across Latin America, Catholicism tended to have a better functioning ministry in urban areas and a pattern of pastoral neglect in rural areas.[47]

Thus, of all these challenges, obstacles, and problems that faced the church in Latin America in 1959, the agenda, set by CAL, at the Inter-American Episcopal Conference included only three topics that were discussed at length: the clergy shortage, communism, and Protestantism. Perhaps the strategy employed by CAL in this selection was that of starting a conversation among Latin American, Canadian, and U.S. bishops; the three topics selected were certainly understood as urgent, major, and also the ones that could most easily be understood by the non-Latin American participants in the conversation.

Yet the purpose of the meeting was not simply to get acquainted so that further and more in-depth conversation might take place later. The purpose of the meeting, from CAL's point of view, was to motivate the church in North America to offer ever-greater aid to the church in Latin America in the form of personnel and funds. This meeting marked the beginnings of the North American Catholic mission to Latin America in the 1960s. Thus, it is fair to ask, as Garneau does, just how such an Inter-American relationship could work out in the end, given the fact that crucial matters of context that were well known to the Latin American bishops were left off the agenda, matters about which the North American bishops knew very little.[48]

---

46. David E. Mutchler, *The Church as a Political Factor in Latin America: With Particular Reference to Colombia and Chile* (New York: Praeger, 1971), 52ff.

47. John J. Considine, "Horseback and Shank's Mare," August 20, 1945. MMA, Considine Papers, 8:8.

48. For example, Latin American bishops would have had some sense of how the

More pragmatically, the goals of the mission itself were beginning to be defined, though, in the case of the North American bishops, without a very informed sense of the Latin American church's past. The initial stages of the mission were therefore somewhat chaotic. Gerald Costello's *Mission to Latin America* remains a good guide to the confusion that ensued in the first half of the 1960s when North American dioceses, religious orders, and lay organizations that had no previous foreign missionary experience selected sites for ministry in Latin America with very little knowledge of the local scene. Costello described the case of Mary Conroy, a Papal Volunteer who worked in a medical lab in Lima while coming to grips with the fact that Latin America did not really need lab technicians like herself, as there were many such trained Peruvian Catholic technicians who were out of work.[49] Similarly, some religious groups that were eager to respond to the pleas of the popes for aid to Latin America found out only later that they had, for example, selected a middle-class area of a large city as a place of ministry mainly based on the idea of its perceived similarity to places of ministry in the United States. Later on they understood that they had displaced local Latin American church personnel by picking a choice location.

From the Georgetown Meeting to the LAB

Two weeks later, Archbishop Samorè was still on hand for the annual assembly of the NCWC. Even though Archbishop Alter, president of the NCWC in 1960, had expressed hesitancy in regard to an expanded mission to Latin America at the Georgetown meeting,[50] the establishment of the Latin America Bureau was approved by the NCWC.

Because of his mission study tours to Latin America and his books on the region, Considine could easily have been considered "Mr. Latin America" in the U.S. church at the end of 1959. He had the cachet of being able to embody the foreign mission ideas, efforts, and concerns of U.S. Catholics. After *Call for Forty Thousand* (1946) and *New Horizons in Latin America* (1958), he was viewed as an expert on the church in the Western Hemisphere. Yet Considine was not the first choice of the NCWC admin-

---

current shortage of clergy and struggles with Protestantism and communism could be understood as tied to the nineteenth century struggles of the church in their countries, a historical context with which North American bishops were much less familiar.

49. Costello, *Mission to Latin America,* 124. Costello features a long list of problems from the early years of the mission to Latin America in the 1960s: the Papal Volunteers did not have field representatives and thus no way to monitor the progress or problems of new missioners (p. 123); most missioners were not properly trained in language and culture (p. 230); selection of candidates for the mission was not properly done (p. 232); missioners had unrealistic expectations about what they could achieve (p. 232); missioners were unwilling to trust Latin Americans with key tasks (p. 233).

50. Garneau, "First Inter-American Episcopal Conference," 675.

istrative committee for the directorship of the LAB; that such a qualified individual was not immediately considered is perhaps the strongest indicator that in 1959–1960 the U.S. bishops did not have a clear idea in regard to what they would be trying to accomplish in Latin America. The first person pursued for the job was instead Fr. Andrew Kennedy of the Archdiocese of St. Louis, whose qualifications for the position included a few years of missionary service in Bolivia in the St. Louis archdiocesan mission. When Archbishop Ritter did not release him, the committee did not immediately have a second choice to approach. On December 16, 1959, Cardinal Ritter wrote to NCWC secretary general Paul Tanner with the news that he would not release Fr. Kennedy; as an alternative, he suggested the names of two priests in Texas who were fluent in Spanish.[51]

In a letter of January 15, 1960, Msgr. Ivan Illich recommended to the NCWC secretary general Msgr. Paul Tanner that Considine be hired for the LAB directorship.[52] As the archival record does not contain any other item from this period, it is hard to avoid coming to the conclusion that the NCWC administrative committee did not have a short list for the director of the new LAB. Tanner took Illich's suggestion seriously and wrote to Cardinal Cushing, and Cushing wrote to Bishop John Comber, the superior general of Maryknoll with the request that Considine be made available for service in the LAB. Comber consulted Considine and then signaled Considine's acceptance of the position to Cushing. Comber spoke of it as a "loan" of Fr. Considine to the NCWC for a year.[53]

A Cardinal's Concern

Cardinal Cushing was both happy and concerned that John Considine would be heading the new U.S. bishops' Latin America Bureau. At that time, the cardinal wrote to the superior general of Maryknoll:

> Confidentially, let me tell you that there is not much enthusiasm among the Hierarchy, at least those on the top level, with regard to the extensive activity on the part of the Church in the United States towards the revival of the Church in Latin America.
>
> As you know my interest in the Church in Latin America is over and above my ordinary routine duty. Nevertheless I'll do everything in my power for Father Considine.

51. Joseph Ritter, St. Louis, to Paul Tanner, Washington, December 16, 1959. ACUA, NCWC General Secretary, Box 43, Folder 21.

52. Ivan Illich, New York, to Paul Tanner, Washington, 15 January 1960. ACUA, NCWC General Secretary, Box 43, Folder 21.

53. CD, January 25, 1960.

In the light of all this, while I am thrilled that Father Considine will be available, I will insist that he should not accept this position unless he is absolutely convinced that he is going to be busy.[54]

Being busy would never be a problem for Considine at the LAB. Because Considine's initiatives at the LAB were so many in number, it is difficult to give an accurate account without providing tediously long lists. During his time at Fides in Rome, Considine's life was a whirlwind of activities that included little time for rest. He would reprise that performance during his years at the LAB, a time in which it seemed as if Considine would have organized just about anything that held promise of being of real assistance to the church in Latin America.

At the same time, Cardinal Cushing's warning was well taken; Considine understood that he would have to use all his talents of persuasion—and all the leverage he could muster from Rome—to get the U.S. bishops to support a large-scale mission to Latin America. Even if influential members of the hierarchy were not well disposed to support an expanded U.S. Catholic mission to Latin America, in Considine's appointment they were getting someone who would persistently and diplomatically hold their collective feet to the fire to gain the resources, financial and human, that the mission required.

If speed-dial had existed in 1960, Considine most likely would have had Richard Cardinal Cushing (1895–1970) on his. During Considine's tenure at the LAB, Cardinal Cushing was his constant ally, and very frequently the one LAB benefactor Considine could count on in a pinch. Cushing was a patron of the United States Catholic mission to Latin America in the 1960s unlike any other. For that mission, he put his prestige and his considerable fundraising abilities on the line over and over again, raising over $4 million for projects in Latin America during Considine's first three years at the LAB.[55]

Within the NCWC, Cushing chaired the Bishops' Committee on the Church in Latin America, and Considine could count on the cardinal to put his name on LAB pamphlets that described "The Papal Program for Latin America," and LAB fundraising projects. [56] Similarly, Cushing could

---

54. Richard Cushing, Boston, to John Comber, Ossining, NY, January 27, 1960. MMA, Considine Papers, 3:3.

55. John J. Considine, Washington, to Richard Cushing, Boston, March 23, 1963. ACUA, NCWC General Secretary, Box 187, Folder 20.

56. Richard Cushing, "On the Call of the Holy See for Papal Volunteers for Latin America" (Washington, DC: Latin America Bureau, n.d.); Cushing agreed to Considine's plan for a "Cardinal Cushing Recruitment Fund" to raise money for the recruitment of

call on Considine to ghost-write speeches and articles on Latin America for him. In all of this, Cushing may have felt like a lonely crusader. After expressing frustration with the bureaucracy of the NCWC, he scribbled in the margins of a letter to Considine: "God be with you John—we would be better off and more successful as an independent Mission Aid Organization. RJC."[57]

After his passing in 1970, who took over as a patron of the mission in Latin America? No one, really, and this lack of strong voices of support for the mission to Latin America within the U.S. hierarchy may explain much about the fortunes of the mission and the post-Considine LAB after Cushing's death.

Considine's official start date was set for September 1960, but he actually got to work right away in February 1960, by visiting various people who would become important to him in his new position. In Washington he met with Msgr. Tanner and with the Apostolic Delegate, Archbishop Vagnozzi. He also visited with his old friend Fr. Fred McGuire, C.M., Director of the Mission Secretariat; for three years Considine and McGuire would share quarters at the National Catholic Education Association (NCEA) staff house on V Street near the Potomac River in northwest Washington. He then caught a plane to Boston to call on Cardinal Cushing; in March he visited Cardinal Ritter in St. Louis. Cushing and Ritter were the two U.S. cardinals who were most committed to mission in Latin America; both of them sent diocesan clergy to work in the region beginning in the second half of the 1950s.

During the Transition, an International Lay Volunteer Movement Is Founded

Because of Considine's many years of experience with Fr. Al Nevins at *Maryknoll* magazine, he felt he could leave the work there in Al's good hands. Though he did not quite disengage from his job at Maryknoll, February to September 1960 were busy months of preparation for Considine's new job at the LAB, months in which, among other things, he hatched and got approval for the founding of a new lay mission movement, the Papal Volunteers for Latin America (PAVLA).

As was the case with the founding of Fides in the 1920s, it is hard to tell when the idea of an international Catholic volunteer corps for Latin America first occurred to Considine, but by March 1960, almost one year before Sargent Shriver would be working on founding the Peace Corps,

new missioners to Latin America. John Considine Diary, 12 January 1962. MMA, Considine Papers, 7:1.

57. Richard Cushing, Boston, to John Considine, Washington, December 29, 1961. ACUA, NCWC General Secretary, Box 187, Folder 19.

the idea of sending "lay apostles" to Latin America was included in Considine's initial drafts of the functions of the LAB.[58] Then in May 1960, Considine was called to Rome to meet with CAL vice president Archbishop Antonio Samorè; Considine submitted his outline of the functions of the LAB to Samorè, and the two of them met on several occasions to discuss revisions. Considine was thus able to leave Rome that same month with an approved plan of action for the LAB, and that plan included PAVLA.

By July 1960, Considine had prepared a letter to be sent out by the NCWC general secretary to all U.S. ordinaries:

Your Excellency,

You will be impressed, I believe, by the unusual tenor of the accompanying document issued by the Pontifical Commission for Latin America.

It is a call to Catholic laymen and lay women of the various countries of the world to consider giving a number of years of their life for service in Latin America. Pope John XXIII has approved the bestowing on each such worker the title of *Papal Volunteer for Latin America.*

As the document explains, the recruitment of these Papal Volunteers is to proceed in each country[59] through the initiative of the already existing organizations of the Church, parochial and non-parochial, through Catholic colleges and universities and through other groups specifically devoted to the lay apostolate. All of these, however, are to act, the document reads, "in response to the appeal of their bishops."

Your Excellency will decide what form this call for volunteers should take in your diocese. It may even be that you would not favor making a formal promulgation of this document at this time. You might prefer to leave its divulgation to the Latin America Bureau of the NCWC, which is the national center from which any action on this matter will be handled.

---

58. "Outline of Functions of Latin American Bureau, NCWC," March 3, 1960. ACUA, Office of the General Secretary of the NCWC, Box 43, Folder 21; "Outline of Functions of Latin American Bureau, N.C.W.C.," May 6, 1960. ACUA, Office of the General Secretary of the NCWC, Box 43, Folder 4.

59. Though there were Papal Volunteers of several nationalities, it seems clear that the United States had the only national program. Considine's diary records the reception of proposals from Chile and Peru for Latin American Papal Volunteers (CD, December 29, 1961), and he also received a letter describing the possibility of organizing a program in Portugal (Betsy Hollants, Lisbon, to John Considine, Washington, October 17, 1962. ACUA, NCWC General Secretary, Box 186, Folder 62).

If this be the case, it will prove a source of guidance to me if you will express your desires by means of the accompanying form. This will assure us in our procedures here.

Most respectfully yours,

Paul C. Tanner, General Secretary[60]

Thus PAVLA was launched by Considine in the summer of 1960, more than a month before he officially took up his duties at the LAB, and three months before presidential candidate John F. Kennedy gave the speech that sowed the idea of the Peace Corps. Kennedy received a wild response from University of Michigan students when he asked them if they would volunteer to serve as teachers, doctors, and engineers in Ghana and other parts of the Global South.

While there can be no doubt that Considine alone created PAVLA and that the enterprise garnered his clear support throughout his tenure at the LAB (1960–1968), PAVLA was from the beginning so decentralized that Considine could not be thought of as a "founder" in the typical sense of founders of religious organizations. For example, he was not a mentor to the new recruits—indeed, the recruits emerged through the efforts of any one of four different institutional sponsors: a diocesan office; a religious community of men or women; lay organizations for overseas service; and Catholic colleges or universities. In the PAVLA plan, those institutions were responsible for recruitment and maintenance of Papal Volunteers, and it was in those institutions that these lay vocations were nurtured.

Thus, when a lay person wanted to join PAVLA, he or she would do so through one of the organizations that had decided to sponsor Papal Volunteers; the volunteer normally did not come in contact with other Papal Volunteers recruited by a different organization. Furthermore, the LAB coordinated the training and the assignment of Papal Volunteers to place them directly in Latin American apostolic works for periods of "two to five years."[61] Time spent in a language school or in cultural training before beginning one's assignment might conceivably be a place where Papal Volunteers from different parts of North America would meet, but apart from that there was no sense of an annual "class" of PAVLA recruits and no corresponding cohesiveness of the membership—the decentralization built into the program pretty much prevented all of that. For example, Raymond Plankey's itinerary within PAVLA began entirely in the Archdiocese of Omaha, where he was recruited and trained in 1961–1962, was followed

60. John J. Considine, "Proposed Letter to Hierarchy," ACUA, NCWC General Secretary, Box 43, Folder 4.

61. Richard Cushing, "On the Call of the Holy See for Papal Volunteers for Latin America" (Washington, DC: Latin America Bureau, n.d.).

by Spanish language and cultural training at the Center of Intercultural Formation in Cuernavaca, Mexico, and continued on to his assignment at the Instituto Indígena in Temuco, Chile. During the nine months of evening training sessions in Omaha and the four and a half months of language school in Cuernavaca, his only contact with other Papal Volunteers was with the other four that made up the Omaha group that year.

When Plankey arrived in Chile, he and his PAVLA confreres from Omaha did not have a chance to mix with the other six or seven Papal Volunteers who were already at work in the country. Chilean Jesuit Fr. Renato Poblete was the PAVLA National Coordinator for Chile, and Plankey recalled that the new group of four—one had dropped out at Cuernavaca to marry a language teacher—met some of the other Papal Volunteers during orientation sessions conducted by Fr. Poblete. Plankey also understood that there was at that time a PAVLA National Office in the United States that coordinated all the Papal Volunteers, but he did not meet Fr. Considine or the PAVLA national director before departing for Cuernavaca in 1962.[62]

Considine conceived of PAVLA as a "general lay movement,"[63] not an organization. In fact, in its earliest iteration it functioned more as an international volunteer placement agency, but with time a more firm organizational structure—expanded guidelines for recruitment and regular meetings of directors in the United States—was added. When compared to the level of complexity in the Maryknoll organizations that Considine had previously managed, PAVLA represented a step in the opposite direction. It operated initially from a minimalist organizational perspective but allowed for expansion as needed.

Although a full history of PAVLA has yet to be written, the success of the "movement" has been uneven—some recruitment and training programs were carried out well, and others were not. Many Papal Volunteers had life-changing experiences in Latin America, experiences that helped them to orient their lives with a global perspective on world poverty and the ways the church attempts to address that problem. Others fell through the cracks of poor training and a lack of good communication between the many concerned parties (local bishop and pastor, Papal Volunteer, sending organization in the U.S., and the PAVLA National Office), which sometimes resulted in placements in which the skill set of the volunteer could not be utilized. The result was that some volunteers had little to do.[64]

PAVLA itself was always subjected to criticisms from many angles. For

---

62. Raymond Plankey, interview with author, November 27, 2011.

63. John J. Considine, "Papal Volunteers: More about Them," *The Shield-Collegian* 40, no. 3 (January 1961): 4–5, 21.

64. Costello, *Mission to Latin America*, 95–102.

example, Considine was surprised to learn in 1960, during his first visit to Latin America, that the name itself—Papal Volunteers—was politically problematic. In Colombia, it seemed to carry the inference of the pope interfering in Colombian politics.[65] In the beginning, Considine had hoped that the acronym VOPAL—Voluntarios papales para América Latina—might make it more international,[66] but that name did not catch on.

In 1965, Ivan Illich judged the idea of sending U.S. lay volunteers for a three-year commitment to Latin America to be too expensive and called for the organization to be transformed into a foundation that would instead support Latin American lay people who were taking up ministry in their own churches.[67] At the fourth CICOP in January 1967, Thomas Quigley urged a change of mentality for PAVLA—Papal Volunteers, regardless of their intentions, too often were operating out of a sense of American superiority or paternalism.[68]

Considine's successor at the LAB, Rev. Louis Colonnese, in 1969 took the decisive step of dismissing the PAVLA national director, Fr. Raymond Kevane, in order to seek guidance from CELAM on how the program might or might not be improved.[69] PAVLA was disbanded in 1971; however, during its more than ten years of operation, over eleven hundred people had served in Latin America as Papal Volunteers.

Living in DC

From the fall of 1960 until October of 1963, Considine lived at the NCEA staff house in a Northwest Washington neighborhood. He shared the house with a close friend, Vincentian missioner Fr. Fred McGuire, and also Norbertine Fr. Al Koob. McGuire and Considine had worked on the founding of the U.S. Mission Secretariat, and Considine's diaries from the 1950s and 1960s are peppered with references of warm friendship with McGuire. Fr. McGuire was also one of Considine's successors at the LAB, becoming the director in 1971.

Considine did not own a car, and so he usually commuted by bus to the LAB, located near "embassy row" on Massachusetts Avenue. In October 1963, when the NCWC decided to open a new and larger staff house located near Catholic University in Northeast Washington, Considine chose to move in there; it was a closer commute, and Considine could

65. John J. Considine Diary, 5 September 1960. MMA, Considine Papers, 7:1.

66. CD, May 9, 1960.

67. Ivan Illich, *The Church, Change, and Development* (Chicago: Urban Training Center Press, 1970).

68. Costello, *Mission to Latin America*, 94.

69. "Future Role Of PAVLA Is Studied," *The Washington Post,* August 30, 1969, A13.

more easily catch a ride to work with one of the several priests living there who had cars.

The residents of the NCWC staff house were a virtual who's who of Catholic clergy in the United States: Msgr. George Higgins, expert on labor relations and long-time director of the NCWC Social Action Department; Msgr. Paul Tanner, general secretary of the NCWC/USCC and later Bishop of St. Augustine, Florida; and Msgr. Frank Hurley, who succeeded Tanner as general secretary and would later become archbishop of Anchorage. Jesuit Fr. John Courtney Murray, considered the intellectual author of the Second Vatican Council's Declaration on Religious Liberty (*Dignitatis Humanae*), was also a frequent visitor. Considine's diary entries reveal that the NCWC staff house was a place where churchmen often socialized with each other and discussed the state of the church during the Second Vatican Council and in the immediate postconciliar years, many times until way past midnight.

Maryknollers also came for visits, and Considine even encouraged the vocation to Maryknoll of William McIntyre, who sought out Considine in 1961 while working at the Labor Department.[70] Fr. McIntyre was later elected vicar general of Maryknoll. In regard to his own family, one of Considine's nieces, Mary Lou Considine, also lived in Washington, and from time to time he would visit her or even borrow her car. And almost every year in the late summer he would spend a couple of weeks with his brother George near New Bedford.

Welcoming Vatican II

In the 1960s, Fr. Considine did not write a great deal about the Second Vatican Council as such. While there are many indications that he took great interest in the Council and received its teachings positively, his lack of commentary on the Council probably came from being very busy with his work at the LAB.[71] Even so, his diary records his appreciation of the positive impact the Council was having on the church. This was especially true about the liturgical reforms.

In terms of personally receiving the liturgical reforms of the Council, his diary from December 1964 relates his excitement at beginning to pray the Liturgy of the Hours in English, along with a crestfallen note about how much was lost in the past by not using the vernacular:

---

70. CD, February 17, 1961.

71. At the end of 1966 he wrote the following in his diary: "To Jim McHugh's room at 11. for one more of the very interesting sessions on post-Conciliar happenings. Much talk and soliloquizing. . . . Meanwhile we keep grinding away at building Latin America (CD, December 27, 1966).

The vernacular office today was the feast of O.L. of Guadalupe, the most beautiful I've ever experienced as an office. It is pitiful to look back on over 40 years of Latin breviary.[72]

But in other ways, the transitions in the church's liturgy were not so easy for Considine to navigate.

Said Mass at 9:30 this eve and John Courtney Murray, who happened to be in the chapel, served it. The new rules and the vernacular give a new dimension to the Mass, though I'll never have ease in the presence of others since it all comes so late in life.[73]

Did that combination of excitement and lack of ease characterize Considine's reaction to the Council? Certainly if one looks at Fr. Considine's life and work in the light of Karl Rahner's notion that the Second Vatican Council was an event carried out by a world church, then that central meaning of the Council was undoubtedly nothing new for Considine. Indeed, the case can be made that his writings on World Christianity, his efforts to take seriously the cultures of the world, and his efforts to counter prejudice and organize missionary work within a framework of respect for peoples and cultures were contributions that assisted the church at Vatican II to meet as a world body.

Nonetheless, as the Council concluded, Considine was sixty-seven—not exactly a time in life when one relishes attempting to make fundamental changes. A 1966 essay by Considine betrays something of his struggle to stay in step with the new pastoral and ecclesial thinking that marked the immediate postconciliar period. The essay urges young sisters in training and religious superiors alike to maintain a consciousness of the needs of the entire world, and his choice of words gives evidence that he was incorporating the concepts and terminology of Vatican II into the older theme of mission-mindedness.

Most of us now recognize that in this age, when all of us regardless of circumstances must rub elbows with the whole human race, it is essential to the day's work that each and every one of us keep our eyes focused on our obligations as members of an ecumenical church.[74]

---

72. CD, December 12, 1964.

73. CD, January 13, 1967.

74. John J. Considine, "World's Work in the Day's Work," in *Revolution in Missionary Thinking: A Symposium,* ed. William Jerome Richardson (Maryknoll, NY: Maryknoll Publications, 1966), 175.

The Second Vatican Council invited every believer to cherish the continuity with the past while embracing a way forward of living the gospel in such a way as to meet, rather than avoid, the challenges of the present day. Considine throughout this period remained busy with his work on behalf of Latin America and welcomed what was new in the teaching of the Council while incorporating it into his lifelong commitment to the growth of the church around the world.

It was for Considine a big advantage to have the chance to think about this with some of the best minds in the church in the United States—digesting the Council and thinking through its implications was a constant topic of conversation among the residents and visitors at the NCWC staff house.

> Very spirited and enlightening discussion of the Council after the buffet supper, with John Courtney [Murray] and George [Higgins] the outstanding contributors.[75]
>
> At the supper table the group may be large or small but we turn . . . to a discussion of the events within the Church touching change. I find myself believing even more strongly that it all means great new strength for the world Church.[76]

Considine in Camelot

With the election of John F. Kennedy, the early 1960s turned into a most interesting time to be running an office in Washington, DC, that focused on Latin America. The Kennedy administration was also turning its attention to Latin America, launching the Alliance for Progress and sending many volunteers from the new Peace Corps to the region. Considine was called upon to be a member of the advisory board of the Peace Corps, an official responsibility that brought him to the White House to meet Presidents Kennedy and then Johnson. It was especially during the Kennedy administration that he rubbed elbows with Teodoro Moscoso, head of the Alliance for Progress. He also had a fluid relationship with mid-level officials at the State and Labor Departments.

Considine felt that there was a natural fit between Kennedy's Peace Corps initiative and PAVLA. In a 1963 interview in *Sign*, Considine noted

---

75. CD, May 26, 1965.

76. CD, December 27, 1966. In another matter related to the Council, Maryknoll superior general Bishop John Comber in 1963 asked Considine to prepare "proposals for an improved prosecution of the missionary enterprise in the Church," which Comber would take to the Second Vatican Council (CD, May 14, 1963). As a consultor for Propaganda Fide, in 1964 Considine presented his Schema de Missionibus to Cardinal Agagianian, the prefect of Propaganda. However, Agagianian told Considine that he could not put forward the proposals at the Council, as they called for an increased role for Propaganda Fide (CD, April 16, 1964).

that the Peace Corps recruited volunteers for civil projects and PAVLA for religious ones, though because placements in both organizations are responses to local needs, in actual fact volunteers in the Peace Corps and in PAVLA might end up doing very similar work. Both programs are "working for good," and so Catholics can do well by participating in either program. At the same time, Considine recognized that the recruitment efforts of the Peace Corps were better funded and more extensive than those of PAVLA. Nonetheless, the publicity given by the Peace Corps to the option of becoming an overseas volunteer helped PAVLA indirectly—people needed to be made aware of the importance of such work.[77] Sargent Shriver read the interview and called Considine to congratulate him. The two were not in frequent contact, but consultations between the two took place from time to time while Shriver headed the Peace Corps. For example, in 1963, Shriver asked Considine to review a speech he was to give at Fordham University. Since not all the members of the Peace Corps advisory board resided in Washington, Shriver's office would call on Considine several times a year to participate in Peace Corps events.

The NCWC opened a Peace Corps Desk in 1961, and it was located in the LAB office in Washington. The main task of the Peace Corps Desk was to respond to requests for information on the Peace Corps from Catholics and to coordinate Peace Corps recruitment activities on the campuses of Catholic colleges and universities. There had also been the hope that Peace Corps volunteers might work on projects run by U.S. missioners overseas, but in December 1961 Shriver made the determination to prohibit Peace Corps contracts with religious groups. At the time, there were Protestant and Jewish objections in regard to a government agency having close ties with Catholic entities. Bishop Swanstrom, head of Catholic Relief Services, lodged a protest,[78] but the issue was effectively closed. The NCWC Peace Corps Desk was shut down shortly thereafter.

Then there was Considine's "big fish" that got away too soon—Teodoro Moscoso and the Alliance for Progress. Considine had been an admirer of Moscoso's work in Operation Bootstrap, the 1950s government development program in Puerto Rico that had effectively ignited a modernization of the island's economy. At the Alliance for Progress, Moscoso was charting a new foreign policy course for the United States in Latin America, and he did so with the confidence of the president.

---

77. John Considine, "Two Ways to Aid the Latins: An Interview with Father John J. Considine, M.M.," *Sign* 42, no. 10 (May 1963): 12–13.

78. "Peace Corps won't sign contracts with church groups, Shriver says; stand deplored by Bishop Swanstrom," NCWC Press Release, December 18, 1961. ACUA, NCWC General Secretary, Box 194, Folder 3.

For example, Latin Americans in the postwar period had grown weary of U.S. economic policy. The region had accumulated $3.4 billion dollars in credits during World War II by supplying price-controlled commodities to the Allies. After the war, the United States raised the prices on capital-goods exports, leading historian Steven Rabe to surmise that "Latin America made a $3-billion non-interest bearing loan to the United States and could not collect on the principal."[79] JFK's Alliance for Progress was the first offer of real assistance in the entire postwar period. Considine was very interested in meeting Moscoso.

During the fall of 1962 Considine had been through a round of consultations on USAID funding, and the result was always the same. Overseas, U.S. government aid could be applied for by private organizations—including churches—but the applications were made by organizations to the national USAID office in each country. For Considine, this arrangement was too dispersed; it did not allow CELAM to coordinate the distribution of USAID goods throughout Latin America in a way that would bolster pastoral objectives.

It is unclear who set up the meeting, but Considine finally met with Moscoso in January 1963. The two hit it off—Considine proposed a combined action wherein the Catholic bishops in Latin America could offer guidance to organizations seeking Alliance for Progress assistance, and Moscoso agreed to work with Considine in the preparation of a procedural manual for citizen groups in Latin America.[80] The manual was produced, but Moscoso was replaced after the Kennedy assassination. Unfortunately for Moscoso and for Latin America, the Alliance for Progress under the Johnson administration would be tied much more tightly to U.S. Cold War objectives in Latin America. The end of Camelot was felt sharply by Considine when he lost this ally at the Alliance for Progress.

In relation to the Peace Corps, Considine was invited to various White House functions during both the Kennedy and Johnson administrations. Nonetheless, Considine could not be considered a Kennedy insider. Cardinal Cushing, however, did have significant access to the Kennedys, and Considine could query him on Kennedy questions. Cushing also got Considine to help with a Kennedy matter. In June 1961, Cushing asked Considine to suggest an itinerary for Ted Kennedy's South American tour. Cushing told Considine that the trip "is unofficial or personal but it has the approval of the President."[81]

---

79. Rabe is quoted in Peter H. Smith, *Talons of the Eagle: Dynamics of U.S.–Latin American Relations* (New York: Oxford University Press, 1996), 147–48.

80. CD, January 19, 1963.

81. Richard Cushing, Boston, to John Considine, Washington, June 8, 1961. ACUA, NCWC General Secretary, Box 187, Folder 18.

Considine experienced the Kennedy years as a time when there was a lot of common cause going on. Public service was understood as a worthwhile activity, if not a calling. When the Peace Corps was founded, unprecedented numbers of volunteers expanded the notion of public service into the international arena, and official Washington was dedicating resources to a new focus on Latin America and other parts of the "developing world," as the Global South was referred to at that time.

Apart from the funding issues, no church–state tension in Washington can be found in Considine's writings of the time. Certainly the larger frameworks of postwar U.S. ascendancy in world affairs and anti-communism created for Considine a cordiality of shared interests with government officials and their offices.

The Latin America Supper Club

To keep conversation on Latin America going between government and church people in Washington, Considine in early 1963 established the Latin America Supper Club. An idea that Considine came up with and simply decided to do, the Latin America Supper Club was an informal though regularly running series of evening discussions. Participation was by invitation only, with the LAB in charge of sending out invitations. The list of participants over the years tended to be a mixture of Catholic Church officials—mostly from the staff of the NCWC—along with mid-level U.S. government officials who dealt with Latin America, officials of international agencies such as the Organization of American States and the Inter-American Development Bank (IDB), and diplomats or diplomatic staff accredited to Washington from Latin American countries. Occasionally someone working in an academic institution might attend or be invited to speak.

At the time, there were few Catholic "think-tank" or lobbying agencies in Washington, so the meetings of the Latin America Supper Club provided a way for church people to network and to stay up on topics of interest with colleagues working in government. The group thus provided church people who were focused on Latin America with a space for meeting each other and for engaging government people on topics of concern to both. Though Considine traveled a lot, he did not often miss a meeting of the Latin America Supper Club.

The Latin America Supper Club especially attracted Latin American Catholics who were mid-level officials at work in governmental or intergovernmental agencies. Emilio Mignone, originally from Argentina, was at the time working at the Organization of American States; René Otero, originally from Bolivia and also a frequent participant, worked in the 1960s for the IDB. The group met every second Tuesday evening of the month for a "Dutch-treat" supper at the Manger Hamilton Hotel in Washington, and supper would be followed by a speaker and discussion. The topics covered many different areas of Latin American life, ranging from the ecclesial ("The Christian Outlook in Bolivia") to the socioeconomic (a report on Latin American initiatives from an IDB official) to the political (a recap of recent Chilean elections). Over the six years that Considine coordinated this group, the attendance was usually between fourteen and twenty-one participants, though the invitation list boasted approximately thirty names.

A Million Dollars for the Church in Latin America

Alone among the activities of the LAB that was not invented by Considine, the annual "million-dollar fund" was set up by the U.S. bishops in 1959 as part of the responsibilities of the LAB. The fund did not have to be raised; instead, it was diverted from funds already gathered by the Society for the Propagation of the Faith to be put at the disposition of CAL. The fund was thus under the care of the LAB beginning in 1960. The initial arrangement was that the LAB would submit allocations for the use of the fund each year to CAL for approval. But Considine was convinced that more fundraising was needed, and with Cushing's help he set up several fundraising campaigns to support PAVLA, recruitment efforts in general for Latin America, and development projects. In 1966 the "million dollar fund" was replaced with an annual national collection for the church in Latin America.[82]

Nonetheless, since the LAB operations and various projects outside the scope of the million-dollar fund[83] required financing, fundraising was an endless task for Considine as LAB director. On the one hand, fundraising presented limitless opportunities; his thinking was that Catholics, when challenged to support the good work of the church in Latin America, would respond generously and that generous support would make even greater efforts in the region possible. On the other hand, the "limitless" side to fundraising took its toll on him: "I'm tempted to feel overwhelmed by the immensity of the opportunities and the puny forces I can rally to achieve anything."[84] Though he was a consistent fundraiser, by 1965 Con-

---

82. Bound Minutes of the Administrative Board of the NCWC, November 13–14, 1965, p. 14 (1167).

83. For example, in early 1963 Considine was trying to found the Kellenburg Center for Latin American Studies in Ponce, Puerto Rico (CD, February 18 and March 14, 1963); during this same period he was working on the Catholic Latin American Student Project (CLASP), which also required funding. The project tried to coordinate short-term projects in Latin America for U.S. students. "File Memorandum from John Considine," February 25, 1963. ACUA, NCWC General Secretary, Box 187, Folder 2.

84. CD, June 21, 1961.

sidine's diaries record a greater and greater preoccupation with being able to do enough fundraising to keep the LAB and its many enterprises afloat.[85]

Managing Relationships among Bishops

One of Considine's more delicate responsibilities was trouble-shooting the relationships between various members of the hierarchy—bishops from the United States and Latin America, and also representatives of the Vatican's Pontifical Commission for Latin America (CAL). Of course, this was something for which Considine was well qualified, having worked in Rome for ten years in his youth and having spent the previous twenty-four years managing Maryknoll's public relations. Even prior to officially assuming his duties, Considine became aware of tension between CAL and the leadership of CELAM. The Vatican was acting like an indecisive boss; before there was a CAL, the Vatican was anxious to get the Latin American hierarchy organized. Archbishop Antonio Samorè had been dispatched to Rio de Janeiro in 1955 for a meeting of the Latin American Bishops. His official role at that meeting was to extend the blessing of the pope on the founding of the Latin American Conference of Bishops (CELAM). Yet once CELAM was formed, the Vatican began to worry that it seemed too independent.

By 1960 when Considine came on the scene, the issue from CELAM's point of view was that the Latin American bishops had no voice in the allocation of the new financial resources from the United States—the process that was set up involved the LAB and the NCWC in Washington making proposals to CAL for the use of the funds. Considine was greatly concerned how this "stern position" on the part of Samorè was poisoning his own efforts to work cooperatively with CELAM.[86]

What was needed was a letter to Archbishop Samorè, but it would take several rounds of consultations with the right parties to come up with what to say and how to say it so that a real change of policy would become possible. Considine met with Msgr. Tanner, with Cardinal Cushing, and with Archbishop Vagnozzi, apostolic delegate to the United States. Then, in a driving snowstorm in December 1960, Bishop Larraín arrived in Washington, and he, Considine, and Tanner set out for Cincinnati to meet with Archbishop Karl Alter, chair of the NCWC Administrative Committee. The four of them agreed to remove Vagnozzi from the process and came up with a different draft of the letter, which was finally sent.[87] Within two months news had come from Samorè that a change in policy had been

---

85. CD, July 31, 1965.
86. CD, December 5, 1960.
87. CD, December 12, 1960.

effected: CELAM would have to approve of any proposed funding of a project before it could be considered by the NCWC.[88]

It was a victory Considine could have predicted. While it was purely Samorè's decision to make, drafting the right letter with the right people in the right way so as to effect the optimal possibility of a favorable outcome was a diplomatic exercise that Considine had performed over and over during his career. Nevertheless, this sort of a slam-dunk success was not always in the offing during his years at the LAB; sometimes it was simply not possible.

A particularly thorny problem was keeping U.S. bishops in line with a program to aid Latin American bishops. Considine found this to be more problematic—the U.S. bishops furnished the resources that greased the wheels of inter-American Catholic cooperation, and keeping them happy about doing that was not a simple matter. Upon arrival in Rome in late September 1964, Considine was greeted with the news that Cardinal Cushing was angry; Considine described the moment in his diary:

> At 7.30 to Mons. Samore at Vatican where I learned that Cardinal Cushing gave him the line yesterday that neither priests nor lay persons from abroad counted in L.A. This is a problem for us that we discussed after my meeting with Samore over dinner as guest of Bishop McNulty at the Hotel Michelangelo. All are convinced we must change the Card.'s mind tomorrow.[89]

When Considine found Cushing, the cardinal was still angry, but he learned that the source of the comment that had upset him was Bishop Larraín. Two days later, Considine met with Larraín, who confirmed that Cushing had misunderstood his remarks. Considine suggested a public interview with Bishop Larraín to clear the air; Larraín agreed with Considine's plan. Considine later drafted the interview and sent it to Larraín. In mid-November he received it back from Larraín, but found it "to be so watered down that it will be of little use."[90] Considine later sent a version of this on to Cushing, but the document failed to resolve the issue. In December, Cushing responded, saying that he found Larraín's remarks "defensive."[91] The issue appears to have blown over and been forgotten after that.

In retrospect, Considine perhaps understood that even his best diplomatic efforts could not settle this one, as the stakes were too high for each

88. CD, February 12, 1961.
89. CD, September 30, 1964.
90. CD, November 9, 1964.
91. CD, December 7, 1964.

of the two bishops. Cushing could be thin-skinned, but, from his perspective, he was daily putting his prestige and financial resources on the line to back the U.S. Catholic mission to Latin America. He may not have expected thankfulness for his efforts—he, like Considine, was aware of anti-Yankee feeling in Latin America—but he did not expect to be told by a leading Latin American bishop that the people he was sending to Latin America did not "count." From Larraín's perspective, even though he was a well-known supporter of U.S. church personnel (clergy, religious, and lay) working in Latin America, he had to show that he was capable of speaking for the church in Latin America, a church that could not be beholden to U.S. missioners at work in Latin America. Yes, Latin American bishops had extended an invitation to North American missioners to come and work in Latin America, but they needed to be clear that they, the Latin American bishops, were in charge in their own church. For as much as Considine felt it to be his job to keep these two important church leaders in constructive relationship, the best he could do in this case was to clarify rather than resolve matters.

Finally, there are signs of weariness in Considine as he came to understand that, in spite of his best efforts and the very large support of Cardinal Cushing, some key U.S. bishops would simply not get on board the train of mission to Latin America. One of these was Bishop Coleman Carroll of Miami. As bishop of the diocese with the largest Cuban-American population, Bishop Carroll seemed to resent the prerogatives of the LAB. Perhaps because Miami was the southernmost diocese in the U.S., he may have felt that he, not the LAB, had the prerogative of setting the U.S. church's course in regard to Latin America.

Normally, Considine's interactions with Carroll were limited to the meetings of the U.S. bishops' Committee on the Church in Latin America; the committee met twice a year, and so Considine was usually well prepared in advance for dealing with him. But in May of 1965 at the inauguration of the brand-new regional seminary in Recife, Brazil, Considine found himself with the onerous task of accompanying Bishop Carroll for a full day in the tropics, a situation that must have felt trying to Considine. The bishop kept complaining about the timing of the seminary inauguration—the building itself was not yet fully constructed:

> I've seldom been as completely exhausted as at the end of this day, principally because of the long discussions led by Bish. Carroll. He has become deeply involved in the L.A. question and talks of inaugurating confrontations of U.S. and L.A. bishops for proper planning.[92]

---

92. CD, May 2, 1965.

Conclusion

The years between 1960 and 1964 were years of success for Considine at the LAB, even if progress was slow at times. These were the years in which he laid the groundwork for further LAB work on the U.S. Catholic mission to Latin America in the second half of the 1960s and beyond. With Cushing's help, he educated the U.S. hierarchy on Latin America, which led to the Bishops' Committee on the Church in Latin America moving from ad-hoc to permanent status. In 1967, the U.S. bishops began annual inter-American meetings, attended by representative bishops from the United States, Canada, and Latin America. During Considine's eight years as director of the LAB, the number of U.S. missioners serving in Latin America approximately doubled,[93] and the pocketbooks of the U.S. bishops and of Catholics in general were opened to financially support the church in Latin America as never before. Considine also created PAVLA, in addition to events such as CICOP for educating U.S. Catholics on the church in Latin America.

The mid-1960s, however, would produce social and political changes in the Americas that would challenge the work of the LAB in new ways, and we turn to those years next.

---

93. According to LAB statistics, the numbers of U.S. missioners working in Latin America *more than doubled* between 1960 and 1967, from 2,405 to 5,369. U.S. Bishop's Committee for Latin America N.C.C.B. "Third Biennial Report of the Church in the United States: U.S. Personnel Serving the Church in Latin America." Washington, DC: January, 1967, p. 4. According to USCMA Statistics cited by Dries, the numbers of U.S. missioners working in Latin America *nearly doubled* between 1960 and 1968, from 2,405 to 4,589 (*Missionary Movement in American Catholic History,* 273).

CHAPTER 10

The Seamy Side of a Conflict
1965–1968

FATHER CONSIDINE'S DIARY entry for Thursday, January 26, 1967, reveals a boiling cauldron of contention in Boston on the first day of the fourth Catholic Inter-American Cooperation Program (CICOP). Richard Cardinal Cushing of Boston, a huge supporter of both the Latin America Bureau (LAB) and Ivan Illich's Center of Intercultural Formation (CIF), was irate; Illich had just published "The Seamy Side of Charity," an essay that called for an end to the U.S. Catholic mission to Latin America.[1]

The mission had been formulated in terms of bringing in foreign priests and pastoral personnel to alleviate a clergy shortage in Latin America. In "Seamy," Illich questioned both the success of and the rationale for the mission. He argued (a) that such aid was not needed—in his view, Latin America was not experiencing a shortage of clergy; and (b) in the case of missioners from the United States, their presence hopelessly changed the pastoral focus to Cold War anti-communism, diverting energies that would be needed for the creation of pastoral approaches to social change in Latin America. Illich also noted that a perception was abroad in 1960s Latin America that the U.S. Catholic mission was allied with U.S. government interests in the region, that it was the religious arm of the Alliance for Progress. "Seamy" also decried the infusion of U.S. money to fund the missionaries as unsustainable for the church in Latin America and called for a moratorium on the sending of new missioners to the region.[2]

---

1. Ivan Illich, "The Seamy Side of Charity," *America* (January 21, 1967): 88–91.

2. "Seamy" also explored several other large issues related to the mission, and space will only permit a brief mention of these: the tendency of North American missioners to replicate in Latin America parish structures—for example parochial schools—from their home countries; the seeming incomprehension on the part of North American missioners of the relational burdens their acts of generosity placed on Latin Americans; a stunning lack of awareness on the part of North American missioners about the already-mentioned

Illich also used "Seamy" to lob a veiled but unmistakable attack at Considine and the LAB, describing PAVLA, CICOP, and the opening of diocesan missions in Latin America as part of an "outburst of charitable frenzy" in the U.S. church.[3] The second paragraph of the essay mentions a "call for 20,000," a not-so-subtle lampooning of the title of Considine's first major book on Latin America, *Call for Forty Thousand*.[4] Considine, however, chose not to take any of this personally and did not himself publish a response to "Seamy." In any case, judging from the responses to "Seamy" published in *America*, it seems apparent that Considine and the LAB were not under immediate scrutiny.[5] All of this points to the oddity of Illich's attacks on Considine. While "Seamy" created a lot of discussion about whether the mission was necessary or should instead be discontinued, no one seems to have believed Illich's basic contention that Considine and the LAB had sold the U.S. church a bill of goods.

Considine and Illich had had a formal working relationship since 1961. Considine at the LAB recruited new U.S. missioners for Latin America who were then trained in language and culture at CIF, led by Illich in Cuernavaca, Mexico.[6] Both Considine and Illich had worked together to establish CIF under the auspices of Fordham University; their working relationship ended on March 31, 1966, when Considine resigned from the CIF Board, withdrawing the LAB's endorsement of CIF.

Considine's diary entries during the January 1967 CICOP meeting recalled how Cushing publicly read a response to "Seamy" from Archbishop Vagnozzi, the apostolic delegate to the United States, doing so "with long harangues and dubious emotional outbursts." Both Cushing and Considine had received advance copies of the article. Their plan had been to draft a response that Latin American and U.S. bishops present at CICOP

---

perception that they were the religious arm of U.S. government efforts such as the Alliance for Progress.

3. "The Seamy Side of Charity" also fixed blame on Considine and the LAB for the shortcomings of the North American Catholic mission to Latin America in a couple of indirect references. Illich called on U.S. church policy makers to "face up to the sociopolitical consequences" of the mission (p. 88); Considine was perhaps the most significant policy person for the U.S. church in regard to Latin America during the 1960s. Later in the essay, Illich said, "A large measure of the blame lies with the underdeveloped ecclesiology of U.S. clerics who direct the 'sale' of American good intentions" (p. 91). While any ordained person (bishop, priest, deacon) is a "cleric," in the article Illich avoids blaming bishops. Who was the U.S. priest who directed organizing efforts for the mission if not Considine?

4. *Call for Forty Thousand: On the Condition of the Roman Catholic Church in Latin America* (Toronto: Longmans, Green & Co., 1946).

5. "Letters to the Editor," *America* (March 4, 1967): 296–98, 317–19.

6. From 1961 to 1966, Illich was also responsible for a branch of CIF in Brazil; it was first located in Anapolis, and then relocated to Petropolis and provided Portuguese language study and the study of Brazilian culture for new Catholic missioners to that country.

could sign, but the prepared text "was declared inadequate before the end of the day and was taken over by a committee of writers."[7] In the end, no such unified response from bishops, from CICOP, or from the LAB would be forthcoming. Instead, discussion of the value of the mission continued in the letter section of the Jesuit weekly *America*, which had published "Seamy." *America* also published "What Is He Getting At?," an article-length companion piece by Joseph Fitzpatrick, S.J., that sought to explain Illich's commentary.[8] Ivan Illich had put the value of the U.S. Catholic mission up for grabs, and through the end of the 1960s the noise from this debate would drown out other U.S. Catholic voices on Latin America, including Considine's.

Readers who are familiar with the sensation caused by "Seamy" may also recall that the story of the LAB begins to drift at this point. As Gerald Costello told it in *Mission to Latin America*, that chilly January in Boston was the "beginning of disenchantment."[9] Todd Hartch makes the much larger claim that Illich and the CIF were responsible for the failure of the U.S. Catholic mission to Latin America.[10] The suggestion seems to have been that the mission was faltering, and that Illich handed Considine his Waterloo. Considine retired in July 1968.

I would like to suggest that the framework of a Latin American church victory over an invasive—or at best a well-intentioned but mismanaged— U.S. Catholic mission was an intentional and long-standing rhetorical ploy on the part of Illich that has outlived its usefulness. For example, Illich may have been successful in spinning the narrative that the mission was counterproductive for the church in Latin America, but what kind of a Waterloo was it when the "victor," Illich, was himself forced out of the priesthood he loved by the Vatican in 1969? In Considine's case, his 1968 retirement had nothing to do with "Seamy"—he had made the decision to retire at the beginning of 1966.[11]

As long as twenty-five years ago, Stephen Judd commented that "Seamy" was just the beginning of a stronger identification of U.S. Catholic missioners with Latin America's poor and that Illich's predictions were essentially incorrect. That is, the violent deaths of four U.S. Catholic women

---

7. CD, January 26, 1967.

8. Joseph P. Fitzpatrick, "What Is He Getting At?" *America* (March 25, 1967): 444–46, 448–49.

9. Gerald M. Costello, *Mission to Latin America: The Successes and Failures of a Twentieth-Century Crusade* (Maryknoll, NY: Orbis Books, 1979), 122.

10. Todd Hartch, "Ivan Illich and the American Catholic Missionary Initiative in Latin America," *International Bulletin of Missionary Research* 33, no. 4 (October 2009): 187.

11. CD, January 1, 1966. In March 1966, Considine informed Bishop Tanner, general secretary of the USCC, of his intention to retire in July of 1968 (CD, March 9, 1966).

missioners in El Salvador in 1980 was concrete evidence of a depth of missionary commitment, not the lack thereof that was decried by Illich. In Judd's telling, 1967 perhaps marked a corrective moment for the mission, but certainly not its end. More recently, Hartch concurred that Illich did not understand "the deeply transformative nature of missionary experience" for both missioners and the people to whom they are sent.[12]

In 1967, "Seamy" was certainly not the only noticeable call for change in the U.S. Catholic mission to Latin America.[13] The previous chapter noted Thomas Quigley's call for a reform of PAVLA, and Gerald Costello described the mid-1960s as a time when the initial mission parishes and works accepted at the beginning of the decade by U.S. missioners were reconsidered. Some missioners who had selected a mission in a middle-class area when new to Latin America at the beginning of the decade, by the middle of the 1960s were making a correction and moving to rural or slum areas.[14]

Although it is true that the number of U.S. missioners in Latin America began to decline after 1968, that same year the number of U.S. missioners serving abroad in any part of the world also declined at a comparable rate. The numbers also need to be viewed within the overall post–Vatican II climate in which U.S. vocations to the priesthood and religious life began a decline that lasted for many years.[15]

As was discussed in the previous chapter, James F. Garneau has suggested that the problems of the mission can be traced back to the Georgetown meeting. All of the above makes it rather implausible to draw a direct line of causation connecting the publication of "Seamy" in 1967 and the post-1968 decline in the number of U.S. missioners working in Latin America. Additionally, I want to suggest that "Seamy" had it wrong in regard to the relationship of Considine and Illich to the church in Latin America:

1. Illich unfairly targeted Considine for criticism in "Seamy"; as should be clear from the previous chapter, Considine was not an independent operator foisting U.S. personnel and resources on the Latin American church, but rather someone who knew the bishops of Latin America and worked cooperatively under their leadership.

---

12. Hartch, "Ivan Illich," 188.

13. I am grateful to Charles Strauss for suggesting this line of thinking.

14. Costello, *Mission to Latin America,* 229–48.

15. Between 1968 and 1970, the total number of U.S. missioners engaged in missions around the world dropped by 13 percent; in the same time period, the reductions were 15 percent for Latin America (South and Central America and the Caribbean) and 13.5 percent for East Asia (Angelyn Dries, *The Missionary Movement in American Catholic History* [Maryknoll, NY: Orbis Books, 1998], 273).

2. Conversely, Illich's implied claim in "Seamy" to speak on behalf of the church in Latin America should be understood as something of a stretch; it was especially Illich's thought-provoking notion of Latin America as "priest-ridden" that could not be understood as representative of the position of the bishops and other leaders of the church in Latin America at the time.

This chapter tells the story of Considine and Illich's relationship and graphs the genesis and development of their feud. Along the way, representative texts from each are analyzed in order to probe how each understood the history of the church in Latin America. Both churchmen proposed solutions to address the problems of the church in the region; I will suggest that fundamental differences in the understanding of the historical development of the problems of the church in Latin America contributed greatly to the exacerbation of their conflict.

At the outset it needs to be stated that "The Seamy Side of Charity" was not without important criticisms of the U.S. Catholic mission to Latin America. For example, a general charge in the essay is that the mission operated without consideration of its being viewed by some Latin Americans as the religious arm of U.S. government's Alliance for Progress, making the mission seem to be part of U.S. imperialistic designs on the region. This chapter is not a defense of Considine against such a charge—his largely unsuccessful efforts to seek U.S. government aid for the mission from the Alliance for Progress during the Kennedy administration has already been discussed in the previous chapter. Additionally, sometime between the second and fourth CICOP (January 1965 and January 1967), Considine's ability to track the shifting interests and priorities of the Catholic Church in Latin America had declined. Care is taken in this chapter to acknowledge the justifiable criticisms of Considine, the LAB, and the U.S. Catholic mission to Latin America found in "Seamy."

The Considine–Illich Conflict in the 1960s
"Ghastly" was the adjective that Ivan Illich chose to describe the letter that Maryknoll Fr. John J. Considine purportedly ghost-wrote in 1961 for Pope John XXIII, a letter that bade all North American religious superiors to send ten percent of their personnel to Latin America.[16] A little chronology in descending order is called for: Illich's remark was from the late 1980s,[17]

---

16. Ivan Illich and David Cayley, *Ivan Illich in Conversation* (Concord, Ontario: Anansi, 1992), 93.

17. The exact date of the remark is not given; Cayley based his book on radio interviews with Illich that were conducted in the second half of the 1980s on more than one occasion.

not from "The Seamy Side of Charity," in 1967. By the late 1980s, Considine had been dead for several years. The passing of years had sharpened, not mellowed, Illich's perspective on Pope John's letter and the mission to Latin America upon which the letter placed a papal stamp of approval.

Illich's stance was not based on hyperbole nor rage-filled folly. It represented instead the clashing of two different generations as the mission to Latin America played out in the 1960s. Considine had ridden the wave of postwar U.S. optimism that saw the election of John Kennedy and the launch of the Alliance for Progress. Illich, on the other hand, was well disposed to understand the critique of U.S. power that came about as human rights abuses in Vietnam and during the civil rights movement came to light. Considine's view of mission was buttressed by abundant vocations to the priesthood and religious life, which the U.S. Catholic Church experienced in the postwar period through the early 1960s. Illich understood the ministerial structure of the church as entering into crisis in the post–Vatican II era as the number of new recruits to the priesthood and religious communities declined and defections from ministry increased.

The mid-1960s was the moment when Considine's "innocence" and optimism were overcome by the cultural forces that brought about a questioning of U.S. power; after the publication of *Humanae Vitae* in 1968, a similar questioning of hierarchical structures took place within the church. Illich seemed to be much more aware of the mood of such a transition than Considine was. Thomas Quigley, a much younger colleague of Considine at the LAB, suggested that the times were revolutionary, and while Considine was certainly capable of working alongside the revolutionaries, it was clear to Quigley that Considine did not have a revolutionary temperament.[18]

As a critique of the U.S. Catholic mission to Latin America, "Seamy" has been read by many missioners and is, even today, a resource for cross-cultural work. Today what seems less obvious is that the article was the most public moment of the long-running conflict between Ivan Illich and John Considine.[19]

Considine and Illich

Msgr. Ivan Illich (1926–2002) was born in Vienna, the son of a Croatian father and a Sephardic Jewish mother who had converted to Catholicism.

---

18. Thomas Quigley, interview with author, August 22, 2009.

19. At the beginning of the essay, Illich identifies several activities as problematic: "Let us coldly examine the American Church's outburst of charitable frenzy which resulted in the creation of 'papal' volunteers, student 'mission crusades,' the annual CICOP mass assemblies, numerous diocesan missions and new religious communities" (p. 88). All but two (student mission crusades and new religious communities) were directly carried out or encouraged by the LAB.

The family had to flee to Rome to escape the coming persecution of Jews in Austria after the Anschluss. Illich continued his education in Rome and earned a doctorate in history from Salzburg; he decided to become a priest, and studied theology in postwar Rome, where for a time he came under the influence of Jacques Maritain. He was ordained in 1951 in Rome.[20] He traveled to New York where his mother was living after his ordination, and when he stepped out of her Upper West Side apartment to buy something, he heard Puerto Rican Spanish spoken for the first time. His view of New York was instantly changed; he became fascinated by the growing population of Puerto Rican migrants who were changing the character of the Yankee metropolis. He spent a month in Puerto Rico and learned Spanish, visiting all parts of the island.[21]

Illich's initiation to Puerto Rican culture was like falling in love, and he tore into study of the history and literature of the island. But the early 1950s also marked the development of Illich's strong convictions about ministry among Puerto Ricans in New York. To be effective, that ministry needed to be in Spanish and have the same style and feeling of the way Puerto Ricans were accustomed to worship on the island. Illich decided to stay in New York and was incardinated into the archdiocese; he began to raise his concerns about Puerto Rican ministry to Cardinal Spellman, to his pastor at Incarnation Parish in northern Manhattan, and to just about anyone else who would listen.[22]

Illich organized ministries among Puerto Rican Catholics in the Archdiocese of New York and was instrumental in raising their profile among the many Catholic ethnic populations of the archdiocese. In 1956, he was appointed vice-rector of the Pontifical Catholic University of Puerto Rico.[23] During the summers of 1956–1960 he organized and ran the Institute of Intercultural Communication (IIC), a successful program for teaching Spanish and Puerto Rican culture to priests, religious, firefighters, teachers, police officers, and social workers from New York. In 1961, Illich founded the Center of Intercultural Formation (CIF) in Cuernavaca, Mexico, under the auspices of Fordham University.

Todd Hartch has suggested that Illich used his position at the CIF to subvert rather than support the mission to Latin America; he also suggested

---

20. Theodore Cardinal McCarrick said that Illich was ordained for a Hungarian or Croatian diocese (interview with author, December 8, 2010).

21. Joseph P. Fitzpatrick, "Ivan Illich as We Knew Him in the 1950s," in *The Challenges of Ivan Illich: A Collective Reflection,* ed. Lee Hoinacki and Carl Mitcham (Albany: State University of New York Press, 2002), 35–36.

22. Joseph P. Fitzpatrick, *The Stranger Is Our Own: Reflections on the Journey of Puerto Rican Migrants* (Kansas City, MO: Sheed & Ward, 1996), 16–17.

23. Fitzpatrick, "Ivan Illich as We Knew Him," 39.

that Considine was unaware of Illich's intentions, calling into question Considine's decision to assist Illich to set up the CIF.[24] How can these two claims be assessed?

The first of Hartch's claims runs contrary to the high regard in which Illich has consistently been held by missioners to Latin America at the time. Far from undermining their mission, missioners understood Illich as offering important correctives for mission work. Philip Berryman comments: "The notion that in 1960 Illich foresaw and plotted to undermine the mission does not ring true."[25] Theodore Cardinal McCarrick says that he "never heard" Ivan Illich mention anything close to what Hartch presents.[26] Cardinal McCarrick had served during the summers of 1959 and 1960 under Ivan Illich at the IIC in Ponce, Puerto Rico.

While Illich had admirers among U.S. missioners in Latin America—and among Latin American bishops and theologians—it was a different story among those whom Illich determined not to be fit for mission in Latin America. For example, Illich and his team dismissed a high number of missioners-in-training during the inaugural session of CIF in 1961. In November 1962, Fr. Vic Fernandez, S.J., the national coordinator of PAVLA, wrote to Considine:

> I received a letter from the Chancellor of the Amarillo Diocese— same old story. Ivan wrote a strong letter to the Bishop, telling him the priest from the diocese, (who just failed at Cuernavaca) is not fit to go to Latin America. . . . The Bishop is disturbed, and so is the Chancellor. The priest insists Illich and Cuernavaca are no good.[27]

Since the priest in question was not identified, it is difficult to ascertain if Illich's judgment of his abilities to adapt to cross-cultural mission in Latin America was correct or not. What does seem to be clear is that Illich was not persuasive with this particular bishop about the problems he encountered with the priest in question, and that for the bishop, Illich himself had become the problem. Seemingly ignored in this brief discussion was an appreciation of the difficulty of the task of becoming a missioner in Latin America.

It was therefore unfortunate that Illich became such a lightning rod while serving in Cuernavaca; apparently, his approach at the IIC in Ponce

24. Hartch, "Ivan Illich," 185–88.
25. Philip Berryman, telephone interview with author, February 21, 2011.
26. Theodore E. McCarrick, Hyattsville, MD, to Bob Hurteau, Los Angeles, February 18, 2011. Personal correspondence.
27. Vic Fernandez, Chicago, to John Considine, Washington, November 9, 1962. ACUA, NCWC General Secretary, 187:31.

did not have the same confrontational tone. In the work of cross-cultural training for ministry, it would have been invaluable if someone like Illich could have helped a bishop to understand the aptitudes—or the lack thereof—that his priests displayed for work in a different culture. However, during Illich's tenure at Cuernavaca, the decision to declare someone "not fit to go to Latin America" was frequently received by U.S. missioners and their backers instead as an indication that Illich himself was a problem.

Regarding Illich's views on the value of the mission to Latin America, it is difficult to ascertain exactly what Illich's intentions were at any one point. For example, he did give three interviews between 1969 and 1976 in which he spoke about having the intention from 1960 to stop mission-ers from going to Latin America, but oddly enough, both prior to and after those interviews, this particular claim is absent from Illich's writings. Cer-tainly, "The Seamy Side of Charity" represented a strong moment of oppo-sition to the mission for Illich, yet the following year he reflected a more ambiguous stance toward the mission in his essay "Violence: A Mirror for Americans." Illich wrote that in 1960

> I told the late Bishop Manuel Larrain, the president of the Confer-ence of Latin American Bishops, that I was prepared if necessary to dedicate my efforts to stop the coming of missionaries to Latin America. His answer still rings in my ears: "They may be useless to us in Latin America, but they are the only North Americans whom we will have the opportunity to educate. We owe them that much."[28]

Did Illich agree with Larraín that the mission was important because it gave Latin Americans the chance to educate people from the United States about how the other half lives? Did he agree in 1960, but by 1967 had changed his mind? He did not say. Berryman offers an explanation: "Illich's opposition to the mission to Latin America came over time; it was not instantaneous."[29]

Even if Illich did not plot to undermine the mission to Latin America from 1960, the high rate of attrition among students from the CIF program in 1961 became a serious friction point with Considine: more than a third of the fifty-nine students in the inaugural program in June 1961 did not finish the full course, which ended in October 1961. Additionally, among those who did not finish the course were eight of the inaugural group of nineteen Papal Volunteers to Latin America (PAVLA), members of the lay mission movement that Considine created in 1960.

---

28. Ivan Illich, *Celebration of Awareness: A Call for Institutional Revolution* (Garden City, NY: Doubleday, 1970), 12.

29. Berryman, interview, February 21, 2011.

Considine was not pleased. While he understood that some of the students left voluntarily, during the course he had received a document from Illich, "The C.I.F. Puzzle,"[30] which laid out the problem from his perspective. At issue was what kind of lay volunteer was needed—or not—in Latin America. The Papal Volunteer program proposed to send volunteers who were "well trained in specialized fields"[31] to serve in Latin America, but apparently that norm was not respected, and Illich explained there was no contribution to be made in Latin America by "generous Catholics" who brought good will but no useful skill to their volunteer service.

Since PAVLA was so new and so decentralized, it was not surprising that this sort of trial-and-error would occur in its first group of Papal Volunteers. For example, who, in Kansas, had made sure that the skill sets of the new PAVLA recruits were matched to specific needs in Latin American placements? If they had read about those needs—in English—while accepting the new recruits, who had made sure that the Kansas supervisor had correctly understood the needs of the church in a Latin American context, so as to be able to match the skills of specific volunteers to specific placement options? It was probably an impossibly complex task for a PAVLA recruiter who, in 1960–1961, likely had no experience of Latin America him or herself.

What happened next is quite curious for Considine, who in his work up to this point had not been supportive of unskilled "generous Catholics" going into mission work. He was the architect of the PAVLA "specialists only" policy, and in 1946 had argued that the pioneer Maryknoll missioners in Tanganyika first train with and then work under the White Fathers there. But in the fall of 1961, rather than agreeing with Illich that, in the future, greater care would be taken to recruit only people with specialized skills, Considine instead remonstrated with him for his negative attitude toward the Papal Volunteers[32] and argued for the usefulness of "hardy workers"[33] going to Latin America who may not have had the intellectual capacity for the CIF course Illich had developed.

While at Cuernavaca for the end of the first course in October 1961, Considine told Illich of his desire for a "craftsman's course" in Spanish to be offered solely to Papal Volunteers, and that he was looking into holding such a course in Lima, Peru. The exact meaning of "craftsman" was not defined; neither had PAVLA defined the category of "specialist." On the

---

30. ACUA, NCWC/OGS 186:61.

31. Richard Cushing, "On the Call of the Holy See for Papal Volunteers for Latin America" (Washington, DC: Latin America Bureau, n.d.).

32. CD, September 22, 1961.

33. John Considine, Washington, to Laurence McGinley, New York, October 11, 1961. ACUA, NCWC General Secretary, 186:51.

other hand, "The CIF Puzzle" contained a list of specialized skills needed in Latin America, but the list contains nothing remotely similar to a "craftsman" or "hardy worker."[34] For unknown reasons, Illich seemed to have forgotten the criteria he himself elaborated in "The C.I.F. Puzzle" and accepted to develop a three-month "craftsman's" course, which would have begun in February 1962. However, the course was never held.[35] After the fall of 1961, Considine and Illich remained at odds over PAVLA.

I will return to the specific disagreements between Considine and Illich over PAVLA presently. But what of Hartch's second claim: Did Considine naïvely allow Illich a significant platform for undermining mission efforts like PAVLA?

The picture from Considine's diaries is hardly one of naïve trust. In 1960, Considine sought Illich's expert services to run the training of new missioners to Latin America, while remaining cautious about some of Illich's obvious baggage—for example, Illich had just been expelled from the Ponce Diocese for publicly disagreeing with his bishop's views on candidates in the 1960 race for governor of Puerto Rico.[36]

The 1960 governor's race in Puerto Rico was won with more than an absolute majority by the incumbent, Luis Muñoz Marín of the Partido Popular Democrático (PPD). In addition to candidates from the Puerto Rican statehood party and the independence party, the newly formed Partido de Acción Cristiana (PAC) also fielded a candidate to oppose Muñoz Marín. The PAC was formed as a "Catholic" political alternative that had the support of the bishops of Puerto Rico, who had objected to the Muñoz Marín administration's role in allowing divorce and access to birth control.[37]

During most of the 1960 electoral campaign, there were only two bishops in Puerto Rico, both of whom were originally from the U.S. mainland: Archbishop James Peter Davis of San Juan and Bishop James Edward McManus of Ponce.[38] As the campaign heated up near election day, the bishops issued a statement prohibiting Catholics from voting for the PPD

34. "The C.I.F. Puzzle," 4–5. The list of skills needed in Latin America does include "teaching electricity to boys or teaching home economics to girls."

35. CD, October 10, 1961.

36. Sherman Goldman, "Ivan Illich: Learning Is Unlearning," *East West Journal* 4 (April 27, 1976): 34–35.

37. "Catholic Party Hits Foes in Puerto Rico," *New York Times,* July 16, 1960, p. 2.

38. A third bishop was Puerto Rican—Luis Aponte Martínez was consecrated auxiliary bishop of Ponce on October 12, 1960, less than a month before the general election (see http://www.catholic-hierarchy.org/bishop/baponte.html). A fourth bishop came a couple of weeks later: Alfredo José Isaac Cecilio Francesco Méndez-Gonzalez of the newly created Diocese of Arecibo was consecrated October 28, 1960, less than two weeks before the general election. Bishop Méndez was born in Chicago but was of Puerto Rican descent.

because of their immoral policies. However, this view was publicly contradicted by Cardinal Spellman of New York, who spoke to the press about his view that there could be no penalty for Catholics who voted for the PPD.[39]

It was in this political climate that Illich had made public statements in the summer of 1960 about his view that Catholics should feel free to vote their consciences in the upcoming election, which led to Bishop McManus expelling him from the Ponce Diocese in September 1960. Because of Illich's background in Puerto Rico, NCWC general secretary Msgr. Paul Tanner would not accept Illich in the LAB.[40] Considine therefore worked with Fordham University president Fr. Laurence McGinley, S.J., to establish CIF under Fordham's sponsorship. However, Msgr. Tanner later modified his stance and, in early 1961, agreed to channel $40,000 through the NCWC to support the establishment of CIF; the funds had been sent by CAL. Similarly, it was probably helpful that Illich never lost the confidence of his archbishop, Cardinal Spellman.

Additionally, since the PAC came in a distant third in the 1960 election, the election results could have been interpreted as exonerating Illich's view that the church should stay out of partisan politics. Even so, during late 1960 and the first part of 1961, as Considine worked to establish CIF, Considine's diaries record his concerns about the decision to work with Illich.[41] Considine's decision appears to have been one of those personnel gambles that managers sometimes make—a certain person has all the right skills for a job, and so one takes a chance on the person in the hope that the candidate's less favorable traits can be kept under control—and one main-

See José Dimas Soberal, "Mons. Alfredo F. Méndez, C.S.C.: Primer Obispo y Fundador de la Diócesis de Arecibo," *El Visitante* (January 22–28, 2006): 23.

39. John Wicklein, "Spellman Sees No Sin by a Voter Who Defies Puerto Rico Bishop," *New York Times,* October 24, 1960, p. 1. Spellman also met with Governor Muñoz Marín during the campaign and attended a dinner to honor Archbishop Davis at which the governor was also present; McManus had boycotted the event and forbade his priests to go. Illich, however, attended the dinner with Spellman (Fitzpatrick, *Stranger Is Our Own*, 29). Spellman visited the Maryknoll Sisters' Cloister on October 30, 1960—about a week before election day—and when asked if he supported a certain change in the liturgy, Spellman wryly commented that he knew the Puerto Rican bishops had not pronounced on that yet. See John Donovan, Ossining, NY, to John J. Considine, Washington, DC, November 3, 1960. MMA, General Council Correspondence with Organizations, 9:14 (Latin America Bureau 1960–1962).

40. CD, September 8, 1960.

41. CD, September 15, 1960, and February 10, 1961. The latter date refers to a sheet of paper stuck into Considine's diary, which is entitled, "Diary entries having to do with John Illich," a hand-written copy of details from eight previous entries over the previous eight months. The date of the sheet is just subsequent to one of the early meetings at Fordham to organize CIF.

tains vigilance. Meanwhile, one of Illich's principal concerns throughout 1960–1962 was for CIF to remain the only training site for U.S. Catholic missioners headed to Latin America.[42]

Then, in February 1962, the game changed completely for Considine when Illich wrote a memo that outlined goals for CIF that Considine could not abide. The memo is apparently now lost, but Considine's reply to it on April 19, 1962, decried Illich's idea that CIF is "becoming a powerful institution" capable of preparing people to exercise political power in the Church; Considine said the idea has "the air of a conspiratorial cabal."[43] In Rome for other business, Considine first discussed the memo with Archbishop Antonio Samorè, then serving as vice president of the Pontifical Commission for Latin America, and then he resolved to take action.[44]

Because Illich's February 1962 memo cannot be found, it is hard to know exactly what issue was the tipping point for Considine. However, it is clear from Considine's reply that Illich had crossed a line: he had spoken of the purpose of CIF as beyond that of preparing missioners to be effective apostles in Latin America, hinting that the mission of the Center was to prepare people to use power to effect needed changes in the church. Considine no longer found himself enthralled by Illich's enormous knowledge of Latin America. The spell had been broken; Considine demystified Illich. He now understood that Illich's adoption of a different agenda presented him with a serious problem. By this time Considine had already expressed his displeasure to Illich about student evaluations and fiscal matters, and he never felt comfortable with the caustic tone in Illich's approach to intercultural learning.[45] After all that, Illich's adoption of an unspecified new purpose for training at CIF served as the catalyst for Considine to begin to extricate himself and the LAB from a relationship with Illich.

Illich, meanwhile, was furious. Considine had suggested that CIF retain an executive director—a person in charge of fundraising—and that it be someone other than Illich.[46] Illich interpreted this as a call for his resignation; he protested to McGinley that Considine was demanding that he "be replaced by Father McGuire as Chief Executive of CIF."[47]

---

42. CD, February 10, 1961. MMA, Considine Papers, 7:1.

43. John J. Considine, Washington, to the CIF Board, April 19, 1962, ACUA, NCWC General Secretary, 186:51.

44. CD, April 9 and 10, 1962.

45. For a description of Illich's pedagogy at CIF, see Hartch, "Ivan Illich," 185–87.

46. John J. Considine, Washington, to the CIF Board, April 19, 1962, ACUA, NCWC General Secretary, 186:51.

47. Ivan Illich, Cuernavaca, Mexico, to Laurence McGinley, New York, May 8, 1962. Fordham University Archives, McGinley Papers, Box: 7, Folder: CIF 1962.

But the situation presented a dilemma for Considine. On the one hand, Considine was increasingly uncomfortable with Illich's leadership at CIF, but, on the other, he had worked hard to establish CIF. Additionally, Fordham University had invested time, resources, and prestige in CIF at the request of Considine and Illich, which meant that extricating himself and the LAB from Illich's operation would not be easy. He pressed ahead anyway, and in late 1962 Considine was working hard to establish a new missionary training institute at Ponce, Puerto Rico; the first classes at Ponce began in August of the following year.

As in most human affairs, the conflict that developed between the two priests in 1962 also had much to do with temperament, money, and management. Nonetheless, conflicting visions of what the mission to Latin America needed to be were also in play. Three issues stand out: a disagreement about the needs of the church in Latin America, PAVLA, and the problem of U.S. missioners being viewed by some in Latin America as an extension of U.S. government interests in the region.

What did the church in Latin America need? Considine understood the mission to be that of support to the institutions of the church in Latin America; he especially understood that Latin America needed many more thousands of priests than were available at the time on the continent.[48] Illich, on the other hand, understood that the church in Latin America was undergoing thorough reform and so it would not be enough to support existing institutions—those institutions needed to be updated according to the needs of the church in a situation of radical social change. Additionally, this is the beginning of Illich's critique of the main institutions of Western societies, critiques that would eventually extend to societal structures built around the concepts of development, medicine, and education.[49]

Regarding PAVLA, Considine and Illich would never find common ground. Considine was the creator of PAVLA and cared deeply about its development; it represented for him an opportunity for lay people to follow a missionary calling.[50] For Illich, it was a waste of the Latin American

---

48. This is the principal thesis of Considine's *Call for Forty Thousand*.

49. Ivan Illich and David Cayley, *The Rivers North of the Future: The Testament of Ivan Illich* (Toronto: House of Anansi Press, 2005), 1–44.

50. In 1960 or 1961, the essay "On the Call of the Holy See for Papal Volunteers for Latin America," by Richard Cardinal Cushing, was published by the Papal Volunteers for Latin America under the direction of the Latin America Bureau. Cushing makes the following comment, with which Considine was surely in agreement: "The call has come directly from the Holy See through the Pontifical Commission for Latin America. It is indeed a great challenge. Lay missioners, the best spiritually and intellectually, have been in the planning stage long enough."

church's resources to train and employ foreign volunteers for a three-year term rather than hiring local lay people.[51]

Finally, there was a danger of missioners being perceived as too close to the U.S. government. For Illich, North American missioners going to Latin America were almost totally unaware of a political perception, held by some sectors in Latin America, that their mission was the religious arm of the Alliance for Progress.[52] Considine seemed unconcerned about such a perception, and he never tired of finding ways to attempt to marshal Alliance for Progress or USAID money to CELAM or other international church agencies for the mission, though apparently no initiative of that sort became reality.[53]

Beyond such specific disagreements were the deep convictions held by each. For Considine, the North American mission to Latin America was a "Papal Program" and carried a divine mandate;[54] for Illich, the mission was a misguided effort that would do serious harm to the church in Latin America by setting up a foreign structure that was unsustainable.[55]

When Illich sent out his open letter on PAVLA in 1965, saying that PAVLA had outlived its purpose and should either be disbanded or become a foundation to support Latin American lay ministers,[56] that was probably the last straw for Considine in terms of trying to get along with Illich. In the spring of 1966, Fordham University decided to end its sponsorship of CIF, and Considine used that occasion to resign from the CIF board.

Illich composed "The Seamy Side of Charity" in the fall of 1966, but it was not accepted for publication by the *National Catholic Reporter*.[57] Considine and Illich saw each other one more time in November 1966; Illich visited Considine's Washington office, and by all accounts it was a stormy meeting and the subject, again, was most likely financial support for CIF.[58]

51. "Dear Father Kevane" is Illich's 1965 open letter on PAVLA (Ivan Illich, *The Church, Change, and Development* [Chicago: Urban Training Center Press, 1970], 33–41).

52. Illich, "Violence: A Mirror for Americans," in *Celebration of Awareness*, 9–16. The first sentence of "The Seamy Side of Charity" also carried a sarcastic remark that could only contribute to such confusion: "Five years ago, U.S. Catholics undertook a peculiar alliance for the progress of the Latin American Church" (p. 88).

53. See the previous chapter; CD, July 26, August 1 and 13, and November 26, 1962. Apparently, such aid could only be permitted between local churches (and other private agencies) and the national offices of USAID or the Alliance for Progress within each country, and not at an international level. From Considine's perspective, this localized approach did not allow CELAM the ability to coordinate the effort.

54. "The Papal Program for Latin America" (Chicago: Papal Volunteers for Latin America, n.d.).

55. Illich, "Seamy Side of Charity."

56. Illich, "Dear Father Kevane."

57. Costello, *Mission to Latin America*, 124; CD, January 16, 1967.

58. Illich's correspondence reveals continuing financial trouble at CIF; it was a theme

One of the LAB secretaries later commented that it was the only time she had ever seen Fr. Considine lose his temper.[59]

America accepted "Seamy" for publication; the article appeared in their January 21, 1967, issue, just days before the start of the LAB's annual CICOP meeting. Illich made sure hundreds of copies would be available at the meeting.

Perspectives on the History of the Church in Latin America

Both Considine and Illich understood the church in Latin America to be in a process of reform, and both of them understood their efforts as auxiliary to that of the Latin American bishops in that process. Members of every reform movement hold a perspective or perhaps several perspectives on history. If an appeal is made for action to be taken to change the current state of affairs toward the realization of some desired end, then a judgment has been made about current or past realities, a judgment that often is unexamined as the focus shifts to a changed-for-the-better future.

What can we understand about the judgments made by Considine and Illich concerning the past and present of the church in Latin America? We know that Considine called for a modernization of religious practice, and Illich urged Latin American Catholics to solve their own problems without importing foreign clergy. As Considine and Illich—and others, of course—made these calls for reform, did they understand the Latin American church's past as continuous or discontinuous with the desired change proposed? Were Considine and Illich calling on Latin American Catholics to break with their past, rejecting (or at least putting aside) significant pieces of their history, or were they attempting to propose a way that was continuous with their past, that would build on the strengths of the faith as Latin American Catholics lived it? What follows is an analysis of the views on the history of the church in Latin America held by John Considine and Ivan Illich in the 1960s.

Apart from the fact that in November 1961 Considine and Illich could not agree on how to hold a dialogue on the church in Latin America,[60] no records remain of the two of them carrying on a discussion with each other in the 1960s about their judgments of the past of the church in Latin America. The absence of such an airing of views is perhaps symptomatic of the intractability of their conflict. As we have seen, before the first CICOP in 1964 the two had simply decided to go their separate ways.

---

of frequent dispute between Considine and Illich (Ivan D. Illich, Cuernavaca, Mexico, to Leo Mahon, San Miguelito, Panama, November 8, 1966. UNDA, San Miguelito Papers [CSMM], Box 2, General Correspondence, A-L; Jan - Dec 1968).

59. Magda Eccles, interview with author, August 22, 2009; CD, November 22, 1966.

60. See chapter 9.

It is important to note that the theological visions of the two men were parallel in important ways. Angelyn Dries has noted that Considine's theological framework for understanding World Christianity sought to have the voices of believers around the world taken seriously and so serves as an important precursor for later developments such as liberation theology.[61] This was a notion that Illich shared completely. In 1964 Illich helped organize a meeting in Petropolis, Brazil, on the topic of Latin American theology which featured keynotes by several theologians who later would become important voices in liberation theology, Gustavo Gutiérrez among them.[62]

It should also be noted that both Considine and Illich were on good terms with bishops and other church leaders in Latin America: Cardinals Silva and Landázuri, Archbishop (later Cardinal) Miranda, Archbishops Helder Câmara and McGrath, Bishop Manuel Larraín and many others who served in the leadership of CELAM—they all knew Considine and Illich in the 1960s. As has been noted, Considine's ability to track the vision of the CELAM leadership diminished around 1965; however, Illich would have the same problem beginning in 1968. Even so, judging by their continued contact with Latin American bishops, both churchmen apparently stayed on good terms with Latin American church leaders through 1968.

A close reading of selected texts by the two churchmen reveals significant areas of agreement. For example, one part of the critique offered by Illich in "The Seamy Side of Charity" focuses on U.S. missioners who ignore the concerns of the Latin American churches they purport to serve and out of ignorance set up unsustainable U.S. church institutions. Yet Cardinal Cushing's keynote at the first CICOP conference in 1964 addressed this situation. In a text drafted by Considine, the cardinal called on U.S. missioners to work under the guidance of the Latin American church. The speech holds to the view that the North American mission to Latin America is one of solidarity with *and* in the church in Latin America, and must be accomplished under the leadership of the bishops of Latin America.[63]

Considine and "the Passing Emergency"
Considine first traveled to Latin America in 1945 for an extended study tour that focused on the needs of the Catholic Church in the region; after

61. Angelyn Dries, "A Theology of Global Christianity: The Mission Thought of John Considine, M.M. (1897 – 1982)" (Philadelphia: American Catholic Historical Society Meeting, April 16–17, 1993, photocopied), 5.

62. Gustavo Gutiérrez, interview with author, July 22, 2011. See Roberto Oliveros Maqueo, "Meeting of Theologians at Petrópolis (March 1964)," in *Liberation Theology: A Documentary History*, ed. Alfred T. Hennelly (Maryknoll, NY: Orbis Books, 1990), 43–47.

63. John Considine, Washington, to Richard Cushing, Boston, December 27, 1963. ACUA, NCWC General Secretary, 187:20.

that trip he published *Call for Forty Thousand*. The text aimed to introduce a U.S. Catholic audience to the church in Latin America and covers a wide variety of topics: the socioeconomic situation, social and religious customs, some aspects of politics, and some concerns about the possible advances of communism and Protestantism in the region. The book tells many stories about Latin American church people and enterprises and was a Catholic best-seller. Considine traveled again to Latin America in 1954 and 1955, and in 1958 published an updated volume with similar themes: *New Horizons in Latin America*.

What can we derive from these texts that will enable us to understand Considine's overall view of the past of the church in Latin America? Concern for the clergy shortage in Latin America looms largest for this author of *Call for Forty Thousand*—forty thousand priests—published in 1946. That book proposes that greater numbers of missionary priests be sent to Latin America to assist in this "passing emergency." However, it is important to clarify here that Considine did not believe that forty thousand priests should be suddenly exported to Latin American countries. To the contrary, he writes:

> The countries of Latin America have no desire for large numbers of foreign priests. In particular, there is no desire for many thousands of priests from the United States. . . . Each country should receive the minimum of outside priests required to care for the passing emergency as would be decided upon by the local hierarchy.[64]

His view of Latin America from that time through 1968 is consumed with unease about the current priest-to-Catholic-faithful ratio (1 priest for nearly 6,000 Catholics in 1946). Considine viewed this as an urgent problem, one emerging as the residue of the nineteenth-century decline of the church after the independence of most of the Latin American republics; the priest-to-Catholic-faithful ratio in the United States in 1946 was 1 to 650.[65] In Considine's view, this was not Latin America's greatest problem—but it was indeed the greatest problem of the church in Latin America.

---

64. Considine, *Call for Forty Thousand*, 14, 16. A quick clarification about the mathematical terms is in order: the influx of foreign priests to Latin America, through 1968 when it peaked, was never as high as forty thousand, nor was the "ten percent" of the membership of North American religious communities requested by John XXIII in 1961 (see the previous chapter) ever remotely attained. There was, however, a dramatic increase in foreign priests (and religious) in Latin America during the 1960s (see chapter 9, n. 93).

65. John J. Considine, "Latin America Needs Priests," *The Missionary Union of the Clergy Bulletin* (September 1946): 9–15. In *Call for Forty Thousand*, Considine explains historical details such as the 1755 decree by Pombal that hobbled mission efforts in the Amazon by closing one hundred Jesuit missions there.

Notwithstanding his assessments, Considine portrays the life of faith that Latin Americans lived without priestly ministers in a most sympathetic light. In *New Horizons in Latin America*, Considine described a large parish in an area called Vila Alpina, located on the periphery of São Paulo, Brazil. Fr. McCann, one of the American Oblate priests at work in the parish, spoke about Brazilian Catholics who do not come to Sunday Mass: "This does not mean that they are not interested in religion."[66] Considine quoted Fr. McCann at length:

> In the case of most of the people . . . the habit of going to Sunday Mass has never been acquired. If it ever existed in their families it was lost generations ago. Many of them have worked out a way to get along in religion almost entirely without the priest.[67]

Fr. McCann then refers to a parishioner, Narciso, who is a *rezador*:

> A rezador is the reciter of prayers among these people. . . . It is a species of neighborhood catechist, a local institution in the villages of Brazil. It is another outcome of the scarcity of priests.[68]

Thus, Considine's descriptions of aspects of Latin American Catholicism strike a sympathetic note; the English-speaking reader is frequently invited to understand differences on a point like Sunday Mass attendance, for instance, as a situation that is related to the historical context of Latin America. Considine continually takes pains to contextualize in order to combat the tendency of many religious people to judge such differences in a moralistic way.

Nonetheless, Considine still brings the pages on Vila Alpina to a close with the hope that that situation might change. Fr. McCann encourages a woman to soon begin to come to Sunday Mass, and Considine concludes the vignette with these words:

> The simple housewife did not reply but a new light lit her eyes as she stared sharply at the priest. Perhaps it was only my lively imagination; yet I saw a new-born resolution in that look. Thus the unchurched

---

It was a mortal blow from which the Church has not recovered to this day. . . . All during the nineteenth century, worthy but hopelessly inadequate efforts were made to regain the vigor of former centuries, but Catholic life in the Amazon today is for the most part anemic. The Salesians, with notable aid from others, are the modern-day successors to the Jesuits, but the sad fact is that they are all too few in number (p. 28).

66. Considine, *New Horizons*, 31.
67. Ibid., 32.
68. Ibid., 35.

millions of Latin America are slowly moving back toward the practice of the Faith that is so deeply entrenched within them.[69]

Of course, it is not clear that by "the *practice* of the Faith," Considine meant to imply that an abiding awareness of "the Faith" proper persisted within this community, that is, with or without regular practice. It would also seem that the emergence of *rezadores* in response to the scarcity of priests could have been seen by Considine as indicative of fertile ground for the expansion of Protestant sensibilities; Protestantism traditionally had a stronger idea of the priesthood of all believers than Catholicism did.

Even as Considine was appreciative of the strength of the faith of Catholics in Latin America, apart from the priest shortage, his principal concern was directed toward the modernization of the church in Latin America. This concern allowed him to be somewhat agnostic in evaluating the past—what mattered was not so much how to evaluate the past as how to go about modernizing the Latin American church. In Considine's case, it was not out of ignorance—Considine had read the history of Jesuit missions in the Amazon from the seventeenth century and was also current with major anthropological works on Latin America and the Caribbean.[70] Considine was a genuine student of church history in Latin America, but like so many modernizing agents, his view of the past was partially eclipsed by his concerns for the present and desires for the future of the church in this region.

In Considine's writings, what are the elements of a vision of the way faith should be lived in contemporary Latin America? His was an enthusiastic program aimed at assisting the Latin American church to transition from a premodern era to a modern, industrialized one, much as the church had done in the United States over the previous seventy-five to one hundred years. Moreover, Considine deems this transition good and necessary—necessary even for the very practice of Catholicism in the region. In *New Horizons*, Considine records a conversation he had with Bishop Perres Hernandez, auxiliary of Bogotá—surely Luis Pérez Hernández, C.I.M.—who once told Considine that bishops and priests are

concerned with what makes people stronger, healthier, better fed, better schooled, better prepared to live life wisely, better able to be faithful to their religion. Anyone genuinely interested in man as man knows that a people that is broken by social wrongs and weaknesses can't properly worship its God.[71]

---

69. Ibid.

70. Considine, *Call for Forty Thousand*, 309.

71. Considine, *New Horizons*, 283. Considine happened upon Bishop Pérez while visiting the Inter-American Institute of Agricultural Sciences near San José, Costa Rica.

With such concerns in mind, Considine argues that modernization makes pastoral sense and encourages the church to promote this process, thereby enabling it to remain in unison with the present needs of the Latin American people.

The programmatic elements to Considine's vision include: the need for education at all levels;[72] cooperatives; credit unions; and agricultural improvement projects.[73] Necessarily, this vision entails attending to less tangible factors so that change can take place. For instance, pastoral workers must gain the trust of the people so as to be able to help them take advantage of the aforementioned agricultural projects, cooperatives, and credit unions;[74] priests in Latin America's rural areas should not be suspicious of technicians brought in to work on modern projects but rather should be respectful of them. Similarly, technicians are needed who will respect religion and the clergy;[75] and a spiritual understanding that souls are real people of immense value is needed.[76]

Coupled with Considine's modernizing tendency was a political stance of the church engaging society through its social teaching. Considine described how Latin American communists in the late 1950s were no longer enjoying the political prominence they had held in the mid-1940s when Argentina, Chile, Uruguay, Peru, Venezuela, and Colombia all had communist members elected in their respective congresses. But he also speaks of a social strategy for the church. In Colombia, Considine captured the words of Jesuit Fr. Juan Álvarez Mejía, who maintained that the only way to stop a

> Communist revolution is for the Christians to lead the revolution themselves. We must call for reforms and fulfill the dreams of world social justice that our Latin American brothers who are in want are so rightly seeking.[77]

Considine found an example of such a strategy in the many issues raised by the Colombian Catholic hierarchy in their April 1958 pastoral letter, calling for

> reform in property ownership, worker's wages, labor-management relations and housing. The pastoral urged the Colombian government to expropriate the land from large properties for less fortunate citi-

---

72. Ibid., 280–81, 310–19.
73. Ibid., 286–89.
74. Ibid., 287.
75. Ibid., 283–86.
76. Ibid., 292.
77. Ibid., p. 233.

zens. It reminded workers of their obligations as well as their rights but enjoined employers "not to treat workers as slaves." "The first obligation of management," said the Bishops, "is to provide a just salary to workers."[78]

This is an extraordinarily radical list of social reforms, and Considine, the anti-communist, was able to embrace it because it had the stamp of approval of the bishops. Evidently, the crisis of social and economic reform in Latin America had not yet sharpened to the degree it would in the 1970s, when church calls for social or economic reform would be labeled communist.[79]

Considine's position is that the church in Latin America was able to resist communism[80] by being a strong voice for social reform. In this way, Latin America—and certainly the Catholic Church in Latin America—was not in need of aid that would be applied directly to efforts to ward off communism as an external threat. Instead, Considine believed that aid to the church in Latin America would help the church to live up to its full potential, providing it with the capacity to tackle the social problems of the day. For Considine, it followed that if the church can engage the people's legitimate desires for social change by living up to the full potential of its own social teaching, the communists will have no ammunition for their activities.

Earl Boyea has argued that in certain meetings of the NCWC, the U.S. bishops opted for a "two-front" stance of opposition to communism. This stance included (1) direct confrontation, and (2) taking steps to address the social ills that nurture the rise of communism. By the mid-1950s, Considine was in touch with and sympathetic to the tendency of the church in Latin America to operate mainly on the second front.[81]

---

78. Ibid., pp. 231–32. He closed the chapter with a similar quotation from Bishop Manuel Larraín, who was at the time serving as the second vice president of the Latin American Bishops' Conference: "Latin America is on the threshold of imminent and radical reforms," he explained. "Shocking social inequality, the existence of immense proletarian and subproletarian masses living in inhuman conditions, the monopoly of land-ownership . . . and the general lack of social awareness on the part of well-to-do Catholics—all show how urgent it is to take a definite stand in this regard. With us or without us, social reform is going to take place; in the latter event, it will take place against us" (p. 233).

79. "Quando dou comida aos pobres chamam-me de santo. Quando pergunto por que eles são pobres chamam-me de comunista" (When I give food to the poor they call me a saint. When I ask why they are poor they call me a communist; cited in Albert Nolan, "Eles me chamam de comunista," in *Helder, o dom: uma vida que marcou os rumos da Igreja no Brasil*, ed. Zildo Rocha [Petropolis, Brazil: Editora Vozes, 2000], 53).

80. And also arrest the growth of Protestantism, but that is covered in other chapters of *New Horizons*.

81. Earl Boyea, "The National Catholic Welfare Conference: An Experience in

Illich: Latin America as "Priest-Ridden"

As has been noted, "The Seamy Side of Charity" appeared in *America* on January 21, 1967, just days before the opening of the fourth annual Catholic Inter-American Cooperation Program (CICOP), which gathered more than two thousand church people interested in the North American Catholic mission to Latin America. The article questioned both the success of and the rationale for the mission and was therefore an instantaneous bombshell at the meeting.[82] In the article, Illich had stuck to sweeping generalities about the overall purpose of the mission without going into detail. He added the provocative claim, enunciated in the first paragraph, that the mission should be judged a "flop." Illich had a flair for the dramatic and an ability to grip a reader's attention with an idea that could not be proven but at the same time could not be dismissed.[83] Illich would employ this technique in the coming years as he took on other weighty topics such as schooling, transportation, gender roles, and the medical profession.[84] More than anything, it was a pedagogical style that got people thinking. For example, exactly one year prior to "Seamy," Ronan Hoffman published in *America* a critique of the mission to Latin America, a very thoughtful piece that contained several arguments that Illich would repeat in "Seamy."[85] The essay was accompanied by a response from Fr. (later Cardinal) Theodore McCarrick but did not create a widespread discussion of the purposes of the mission to Latin America the way Illich's "Seamy" did.

I turn now to an in-depth analysis of "The Seamy Side of Charity." Though at times it may seem as though a switch has been made—a biography of Ivan Illich has been substituted for one of Fr. Considine—the intent is to offer as clear a picture as possible of the two individuals during the

---

Episcopal Leadership, 1935–1945" (Ph.D. dissertation, Catholic University of America, 1987–88), 392–425.

82. George Hall, "Catholic Inter-American Cooperation Conference," *The Christian Century* 84, no. 8 (February 22, 1967): 252–54.

83. Indeed, several thoughtful responses from readers were published in subsequent issues of *America*, and many of those attempted to dismiss "Seamy" for its lack of specificity. This prompted Joseph Fitzpatrick, S.J., Illich's longtime collaborator and "explainer-in-chief" to write a subsequent essay that provided more detail for the kinds of claims Illich made in "Seamy": Fitzpatrick, "What Is He Getting At?" *America* (March 25, 1967): 444–46, 448–49.

84. Ivan Illich, *Deschooling Society* (New York: Harper & Row, 1971); idem, *Tools for Conviviality* (New York: Harper & Row, 1973); idem, *Gender* (New York: Pantheon Books, 1982); idem, *Medical Nemesis: The Expropriation of Health* (New York: Pantheon Books, 1976). This latter work began with this sentence: "The medical establishment has become a major threat to health."

85. Ronan Hoffman, "Latin America in the Church's Global Mission: What Priority?" *America* (January 15, 1966): 68–70; Theodore McCarrick, "Top Priority: A Reply," *America* (January 15, 1966): 70–71.

1960s in order to have a better grasp of the impact that their distinct points of view have had on the relationship of the church in North America with the church in Latin America.

Uncritical Imagination and Sentimental Judgment

"The Seamy Side of Charity" has often been read as a treatise on missionary work, if not an anti-missionary text,[86] yet I would like to suggest that its subject matter is instead an analysis of the Latin American church and how that church is impacted by Vatican policies and U.S. hemispheric ambitions—the latter allegedly experienced by the Latin American church leaders through the presence of missioners from the United States. It is far from clear that the content of "Seamy" could be understood as representative of the thinking of the leadership of the church in Latin America in 1967. Nonetheless, the text of "Seamy" was designed by Illich to articulate concerns in the Latin American church; the essay's main question is, simply, what should the Latin American church do?

For example, Illich understood the present-day difficulties of the church in Latin America in relation to the history of the nineteenth and early twentieth centuries:

> In the more than a century since Spain lost Latin America, the Church has steadily lost government grants, patrons' gifts and, finally, the revenue from its former lands. According to the colonial concept of charity, the Church lost its power to help the poor. It came to be considered a historical relic, inevitably the ally of conservative politicians.[87]

Illich then argued that all of that was suddenly changed with the influx of money and personnel due to the North American Catholic mission to Latin America. But the change came with a price, and the price is that Latin American beneficiaries of church projects will understand that the church is "on the side of W.R. Grace and Co., Esso, the Alliance for Progress, democratic government, and whatever is holy in the Western pantheon."[88] For these reasons, Illich understood the decision to send personnel and aid to Latin America as "an impulse supported by uncritical imagination and sentimental judgment."[89]

The heart of the analysis of the situation of the Latin American church in "Seamy" was twofold: there was a danger of allying the church with a

---

86. Hartch, "Ivan Illich," 185.
87. Illich, "Seamy," 89.
88. Ibid.
89. Ibid., 88.

specific political project—the anti-communism of U.S. hemispheric ambitions; and Latin America simply did not need all this influx of money and of people who would not understand the context. More than just a simple rethinking of the North American Catholic mission to Latin America, "Seamy" stressed that a moratorium on the mission was needed.[90]

And what about communism? Illich had two answers. First, Illich argued that it is not the concern of the church: "it is blasphemous to use the gospel to prop up any social or political system."[91] Second, at the end of the essay he offered assurance that the church "is in no critical danger."[92] For people with anti-communist tendencies in 1967, their reaction to such assurance was probably incredulity. But I would like to suggest that, if one stays within Illich's attempt to present an analysis of the Latin American church, Illich was echoing a view held by some Latin American church leaders. At the 1959 Georgetown meeting, then bishop Helder Câmara had urged that the reform of the social order—and not Cold War anti-communism—was the most effective framework for pastoral programs.[93] As has been noted, Bishop Manuel Larraín also believed that the church must take a "definite stand," on issues such as social inequality and land ownership.[94]

Interestingly, Protestantism was given no mention in "Seamy."

Illich made the surprising claim that Latin America had a "chronic surplus of clergy."[95] He did not explain how he arrived at that conclusion;

---

90. "Seamy" mentions that Daniel Berrigan, S.J., had already called for such a moratorium (p. 90). Although mission moratoria were discussed in many places in the 1960s, when "Seamy" was published in January 1967 it became perhaps the most well-known Catholic call for a mission moratorium to that date. Regarding the prevalence of serious rethinking of mission in the mid-1960s, William B. Frazier in 1967 cogently formulated the post–Vatican II mission questions for Catholics by asking if, in a world already embraced by God's Spirit, a missionary still had anything to do? Frazier answered his own question in the affirmative by articulating a theology of mission as "sign" of God's outreach to people. Additionally, the article is a barometer of the kind of soul-searching about mission that was going on immediately following Vatican II. See William B. Frazier, "Guidelines for a New Theology of Mission," in *Mission Trends No. 1: Crucial Issues in Mission Today*, ed. Gerald H. Anderson and Thomas F. Stransky (New York: Paulist Press, 1974), 23–36. Frazier's essay was first published in *Worldmission* (Winter 1967–68).

91. Illich, "Seamy," 90.

92. Ibid., 91.

93. James F. Garneau records how, during the 1959 Inter-American Episcopal Conference, Bishop Helder Câmara proposed that "the task ahead of us is not to mobilize alms. Our first object is to lead public opinion to understand that raising the underdeveloped world is a much more serious and urgent problem than the East-West conflict itself" ("The First Inter-American Episcopal Conference November 2–4, 1959: Canada and the United States Called to the Rescue of Latin America," *Catholic Historical Review* 87, no. 4 [2001]: 680).

94. Considine, *New Horizons in Latin America*, 233.

95. Illich, "Seamy," 90.

my own analysis is that he was referring to the fact that the church in Latin America could not afford the priests and bishops who worked in the region at the time. This point is taken up in the paragraph that follows the "chronic surplus" comment:

A large proportion of Latin American Church personnel are presently employed in private institutions that serve the middle and upper classes and frequently produce highly respectable profits; this on a continent where there is a desperate need for teachers, nurses and social workers in public institutions that serve the poor. A large part of the clergy are engaged in bureaucratic functions, usually related to peddling sacraments, sacramentals and superstitious "blessings." Most of them live in squalor. The Church, unable to use its personnel in pastorally meaningful tasks, cannot even support its priests and the 670 bishops who govern them.[96]

An important thread running through "Seamy" was that the importation of foreign clergy propped up this state of affairs artificially. The Latin American parishes served by foreign clergy could not pay their expenses, so the priest's home church in a foreign country footed the bill. But for Illich, the most reprehensible part of this arrangement was that, in his view, none of it was needed. The church in Latin America—or anywhere else—did not need any level of service that it could not afford in order to be a Catholic community in Christ, and the influx of foreign clergy only perpetuated the false idea that an institutionalized priestly ministry was essential for church life. Illich mentioned several possible alternatives to the clerical status quo that were not being considered in a climate in which the importation of foreign clergy was ongoing:

If North America and Europe send enough priests to fill the vacant parishes, there is no need to consider laymen—unpaid for part-time work—to fulfill most evangelical tasks; no need to re-examine the structure of the parish, the function of the priest, the Sunday obligation and clerical sermon; no need for exploring the use of the married diaconate, new forms of celebration of the Word and Eucharist and intimate familial celebrations of conversion to the gospel in the milieu of the home.[97]

Thus, in Illich's view, the church in Latin America found itself impacted by two forces: the policies of the church universal, which stressed the role

---

96. Ibid.
97. Ibid.

of the ordained priest and, through the presence of U.S. missioners, the unique geopolitical situation of the United States. How was the church in Latin America impacted by these forces? In the case of the former, Illich understood the normativity of the institution of the priesthood as having an adverse impact on the church in Latin America. In the view of Vatican authorities, because the priesthood is essential for practice of the faith, Latin America was at a spiritual deficit with its unfavorable priest-to-Catholic-faithful ratio. Regarding the impact of the United States, the problem in Illich's view was that the anti-Castro and anti-communist pretensions of the U.S. government were too easily embraced, even at an unconscious and otherwise well-intentioned level, by U.S. missioners. In such a situation, the church's gospel message was getting lost and the church was being seen as an ally of U.S. power.

How did Illich arrive at such a critique? Under Illich's leadership, CIF became more than just a place where a new missioner received initial language and cultural training for work in Latin America. David Cayley would later describe it as a "free university," a place where Illich would gather scholars and encourage the discussion of ideas on pedagogy, church, mission, development, poverty, health and health care, gender, social justice and so on.[98] During his years at CIF, Illich formulated poignant critiques of Western institutions and categories: the school system, the medical profession, "development," and gender. He eventually formulated a critique of the church as an institution. For Illich, the effort to institutionalize love—that is, the idea that the call of Christ to love God and neighbor must necessarily be mediated by a church institution—amounted to a serious and particularly modern perversion of the gospel.[99] In this respect, he saw the U.S. church as particularly committed to institutions and thus particularly corrupt.[100]

Regarding the institution of the priesthood in particular, Illich understood four characteristics to have taken prominence, none of which he viewed as essential: (1) trained in a seminary; (2) lifetime commitment to celibacy; (3) employed full-time in the church; (4) supported by the church.[101]

It is clear that by 1967 Illich did not believe that the North American Catholic mission to Latin America should be continued. To make his case, blame would need to be assigned for this state of affairs. Perhaps a process

---

98. Illich and Cayley, *Rivers North of the Future*, 10.

99. Ibid., 33–34.

100. The author is grateful to Todd Hartch for this interpretation of Illich's thinking.

101. Fitzpatrick, "Ivan Illich as We Knew Him in the 1950s," 40. Fitzpatrick's comments are based on Illich's essay "The Vanishing Clergyman," which was published in *The Critic* in 1967 and can be found in Illich, *Celebration of Awareness*, 57–83.

of elimination led him to blame Considine and the Latin America Bureau; since he was trying to make his case to bishops and religious superiors about the inadvisability of the mission, he could not blame them. Neither would they accept arguments that blamed Pope John—or Pope Pius before him—for calling for aid to church in Latin America. So why not blame Considine, the articulator and organizer of the mission in the United States and beyond? It was also true that, at the time that Illich drafted "Seamy," he and Considine were in another of their periodic feuds.[102]

This was certainly a weak point in Illich's argument, for Considine was by no means the only person who believed that more priests were needed in Latin America. Indeed, Illich's view of Latin America as "priest-ridden" was what set him apart from nearly every other church leader in Latin America at the time, making it hard to understand the expression of this view in "Seamy" as representative of the views of the Latin American church. It was true that by 1967 some Latin American bishops might have wearied of importing foreign clergy, but it remained a stretch to think that any Latin American bishop could have agreed with Illich's larger point that fewer priests, not more, were needed in Latin America.

Considine Declines to Respond to "Seamy"

Although Considine made no public response to "Seamy," his diary entries during the first two months of 1967 portray someone actively seeking to understand and minimize any adverse effects the essay could have on the U.S. Catholic mission to Latin America. At first Considine hoped for a positive outcome, as the essay would put "Illich on public record" as against the movement for Latin America in the U.S. church.[103] He also received an offer from Renato Poblete, S.J., to write a response, which could be signed by Latin American cardinals and bishops.[104] At the CICOP meeting, a different letter by Fr. Felipe MacGregor, S.J., was considered but rejected by the three cardinals (Landázuri of Lima, Silva of Santiago, and Cushing of Boston) who had been called by Considine to discuss the Illich article.[105]

Understandably, during CICOP itself Considine was in a damage-control mode, meeting with as many people as he could to answer questions. Back in Washington just a few days later, his diary portrays someone who had found a way to think clearly:

Got off the Illich study to [apostolic delegate to the U.S. Archbishop]

---

102. CD, November 22, 1966. The dispute was probably related to finances of CIF, which were always running short (CD, November 20, 1966).

103. CD, January 16, 1967.

104. CD, January 17, 1967.

105. CD, January 26, 1967.

Vagnozzi as he requested, carefully avoiding any unfair interpretation; to me his only fault lies in the order of ideas.[106]

On the surface, this is a curious statement, since there is no evidence that Considine at any time agreed with Illich's call for an end to the mission. Even so, we have already noted that the issues raised by "Seamy" were for the most part explored by Ronan Hoffman a year earlier in a separate article in *America*.[107] At the level of content, Considine and the LAB staff were aware of and worked on the many thorny issues involved in a large international operation like the mission.

Demystifying Illich

As has been shown, in "The Seamy Side of Charity" Ivan Illich made use of a provocative style to instigate a large debate in North America about the value of the mission to Latin America. If "Seamy" has wrongly been understood as a watershed in the U.S. Catholic mission to Latin America during the 1960s, one reason is that Ivan Illich remains shrouded in a rhetorical style that made use of both facts and generalizations in combination with wit and sarcasm. This style allowed Illich to occupy the center of attention, if not set himself up as the authoritative voice on a topic. It is therefore important to demystify Illich—as Considine did in 1962—patiently seeking the facts behind the rhetoric.

While Illich's published writings could be provocative and seemed to produce an almost larger-than-life impact, a different version of who he was emerges when one speaks with someone who knew him as a colleague. For example, one of Illich's colleagues understood his polemical style as just a way of making an important point. In regard to "The Seamy Side of Charity," Gustavo Gutiérrez has commented:

> Well, there were bad ways of being in mission to Latin America, and so it was important to say so. If it were me, I would not have painted with so broad a brush—there are missioners who have given their lives for the people of Latin America. But Illich was not so concerned—he was concerned instead about making a strong impact with his reflections, reflections that were needed at the time.[108]

Fr. Gutiérrez went on to paint a picture of the Ivan Illich that he knew as a colleague in the 1960s. Illich had a real gift for gathering scholars concerned about church and social change. He offered great hospitality

---

106. CD, January 30, 1967.
107. Hoffman, "Latin America in the Church's Global Mission: What Priority?"
108. Gustavo Gutiérrez, interview with author, July 22, 2011.

and true friendship, used warm humor, and held to a persistent belief that, together, a new way forward through the uncharted waters of social change in Latin America could be found. With students, he could be extremely demanding, but with colleagues he was very much at home. Illich was a man of ideas, but he was almost equally one who valued his relationships with colleagues.

This perspective of Illich as a colleague is something of an antidote for anyone who has taken Illich too literally. The provocative claims found in his writings served a rhetorical or pedagogical purpose and were often intentionally exaggerated. Sometimes they were also playfully misleading, as a favorite Illich story about the day he quit the Second Vatican Council illustrates:

> During the Second Vatican Council I worked with a man named Sue-nens, then the cardinal of Malines-Brussels. The Pope had asked him to be the president of a group of four cardinals who moderated the Council. Much earlier, Suenens had known me pretty well through a variety of circumstances, and he asked me to come to Rome as one of the direct advisors of this committee. We met every day during the second and third sessions. One morning, I asked him if we could have a cup of coffee together up at Quattro Fontane, where he was staying at a little Belgian college. I said to him, "I'm leaving now. Yesterday you proved to me that this Council is incapable of facing the issues which count, while trying hard to remain traditional."
>
> The day before, in the aula of St. Peter's, the bishops had accepted the fact that the document which would come out on the Church and the world would say that the Church could not yet condemn governments for keeping atomic bombs, that is, for keeping tools of genocide . . . for the moment.
>
> It was a wise decision, *world*-wise.[109]

Since the story seemed to make a somewhat large claim about Illich's place in the history of Vatican II, I wanted to verify as much as I could. A series of inquiries led me to Fr. Leo Declerck, a bibliographer of the Second Vatican Council. Fr. Declerck confirmed that he had seen Illich and Suenens meet on a couple of occasions at the location Illich mentioned. But he went on to enumerate several "mistakes" in the story. First, Suenens was not the president of the four moderators—there was no president. Fr. Declerck added:

---

109. Illich and Cayley, *Ivan Illich in Conversation*, 100. The same story is found also in Illich and Cayley, *Rivers North of the Future*, 7–8.

When Illich said he met Suenens daily during the second and third sessions of the council, he is very exaggerated.

When Illich said that the text of Gaudium et Spes on the possession of nuclear weapons and the use of strategic nuclear weapons (Gaudium et Spes 80 and 81) has been changed, he is mistaken. The text has been maintained despite the protest on December 2, 1965 by Cardinal Spellman and some American bishops.[110]

After reading Declerck's comments, I reread Illich's text and the relevant chapters of Gaudium et Spes; Illich did not actually claim to meet daily with Suenens—he met daily with the committee—so Declerck was perhaps too quick to call him "exaggerated." Moreover, it would also seem that Declerck misunderstood what Illich said about Gaudium et Spes 80, which indeed does not condemn the possession of nuclear weapons, just as Illich stated (it does condemn the use of nuclear weapons). Illich, though dead for several years, was still able to confound those who read him too literally—the present writer included!

I later found out that Illich did not abandon Vatican II at that point, never to return. According to Fr. Gutiérrez, Illich was in Rome the following year during the Fourth Session of the Council, still getting together with colleagues over food and wine, still thinking the council through with them.[111]

The point is that trying to pin Illich down on details leads to unexpected results; at the same time, the larger points he wrote about—questioning the morality of nations possessing nuclear weapons in this case—remain as his contribution. I would like to suggest the same is true about a too-literal reading of "Seamy."

In June 1968, Illich was called to Rome for hearings at the Congregation for the Doctrine of the Faith (CDF), and as a result of those proceedings, Illich withdrew from public ministry in the late spring of 1969. In January 1969, Illich received word that the Vatican had prohibited priests and religious from attending courses at CIF.[112] One month later, Illich decided to publish accounts of his Vatican process in Excelsior of Mexico City, and in The New York Times. However, because the CDF as a matter of procedure does not make its records of such cases public, almost the entire record of this episode is based on Illich's accounts.[113]

110. Leo Declerck, Bruges, Belgium, to Robert Hurteau, Los Angeles, February 7, 2011. Personal correspondence.

111. Gustavo Gutiérrez, interview with author, July 22, 2011.

112. Francine du Plessix Gray, Divine Disobedience: Profiles in Catholic Radicalism (New York: Knopf, 1970), 307.

113. In the New York Times coverage, the only evidence cited that was not generated by

That is certainly not his fault—the procedures of the CDF do not provide public transparency, even when requested by the individual, as Illich said he did. But it is important to note that without access to the Vatican's records of the proceedings, it is doubtful that the facts of the case can be credibly established. Ever since he took his story to the press, Illich has had control of the narrative of the end of his priestly ministry. Later reporting on the proceedings against Illich at the CDF implied that the handling of his case produced sackings at the CDF, [114] which apparently was not true. The Vatican official named by Illich as his principal interrogator, Giuseppe Casoria, was promoted to archbishop in 1972 and elevated to cardinal in 1983. Another official named by Illich, Luigi de Magistris, became an archbishop in 1996. There is a measure of bravado in the character of Illich portrayed in the press at the time—Illich was someone who withstood all that the Vatican could throw at him with a degree of skill and grace. Less discussed was Illich's love of the church and the priesthood.

Illich's love of the church pervaded his writings, even as late as April 1968 in his essay "Violence: A Mirror for Americans." Illich observed that the roots of social and political violence could be found in the theological category of idolatry—the world's poor majorities were rebelling against the false "gospel" of American prosperity, and he railed against the use of the priesthood to prop up such an aberration:

> I submit that foreign gods (ideals, idols, ideologies, persuasions, values) are more offensive to the "poor" than the military or economic power of the foreigner. It is more irritating to feel seduced to the consumption of the overpriced sugar-water called Coca-Cola than to submit helplessly to doing the same job an American does, only at half the pay. It angers a person more to hear a priest preach cleanliness, thrift, resistance to socialism, or obedience to unjust authority, than to accept military rule. [115]

A more explicit exposition of Illich's high regard for the importance of priestly ministry can perhaps be found in his earlier writings, [116] but the late date of "Violence" (a couple of months before his proceedings at the CDF)

Illich was the "highly classified documents" covering eighty-five accusations against Illich. Illich had requested that the accusations against him be put in writing. See Edward B. Fiske, "Head of Cultural Center Tells of Secret Hearing in Vatican," *New York Times,* February 4, 1969.

114. Gray, *Divine Disobedience,* 240.

115. Illich, *Celebration of Awareness,* 14.

116. Two examples are "Missionary Poverty" and "Missionary Silence," in Ivan Illich, *Church, Change and Development,* 112–25.

and its appeals to a theological, ecclesiological, and ministerial framework give the lie to some of Illich's post-"Seamy" remarks in which he essentially said that CIF and CIDOC may have started as ecclesiastical institutions but they neatly transformed themselves into secular entities.[117] No such smooth transition was possible—it was probably not even desired by Illich himself. With Illich so personally invested in theology, in the church, and in ministry, could it have been otherwise?

Privately with colleagues it was a different story as Illich faced Vatican pressure to withdraw from ministry. With a colleague, Illich could be vulnerable. In July or August of 1968, Illich visited Gustavo Gutiérrez in Lima. Fr. Gutiérrez recalled their visit:

> It was a little before [the] Medellín [Conference] that Illich came for a visit. What I can recall are impressions—he was dejected, feeling some loss. I had a distinct impression that he was moving away from Latin America, that he was shifting his focus to Asia.[118]

For someone who had invested so much of himself in the church's ministry, the prospect of having to withdraw was certainly a fateful decision. Afterward, he put on a strong face and moved on, but it is hard to imagine that the result was anything he had desired.

Moving Aside So That Others Can Take Over

Considine was 68 years old in January 1966 when he made the decision to retire, with the effective date two and a half years into the future. Some months before making the decision, his diary records a note about his boss, NCWC secretary general Msgr. Paul Tanner: "Tanner keeps talking about men's obligation to retire at 65."[119] Though it might sound as if Considine felt some pressure from his boss, the pressure could not have been too great, since apparently Tanner was agreeable to Considine making his exit in 1968.

It is probable that during 1965 Considine was pondering this significant change. Unfortunately, the unavailability of archival records[120] makes

---

117. Wayne Cowan, "An Interview with Ivan Illich," *Christianity and Crisis* 29 (August 4, 1969): 213–15.

118. Gustavo Gutiérrez, interview with author, July 22, 2011.

119. CD, May 29, 1965.

120. The LAB records for 1960–1963 are at the American Catholic History Research Center and University Archives at the Catholic University of America (ACUA). The LAB records for 1964–1968 are held at the U.S. Conference of Catholic Bishops, and come under the fifty-year ban that is standard practice in that archive.

it difficult to pinpoint exactly what circumstances surrounded Considine's decision.

A Maryknoll colleague who lived with Fr. Considine at the USCC staff house in Washington (1965–1968) commented that he noticed at that time that, in table conversation, Considine would display forgetfulness, repeating things he had already said just moments before.[121]

Additionally, Considine's 1965 and 1966 diaries reveal the pressure-cooker pace of work at the LAB. In April 1965, the U.S. invaded the Dominican Republic, a move that once again tested north–south relations in the hemisphere. In the LAB offices themselves, another sort of turmoil persisted, as the bureau experienced constant financial strains; apparently the staff had grown as initiatives like PAVLA, CICOP, and the various publications were begun. Considine's attention was often taken away from Latin American affairs to be caught up in fundraising.

Around 1965 a subtle shift seems to have taken place. As his diary filled up with administrative concerns about the LAB, in 1965 there was a noticeable absence of diary entries that record Considine finding pleasure in his relationships with Latin Americans. In regard to Considine's attention to the complexity of inter-American church relations, his ability to empathically anticipate the concerns of Latin American Catholics seemed to decline.[122] There is every indication that at this time he was still as courteous and diplomatic as he always had been, but he simply seemed much more harried and perhaps less curious about others than he had been prior to this time.

For example, in May 1965 he made a trip to Recife, Brazil, as part of a U.S. delegation for the opening of a new regional seminary; the LAB had helped raise funds for its construction. His diary entries before, during, and after this trip give customary detail about the new facility that was inaugurated, along with visits to a couple of Brazilian church institutions. But the entries lack a sense of wonder, delight, or enthusiasm that was there in his earlier trips south of the border. Rather than seeing himself as a work-

121. Laurence Murphy, interview with author, November 22, 2008.
122. Considine provided his own benchmark on this point early on. In 1944, when Considine was vicar general of Maryknoll and the mission society had only two years of experience in Latin America, Considine wrote a convincing memo to the superior general and his council on the need for U.S. missioners to Latin America to understand the depth of Latin American resentment at U.S. condescension. The memo was written after Considine spoke with Bishop John M. Gannon, who had recently traveled to Latin America and had returned convinced that Latin Americans will accept U.S. priests only if the Pope calls on both North America and Latin America to enter into such a cooperative arrangement. Any effort initiated in the U.S. will hit a wall of resentment in Latin America. (John J. Considine, Memo to the General Council, December 16,1944. MMA, General Council Reports Memos 1936–1983, 1:6 [Memos 1944–1946]).

ing partner with Latin Americans—Dom Helder Câmara was his host for the event—Considine on this trip seemed accepting of the role of a U.S. fundraiser whom grateful Latin Americans wined and dined along with the other U.S. visitors.

Indeed, the world was changing too—when Considine started at the Latin America Bureau in 1960, U.S. ascendency and optimism were the order of the day, and Considine found himself well received in Latin America as an energetic and optimistic American. Vietnam and the invasion of the Dominican Republic had sparked a new round of questioning about U.S. leadership in world affairs. Considine's decision to retire appears to have been a mature one; aware that his effectiveness was no longer what it once had been, he opted to get out of the way and make room for others.

The Legacies of Illich and Considine

It was probably inevitable that Considine, a builder of institutions, and Illich, an iconoclast, were to enter into conflict as they both contributed to the Catholic Church in Latin America during the 1960s. While it is true that the church can benefit from the efforts of both iconoclasts and institution builders, it is perhaps unrealistic to expect that both can make common cause for a sustained and large effort over several years. [123]

Both Illich and Considine had extensive knowledge of and respect for the complexity of the history of the church in Latin America. While working at Cuernavaca, Illich established the Centro Intercultural de Documentación (CIDOC), and one of the series produced, *Sondeos*, focused exclusively on religion in Latin America dating from the time of the first European contact. [124] Considine, too, was a student of Latin American religion and history. Unlike the North American bishops at the Georgetown meeting, both churchmen had extensive knowledge of the church in Latin America and the complexities of history in the region.

Did Considine and Illich attempt to understand their work with the Latin American church as continuous with the church's past? It is apparent that both churchmen not only understood but had great sympathy and respect for the way Catholicism had been lived in Latin America over the preceding four hundred years, and in good faith each saw his efforts as building on the strengths found in the way Latin American Catholics lived their faith. But it should be equally apparent that the two diverged on at

---

123. The author is grateful to Wilbert Shenk for suggesting these juxtaposed roles for Considine and Illich.

124. For an excellent bibliographical guide to the work of CIDOC, see Carl Mitcham, "The Challenges of this Collection," in *The Challenges of Ivan Illich: A Collective Reflection*, ed. Lee Hoinacki and Carl Mitcham (Albany: State University of New York Press, 2002), 9–32, especially 20–28.

least two issues: the necessity of the priesthood for Catholic life and the pastoral ministry of the church, and the inevitability of the modernization of Latin America.

On the first issue, Illich's stance—that more priests than a church can support are not needed in Latin America—appeared to be an innovation. Considine's position—that priests are constitutive of Catholic pastoral life and so the church should do all it can to maintain a sufficiently large clergy to serve the flock—reflected the institutional stance held widely in the Catholic Church. Historically, their divergence can be seen as a discrepancy in the evaluation of the Latin American church's nineteenth century process of secularization. Did the resulting decrease in clergy reflect a situation that was to be regretted and corrected (Considine's position), or did it present instead an opportunity to reform ministry by concentrating on essentials (Illich's position)?

The question of modernity was also a significant point of divergence between the two. Could Considine ever imagine that Latin America would not follow a course of modernization similar to that of the United States? Conversely, was the perception of a lack of a modernization process in Latin America something Illich valued—his remark in "Seamy" about "superstitious blessings" notwithstanding?[125] Can the insistence in "The Seamy Side of Charity" that the church in Latin America go without the services—and influences—brought in by foreign clergy and religious be understood as Illich's defense of a space untouched by modernity?

One way to gauge their views on modernity would be to attend to what the two of them said about the "Indian problem." The 1960s were still decades before the emergence of indigenous theology ("teología india") in the Latin American church. Even so, what can be learned from their writings about the social, ecclesial, and theological climate that would eventually see the emergence of indigenous theology?

Regarding missions among Latin America's indigenous peoples, both Illich and Considine receive high marks for urging missioners to be respectful of the indigenous peoples and to strive to understand the values found in indigenous cultures. Illich spoke of the need for missioners to shed their desire to share "the magic of Western technology" with indigenous peoples in order to learn from rather than teach those peoples.[126] Elsewhere, I have argued that Considine, at the 1954 Lima Methods Conference, confirmed a set of pastoral options that put missioners on the side of indigenous people in conflictive social situations.[127]

---

125. Illich, "Seamy," 90.

126. Philip Toynbee, "Pilgrimage to a Modern Prophet," *Observer* (February 24, 1974): 32.

127. "What Happens When Church Elites Begin to Take Seriously the Perspective of

In terms of a vision of the future for indigenous peoples, the opposing
views held by Considine and Illich about the importance of modern institutions put them both at odds with the views of indigenous peoples. Illich's
arguments against universal schooling and the spread of Western health care
institutions among developing nations might have appeared to position him
as an ally of indigenous communities who have felt encroached upon by
Western cultures. However, it did not actually turn out that way. There is a
risk of oversimplifying a complicated matter, and it is true that indigenous
communities have frequently experienced modernity and its institutions
as being forced upon them. Nonetheless, the proponents of teología india,
like most Latin American church leaders, have in general not agreed with
Illich that schools and medical care are invasive to indigenous peoples and
are not needed; they have instead argued that their communities should
get their fair share of these resources and have some control over how they
are operated.[128] Considine had the opposite view—that indigenous peoples
themselves will welcome the opportunity to adopt modern institutions and
modern ways, seemingly without hesitation.[129] Considine as a matter of
principle understood modern education and medical care as a good to be
shared.[130] Again, indigenous communities have been much more skeptical than Considine about these goods or services, principally due to their
experience of not being able to gain sufficient access to them.

What of the question of the value of the mission itself? Illich's prophe-

Indigenous Peoples? John J. Considine, M.M., and the 1954 Lima Methods Conference
of the Maryknoll Fathers" (paper given in the World Christianity Group at the Annual
Meeting of the American Academy of Religion [Chicago], November 3, 2008).

128. This is a sensitive point, as it is abundantly clear that many indigenous communities
experience modernity as the aggressive harbinger of processes of change over which they
have had little control. Diego Irarrázaval has pointed out a range of indigenous attitudes
lying between a principled rejection of modernity and accepting integration to modernity
at the cost of one's indigenous identity: some rethink modernity according to indigenous
and *mestizo* patterns; some keep one foot in the indigenous world and another in the
modern world; and some engage the modern world for some of their affairs (for example,
business) while staying rooted in the indigenous world when it comes to family life and
communal celebrations (Diego Irarrázaval, "El saber indígena sopesa la modernidad," in
Sabiduría indígena: fuente de esperanza. Teología india, vol. 2, *Aportes*, ed. III Encuentro Taller
Latinoamericano de Teología India [Puno, Cusco, Peru, and La Paz, Bolivia: IDEA, IPA and
CTP, 1998], 276).

129. In a chapter called "Agoliagbo and the Men of Tomorrow," in the African context
Considine simply juxtaposed traditional and modern role models, presenting the latter as
clearly the way Africans are choosing to go in the future (*Africa: World of New Men* [New
York: Dodd, Mead & Co., 1954], 13–23).

130. Lima Methods Conference of the Maryknoll Fathers, *Proceedings of the Lima
Methods Conference of the Maryknoll Fathers, Maryknoll House, Lima, Peru, August 23–28, 1954*
(Maryknoll: Maryknoll Fathers, 1955), 271.

cies that hemispheric Catholic relations would only follow a pattern of Yankee imperialism did not come true. And while the presence of U.S. missioners in Latin America in 2009 reflected the reduced numbers and graying of the priesthood and religious life in the United States, the 721 U.S. missioners serving that year in Latin America and the Caribbean still represented 21.5 percent of all U.S. missioners, a relatively high proportion.

Edward L. Cleary has pointed out that the Catholic Church in Latin America experienced a significant revival in the second half of the twentieth century. Of course it is not possible to draw any causal relationship between the U.S. Catholic mission to Latin America and the transformation of Latin American Catholicism during the period. Nonetheless, it is hard to not imagine Considine delighting in the way the statistics have shifted so positively:

- In 2000 there were 61,000 priests serving in Latin America, up 144% from the 25,000 which Considine estimated to be serving in the region in 1945. Cleary notes that the increase "stands in marked contrast to the well-publicized decline in the United States and Europe."[131]
- The number of seminarians in post-secondary studies for the priesthood has increased dramatically in all Latin American countries between 1972 and 2000, with the lowest percentage of increase occurring in Puerto Rico (96%) and the highest in Bolivia (1,322%).[132]
- In contrast to seminarians, the numbers of religious women working in the region showed a more modest increase, to a total of 128,000 in 2000. Again, it is of note that women's religious life has been in statistical decline during the same period in the United States.[133]
- More than one million lay Catholics served as catechists all across Latin America in 2000.

A familiar Latin American Catholic cliché from the 1980s goes like this: the church opted for the poor, and the poor opted for the Pentecostals. While it is true that millions of Catholics, many of them inactive in the practice of their faith, did leave the Catholic Church to become Pentecostals and Evangelicals, the statistics present a picture of ecclesial vitality that cannot be so easily dismissed. Cleary sums up his analysis of the trans-

131. Edward L. Cleary, "The Transformation of Latin American Christianity, c. 1950–2000," in *World Christianities, c. 1914–c. 2000,* ed. Hugh McLeod (Cambridge: Cambridge University Press, 2006), 372.

132. Ibid., 374.

133. Ibid., 375.

formations in Latin American Catholicism during the second half of the twentieth century in this way:

> The church had especially lacked a laity well educated in religion and its social implications. In providing adult education and building a sense of community, and by making Bibles available to millions, the church produced a core group of committed Catholic parents. They, in turn, fostered among their children large increases in vocations to the priesthood and religious life.[134]

Were he alive, John Considine the institution-builder might today point to these statistics with satisfaction and a sense of accomplishment—the U.S. Catholic mission to Latin America in the 1960s was able to contribute to substantial growth in the church's pastoral capacity in the region. He would be much too modest to think of the matter this way, but we might ask if, in some sense, the revitalization of the church represented in the statistics can be considered the legacy of Considine's service at the Latin America Bureau.

Illich, on the other hand, today might be quick to point out that the growth graphed by Cleary has not kept pace with population growth—in fact, the priest-to-Catholic-faithful ratio is more unfavorable now than it was in 1945. Illich's legacy, therefore, cannot be statistically measured, but it is just as valuable as any that can be attributed to Considine. The value of a healthy skepticism for a church in a process of growth cannot be under-estimated. In regard to the statistics, were he alive today, Illich might ask more about the quality of Latin American pastoral ministry rather than the quantity of the church's pastoral ministers. Is the church today better able to communicate the gospel in the context of Latin America?

By now it should be apparent that it would be pointless to ask who was right about the church in Latin America, Considine or Illich? If Cleary was correct and the numerical gains have something to do with an educated laity, Illich during his time in Latin America also contributed mightily on that front. He was not the institution-builder that Considine was, but the research and bibliographic work accomplished by CIDOC created neces-sary resources for the church's pastoral and theological reflection in the region. Additionally, during the 1960s both Considine and Illich offered encouragement and friendship to the pastoral leaders of the church in Latin America and worked in partnership with them, all of which contributed to a climate of ecclesial revitalization.

---

134. Ibid., 372.

Conclusion

Are we now seeing fruits of the kind of hemispheric Catholic integration that Considine sought to establish? Hemispheric migration in the twenty-first century continues with a strong northward flow; in the particular case of Catholicism in the United States, immigration from Latin America has been the principal engine of growth for that church.[135] As Manuel Vásquez and Marie Friedmann Marquardt have argued, it is a mistake not to study religion as a factor in migratory and economic integration processes of the Americas; religious institutions provide social services and breathing space for immigrants, and the faith of Latin American immigrants is frequently mentioned by them as a resource for finding their way in a strange environment. The Latin American religious imagination is ever engaged as migrants make the hazardous journey north.[136]

Additionally, the flow of Catholic clergy in the Americas has been reversed, as priests from all corners of Latin America serve in U.S. parishes in increasing numbers at the beginning of the twenty-first century.[137] From the perspective of building up the church in Latin America, it would be hard to understand Fr. Considine welcoming this situation. After all, North America currently has a priest-to-Catholic-faithful ratio of 1 for every 1,590, while in South America, despite the gains just noted, it is 1 for more than 7,000.[138] If Latin America today remains in need of more church personnel, Fr. Considine's past efforts would seem to give evidence that today he would still be concerned about the needs of the Catholic Church south of the Rio Grande, and therefore would be apprehensive about a "brain drain" of Latin American clergy who have immigrated north and found work in U.S. parishes.

However, the situation of priests from Latin America presently serving in U.S. parishes is a bit more complex. A mitigating factor is the general situation of immigration: many priests from Latin America who are presently serving in U.S. parishes have responsibilities for the pastoral care of immigrants from Latin America. In this way their presence in the United States has assisted the church of this country in a key pastoral task. Additionally, as the pastoral leaders of communities of Latin American immigrants, they

---

135. Robert D. Putnam and David E. Campbell, *American Grace: How Religion Divides and Unites Us* (New York: Simon & Schuster, 2010), 268.

136. Manuel A. Vásquez and Marie Friedmann Marquardt, *Globalizing the Sacred: Religion across the Americas* (New Brunswick, NJ: Rutgers University Press, 2003), 9.

137. Dean R. Hoge and Aniedi Okure, *International Priests in America: Challenges and Opportunities* (Collegeville, MN: Liturgical Press, 2006).

138. Tom Roberts, "New CARA stats on deacons, priests, sisters, and parishes," NCR Online, August 31, 2010 (http://ncronline.org/blogs/ncr-today/new-cara-stats-deacons-priests-sisters-and-parishes [accessed November 21, 2012]).

have played an important role in educating the church in the United States about the importance of this immigrant community for the future of the church in this country.[139] Would not Considine be enthusiastic about this profound transformation of U.S. Catholicism? Would he not desire to be engaged with the contributions of Latin American clergy and faithful to the life of the church in the United States?

In such a climate, a hemispheric integration of Catholic leadership is useful today more than ever, and it is hard to imagine that both Considine and Illich would not be pleased at such a prospect. What Considine said about Latin America and the United States in the context of the Cold War appears to be equally important today in a Western Hemisphere connected by constant migration: "Their destinies and ours are at stake."[140]

---

139. Given the strong demographic growth of Hispanics in the United States, scholars have been pointing out the characteristics of Latino/a migration and religion. Allan Deck has noted that Latinos/as who have migrated northward from Latin America represent a phenomenon that has been in place for several centuries ("Towards a New Narrative for the Latino Presence in U.S. Society and the Church," *Origins* 42, no. 29 [December 20, 2012]: 457–64). Timothy M. Matovina has pointed out that, similar to the experience of African American and Native American Catholics, the experience of Hispanic Catholics does not fit the historical narrative of "Americanization" that has so characterized historical studies of American Catholics of European descent (*Latino Catholicism: Transformation in America's Largest Church* [Princeton, NJ: Princeton University Press, 2012], 5–6).

140. Considine, *Church in the New Latin America,* 139.

CHAPTER 11

No One Remembers
Who Planted the Seed
1968–1982

WHEN JOHN CONSIDINE retired from the Latin America Bureau, he first landed in the Big Apple, taking up residence at the Maryknoll Society house in New York City. He did not stay long; by the summer of 1969 he was at Maryknoll College at Glen Ellyn, outside Chicago. The college was a seminary, set up to give a liberal arts education to Maryknoll seminarians. However, enrollment had been dropping off in the late 1960s. For a time, there was a plan to organize a Maryknoll School of International Service at the campus. Considine believed there was a future for the college as open to the public, but "with a specifically missionary bent."[1]

In 1969, Maryknoll Fr. Frank McGourn was assigned to Maryknoll College. He had just finished a doctorate at Stanford in Spanish and linguistics. In his doctoral program he had done fieldwork in the Peruvian highlands; his research focused on the spoken Spanish of indigenous Quechua and Aymara people. McGourn would later comment about Considine at Glen Ellyn, "I remember [him] kind of looking around the place and saying, 'You could walk in here and never have a clue that this is a missionary place.'"

For Considine and McGourn, the very first step toward making a missionary center was to make something visible. "So they gave [Considine] a budget, they gave him the basement rec. room, and the third thing they gave him was me." Fr. McGourn taught Spanish in the college but also went to work from the summer of 1969 to the summer of 1970 helping Fr. Considine to set up a photographic display. The theme of the display was "Development is the new word for mission." The basic idea was that mis-

---

1. Francis McGourn, interview with author, November 23, 2008. All quotations from Fr. McGourn in this section are from this interview.

sion was not saving people's souls but assisting their overall development as
people. McGourn found it most congenial to be working with Considine
on the project. There were, however, those who criticized the title, asserting
that the term "development" was paternalistic.

But to McGourn it was obvious that Considine was far from paternalistic. They discussed evangelization in relation to cultural and linguistic
structures. As they selected photographic images, the question of what kind
of development—what meaning to give the concept—came up. Development might sometimes be understood as building latrines or other public
health projects, but other times it was helping people to gain an awareness
or a consciousness of who they are as people.

They also discussed the 1954 Lima Methods Conference. Fr. McGourn
had been reading the *Proceedings* and complained that it must have seemed
annoying to know that, even though back in 1954 Maryknollers in Latin
America were taking the culture of the people seriously, so often such a
perspective is simply unheeded by missioners.

> I remember him sort of chuckling, and saying to me something to
> the effect of, "In Maryknoll and in the church in general, usually you
> have to plant the seed and wait for twenty years, and then it starts to
> mature and then comes breaking through. And by that time, no one
> remembers who planted the seed. But who cares, as long as it's grow-
> ing?"

Fr. McGourn later went on to found the Institute of Aymara Studies in
Chucuito, Peru, an institute set up specifically to focus on issues of culture
and faith for the mostly rural Aymara people of southern Peru. And to
make the case for the establishment of the Institute, Fr. McGourn quoted
liberally from the *Proceedings* of the Lima Methods Conference.

The international school at Glen Ellyn was never established; the college graduated its last class in 1971 and closed its doors in 1972. After the
summer of 1970, Considine was reassigned to Maryknoll headquarters near
Ossining, New York. But during 1969–1970, Considine was still sowing
seeds that would bear fruit later in southern Peru.

The Mission Department
It was during the period after Considine's return from Glen Ellyn in
1970 that he joined forces with Fr. Eugene F. Higgins, M.M., to found
the Maryknoll Mission Department. After the Maryknoll Society's Sixth
General Chapter in 1972, the Mission Department was subsumed into the
Mission Research and Planning Department (MRPD), and Fr. Thomas
Cronin, M.M., became the first MRPD Director.

Gene Higgins and Considine knew each other well—in the late 1920s, Higgins had been one of the Maryknoll students sent to Rome to complete his theological studies and be ordained. When Considine arrived at Maryknoll in 1970, Fr. Higgins already had been running the Maryknoll Overseas Extension Service (MOES), a library on missions that carried subscriptions to over three hundred periodicals.

What was the purpose of the Mission Department? Sister Camille Marie Black, M.M., who served as Fr. Higgins's assistant at MOES from 1972 to 1988, described it this way:

> Fr. Considine wanted a Mission Department that would think and breathe mission. . . . I recall Fr. Considine telling Fr. Higgins: "Gene, we can't plan on just tomorrow; we have to plan on twenty years from now."[2]

Within the Mission Department, Considine was responsible for the *Bulletin*, which was sent to Maryknoll priests, brothers, and students around the world. The *Bulletin* certainly carried a Considine stamp, for it was based on missiography—offering views of the world's peoples and the church's efforts to be in mission among them. Circulating as it did among missioners, its special focus was on church and theology news taking place in Asia, Africa, and Latin America.

While the MRPD had a mandate to assist the superior general of the Maryknoll Society with strategizing mission initiatives, the *Bulletin* was a free service offered to those who would read it. Considine at this point in his life had moved into a supportive role in the operation of Maryknoll. This afforded him great freedom to research and write on topics of his own choosing. For example, issue number 1 (October 1971) carried a lead article that summarized the ideas on liberation theology that had emerged from an all–Latin America study workshop conducted by Maryknoll on the topic. Another page carried two short articles: Considine summarized the conclusions of the Maryknoll Central America Regional Meeting of June 1971 in one and described the formation of the Mission Institute London by seven different mission-sending societies. An ecumenical perspective was offered in an article on mission training methods at Trinity Evangelical Divinity School. On page 9, "Understanding Slow Growth in Japan" was featured; this article carried an acknowledgment to Pro-Mundi Vita and offered this salient piece of contemporary ecclesiological and missiological analysis:

---

2. Camille Marie Black, interview with author, November 20, 2008.

Today, both the West and Japan have left behind feudalism but the structure of the Church is suffering from a serious culture lag, recognized by Vatican II. The lag is particularly striking in Japan, which is now industrially one of the most advanced nations in the world.

Considine was still thinking expansively about the church's ability to have an impact around the world.

The issue concluded with what would become a regular feature: "Annotations on Useful Books." Latin America was the theme of this first edition; over three pages, fifty-four different works were described. Additionally, a Book Service Department at Maryknoll was instituted, making it easier for overseas missioners to acquire the titles described.

Most of the articles in this in-house publication were unsigned, but Considine worked on nearly everything in each issue until his health forced him to retire from this work in 1976. According to Sister Camille Marie Black, Considine was the author of all the unsigned articles during this period, and other types of material that appeared in the pages of the *Bulletin* (reports of meetings or texts of talks) were edited or summarized by him. Once a year Considine's name appeared in the *Bulletin*, on a list of the four or five members of the Mission Department staff.

Considine in the Post–Vatican II Years

In the fifty years that have passed since the opening of the Second Vatican Council, the Catholic Church has held within itself great differences over the meaning of the council. The issues are too numerous to list here, so I focus on a single broad issue, outlined by Karl Rahner: the emergence of a world church. Putting Rahner's observation into other words, fifty years after Vatican II, how open is the church to non-Western culture?

Since the closing of the council in 1965, has the church's oneness flourished as the many have articulated their ownership of the faith in non-Western terms? Have Africans, Asians, Latin Americans, as well as Polynesian and Melanesian peoples, continued to find a welcome in the church for the expression of Catholic faith in terms that are culturally comprehensible to them? Or has the opposite occurred—has concern for the unity of the church brought the church's leadership to prefer a cultural uniformity rather than pluriformity in the practice of the faith?

Early in the twenty-first century, revisionist evaluations of the council are common. Beginning with the papacy of John Paul II (1978–2005), what has come under discussion is the "authentic" interpretation of the Second Vatican Council for the church today. Under the leadership of John Paul II, proponents of the "restorationist" position have argued that the most authentic interpretation of the council preserves a strong role for centralized authority. According to this view, the tension found in *Lumen Gen-*

tium between the hierarchical order of the church and the notion of the church as the people of God has been resolved in favor of interpreting the latter within the former.[3]

Prior to the papacy of John Paul II, the principal positive and negative positions on the direction of the postconciliar church were tied more closely to the memory of the event itself. On just about any issue, from ecumenism to interreligious dialogue to church–state relations to social communications, the question was, did the council "go far enough" or did it "go too far?"

Fr. Considine's writings need to be understood within this earlier context. Because of ill health, Considine retired from the MRPD in 1976. We therefore have no record of his reactions to the papacy of John Paul II. On the issue of liberation theology, Considine's writings in the *Bulletin* do show approval, but that approval was expressed in the period before the papacy of John Paul II, the time when liberation theology became a contentious issue. In this earlier period, many of the principal liberation theologians had highly placed supporters in the Catholic hierarchy. Thus, it may simply be impossible to understand what Considine thought of the "restorationist" perspective that achieved such prominence after 1978. Moreover, the hypothetical question of how Considine would have reacted to the papacy of John Paul II probably misses other important issues. For example, he probably would have been quite interested in the way migration in the late twentieth and early twenty-first centuries was opening opportunities for sharing the faith. In the United States, it would be easy to imagine him fascinated with the demographic explosion of Hispanic Catholics and their rise to prominence in the U.S. church. Would we have heard Considine lecturing the church on how the business community has seemed to recognize the growth of this population sooner than pastoral planners? Would he have been parsing the question of the importance of a certain culture-bound feeling for the faith among Latino/a Catholics, almost independent of the use they make or do not make of the Spanish language?

When Japanese Americans were interned during World War II, Considine wrote to his colleagues about the mission purposes of the Maryknoll work in the camps. The Maryknollers in pastoral ministry in the camps were not to see their role as only that of ministering to the handful of Japanese Catholics—the Maryknollers had "a duty of justice and charity" to take an active interest in the political, social, and economic needs of the entire population. But they also were to seek opportunities to share the Catholic faith among Japanese Americans.

---

3. Ian Linden, *Global Catholicism: Diversity and Change since Vatican II* (New York: Columbia University Press, 2009).

Catholic work among Japanese-Americans is not to be viewed as
of an uncertain, emergency nature but as an undertaking of definite
scope which represents carrying the faith to 100,000 people living
either in settlements of 5,000 and more population, or scattered in
smaller groups throughout the country.[4]

Considine was always interested in the ways the faith could be made real
among immigrant populations; he was equally fascinated by the way that
cultural and demographic shifts shaped the meaning of the faith for the
church.

Some of the realities of the post–Vatican II church were unexpected for
Considine. Two examples of surprises experienced by Considine during
this period were the decline in vocations to the priesthood and missionary
life, and the situation of conflict between some U.S. bishops and Considine's successor at the Latin America Bureau. It is doubtful that Considine
would have predicted the decline in vocations to U.S. missionary orders
that followed the council; during his career, the Maryknoll Society, like
most U.S. mission-sending groups, had always been growing. Toward the
end of his term on the General Council, Considine circulated memos to
his council colleagues on the expansion of operations at the Maryknoll
headquarters to accommodate the training and governance of growing
numbers of Maryknoll Missioners, and even on the creation of separate
U.S. provinces for Maryknoll.[5]

The drop in vocations was clearly in the background of Considine's year
(1969–1970) at Maryknoll College in Glen Ellyn, Illinois. The college was
not taking in enough recruits to justify the resources required to keep it
open, and the college finally closed in 1972. Fr. McGourn commented that
no one "knew why the number of vocations had dropped off, if it would
be temporary, nor what to do about it."

In relation to Considine's previous position at the U.S. bishops' Latin
America Bureau, it is doubtful that he would have welcomed the end of
CICOP in 1973, and he probably felt disappointment over the direction
of the LAB that was charted by his successor, Fr. Louis Colonnese. Only
one year after taking leave from the LAB, Considine worked behind the

---

4. John Considine, "Maryknoll Work among Japanese-Americans 1944–1950," memo,
July 3, 1944. MMA, General Council Reports and Memos 1935–1983, 1:6 (Memos 1944–
1946).

5. The independent provinces were never created; the Maryknoll Society operates
today under a single governing structure in the United States as it always has. John
Considine, "An Outline for Development," memo, October 28, 1944; and John Considine,
"Should we foresee the creation of homeland provinces for Maryknoll?" memo, May 21,
1946. MMA, General Council Reports Memos 1936–1983, 1:6 (Memos 1944–1946).

scenes with others at Maryknoll to diplomatically uninvite Fr. Colonnese as a Maryknoll Mission Departure Day speaker for 1969.[6] Colonnese's tenure at the LAB was short—he was fired by the USCC general secretary in 1971.

Considine's writings make it clear that the process of a greater and greater inclusion of Catholics from all parts of the world in the church's life, reflection, ministry, prayer, and liturgy was something he welcomed throughout his career. The period of his retirement and illness (1968–1982) is when some indication of his evaluation of the trajectory of his thinking and life's work comes forward as he reacted to the realities of the post–Vatican II church throughout the globe.

The Product of Our Success

How comfortable was Considine with mission in the postcolonial era? "The New Missionary in the New Africa" was the lead article of the December 1973 *Bulletin*, and it is an indication that he embraced the manifold possibilities for fruitful missionary collaboration between non-African missioners with African Catholics. Subtitled, "Father Heigl[7] of the White Fathers has views," the unsigned piece was most likely a recent talk given by the former provincial of the Missionaries of Africa in Tanzania. But the prominence given the piece in the *Bulletin* suggests much agreement from Fr. Considine with the views of the author.

The article enumerated four stages of missionary history in Africa:

- 1840–1880 The missioner as pioneer who "evangelized by building Christian villages and peopling them with redeemed slaves."
- 1880–1919 The missioner as civilizer who evangelized with catechist boarding schools.
- 1920–1961 The missioner as administrator and builder who evangelized by setting up school systems.

---

6. John Considine, Ossining, NY, to John McCormack, Ossining, NY, October 22, 1969; John Considine, New York, NY, to John McCormack, Ossining, NY, October 29, 1969. MMA, Considine Papers, 3:2. At issue were the complaints received about Fr. Colonnese speaking to the press outside an Inter-American Bishops' Meeting in Caracas, Venezuela, in June 1969. Colonnese presented himself as one authorized to speak to the press when in fact he was not authorized by any bishop to do so, and he expressed views that were not in accord with the bishops' thinking. In his letter to Fr. McCormack, Considine said the Caracas incident "shook" him. For a description of the Caracas fracas, see Thomas E. Quigley, "The Great North-South Embrace: How Collaboration among the Churches of the Americas Began," *America* 201, no. 17 (December 7, 2009). While it is unlikely that Considine was able to select Colonnese to be his successor, a January 28, 1966, entry in Considine's diary reveals that he favored that choice. As has been noted, prior to this, Considine had worked on recruiting others for key positions in the LAB: see chapter 9, n. 3.

7. Probably this was Fr. John J. Heigl, M.Afr. (1933–2011).

- 1961–[1973] The missioner as invited guest in independent Africa who backs up the evangelization carried out by African Christians.

Those who were evangelizing in Africa in 1973 found themselves in a situation that was radically different from just a few years before. But both Heigl and Considine were aware that the new moment was exactly what the church had been striving for.

> Before 1961 we came here to die in Tanzania; we felt we were in our new home. We were administering works with great responsibilities. We were in key positions. We were in expansion and we did the planning.
>   Now we have arrived at the point we were always working towards. We are entering a new era of missions, not just a new phase. We are entering a time when Tanzanians will be missionaries to themselves. To conclude, we state the obvious; our role has completely changed and we cannot turn back the clock of history. This is not something to cry about but to rejoice at. It is the product of our success. It is a normal stage of growth in mission work.

Retiring a Second Time

Considine's health continued to slip following his retirement from the Latin America Bureau; the forgetfulness that was noted by his housemate at the USCC staff house in 1966–1968 was also noted by people who knew him in retirement from 1968 to 1976. According to several Maryknollers who knew him during this period, he suffered from dementia. Sister Camille Marie Black, who worked in the office adjacent to Fr. Considine from 1970 to 1976, observed him having serious vision problems and some forgetfulness but did not concur that Fr. Considine suffered from dementia while still at the Mission Department.[8] Because Fr. Considine's medical records are not available, it is difficult to know the exact nature of his health problems during his final years.[9]

A worsening of his condition was noticed in 1976 by Fr. Bill Galvin, M.M., the director of MRPD 1974–1978. Fr. Considine was having real difficulty meeting the publishing deadlines for the *Bulletin*. Fr. Galvin noted that Considine

---

8. Camille Marie Black, Ossining, NY, to Bob Hurteau, Los Angeles, March 6, 2012. Personal communication.

9. Fr. Considine's medical records, like those of most Maryknoll Society members, are under a seventy-five year ban in place at the Maryknoll Mission Archives. His death certificate listed cerebral arteriosclerosis as the immediate cause of death in 1982.

had been working and editing . . . but gradually . . . what took him hardly any time to do became really a chore—longer and longer, because his mind was slowing up. So, we finally reached a point at which we felt it would be better if he would just retire, which was hard, because he . . . didn't think in terms of retiring. He always wanted to keep contributing to the mission.[10]

At the time of his retirement from the MRPD in 1976, Fr. Considine had already been living at St. Teresa's Residence on the Maryknoll Society property, which at the time was a combination retirement home and infirmary for Maryknoll priests and brothers. As was noted, his vision got worse, which had to have been a heartbreak for this voracious reader. Fr. Thomas Wilcox, administrator of St. Teresa's, recalled fondly a birthday party for Fr. Considine a few years before his death. With members of his family along with Maryknoll colleagues present, Fr. Considine stood up and declared, "This is the happiest day of my life."[11]

Fr. Considine remained in residence at St. Teresa's until his death on May 4, 1982.

---

10. William Galvin, interview with author, June 7, 2009.
11. Thomas Wilcox, interview with author, November 19, 2008.

Conclusion

An Early Enlarger of the Story?

In *Enlarging the Story*, Wilbert Shenk and host of colleagues have asked what does the discipline of church history need to do to adequately tell the story of the church in a world that is truly global. If the majority of Christians now live outside of Europe and North America, the story of Christianity has to be on a much larger geographic scale than it has been. Traditionally church history courses tell of a short beginning in the Near East, almost two thousand years of activity in Europe, and then the exportation of church activities to other parts of the world via missions. Christians around the world are beginning to re-think the story of Christianity in terms that are no longer Eurocentric.

In the same volume, Andrew Walls notes that early church history is usually thought of as taking place within the Roman Empire. But what about places outside the Roman Empire? What if, instead of understanding Edessa as the eastern extremity of Mediterranean Christianity it were to be understood as the western extremity of Asian Christianity? Walls then traces the breath-taking early history of evangelization in central Asia, which reached Northern Mesopotamia and Persia and eventually China. Walls then asks: what kind of a church history syllabus do we need to tell the story of a world church?

Considine's fervent Catholicism and devotion to Rome as a mission center seem to mark him as Eurocentric in his understanding of the church as an institution. However, it needs to be added that this practical view of church operations during his lifetime is off-set by his definition of Catholicity, which really meant that everyone and everyone's story counts.

When did Considine become converted to this global sense of Catholicity? I have not been able to pinpoint a single moment. In these pages we have noted that his orientation to World Christianity is early—it can be seen in his Licentiate thesis in theology at Catholic University (1924) and in *The Vatican Missionary Exposition: A Window on the World* (1925). Certainly the 1925 Vatican Missionary Exposition, with clergy and faithful present from around the world at that event, was most likely his first direct

262

experience of non-Western peoples embracing and practicing the Christian faith. Yet, because he held this perspective prior to coming to Rome at the end of 1924, the experience of the Exposition must have been one of confirmation rather than revelation.

So if there was no identifiable moment of conversion, how did it all start for Considine? I would like to suggest that he absorbed a "worldwide heart" from James A. Walsh, the co-founder of Maryknoll. Walsh spoke frequently about indigenization and Christianity's adaptation to new cultures. Considine held the indigenizing perspective to be constitutive to modern mission from the beginning of his time in Maryknoll.

Considine was not the policy innovator on indigenization and post-colonialism in Catholic mission—that honor goes to the seminal figure of Vincent Lebbe (1877–1940) in China.[1] If Benedict XV in 1919 teaches the importance of an indigenous clergy, it is owing to the ground-breaking and conflictive story of Lebbe, who basically took on the missioner-within-colonialism establishment.

Considine is in Rome 1924–1934, and so his time is after the innovation had caught on, and he is representative of a grouping there and in missions around the world that were embracing indigenization and allowing that reality to deepen their understanding of mission and church. What makes Considine important in this group—though not unique among Dindinger, Perbal, Pierre Charles, and, of course Wilhelm Schmidt—is his study of church and mission history and his ability to communicate the new reality to a wide English-speaking audience.

Considine was someone who lived this global vision with great intent and great integrity. As was noted, even as he turned sixty he was still taking copious notes as he listened to John Wu explain the place of Christianity in China and East Asia.[2] Additionally, most of his closest friends in Maryknoll had years of exemplary service in Asia, Africa, and Latin America, and two—Alonso Escalante and Miguel D'Escoto were Latin Americans.

By now, it should be obvious to the reader that a biography of John Considine has opened panoramas beyond the life of this one extraordinarily accomplished individual. Considine's life story has served as a lens for observing two broad areas over the course of two thirds of the twentieth century: the Catholic mission movement in the United States—and in particular, the efforts of Maryknoll—and the growth of Catholic missions worldwide—and in particular, the pivotal moment of the papacy of Pius XI.

Christian mission today is polycentric, and many of today's centers are located in areas that would have been considered "mission lands" one hun-

1. James A. Walsh had met Vincent Lebbe.
2. See the end of chapter 7.

dred years ago, from Seoul to Lagos to Yarumal, Colombia, and from Mexico City to Nairobi to Manila. As John Mbiti first suggested many years ago, the "centers of the Church's universality" have shifted away from Europe.[3] Similarly, the center of gravity of missionary energy has also shifted.

Considine's life and times remain of particular interest because they graph a different earlier shift in the center of gravity of missionary energy. For Roman Catholics, churches of the continent of Europe for centuries were that center of gravity. As the twentieth century dawned, another center—North America—was added.

A noticeable pattern did emerge that allows us to ask if the two major shifts were somehow related. Did the first shift— when North American Catholic mission centers emerged alongside the European Catholic ones—in some way open a pathway for or otherwise influence the second shift—the more recent growth of Asian, African, and Latin American mission centers amidst the decline of North Atlantic ones? Did the emergence of U.S. Catholic mission enterprises in the twentieth century contribute positively to the process of indigenization in the churches of Asia, Africa, and Latin America?

Knocking on Doors—A Midwestern Interlude

Late October and early November was as good a time of year as any to make public relations calls on bishops and diocesan officials in Ohio, Illinois, Wisconsin, Iowa, and Nebraska. The year was 1942, and Considine was on a westbound train, one of several such trips he made that year. In the various dioceses he would knock on doors for Maryknoll, ever hopeful that he would encounter goodwill in the U.S. church for foreign mission.

In Nebraska he visited Boystown, and also spoke at the seminary of the Columban Fathers. When he arrived at the offices of the Diocese of Rockford he found that Bishop Hoban was away, and so he spoke instead with a priest who promised to inform the bishop of Considine's visit.

The concrete results of Considine's efforts on this trip were mixed—he procured permissions for Maryknollers to speak in the Catholic schools of three of the seven dioceses he visited, but received no further permissions from any bishop for Maryknollers to do direct fundraising in parishes. Considine's diary noted that one archbishop "tried to dodge the whole question" of Maryknoll doing fundraising in churches.[4]

---

3. John Mbiti, "Theological Impotence and the Universality of the Church," in *Mission Trends 3: Third World Theologies*, ed. Gerald H. Anderson and Thomas F. Stransky (New York: Paulist Press, 1976).
4. CD, November 7, 1942.

Considine had been working in Maryknoll's promotional efforts since 1935. He was a member of the General Council, was responsible for the editorial work at *The Field Afar*, and had just published his third book, *Across a World*. As a Council member, he had a world of cares on his mind—almost no word had come in regard to the fate of more than a hundred Maryknollers in the Far East who had presumably been interned by the Japanese, and the new missions in Latin America were only slowly getting established.

But public relations work was not something he could put aside for more important concerns. Even when the results were meager, reaching out to representatives of the U.S. church was a practical and ecclesiological priority. On the practical side, both the Maryknoll Society and the Maryknoll Sisters were still in debt, and both organizations were growing and therefore in need of funds for necessary expansions of infrastructure. From an ecclesiological perspective, Considine firmly believed that involvement in foreign missions was key for the future vitality of the church in the United States. Mission, in Considine's mind, was never an ephemeral activity of the church, but rather constitutive of a healthy church.

The Future of Foreign Mission Work?

It is now about a hundred years since the young John Considine began to consider a calling to the priesthood and to missionary life. It is an understatement to say that Catholicism in the United States at the beginning of the twenty-first century varies significantly from the Catholicism lived by Considine at the beginning of the twentieth century. Charles R. Morris has described the historical evolution of a Catholic subculture that featured obligatory church participation by the many into a situation where a smaller number of committed Catholics participate by choice. The composition and operation of most Catholic parishes has changed dramatically in a hundred years, and the hierarchical leadership of the church—the priesthood—is greatly reduced in number.

Suffice it to say that much has changed in the practice of Catholicism in the United States over the last one hundred years. How have the changes affected the outlook for U.S. Catholic participation in the church's global mission? At the institutional level, it is fair to say that since the deaths of Cardinals Spellman in 1967 and Cushing in 1970, U.S. Catholic mission organizations have not had enthusiastic, generous, and influential patrons among the hierarchy of the United States, and that this has been a significant change.[5] In the midst of many changes, pessimistic voices offer the

---

5. I am grateful to Fr. Laurence Murphy, M.M. for directing me to this issue.

interpretation of decline, claiming that U.S. Catholics are simply no longer interested in the subject.[6]

To those who saw the glass as half-empty, Considine had a consistent answer in his own willingness to throw himself into the work of organizing for mission and research and writing on missions themselves. The picture above of Considine traipsing from one Midwestern diocese to another to knock on doors displays a commitment to the cause of mission, even in the face of predictable short-sightedness or apathy. Similarly, in 1963, he wrote to Cardinal Cushing about the Latin America Bureau not making its fundraising goals: "We'll do better next year. We hope eventually to secure funds which your Eminence can distribute in Latin America. . . . . Our slogan meanwhile: HARD WORK, NO WHINING!"[7]

In short, the fact that things were not working out for the cause of mission at any one moment was for Considine never a cause for despair. In his own time, mission changed quite a bit as the mission policy of indigenization and the end of the colonial era paved the way for a church that was truly global. Where was Considine as the church's mission changed? He was studying the changes, and finding ways forward for the advance of the mission as the context changed. More specifically, he continued to offer his gifts and talents as a journalist, striving to interpret the changes to his audiences.[8]

Considine's story also begs the question of how open to innovation the church is today as it seeks to fulfill its mission. For example, Considine was not yet thirty years old in 1927 when he was given the nod by the Sacred Congregation of Propaganda Fide to found Fides Service. That work was begun in the heart of a church bureaucracy that was ready to modernize, even as it remained skeptical of the modern world. Are there parallels to this story today? In what ways does the church need to continue to adapt its methods or structures to the temper of the times, even as it proclaims a message that the church understands to be countercultural? How might such adaptations themselves serve as points of dialogue with the world of our times? Who are today's young Considines? One wonders from what part of the world they might hail. More importantly, will the church empower such young people to be intercultural innovators, much as Considine was empowered to do so in 1927?

---

6. Jim Collignon, "Maryknoll's Micaiah," in *Turns in the Road, Companions on the Journey*, ed. Larry Egan, Tom Fenton, Darryl Hunt, George Laudadio, Frank Maurovich, Bill Murphy, and Al Stumph (Privately printed, 2011), 66.

7. CD, 29 July 1963.

8. John Considine, "The Church's Global Mission and the Future," in *The Global Mission of the Church: Proceedings of the Fordham University Conference of Mission Specialists, Tenth Annual Meeting January 19-20, 1962*, ed. J. Franklin Ewing (New York: Institute of Mission Studies, Fordham University, 1962), pp. IX-1 – IX-7.

Excerpts from Selected Writings by John J. Considine

Bidon Cinq, the Heart of the Sahara[1]

In January 1933, Considine wrapped up his fourteen-month mission study tour of the Near East, Asia, and Africa with a six-day trans-Saharan journey from Gao, French Sudan (present-day Mali), to Colomb Beshar in Algeria. The trip was made in a small bus operated by the Transsaharan Company. Only four people made this particular trip: Considine, another passenger, the driver Cheval, and the radio man Reneau. The excerpt combines the romance of a dangerous journey through a famously remote area with a narrative that gives human and religious context; Considine is the missioner as explorer and interpreter. The excerpt picks up the story on the second day of the journey.

At half past two in the morning, Reneau roused us, gave us some black coffee and a toast biscuit, and we were on our way by three. We had gone sixty miles when the sun popped up, preceded by a pale pink on the clouds. During the morning we crossed some rough ground, the worst of the route, at times causing our car to bounce along as over a fallow corn field and again to whine painfully in first speed through soft sand. Guide signals, which the French call *valises,* were the only construction along the way. They gave the kilometers ahead and the kilometers behind. Our last sight of a human being was that of a Tuareg woman working a field in a small oasis. By afternoon every sign of life, every blade of grass or withered shrub, was gone.

---

1. Excerpted from John J. Considine and Thomas Dickenson Kernan, *Across a World* (New York: Longmans, Green & Co., 1942), 361–64, 366.

Gone, because we were then in the desert of deserts, the classic desert of the world, the Tanezrouft. This is an area six hundred miles from north to south and two hundred from east to west, in great part as smooth as a billiard table. It makes excellent going for an automobile, but for centuries it was dreaded by the caravans, for in all the area there is not a single well. At night we camped in the heart of the Tanezrouft, at a spot bearing the curious name of *Bidon Cinq*. This means Gas Tank Number Five. When the route was first laid out, a series of ten fuel deposits were installed, of which this was the fifth in the line. The others were soon abandoned as impractical, but Bidon Cinq remains; and for those who dream of a great tomorrow for the Sahara, Bidon Cinq has taken on symbolic greatness as signifying the heart of things. It is to the Sahara what Times Square is to New York. When the Trans-Saharan railway will have been built, the station master at Bidon Cinq will boast that he has the honor to command the halfway point.

Meanwhile the boasting is done by Abdul Qader, the hermit of Bidon Cinq—who, however, is a hermit no longer, for he has acquired a wife, Fatima by name.

"There is Abdul!" Reneau cried at twilight, as far in the distance we saw a black spot on the horizon and the faint flickering of a lantern. By the time we arrived, the sun had set and the lantern gleamed brightly. "You must meet Abdul," said Reneau, and his first act on alighting was to call this pleasant little fellow and his bashful wife.

"Abdul was born on the oasis of Reggan," explained Reneau, "and hence is at home in the desert. He's lucky to have his wife with him, so the long days between bus arrivals can be punctuated by an occasional good quarrel to break the monotony.

"One of the company's greatest problems was to secure a guardian for this post. The first man here went out of his mind from the isolation. The second man sold his water supply to a private auto-mobilist who passed through; soon after, as luck would have it, our bus broke down and a trip was omitted. Running out of water, the man started in his frenzy to walk toward Reggan. Our driver found his body along the way, where he had fallen in his tracks and died of thirst. The third guardian also went out of his mind. As we approached one evening, he came within an ace of smashing his lantern into the gasoline tank and blowing us up. Abdul seems to solve the problem, with the help of Fatima."

Our quarters were two dismounted desert busses equipped with beds. Bidon Cinq is memorable, however, not for the accommodations, but for the horizon. This is a single line, a perfect circle, where flat, limitless sand meets the limitless sky. I walked slowly in the moonlight about our little camp, my eyes fixed on the distant joining place of heaven and earth. There are few spots on the globe where material things are reduced to such a simple common denominator. The author of *Kabloona* stood in the Arctic waste and had a similar experience. He was awed by the unearthly silence. So was it here in the Sahara. No wind moved the leaves, for there were no leaves, no trees for leaves. No birds sang, for there were no birds. No water eddied or tapped, for there was no water. No beast took fright and scurried in the darkness, since for hundreds of miles there were no beasts. Only the quintessence of desert: sand under foot, sky overhead. Here was solitude.

Some Frenchman has said, "The dearest wish of the truly unimpeded man is to seek refuge in the desert." At Bidon Cinq I thought of Charles de Foucauld. Along the great camel route from Tunis to Kano, which lay to the east of me, were the desert heights of Ahaggar. In the mountains outside Tamanrasset, he had built a hermitage six feet by twenty feet, and there he long held communion with the All-Present. He had been a brilliant and atheistic French army officer and had made a name for himself in North Africa. But it was not a career he desired; it was Reality. Hence the priesthood, and then the desert.

"Since I was twenty, I have always relished the sweetness of solitude," de Foucauld wrote. "Even in my non-Christian days, I loved the solitude of beautiful nature along with books, but now all the more when the sweetness of the invisible world prevents one's solitude from ever being lonely. The soul is not made for noise, but for meditation . . . Man, however, has launched out into endless discussions: the little happiness he finds in loud debates is enough to show how far they lead him away from his vocation."

This last may sound a bit misanthropic. Was de Foucauld a mere pessimist? Quite the contrary. He called the Sahara Desert his parish, and the ten thousand Tuaregs of its oases his missionary flock.

"You must be simple, affable, and good to the Tuaregs," he wrote. "Love them and make them feel they are loved, so as to be loved by them. Don't be the assistant surgeon, or even the doctor with them; don't take offense at their familiarities or their easy manners: be human, charitable, and *always gay*. You must always laugh even in saying the simplest things. I, as you see, am always laughing, showing my very ugly teeth. Laughing puts the person who is talking to you in good humor; it draws men closer together, allows them to understand each other better; it sometimes brightens up a gloomy character; it is a charity. Always laugh."

Such was the renowned modern hermit of the Sahara. True, he did not convert great numbers; and despite all his efforts, he received, in 1916, the bullet of a Senussi rebel that ended his days. But throughout the desert country, Charles de Foucauld has accomplished more good than all the colonial functionaries. A Moslem writer, Amenokal Moussa ag Amastan, says of him: "The renown of our marabout [Moslem word for holy man] is great in Ahaggar. The folk to whom he did good, and that means all folk of Ahaggar, honor his tomb as if he were still alive."

At El Golea, where de Foucauld once passed some weeks, a Moslem notable spoke of him with reverence for the remainder of his days. "When I called to see him," he used to relate, "he said to me, 'May the Lord be with you!' and that expression moved me to the bottom of my heart."

Next morning we made another early start, fortified with Reneau's treat of black coffee without sugar and a toast biscuit. . . .

★ ★ ★

At Colomb-Bechar, a post of the Foreign Legion, Barre and I said goodby to Reneau and Cheval. There was something stale about the train ride that followed, through busy regions to Oran and Algiers. I kept thinking of the empty desert, of Charles de Foucauld who set up his hermitage deep in the labyrinth of its dunes, who rose at midnight to taste the sweetness of virginal sand, soft winds, and sky.

Mission, Aesthetics, and Architecture: Indonesia (1932) and Cambridge (1939)

Perhaps aware that missioners are often too concerned with practical matters to pay attention to aesthetics or architecture, in the following diary entries Considine broaches these two topics and articulates connections among mission, culture, liturgy, art, and architecture. Considine's comments on art and church vestments offer a perspective on the church's efforts to communicate the gospel in a non-European setting and at the same time reveal something of the depths of Considine's own artistic sensibilities. His comments on architecture display an appreciation of the ability of a church structure to embody a sense of Catholic tradition.

Sept. 18, 1932 Sun. Djokja

Out at 10:00 with Pere Ministre to Catholic hospital of 35 beds constructed by Mr. Schmutzer with splendid, cool operating quarters, prepared for air conditioning. We met Jules Schmutzer here and with him to his 1,200 hectares (3,000 acre) estate at Gandjoeram. We saw the tjandi [shrine], wherein [there is a] statue of the Sacred Heart. Java was dedicated to Sacred Heart in 1927. To chapel where the Sacred Heart again, pair of angels and Madonna and Child, all in Javanese style. Many do not like the style, I was told, particularly the Javanese but, like some of the modern schools of Christian art in Europe, [it is] a question of taste. The trinity was disapproved in Rome because three men were taken to represent [God].

Besides Schmutzer, a certain J. Peltenburg has attempted some paintings in Javanese art while J. Custers of Eindhoven, Holland has made some statues. Custers' work is pronounced as not good and the other items are too heavy; Javanese very fine and delicate in character and in art demand a great delicacy.

Sept. 19, 1932 Mon. Djokja – Batavia

After Mass at 7:00 to minor seminary with Fr. Rector . . . Fr. Rector showed me vestments made in Holland under direction of Fr. Djajasepo-etra; appealed very much to me as they do to most Europeans as adaptation of Javanaese art to vestments. However, Javanese do not like them; those sincere, even among educated, say they are queer and laughable, colours not correct, motifs poorly chosen or erroneous; one design on chasuble is one used on the Javanese skirt and hence quite out of place. Hence we get light on this much discussed subject; it is not Javanese opposition to their own art; seems rather the insuccess of these first infantile efforts of Westerners to penetrate the East and create on Eastern terrain. Naturally it must be tremendously difficult. Perhaps the best we can do is to awaken interest in Easterners and prompt them to seek to correct our blundering essays.

Out about 8:30 with a Dutch and a Javanese scholastic to a bookshop and to Javanese art shops. Leatherwork interesting but particularly the batik work, a process of covering a designed cloth with wax and dying the free space. . . . . Djokja, Solo, Grissee, Pekalongan the batik centers; I noted how rapidly the women work with their pens of liquid wax.

King's Chapel at Cambridge – Sunday, April 23 1939

Cambridge—Today I journeyed out of London in a different direction for some contact work in Cambridge. The city has some 70,000 inhabitants and is dominated by the University, which comprises 17 colleges and has an enrollment of 75,000, about 2,000 more than Oxford. The buildings are intensely interesting as at Oxford, with quadrangles which emanate an atmosphere at once collegiate and ecclesiastical. Particularly beautiful at Cambridge is what is called the "backs," the parkway along the Cam River framed by the property to the rear of a number of colleges.

Trinity and King's Colleges took my particular fancy. King's College chapel is the most outstanding of the university, and compares in certain details with many of the greatest of Europe. The carving of the stalls is pronounced the best this side of the Alps and the windows, in all depicting exactly 100 scenes, are regarded as the greatest and largest extent of the medieval Flemish school. All was Catholic when this and the other chapels were built and they still have a Catholic atmosphere. The organ was playing when I visited Trinity chapel. It provided the setting for some lines of Wordsworth which I found in a leaflet in King's chapel:

Where light and shade repose, where music dwells,
Lingering—and wandering on as loth to die;

Like thoughts whose very sweetness yieldeth proof
That they were born for immortality.

There are ideas in these college chapels which I believe could be incorporated into our future chapel at Maryknoll. Offhand, as it occurs to me now after looking at many chapels over here, ours should be conservative in line, teaching a regard for our rich Catholic heritage; it should be non-modern but not mediocre and obvious in its conception. I would like to follow the general wall structure of that part of King's Chapel within the rood screen. Structural requirements to make the outside of the chapel conform with the rest of the building need not interfere with our having a lofty and almost flat ceiling and an unobstructed sanctuary.

The Creation and World Christianity[2]

In 1944, as many of the world's populations continued at war, outlines of a new universalism capable of embracing all peoples—and thus avoiding future armed conflicts—began to gain currency. Considine was convinced that the church was the world institution with the best ability of seeking a positive universalism. His small volume World Christianity *offers seven chapters on Christian apologetics and theological topics, and in each shows how these matters of faith are intrinsically related to themes of the universality of the human race, the need to overcome racial hatred, and the church's missionary regard for all the peoples of the earth. Here is chapter 5 on the creation:*

God made first the purely spiritual creatures, the angels; then the purely material, the world; and finally the creature that is composed of spiritual and material, of soul and body. Theology explains that the primary purpose of creation was the "formal glorifying" of the Creator, and the next purpose was the eternal happiness of man.

The scholar Lactantius says: "The world was made that we might be born. We were born that we might know God. We know Him that we may worship Him. We worship Him that we may earn immortality. We are rewarded with immortality that, being like unto the angels, we may serve our Father and Lord forever, and be in the eternal kingdom of God."

There are beauty and significance in the simplicity of this picture of the Creation: God, the One and Only, served by man, one and undistinguished. There is no division into white men and colored men; there is no separation between men on the basis of country, or occupation, or education, or even of spiritual accomplishment. All men are intended by God's plan to worship Him and thus find happiness.

---

2. John J. Considine, *World Christianity* (Milwaukee: Bruce, 1944), 24–32.

Then came the Fall, and again there was unqualified application to all men. The consequent Redemption likewise was universal, though conditioned as to the communication of the fruits of the Redemption to each individual man. The Church, the instrument of the Redemption, did not automatically embrace all creation. Its universality was to depend upon the degree to which the Church should be missionary, for it is sterile unless it possesses men within its embrace. Today it would appear to be as yet largely sterile, for seventeen out of every twenty men on earth are still outside its embrace. The beautiful and significant simplicity of the Creation is marred by the fewness of men who are possessed by God's society of worship and redemption, the Church.

Unity of the Human Race. Theology tells us that all mankind is descended from one pair of progenitors, Adam and Eve. There have been "pre-Adamites" and "co-Adamites" who, while to a certain degree concurring in the Biblical statement on the Creation, have sought to explain the differences among men by asserting that men had a multiple origin—some descending from Adam and Eve, and others from other, inferior beings. This made some races substantially at variance with others. The Church has always condemned such theories.

In the Middle Ages, slave traders and others attempted to justify their mistreatment of Negroes and Indians by contending that those "backward" peoples were not men at all. Of course the contentions were condemned unhesitatingly. Bartholomew de Las Casas—to cite a single instance—carried on a long campaign against slave traders in Spanish America. Their very contentions are eloquent testimony of the Church's teaching that all men are one.

Equality of All Men. Men are not only one; they are also equal, as so many beautiful texts of Scripture establish. In our day, racism and nationalism offer special obstacles to the ready acceptance of this teaching—obstacles which did not always exist in days gone by. Happily, human considerations and human testimony have come forward to support the Church in her stand that all men are equal. In the social and political sphere, thoughtful men see the harm which can come from group claims to superiority, and they try to educate people to a proper attitude.

But it is in the scientific field that the evidence has been most conclusive. It could conceivably come to pass that, while men are equal in their spiritual dignity as men, whole portions of mankind (for instance, the Negroes) could be physically or intellectually inferior to other portions. But the general view of scientists today is that, among human beings over the earth, when due allowance is made for physical and social environment, there is essentially no intrinsic difference between one race and another. There are brilliant, mediocre, and weak specimens in one race as well as in another; there are diversities among *all* men, but no substantial difference between group and group.

Taylor, in *Environment, Race, and Migration* (University of Chicago, 1937), makes a typical statement in this regard. "In my opinion," he says, "race prejudice is but another term for ethnological ignorance. Such prejudice is based on very real differences of *culture,* but in the majority of cases the *biological* differences are negligible. For instance, the *racial* difference between some of the broad-headed Yamatos of Japan and the broad-headed Englishmen of Kent is negligible compared with the gap which separates both from the little dark men of Devon or the primitive folk of Central Wales. This is a very encouraging idea, for cultural differences of habit, education, and religion can be entirely changed in a generation, whereas a racial barrier is much more difficult to overcome."

Equal Fellowship of All Men. The doctrine of the Creation teaches us an equal fellowship with all men. The earth, the home of man, was made by God to be held in stewardship by each succeeding generation. Each person's right to private ownership is sacred; but in a world in which all men are one, in which all men are equal, in which all men must love one another, if some men are in desperate want, whether of food or shelter or clothing, their fellows are bound to seek to relieve this need.

Such, incidentally, would appear to be the situation in our world of today; for out of every ten people on earth, two of them, we are told, are chronically hungry from lack of sufficient food—four hundred million people in the world have not enough to eat! For the Eternal God, gazing down from heaven, how incidental it must seem that some of those in want have brown skins, some black, some white; or that some are on the continent of North America, some on South America, some on Europe or Asia or Africa. From the unity of the world's creation is born the unity of all human want.

"Am I my brother's keeper?" Cain asked, and God answered in the affirmative. "Thou shalt love thy neighbor as thyself," says the Gospel. "This is my commandment, that you love one another, as I have loved you" *(John xv:12).* And Saint Paul trumpets: "There is neither Jew nor Gentile, there is neither bond nor free. . . . For you are all one in Christ Jesus" *(Gal. iii:28).*

Unity of the Fall. From the common origin of the Fall, no man is better or worse than his fellow. The infant born of the primitive in the jungle and the unbaptized child of the educated Christian at the summit of civilization are equal in the deprivations caused by original sin: (1) the privation of sanctifying grace; (2) concupiscence; (3) dominion by Satan; (4) liability to suffering, disease, unhappiness, death.

It is Baptism and the other sacraments which bestow on the Christian the spiritual power that arms him with a tremendous and essential advantage over the non-Christian in the matter of doing good and avoiding evil. Apart from this spiritual power, however, which is a gift from God and wholly unmerited by those of us who receive it, there is no essential difference between the Christian and the non-Christian. In considering the doctrine of the Fall, we should consider this common likeness between ourselves and the non-Christian.

The spiritual lack from which every non-Christian suffers possesses an urgency which should prompt us to work ceaselessly for the non-Christian's relief. We must take care, however, to avoid in ourselves any sense of partisan pride or smug superiority which creates in us disdain rather than fraternal regard. God does not wish us to be the enemy of the non-Christian, but his friend. We shall never do God's will in relation to the non-Christian if we regard him in arrogance and vanity, rather than in humble fellowship.

Mr. Cheap

Fr. Considine's 1953 visit to South Africa exposed him to the brutality of the apartheid regime, and a chapter in Africa: World of New Men[3] *relates a lengthy conversation he had with a black South African, George Maruku, regarding the difficult economic situation of black South Africans.*

Johannesburg is THE biggest thing in Africa. It is a mining town with a million people in it. Its core is the congested business center, fringed with crowded apartment and residence areas such as we know in our American cities. Then to the north fan out the attractive suburbs; communities like Houghton where, in the radiance of a California morning, we ride through winding, tree-lined avenues, past expensive homes, country clubs, tennis courts, golf courses, swimming pools. But to the south, lies an infamous arc of appalling slums that rank with some of the worst in the world. Everywhere are the mines, the mine dumps—the hallmark of Johannesburg—the pit-head gear, the paraphernalia of the battle for gold.

A friend loaned me his car and an African acquaintance of his was my chauffeur. Thus I met George Maruku, a young man whose family came from Basutoland more than a generation ago, and whose relatives today are very much at home in the Golden City. George was an interesting individual, a graduate of the Native University at Fort Hare and a writer for Bantu papers. He accepted his place in life, with no illusions about any bright opportunities that might lie before him.

"The gold mines of the Rand are the biggest single employers of Afri-

3. John J. Considine, *Africa: World of New Men* (New York: Dodd, Mead & Co., 1954), 219–30.

can labor in Africa," George observed as we rode. "The eternally pounding stamp-batteries of Johannesburg, which crush the stone that holds the gold, are called the heartbeat of the nation. Every day some 350,000 able-bodied adults, called 'boys' by the white men, are lowered into the shafts. Thus far, they have taken out over six billion dollars in gold."

"How much are they paid, George?" I asked. "They average the equivalent of fifty cents a day in your money, plus their keep," replied George.

"As a man learns his job, does he get a raise in pay?" I asked.

"Very little!" said George. "That's the key to the whole labor problem. You have heard that gold is the most precious thing in South Africa, but the real wealth of the country is cheap labor. Deprive the Union of cheap labor, and it would become bankrupt overnight. The great commandment of the mine owners is, 'Thou shalt employ only cheap migrant labor.' Each of us Africans has a big tag tied to him, or better, a brand on his hide. It reads CHEAP. Every African is named 'Mr. Cheap.' By any other name, no employer wants him."

"But are you sure that, even if a man gets experience in the mines, he can't earn more as time goes by?"

"I'm quite sure of that, Father. While I was at Fort Hare in 1943, there was a statement by the Chamber of Mines, which represents the owners, asserting categorically that this had to be their policy. The statement was much discussed by us Africans. The statement said that the ability of the mines to maintain their Native labor force by means of tribal Natives from the reserves at rates of pay that are adequate for this migratory class of Native but inadequate in practice for the detribalized urban Native, is a fundamental factor in the economy of the gold-mining industry."

"The mine boy, then, is a special class of African," I observed.

"Yes, that's right. Among us Africans, the mine boy is the simple rube from the country. He lives in the mine compounds, one of which you are going to see at Sophiatown. Most of us Africans around Johannesburg live in locations. There is a third category of urban African, the domestic servant. He is regarded by many as the best off, since he lives in quarters supplied by the master and is not confined to the compound or the location."

"Why do the mine companies speak of migrants?"

"Because almost literally that's what the mine worker is. The system brings only the young workers from the kraal. They sign on for 350 days in the mines, during which period each man is well fed and well doctored but, as you will see, has no more home than a concrete bunk in a large dormitory building. He leaves his wife and children back in the reserve, so that the wife can continue to work their little plot of ground. After his term of service, the mine boy goes back to the kraal."

"Does he have anything to take with him, out of such a small salary?" I asked.

"Perhaps the first time back he doesn't have much. When he's green, he makes a particular fool of himself in the city, spending the first money he's ever had. He returns to the reserve with a pathetic collection of flashy and worthless junk, in a tinseled box that he has paid a terrific price for in the bazaar. He takes back, too, a contempt for the old tribal ways and an impatience toward the local chiefs in the reserves. After several trips to the city, he takes home less junk and, if he hasn't learned to gamble, more of the $175 that he has earned in his 350 days."

"Why do the mine workers migrate for fifty cents a day?" I asked.

"Frankly, because the African's economy is so rigged that he has to, to keep from starving. Some white men will tell you that the country boy, the young man from the reserve, comes to the city for adventure, for escape from the cramping restrictions at home. Some will say that a young fellow has to go to Goldieburg for prestige; until he does, the girls of the reserve point the finger of scorn at him and tell him he's not fully blooded yet.

"But apart from these contributing factors, most fellows are at the mines because they have to be. A married man with a plot of land in Transkei Native Reserve, which is one of the best, can with the help of his wife get about $50 a year from his land. If he has five children, the Native Reserve authorities say he needs a minimum of $160 a year. He can hope to get that much money only by leaving home."

★ ★ ★

As we rode home from Moroka, I asked George a question. "What should you say, George, is the thing that the African wants most?"

George thought a moment. "Some people say we'd like most to have cattle and lie in the sun. Others say we want education, money, opportunity. I don't really think that to possess things—either the things of the old Africa or of the new—will really satisfy us, any more than merely possessing things satisfies the white men. I think that we really yearn most to *be* something, rather than to *have* something.

"I think we desire tremendously to be free from the world's disdain. Then as we analyse this desire, we see that merely being externally free of that disdain won't be enough either. I think that, in the end, we want most of all not merely to be free of other men's disdain. We want to see, by looking deep inside ourselves, that we *deserve*, by the right way we do things, to be free of man's disdain. And then, as well, of God's disdain.

"We don't see all this right away. But I think this is what the African wants most of all." I found myself silenced.

But why be astonished that Mr. Cheap, quite as well as any other man on the planet, should exercise his right to spiritual insight? There is in the African a stronger appeal for the non-material than many of us whites realize.

Tribal Gods in Catholic Bahia[4]

In 1954 during his second mission study tour of Latin America, Fr. Considine spent several days in Bahia, Brazil, and later dedicated a chapter in New Horizons in Latin America *to a discussion of Candomblé and Catholicism among the large population of Afro Brazilians in that city. The chapter concludes with a description of a Candomblé ritual, which Considine attended in the company of his Bahia informant, Antonio Lobo. The description is remarkable for the dispassionate tone with which the reader is provided cultural, economic, and religious background for the ceremony. Not many Catholic priests in the 1950s would have had an interest in attending such a ceremony, and those interested may not have easily received proper permission from ecclesiastical authorities to do so. The description provided by Considine displays his comparative religions sensibilities, and only the final paragraph is a slight nod to the standard rejection of Candomblé by church officials of the time.*

"Enough about the gods," said Antonio as we drove away. "Now we must arrange to attend a *candomblé* seance."

For this, Antonio chose a famous house in a convenient suburb that occupied the fazenda of a Frenchman named Gantois. This *candomblé* was once headed by the great "mother" Pulcheria and now belonged to Menininha.

"It is one of the best conducted *candomblés* in Bahia," explained Antonio, "so much so that it is difficult for outsiders to get permission to attend."

We entered the backyard of a rather large house and found half a dozen Negro women. One kindly old lady knitted in a chair. A couple of other women were preparing the supper. One woman was doing some wash while a large-boned, sloe-eyed girl hung clothes on the line. "Is Mother here?" Antonio asked the girl. She stopped hanging clothes, looked at us quite deliberately and without a word went into the house.

"They want to know what you want," she drawled when she returned.

"Antonio began to explain but she stopped him. "Go around to the festal-hall door," she said and returned to her clothes.

As we walked around the house I observed a burly Negro in his undershirt look out the window at us. When we reached the door it was he who opened it a slit and stood looking intently at Antonio. "You remember me,

---

4. John J. Considine, *New Horizons in Latin America: Illustrated with Photographs* (New York: Dodd, Mead & Co., 1958), 46–51.

don't you?" said Antonio. "I've been here for some of the seances. When is the next one?"

"There's one tonight," answered the fellow, looking for all the world like a night club bouncer. He hesitated a moment and made his decision. "Come back tonight. We start at eight."

Thus we had been put under the gleam of the fish eye and voted safe enough not to make trouble. Antonio was delighted; his worries were over. It reminded me of stories of how men used to buy bootleg liquor.

Circumstances made us late and we did not return until nine o'clock.

"The sacrifices will be over," remarked Antonio as we drove along. "To the devotees, remember, feeding the gods, as the sacrifice is called, is more important than dancing to them though to onlookers the dancing and the sight of the dancers becoming possessed is much more dramatic."

"Just how do they feed the gods, Antonio?" "The *candomblé* feast begins with the *matança*, the killing of hens or pigeons or other small animals and the pouring of their blood before the feet of the gods. This ceremony is private as is also the placating of Eshu."

As we crawled gingerly up the very bad road to the hilltop we heard the drums. A couple of other cars were already parked and a hundred or so Negroes milled about outside in an air of excitement. When we reached the door we found the ceremony in full career. The brightly lighted festal hall was packed with over two hundred onlookers and the circle of dancers moved counterclockwise in the hollow square in the center. The drums were lively but I was to find that they were not at all hot as yet.

A tall gentleman of the perfect butler type, neatly dressed in gray suit, came over and conducted us to the section on the wooden bench reserved for the special guests.

"This festal hall is one of the best in Bahia," explained Antonio. "It is a new building constructed for the purpose. Since it corresponds with the plan of Engenho Velho, the master *candomblé* plan in these parts, it's evidently correct. It's made of brick covered with plaster and has a solid tile roof."

The walls of the hall were painted but not otherwise ornamented except for three niches high above the crowd. Each of the niches was illumined with an arc of electric lights. The central one contained a large crucifix. The one to the right contained a statue of Our Lady with a couple of vases of flowers before it. I could not identify the statue in the third niche but it also had flowers before it.

On each side wall were three glassless windows through which the wind blows almost with violence so that the hall remained pleasantly cool all evening. On three sides the crowd filled every foot of space outside the hollow square and black faces peered in through every window. The men occupied one side, the women the other.

Most of the onlookers were neighborhood Negroes but there were special guests. In front of us sat a well dressed Negro with sharp, intelligent face accompanied by two policemen. "He's evidently a high ranking police official," whispered Antonio. There were four Brazilians of mixed blood and several whites. None gave signs of active participation, but a number made large offerings at the end of the evening. Across the hall in the women's section were some well dressed Brazilians and several foreign women.

On the fourth side of the room between the entrances for the participants sat the major officers of the seance. Most important, of course, was "mother" Menininha, the spiritual head of the Gantois *candomblé*. Her Portuguese title is *mãe-de-santo*, "mother in sainthood" which indicates her role as the mother in leading her followers to sainthood. Menininha occupied a double-width chair because she is extremely broad and fleshy. I watched her during the evening. She displayed no air of haughtiness or imperiousness, no attempt at glitter, no smirking sophistication. She gave every bit the impression of being a kindly mother.

On Menininha's right stood the muscle man of the afternoon, now in a dark suit that made him quite proper. His trousers needed pressing, however, and he wore a generally tousled air. Despite his attempts at fervor and unction, I kept my conviction that his greatest opportunity came in the hour of trouble. Several men who sat on Menininha's left were *ogans* of the ceremony; they provided prestige and money. An interesting man was the *iye tebexe,* who directed the dance. He called out the songs, initiated each fresh refrain and with his iron gong fixed the basic rhythm for the music.

Then there were the drums. They were the authentic hollow-log African type, the heads stretched with cow-hide. An official battery of drums is always three: large, medium and small. For me, the most fascinating person at the seance was the drummer boy of the big drum. He used a single heavy stick in his right hand and with his left struck the drumhead with his hand in a marvelous variety of ways. His performance was sheer wizardry. Physically he had the form for a lightweight boxer, lithe as a leopard, with thin hips and no stomach. As the evening wore on the drumming of the entire trio rose from enthusiasm to exultation and of course, as was intended, played a major role in making the seance a success.

And now for the "daughters-in-sainthood," as they are called. As I was taking in the details of the scene they were earnestly concentrating on their quest. Each was seeking to call down the special god, or "saint," to which she was devoted, get him to enter her head and take possession of her, thus riding her as a horse.

Circling before us to the rhythm of chanting and drums were twenty to twenty-five women. I recognized immediately the sloe-eyed girl who, when we came in the afternoon, was hanging out the clothes in the backyard. In the circle also was the white-haired grandma, whom I had seen knitting in the rocking chair. She was probably seventy, with handsome face and large, strong body. The others varied in age from a child of twelve, slight of build, to women in their twenties, thirties, forties, fifties, tall, short, thin, extremely fat.

All were modestly and charmingly dressed in old Empire style, though with no costume jewelry. None gave the least indication of exhibitionism, of melodramatics. One lone girl had modern dress, a loose sweater and a black, tight-fitting skirt. She could have been a university student. She was awkward in her movements, lacked the rhythm of the others, but was deeply absorbed and entirely without pretense.

"They'd make a nice group of ladies for a parish sodality," I remarked to Antonio.

"Most of them are plain women of the city with a religious bent," Antonio observed, "dressmakers, domestics, or sweets vendors. They have little money and yet pay their way in the *candomblés*. In their ignorance they are quite unaware that this is paganism almost as it came from Africa centuries ago."

"I suppose men have traced all these practices to their sources."

"Quite so," noted Antonio. "Half a dozen details have been pointed out to me as African. First, the circle of women rotating in a counterclockwise direction is precisely as it is still done in Africa. Secondly, the worship through specific dances for each specific deity is traditionally African. Thirdly, the method of sounding the basic rhythm with an iron gong is African. Fourthly, stirring the emotions with wild, intricate orgies of drumming is African. Fifthly, the calling of the gods with specific songs is African. Sixthly, the practice of becoming possessed as a means to establish contact with the gods is directly from West Africa's animistic worship."

The drums got hotter, the voices of the singers, which lacked good timbre, became more piercing, the dancing became more furious. Menininha sang a bit part every now and then and her voice was sweet and warm. Meanwhile she watched the revolving line and the evolvement of the emotions of the individuals. Some became quite violent and had to be protected by companions from falling or from snapping their heads too sharply.

Each new song was initiated in a clear fresh voice by the director and continued for fifteen or twenty minutes with alternating solo and chorus, again in traditional African style. As a woman showed signs that her god was taking possession of her the drums took up the specific rhythm of the god—Shango, Ogun, or other of the deities.

Finally Menininha had signaled to eight dancers in the circle who had shown signs of possession to retire to the dressing room. During their absence there was a period of surcease. Then, with a burst of climactic singing and drumming, the strange procession of possessed ones returned in their triumphal finery.

Two were made up as the Christ of Bomfim who identified the god Oshala, one represented St. George who identifies Oshosse, god of the hunt, two represented Santa Barbara, the identification for Shango. Three, then, came out with the ugly hooded costume of St. Lazarus who identifies Omolu. One of these three was the old lady of seventy. A second Lazarus was the child of twelve, and the third a stout woman whose violent energy likewise astounded me.

Each of these eight whom the gods had mounted and were now riding was accompanied by a woman caretaker, and quite wisely so since now came an apogee of violence. The eyes of the group were glassy, the minds evidently in a stupor, but the emotions were afire. As their specific drum rhythm was played, they shook and stamped and were taken by convulsions. One lady had to be held for a minute or so by four of the caretakers till she quieted and then continued in her dancing. The drums came alive with their astoundingly complex rhythms, the singers shouted and the onlookers joined in the surges of excitement.

"What such a night can mean to these people always puzzles me," Antonio commented on the way home, "but one has only to witness a *candomblé* to realize that every last one of the participants experiences a terrific emotional shake-up."

Just what is the explanation for the phenomenon called possession? Herskovits says, "Scientifically, the phenomenon of possession in Negro cultures, at least, is as yet unsatisfactorily explained, largely because of the almost complete absence of adequate reports on the background and incidence of specific cases."

It was one o'clock when finally I reached my room in the beautifully peaceful residence high above Bahia. I looked out on the bay where a silent moon put a gleam of unearthly loveliness on the waters.

It was over four hundred years since the first men of color were brought into this harbor from Africa. Antonio the student dwelt on the emotional impact of the ceremony we had witnessed. The scientist puzzles over the causes of the phenomenon. What can a missionary take away from such a shattering experience, I asked myself, other than a profound realization that after four centuries the Negro in Brazil still represents for world Christianity as well as for the Brazilian Church a great unfinished task?

The Church's Global Mission and the Future

Considine's 1962 address to the tenth Fordham Conference of Mission Specialists is prescient about the coming polycentric reality of Christianity on a global scale. In the first section, he lays out the basis for understanding this new reality by examining those non-Western areas of the world in which Christianity has taken root.

Events in our day have brought myriad changes in our vision of mankind and its goals. As we contemplate the world's future during the next half century or so, the political, cultural, social and economic objectives hold the principal attention of the majority of men. But most fascinating of all, it would seem, are the possibilities which lie ahead in the realm of the spiritual.

In the area of the global apostolate, thoughtful men say that we are witnessing a transition into a revolutionary new "missionary center of gravity" which, despite the threatening aspects in our rapidly changing world, can represent advantages to the Church during the next half century. Let us dwell briefly upon half a dozen or so strong possibilities.

First Characteristic of growth: cross-cultural "break-throughs"
in terms of Christian society

Thus far Christian history has been characterized by the rare instances of "break-throughs" of Christian society. By this we mean the authentically coalescing of Christianity into cultures diverse from the East European and West European cultures of the original Christian world. Now by the year 2000 there is promise that modest islands of such authentically coalesced Christian society may be foreseen in certain areas of Asia and Africa.

In past ages the Church's experiences in the penetration of Christian society into other cultures have been limited. Nestorian Christianity from Persia penetrated into China and, according to the Sianfu tablet, flourished there in modest fashion from the seventh to the ninth centuries. When in the sixteenth century Christianity returned to China, inter-family strife within the Christian body over the application of the principle of accommodation handicapped the Church in ever making itself genuinely Chinese.

In India, the St. Thomas Christians along the Malabar Coast represent the most notable example in the world of the thorough acclimatization of Christianity to non-Western society. This Church, which reached India through the Persian Gulf, and which never during long centuries was other than faithful to Rome though for centuries out of touch with Rome, was discovered by the Portuguese to possess tens of thousands of families congregated in hundreds of villages. Ironically, rather than rejoicing in this Church's substantial harmony with Indian culture, Portuguese officers and clergy sought to Latinize it. Rather than encouraging the building of Christianity on this Church as a possible agency for Indian penetration, a Western Latinism was introduced. Efforts of Robert de Nobili to create an ideal social pattern for Christianity in India were thwarted.

The largest Christian body to date in the Afro-Asian world is the Church in the Philippines, thoroughly at home among its people though colonial and Latin in its traditions. Important enclaves of Christianity in Asia are the Christians of Vietnam, of the Little Sunda Islands in Indonesia, of the Chota-Nagpore area in India, though all of these are predominantly Latin in their culture. Certain Middle East Christian bodies, such as those in Lebanon, are non-Western. They are vital units in Christendom even though they lack any tradition of being self-propagating.

Very promising are large units of Christians in East, Central and West Africa. Despite their colonial origins the tradition of the Church in these areas is such that there is strong hope that the passing of the colonial era will not jeopardize their existence and that their inner vitality will lead them to become thoroughly united with the African culture of their peoples.

The greatest present danger to Christianity in Asia and Africa is not its colonial connection but the strong secularist spirit that has characterized the latter years of the colonial period. Arnold Toynbee, whose opinion does not always conform with Catholic thinking, has strong and convincing words on this.

"The paradox of our generation," says Toynbee[*Civilization in Crisis,* p. 83], "is that all the world has now profited from an education which the West has provided except the West itself." He goes on to explain that the Achilles' heel of Greek civilization was the lack of a strong religion. Now the West suffers from this same malady. In the 1500's and 1600's the West in the persons of the Spaniard and the Portuguese attempted to export the whole of our Western culture, its religion included. During the 1700's and 1800's in the regimes of the Western powers this policy at least officially was dropped.

During the earlier period, Toynbee explains, "our world-storming Western forefathers made a valiant attempt to propagate abroad the whole of our Western cultural heritage including its religious core as well as its technical rind; and in this they were surely well-inspired; for every culture is a whole whose parts are subtly interdependent."

During Europe's reformation quarrels, however, Toynbee explains, a tacit agreement was reached to cut out religious wars by cutting out religion itself. This was deadly, Toynbee notes. "The Western civilization that has since run like wild-fire around the world," he asserts, "has not been the whole of the seamless web; it has been a flare of cotton-waste: a technological selvage with the religious center-piece torn out" [Toynbee, *op. cit.,* p. 85].

Will this technological selvage which now becomes the inherited pattern of the new states of Asia and Africa for the conduct of society, prevent our emergent Catholic Church units from becoming thoroughly at home in non-Western lands? We are optimistic enough to believe that they will gain new strength during the next half century.

Considine goes on to describe four other characteristics of the church's shift of center of gravity: the mutual enrichment of Christian life and non-Western cultures; the increased contribution of a rejuvenated Latin America to the world strength of Christianity; the impact of a well-catechized and active laity; and the growth of the concept of the universality of human rights.[5] He closed the address with a renewed look at ways in which the concept of Western cultural superiority was giving way to the notion of the equality of all peoples:

Sixth characteristic of growth: Abiding concern
for the common good of mankind

Only yesterday we as citizens of the West possessed what may be described euphemistically as a hen-and-chickens concept of the world, the West serving as mother hen and the remaining peoples of the globe as so many chicks in the planetary roost, to be guided, directed, scolded, punished according to how they kept their place as juvenile subordinates in the human family. In short, we lived by a philosophy of arrogant Western superiority.

Today this concept has vanished in [the] face not only of political changes but profound social changes that force men to recognize at least a practical working equality among all the peoples of the planet.

On examination we find that long ago Christian thinkers provided us with a thoroughly sound philosophy of our relations with the human race. By the end of the century, long years of rubbing elbows with the human race in the fashion that our new era demands should make vividly evident at least to Catholics and possibly to many others the wisdom of the Christian philosophy of an abiding concern for the common good of mankind.

St. Augustine taught that there were three natural societies: the family, the state and the society of all men—*domus, urbs et orbis.* St. Thomas Aquinas likewise recognized the idea of a society of all men. But the most complete expression of the universal community of all peoples comes to us from Francisco de Vitoria [J. Brown Scott, *The Spanish Origin of International Law—Francisco de Vitoria and his Law of Nations,* Oxford, 1934; *Obras de Francisco de Vitoria—Relecciones Teologicas,* Biblioteca de Autores Cristianos, Madrid, 1960; *Dictionnaire de Theologie Catholique* Tome XV, 49, Part II, Vitoria, Francois de].

---

5. See chapter 8 for a discussion of the full address.

Vitoria does not treat of a secular political empire or of a theocracy, or of a world federation of states. He concerns himself rather with a social organization of the human race in which all men constitute a *civitas maxima*, a great family which binds its members together by moral and juridical bonds into an ecumenical community that no racial differences or political rivalries can destroy.

Vitoria notes that from God proceeds:

1. the instinct or tendency toward a natural sociability of all men;
2. the right of peoples or nations (using nation in the social rather than political sense) that makes world solidarity and co-operation obligatory;
3. the possession of authority by human society as a whole, it being understood that all power comes from God.

The basic doctrine of Vitoria rests on the concept that humanity is a single whole destined to a temporal sojourn in a common residence, the earth, with vital common necessities and aspirations that cannot be satisfied by national isolation or divisions among peoples. Rather, they require global relations and institutions with obligatory universal cooperation to the end that the common good of the human race may be served.

In Francisco de Vitoria's day this basic concept of the human race represented academic theory. In the year 2000, global communications will have created such a common neighborhood of all men on the planet that Vitoria's teachings can constitute a practical, every-day *vade mecum* for all men possessed of an abiding concern for the common good of mankind.

First Consideration: The classic missionary
of a half century hence

From the foregoing, our image of the classic missionary of a half century hence, rather than that merely of a technical specialist with the task of contributing to the current thirst for modern social superstructure, must be rather that of a thoroughly equipped theoretician. He should, it is true, be au courant with modern techniques but more than ever he needs to be able to imbue local Christian leaders of the younger segments of the world Church with the timeless social and ecclesiological principles of Augustine and Francisco de Vitoria. In short, he must provide the practical social framework for the world-embracing charity of Christ.

APPENDIX 2

Table of Ten CICOP Conferences

CICOP	Year[1]	Place	Author	Book Title
1	1964	Chicago—Edgewater	Considine	*The Church in the New Latin America*
2	1965	Chicago—Edgewater	Considine	*Social Revolution in the New Latin America: A Catholic Appraisal*
3	1966	Chicago—Hilton	Considine	*The Religious Dimension in the New Latin America*
4	1967	Boston—Statler Hilton	Samuel Shapiro	*Integration of Man and Society in Latin America;* also available: *Working Papers*
5	1968	St. Louis	Samuel Shapiro	*Cultural Factors in Inter-American Relations*
6	1969	New York—New Yorker Hotel	Colonnese	*Human Rights and the Liberation of Man in the Americas*
7	1970	Washington, DC—Shoreham	Colonnese	*Conscientization for Liberation;* also available: *CICOP Position Papers*
8	1971	Washington, DC—4-H Center	Quigley	*Freedom and Unfreedom in the Americas*
9	1972	Washington, DC—4-H Center		None published (Communications in the Americas was the theme)
10	1973	Dallas	Quigley	*Poverty, Environment, and Power: Papers on Issues of Justice in the Americas*

1. The CICOP conferences were held in late January.

Works Cited

WORKS BY JOHN J. CONSIDINE

Books

"Blessed Ramon Lull: A Thirteenth Century Missioner." Licentiate in Sacred Theology diss., Catholic University of America, 1924.

The Vatican Mission Exposition: A Window on the World. New York: Macmillan, 1925.

When the Sorghum Was High. New York: Longmans, Green and Co., 1940.

March into Tomorrow. New York: Field Afar Press, 1942.

An Outline of Missiography. New York: Society for the Propagation of the Faith, 1944.

World Christianity. Milwaukee: Bruce, 1945.

Call for Forty Thousand. Toronto: Longmans, Green & Co., 1946.

Africa: World of New Men. New York: Dodd, Mead & Company, 1954.

New Horizons in Latin America: Illustrated with Photographs. New York: Dodd, Mead & Company, 1958.

God So Loved the World: Thoughts on the Maryknoll Cloister. Maryknoll, NY: Maryknoll Cloister, n.d.[1]

The Missionary's Role in Socio-Economic Betterment. Westminster, MD: Newman, 1960.

Fundamental Catholic Teaching on the Human Race. Maryknoll, NY: Maryknoll Publications, 1961.

The Church in the New Latin America. Notre Dame, IN: Fides Publishers, 1964.

Social Revolution in the New Latin America: A Catholic Appraisal. Notre Dame, IN: Fides Publishers, 1965.

The Religious Dimension in the New Latin America. Notre Dame, IN: Fides Publishers, 1966.

Considine, John J., and Thomas Dickenson Kernan. *Across a World*. New York: Longmans, Green & Co., 1942.

---

1. Although *God So Love the World* carries no date, the photos of the Maryknoll Sisters Cloister contained in it are post–1960.

Articles and Chapters[2]

"Agentia Fides." *The Commonweal* 6 (28 September 1927): 498–99.

"Moslem Missions." Acolyte 4 (July 14, 1928): 13–15.

"Protestantism and Self-Government in China." *Ecclesiastical Review* 79 (Summer 1928): 301–4.

"Peter's Mission Money." *Catholic Missions* 6 (September 1929): 262–63.

"A Papal Mission to Ethiopia." *The Acolyte* 6 (November 1930): 12–14.

"Bethlehems of the Missions." *Catholic Missions* 8 (December 1931): 366–69.

"Two Great Missioners Pass." *Catholic Missions* 10 (May 1933): 149.

"Glimpses of Asia's New Bishops." *Catholic Missions* 10 (September–October, 1933): 238–40.

"An Ozanam of China (Lo Pa Hong)." *Catholic Missions* 10 (December 1933): 301–2.

"Where Propaganda Funds Go." *Catholic Missions* 11 (January 1934): 13–20.

"Ethiopia." *The Commonweal* 22 (May 1935): 5–6.

"Local Christian Art in Mission Lands." *Liturgical Arts* 4 (1935): 49–59.

"Homes and Haunts of Him Who Is Pope." *America* 61 (July 1, 1939): 270–71.

"Missioners Stayed." *Catholic Digest* 6 (August 1942): 71–74.

"Missionary Cooperation Plan." *Ecclesiastical Review* 107 (September 1942): 207–14.

"China Plans a Chinese Economy." *America* 69 (April 17, 1943): 36–38.

"Some Points on the Place of Mission Education in General Education." *Catholic Educational Review* 41 (April 1943): 229–33.

"Japan and the Future of East Asia's Missions." *Catholic Mind* 41 (July 1943): 23–25.

"Education to World Christianity." *Journal of Religious Instruction* 14 (December 1943): 405–9.

"World Christianity in the Religion Course." *Journal of Religious Instruction* 14 (January 1944): 483–91.

"World Christianity in the Social Studies." *Journal of Religious Instruction* 14 (February 1944): 516–24.

"World Christianity in Teaching Geography and History." *Catholic Educational Review* 42 (April 1944): 216–21.

"Church and the Unity of the Human Race." *Catholic Action* 26 (October 1944): 6–7.

"Latin America Needs Priests." *The Missionary Union of the Clergy Bulletin* (September 1946): 9–15.

---

2. Considine also wrote countless articles for Maryknoll's mission magazine, *The Field Afar* (later renamed *Maryknoll—The Field Afar*, and then simply *Maryknoll*). At times he used the pseudonym Peter Cosmon.

"Spiritual Bond between the Two Americas." In *Proceedings of the National Council of Catholic Women*, 135–39. NCWC, 1946.

"Goal in Sight." *Catholic World* 164 (January 1947): 365–66.

"Good Neighbors Calling." *Catholic Mind* 45 (February 1947): 75–79.

"Bolivia's Aymara." *Catholic Digest* 11 (March 1947): 20–24.

"Thousand American Missioners a Year." *Catholic Mission Digest* 5 (March 1947): 1–4.

"Catholic Cooperation with Latin America." *Catholic World* 165 (April 1947): 62–65.

"Latin America." *Catholic Mind* 47 (October 1947): 617–20.

"Story of Maryknoll." *Catholic Digest* 12 (March 1948): 81–86.

"Missions of the Catholic Church: 1948." *International Review of Mission* 38 (1949): 165–180.

"Panorama de las Misiones Católicas en 1949." *El Siglo de las Misiones* 36 (1949): 385–94.

"Catholics and World-Consciousness." *Missionary Union of the Clergy Bulletin* 14 (September 1950): 5–11.

"Christian World Outlook." *America* 86 (October 20, 1951): 84.

"Evangelii Praecones." *Homiletics* 52 (February 1952): 420–23.

"Education to World Christianity." In *Scientia Missionum Ancilla; Clarissimo Doctori Alphonso Ioanni Mariae Mulders. Instituti Missiologici ad Universitatem Neomagensem Fundatori Hunc Librum Dedicant Amici Occasione Sexagesimi Eius Anniversarii*, 153–58. Nijmegen: Dekker & Van de Vegt, 1953.

"Maryknoll Projects in Underdeveloped Countries." *Catholic Charities Review* 36 (March–June 1953): 65–66; 118–20; 149–51.

"Letter from Africa." *Catholic Digest* 17 (June 1953): 46–54.

"A World Survey of Contemporary Local Leadership in Mission Lands." *Proceedings of the Fordham University Conference of Mission Specialists* (1954): 27–45.

"Young Man's Day in Africa." *The Shield* 33 (January, 1954): 2–3.

"Challenge of Latin America." In *Forward with Christ: Thoughts and Reflections on Vocations to the Foreign Missions*, ed. Paolo Manna and Nicholas Maestrini, 152–63. Westminster, MD: Newman Press, 1954.

"Señorita Rosario, Social Worker Extraordinary." *Catholic Charities Review* 39 (March 1955): 8–11.

"Charities Leadership at the Grass Roots Level." *Catholic Charities Review* 40 (March 1956): 10–14.

"Mother Mary Joseph." *Mission Digest* 14 (May 1956): 11–16.

"Today's Latin America." *The Shield* 36 (November 1956): 4–5.

"Social Gains in Today's Latin America." *The Shield* 36 (January 1957): 16–17.

"Impressions of a Visit." *America* 96 (February 23, 1957): 582–84.

"Christian Gains in Today's Latin America." *The Shield* 36 (March 1957): 12–14.

"African Gods in Catholic Bahia." *Worldmission* 8 (Winter 1957): 77–95.

"World Goals of the National Conference of Catholic Charities." *Catholic Charities Review* 41 (December 1957): 5–9.

"Special Effectiveness of the International Voluntary Agency at the Grassroots Level." *Catholic Charities Review* 42 (December 1958): 11–12.

"Facts about Cuba." *The Shield* 38 (March 1959): 10–11, 36.

"World Charity and the Vincentian Layman." *Catholic Charities Review* 43 (October 1959): 22–27.

"Africa: Birth of a Great Black Church." *Catholic World* 190 (November 1959): 93–100.

"The Laity in the Church Today." *Perspectives* 5 (April 1960): 4–7.

"Papal Volunteers: More about Them." *The Shield-Collegian* 40, no. 3 (January 1961): 4–5, 21.

"The Church's Global Mission and the Future." In *The Global Mission of the Church: Proceedings of the Fordham University Conference of Mission Specialists, Tenth Annual Meeting, January 19–20, 1962,* ed. J. Franklin Ewing, IX–1–IX–7. New York: Institute of Mission Studies, Fordham University, 1962.

"The Missionary Approach to Urban Problems." *Community Development Review* 8, no. 2 (June 1963): 15–24.

"Two Ways to Aid the Latins: An Interview with Father John J. Considine, M.M." *Sign* 42, no. 10 (May 1963): 12–13.

"Fighting Fire with Fire: The Catholic Reply to Communism in Latin America." *The Shield* 43, no. 2 (December 1963/January 1964): 13, 29.

"The Papal Program for Latin America." *American Ecclesiastical Review* 154, no. 3 (March 1966): 153–169.

"World's Work in the Day's Work." In *Revolution in Missionary Thinking: A Symposium,* ed. William Jerome Richardson, 172–79. Maryknoll, NY: Maryknoll Publications, 1966.

"Latin America: The Church Not Missionary, but in Need of Repairs." In *Readings on the Theology of Mission: A Symposium Tracing the Mission Apostolate from the Old Testament down to the Ecumenical Age of the Present,* ed. J. Paul Spaeth. World Cultures and Religion Series. Cincinnati: CSMC Press, 1968.

"For the Revelation of Events." *Worldmission* 23 (Summer 1972): 30–33.

OTHER WORKS CITED

Allen, Yorke. *A Seminary Survey: A Listing and Review of the Activities of the Theological Schools and Major Seminaries Located in Africa, Asia, and Latin*

America Which Are Training Men to Serve as Ordained Ministers and Priests in the Protestant, Roman Catholic, and Eastern Churches. New York: Harper, 1960.

Aveling, Francis. *The God of Philosophy.* London: Catholic Truth Society, 1920.

Baer, George W. *The Coming of the Italian–Ethiopian War.* Cambridge, MA: Harvard University Press, 1967.

Bedier, Mary Juliana. *Neighbors in One World.* New York: W. H. Sadlier, 1952.

Bedier, M. Juliana, and Frederick K. Branom. *Neighbors in Eurasia: Europe and Asia.* New York: W. H. Sadlier, 1950.

———. *Neighbors Across the World, Eastern Hemisphere.* New York: W. H. Sadlier, 1950.

Bedier, M. Juliana, Frederick K. Branom, and George H. McVey. *Southern Neighbors: South America, Africa, Australia, Oceania: Geography for the Air Age.* Chicago: W. H. Sadlier, 1951.

Borra, Edoardo. *La carovana di Blass: Padre Gaudenzio Barlassina: ricordi di un medico.* Bologna: Missionaria Italiana, 1977.

Boyea, Earl. "The National Catholic Welfare Conference: An Experience in Episcopal Leadership, 1935–1945." Ph.D. dissertation. Catholic University of America, 1987.

Brandewie, Ernest. *When Giants Walked the Earth: The Life and Times of Wilhelm Schmidt, SVD.* Fribourg, Switzerland: University Press, 1990.

Carney, Joseph P. "The History of the Functional Structure of the Maryknoll Mission in Musoma and Shinyanga, Tanzania." Ph.D. dissertation. St. John's University, New York, 1973.

Casey, John J. "The History of Maryknoll Formation/Education, 1911–2011: An Internal History of the Seminaries Built and Run by Maryknoll." Published privately, n.d.

Catholic Association for International Peace. *Latin America and the United States: Preliminary Study Presented to the Catholic Association for International Peace.* New York: Paulist Press, 1929.

Catholic Church. *Conferencia general del episcopato latino-americano: Rio de Janeiro, 25 de julio–4 de agosto de 1955: Conclusiones.* Vatican City: Tipografia poliglotta vaticana, 1956.

Catholic Church. *Missiones catholicae.* Vatican City: Typis Polyglottis Vaticanis, 1930.

Ceci, Lucia. "Chiesa e questione coloniale: Guerra e missione nell'impresa d'Etiopia." *Italia Contemporanea* 233 (2003): 618–36.

———. *Il papa non deve parlare: Chiesa, fascismo e guerra d'Etiopia.* Rome: Laterza, 2010.

Cleary, Edward L. "The Transformation of Latin American Christianity, c. 1950–2000." In *World Christianities C. 1914–C. 2000*, edited by

Hugh McLeod, 366–84. Cambridge, UK: Cambridge University Press, 2006.

Coleman, William J. *Latin-American Catholicism: A Self-Evaluation.* Maryknoll, NY: Maryknoll Publications, 1958.

Collignon, Jim. "Maryknoll's Micaiah." In *Turns in the Road, Companions on the Journey*, edited by Larry Egan, Tom Fenton, Darryl Hunt, George Laudadio, Frank Maurovich, Bill Murphy, and Al Stumph. Privately published, 2011.

Console, Ester Maria. "Incontri tra culture nelle collezioni del Museo Missionario Etnologico." In *I Musei Vaticani nell' 80° anniversario della firma dei Patti Lateranensi 1929–2009*, edited by Antonio Paolucci and Cristina Pantanella, 168–77. Vatican City: Edizioni Musei Vaticani, 2009.

Coppa, Frank J. "Between Anti-Judaism and Anti-Semitism: Pius XI's Response to the Nazi Persecution of the Jews. Precursor to Pius XII's Silence." *Journal of Church and State* 47, no. 1 (Winter 2005): 63–89.

———. "Between Morality and Diplomacy: The Vatican's 'Silence' During the Holocaust." *Journal of Church and State* 50, no. 3 (Summer 2008): 541–68.

Costello, Gerald M. *Mission to Latin America: The Successes and Failures of a Twentieth-Century Crusade.* Maryknoll, NY: Orbis Books, 1979.

Cowan, Wayne. "An Interview with Ivan Illich." *Christianity and Crisis* 29 (August 4, 1969): 213–19.

Croce, Giuseppe M. "Regards sur la Curie romaine de 1895 à 1932." *Trajecta* [Leuven] (2010–2011): 53–65.

Cushing, Richard. "On the Call of the Holy See for Papal Volunteers for Latin America." Washington, DC: Latin America Bureau, n.d.

Deck, Allan Figureroa. "Towards a New Narrative for the Latino Presence in U.S. Society and the Church." *Origins* 42, no. 29 (December 20, 2012): 457–64.

Dennett, Tyler. *Americans in Eastern Asia: A Critical Study of the Policy of the United States with Reference to China, Japan and Korea in the 19th Century.* New York: Macmillan, 1922.

Dries, Angelyn. "A Theology of Global Christianity: The Mission Thought of John Considine, M.M. (1897–1982)." Philadelphia: American Catholic Historical Society Meeting, April 16–17, 1993 (photocopy).

———. *The Missionary Movement in American Catholic History.* Maryknoll, NY: Orbis Books, 1998.

———. "The Context for the Maryknoll Foundations: The Church and the United States in the Post–Civil War South, Urban North, and the Competition for a Foreign Missions Seminary, 1866–1911." Talk given at Maryknoll Centennial Celebration, Ossining, NY (January 26, 2011).

Ede, Alfred J. *The Lay Crusade for a Christian America: A Study of the American*

Federation of Catholic Societies, 1900–1919. New York: Garland, 1988.

Endres, David Jeffrey. *American Crusade: Catholic Youth in the World Mission Movement from World War I Through Vatican II.* Eugene, OR: Pickwick, 2010.

Erlich, Haggai. "Adwa, battle of." *Encyclopaedia Aethiopica,* edited by Siegbert Uhlig. Wiesbaden: Harrassowitz, 2003.

Fattorini, Emma, and Carl Ipsen. *Hitler, Mussolini and the Vatican: Pope Pius XI and the Speech That Was Never Made.* Cambridge: Polity Press, 2011.

Finn, Brendan A. *Twenty-Four American Cardinals: Biographical Sketches of Those Princes of the Catholic Church Who Either Were Born in America or Served There at Some Time.* Boston: Humphries, 1947.

Fitzpatrick, Joseph P. "What Is He Getting At?" *America* (March 25, 1967): 444–46, 448–49.

———. *The Stranger Is Our Own: Reflections on the Journey of Puerto Rican Migrants.* Kansas City, MO: Sheed & Ward, 1996.

———. "Ivan Illich as We Knew Him in the 1950s." In *The Challenges of Ivan Illich: A Collective Reflection,* edited by Lee Hoinacki and Carl Mitcham, 35–42. Albany: State University of New York Press, 2002.

Frazier, William B. "Guidelines for a New Theology of Mission." In *Mission Trends No. 1: Crucial Issues in Mission Today,* edited by Gerald H. Anderson and Thomas F. Stransky, 23–36. New York: Paulist Press, 1974.

Garneau, James F. "Commandos for Christ: The Foundation of the Missionary Society of St. James the Apostle and the 'Americanism' of the 1950s and 1960s." Ph.D. dissertation. Catholic University of America, 2000.

———. "The First Inter-American Episcopal Conference November 2–4, 1959: Canada and the United States Called to the Rescue of Latin America." *Catholic Historical Review* 87, no. 4 (2001): 662–87.

Gigot, Francis E. "Jews and Judaism." In *Catholic Encyclopedia,* ed., Charle G. Herbermann, Edward A. Pace, Conde B. Pallen, Thomas J. Shahan, John J. Wynne et al., 386–404. Vol. 8. New York: Robert Appleton Company, 1910.

Giovagnoli, Agostino. "Il Vaticano di fronte al colonialismo fascista." In *Le guerre coloniali del fascismo,* edited by Angelo Del Boca, 112–31. Rome: Editori Laterza, 1991.

Godman, Peter. *Hitler and the Vatican: Inside the Secret Archives That Reveal the New Story of the Nazis and the Church.* New York: Free Press, 2004.

Goldman, Sherman. "Ivan Illich: Learning Is Unlearning." *East West Journal* 4 (April 1976): 26–28, 33–35.

Gray, Francine du Plessix. *Divine Disobedience: Profiles in Catholic Radicalism.* New York: Knopf, 1970.

Guida delle missioni cattoliche. Rome: Unione Missionaria del Clero in Italia, 1934.

Hall, George. "Catholic Inter-American Cooperation Conference." *The Christian Century* 84, no. 8 (February 1967): 252–54.

Halsey, William M. *The Survival of American Innocence: Catholicism in an Era of Disillusionment, 1920–1940.* Notre Dame, IN: University of Notre Dame Press, 1980.

Harding, Chris. "A legendary Lenten passion play may be revived in Roxbury 'Pilate's Daughter.'" *The Redemptorist Chronicle* (June 1984).

Hartch, Todd. "Ivan Illich and the American Catholic Missionary Initiative in Latin America." *International Bulletin of Missionary Research* 33, no. 4 (October): 185–88.

Heath, Kingston Wm. *The Patina of Place: The Cultural Weathering of a New England Industrial Landscape.* Knoxville: University of Tennessee Press, 2001.

Henkel, Willi. "The Legacy of Robert Streit, Johannes Dindinger, and Johannes Rommerskirchen." *International Bulletin of Missionary Research* 6, no. 1 (January 1982): 16–21.

———. "Perbal, Albert." In *Biographical Dictionary of Christian Missions*, edited by Gerald H. Anderson, 526–27. New York: Macmillan Reference USA, 1998.

Hoffman, Ronan. "Latin America in the Church's Global Mission: What Priority?" *America* (January 15, 1966): 68–70.

Hoge, Dean R., and Aniedi Okure. *International Priests in America: Challenges and Opportunities.* Collegeville, MN: Liturgical Press, 2006.

Hudal, Alois. *Römische Tagebücher: Lebensbeichte eines alten Bischofs.* Graz: Stocker. 1976.

Illich, Ivan. "The Seamy Side of Charity." *America* (January 21, 1967): 88–91.

———. *Celebration of Awareness: A Call for Institutional Revolution.* Garden City, NY: Doubleday, 1970.

———. *The Church, Change, and Development.* Chicago: Urban Training Center Press, 1970.

———. *Deschooling Society.* New York: Harper & Row, 1971.

———. *Tools for Conviviality.* New York: Harper & Row, 1973.

———. *Medical Nemesis: The Expropriation of Health.* New York: Pantheon Books, 1976.

———. *Gender.* New York: Pantheon Books, 1982.

Illich, Ivan, and David Cayley. *Ivan Illich in Conversation.* Concord, Ontario: Anansi, 1992.

———. *The Rivers North of the Future: The Testament of Ivan Illich.* Toronto: House of Anansi Press, 2005.

Irrarázaval, Diego. "El saber indígena sopesa la modernidad." In *Sabiduría indígena: fuente de esperanza: teología india.* Vol. 2, *Aportes*, edited by III

Encuentro Taller Latinoamericano de Teología India, 275–99. Puno and Cusco, Perú, and La Paz, Bolivia: IDEA, IPA, and CTP, 1998.

Just, Mary. *Our Neighbors the Chinese*. New York: Field Afar Press, 1944.

———. *Our Neighbors, the Koreans*. New York: Field Afar Press, 1946.

———. *Our Neighbors in the Andes: Peru, Bolivia, Ecuador*. New York: Field Afar Press, 1947.

———. *Our Neighbors, the Japanese*. New York: Field Afar Press, 1947.

Kennedy, Eugene C. "Didn't You See It? It Happened." *Interchange* 31, no. 2 (2011): 1, 3–6.

Latourette, Kenneth Scott. *A History of Christian Missions in China*. New York: Macmillan, 1929.

———. *Beyond the Ranges: An Autobiography*. Grand Rapids: Eerdmans, 1967.

Lima Methods Conference of the Maryknoll Fathers. *Proceedings of the Lima Methods Conference of the Maryknoll Fathers, Maryknoll House, Lima, Peru, August 23–28, 1954*. Maryknoll: Maryknoll Fathers, 1955.

Linden, Ian. *Global Catholicism: Diversity and Change since Vatican II*. New York: Columbia University Press, 2009.

Luzbetak, Louis J. "Wilhelm Schmidt, S.V.D., 1868–1954: Priest, Linguist, Ethnologist." In *Mission Legacies: Biographical Studies of Leaders of the Modern Missionary Movement*, edited by Gerald H. Anderson, Robert T. Coote, Norman A. Horner, and James M. Phillips, 475–85. Maryknoll, NY: Orbis Books, 1994.

Maclennan, Kenneth. *The Cost of a New World*. New York: Missionary Education Movement of the United States and Canada, 1925.

Maritain, Jacques. "Racist Law and the True Meaning of Racism." *The Commonweal* 38, 0no. 7 (June 4, 1943): 181–88.

Marongiu Buonaiuti, Cesare. *Politica e religioni nel colonialismo italiano (1882–1941)*. Milan: Giuffrè, 1982.

Matovina, Timothy M. *Latino Catholicism: Transformation in America's Largest Church*. Princeton, NJ: Princeton University Press, 2012.

Mazzenga, Maria. "Toward an American Catholic Response to the Holocaust: Catholic Americanism and Kristallnacht." In eadem, *American Religious Responses to Kristallnacht*. New York: Palgrave Macmillan, 2009.

Mbiti, John. "Theological Impotence and the Universality of the Church." In *Mission Trends 3: Third World Theologies*, edited by Gerald H. Anderson and Thomas F. Stransky, 6–18. New York: Paulist Press, 1976.

McCarrick, Theodore. "Top Priority: A Reply." *America* (January 15, 1966): 70–71.

McGlone, Mary M. *Sharing Faith Across the Hemisphere*. Washington: United States Catholic Conference, 1997.

McGurkin, Edward A. "Father John J. Considine." In *Profiles of 12 Maryknollers*. Published privately, 1983.

Morris, Charles R. *American Catholic: The Saints and Sinners Who Built America's Most Powerful Church*. New York: Times Books, 1997.

Mutchler, David E. *The Church as a Political Factor in Latin America: With Particular Reference to Colombia and Chile*. New York: Praeger, 1971.

Nuesse, C. Joseph. *The Catholic University of America: A Centennial History*. Washington, DC: The Catholic University of America Press, 1990.

Oldham, Joseph Houldsworth. *Christianity and the Race Problem*. New York: George H. Doran Co., 1924.

Oliveros Maqueo, Roberto. "Meeting of Theologians at Petrópolis (March 1964)." In *Liberation Theology: A Documentary History*, edited by Alfred T. Hennelly, 43–47. Maryknoll, NY: Orbis Books, 1990.

"The Papal Program for Latin America." Chicago: Papal Volunteers for Latin America, n.d.

Pattee, Richard. *Love Thy Neighbor: Is the Church Failing in the Americas?* Huntington, IN: Our Sunday Visitor Press, 1930.

———. *Richard Pattee's Catholicism in Latin America*. Washington: National Catholic Welfare Conference, 1945.

Price, Stuart. *Media Studies*. Harlow: Longman, 1998.

Prudhomme, Claude. *Stratégie missionnaire du Saint-Siège sous Léon XIII (1878–1903): centralisation romaine et défis culturels*. Rome: Ecole française de Rome, 1994.

Prunier, Gerard. *The Rwanda Crisis: History of a Genocide*. New York: Columbia University Press, 1995.

Putnam, Robert D., and David E. Campbell. *American Grace: How Religion Divides and Unites Us*. New York: Simon & Schuster, 2010.

Quigley, Thomas E. "The Great North–South Embrace: How Collaboration among the Churches of the Americas Began." *America* 201, no. 17 (December 7, 2009): 17–20.

———. "Notes on the History of the U.S. Bishops' Conference in Its Relations with the Church in Latin America." Unpublished manuscript.

Rogers, Mary Josephine. *Discourses of Mother Mary Joseph Rogers, Foundress, Maryknoll*, Vol. III. Compiled by Mother Mary Coleman and Archives Staff, 1982.

Salotti, Carlo. *I Santi ed I Beati proclamati nell'Anno santo 1925: Panegirici tenuti in Roma in occasione dei Tridui solenni*. Turin: Soc. Ed. Internaz., 1927.

Saxon, Wolfgang. "Rev. John Stott, Major Evangelical Figure, Dies at 90." *New York Times,* July 27, 2011.

Sheen, Fulton J. *God and Intelligence in Modern Philosophy: A Critical Study in the Light of the Philosophy of Saint Thomas*. London: Longmans, Green & Co., 1925.

Shenk, Wilbert R. *Enlarging the Story: Perspectives on Writing World Christian History*. Maryknoll, NY: Orbis Books, 2002.

Smith, Peter H. *Talons of the Eagle: Dynamics of U.S.–Latin American Relations.* New York: Oxford University Press, 1996.

Soberal, José Dimas. "Mons. Alfredo F. Méndez, C.S.C.: Primer Obispo y Fundador de la Diócesis de Arecibo," *El Visitante* (January 22–28, 2006): 23.

Society for the Propagation of the Faith. *Little Atlas of Catholic Missions.* Bergamo: Istituto italiano d'arti grafiche, 1926.

Streit, Robert. *Catholic Missions in Figures and Symbols: Based on the Vatican Mission Exhibition.* Society for the Propagation of the Faith, 1927.

Streit, Robert, and Johannes Dindinger. *Bibliotheca missionum.* Münster i.W.: Aachen, 1916.

Tempels, Placide. *La philosophie bantoue.* Paris: Éditions africaines, 1949.

Tentler, Leslie Woodcock. *Seasons of Grace: A History of the Catholic Archdiocese of Detroit.* Detroit: Wayne State University Press, 1990.

Tisserant, Eugène, and Sever Pop. *Recueil cardinal Eugène Tisserant: «Ab Oriente et Occidente.»* Louvain: Centre international de dialectologie générale, 1955.

Toynbee, Philip. "Pilgrimage to a Modern Prophet." *Observer* (February 1974): 29–30, 32–33, 35–36, 39–40.

Trinchese, Stefano. *Roncalli e le missioni: l'opera della propagazione della fede tra Francia e Vaticano negli anni '20.* Brescia: Morcelliana, 1989.

Vandenberghe, An. "Entre mission et science: La recherche ethnologique du père Wilhelm Schmidt SVD et le Vatican (1900–1939)." *Le fait missionnaire* 19 (2006): 15–36.

Vásquez, Manuel A., and Marie F. Marquardt. *Globalizing the Sacred: Religion Across the Americas.* New Brunswick, NJ: Rutgers University Press, 2003.

Walls, Andrew F. "Eusebius Tries Again." In *Enlarging the Story: Perspectives on Writing World Christian History,* edited by Wilbert R. Shenk, 1–21. Maryknoll, NY: Orbis Books, 2002.

Walsh, James Edward. *Maryknoll Spiritual Directory.* New York: Field Afar Press, 1947.

Wells, H. G. *A Short History of the World.* New York: Macmillan, 1922.

Wiest, Jean-Paul. *Maryknoll in China: A History, 1918–1955.* Armonk, NY: M. E. Sharpe, 1988.

Wu, Jingxiong [John C. H.]. *Beyond East and West.* New York: Sheed & Ward, 1951.

———. "The World's Need." In *Texts [of the] Second World Congress for the Lay Apostolate, Rome, 5–13 October, 1957.* Vol. 2, by the World Congress of the Lay Apostolate, 31–59. Rome: Palazzo delle Congregazioni, 1958.

Index

Index